Applying Norm-Referenced and Criterion-Referenced Measurement in Education

Victor R. Martuza
ASSOCIATE PROFESSOR OF EDUCATIONAL FOUNDATIONS
UNIVERSITY OF DELAWARE

Allyn and Bacon, Inc.
boston   london   sydney   toronto

Library of Congress Cataloging in Publication Data

Martuza, Victor R
    Applying norm-referenced and criterion-referenced measurement in education.

    Includes bibliographies and index.
    1. Educational tests and measurements.   I. Title.
LB3051.M456   371.2'6   76-13172
ISBN 0-205-05545-1

Contents

Preface

This text has been prepared for use in a one semester, introductory measurement course. Its focal points are: (a) the distinction between norm-referenced and criterion-referenced measurement and (b) the implications of these two quite different measurement orientations for test construction and test usage. The approach taken in this text is primarily intuitive with a strong "how-to-do-it" flavor. This was done in order to accommodate the varying capabilities and interests of: (a) pre-service undergraduate students in teacher education programs, and entry level graduate students being formally introduced to measurement for the first time, and (b) in-service educational practitioners (e.g., teachers, counselors, and administrators), whose knowledge of measurement theory and techniques has slipped away or become dated.

At the introductory level, students in teacher-preparation programs tend to vary a great deal in statistical sophistication. Many have, at best, an incomplete understanding of how and why certain statistics are used or what factors affect their interpretation within various educational measurement contexts. In an attempt to ameliorate this problem, a short course in descriptive statistics (Chapters 2–7) has been included in this text. Many of the statistical concepts and techniques utilized or referenced in the remainder of the text are discussed in these chapters. Examples and illustrations are used wherever they seem to purchase additional clarification of the verbal presentation. Additionally, numerous exercise sets are included with each chapter to provide opportunities to practice procedures as they are encountered and, in some cases, to prompt the reader to think about the material in a slightly different way than discussed in text.

Once the concepts and techniques presented in Chapters 2 through 7 have been mastered, the student should be ready for the measurement theory and techniques discussed in the remainder of the text. For an overview of the entire text, consider the following brief outline.

Chapter 1 is intended to introduce some basic terminology and to establish a framework within which the remainder of the text may be sensibly viewed. Here we define measurement, discuss the levels of measurement, differentiate among the terms domain-referenced, criterion-referenced, and norm-referenced, and, finally, examine briefly the important concepts of reliability and validity.

Chapters 2 through 7 focus on statistical procedures that are especially useful in norm-referenced measurement. Here, an attempt is made to provide an explanation of how and why these statistics work, and, hence, of their different degrees of utility within norm-referenced and criterion-referenced measurement contexts.

Chapter 8 is an introduction to classical measurement theory. It provides a basis for subsequent reliability, validity, and norm-referenced test interpretation discussions that follow; and, also, it provides a useful backdrop for the criterion-referenced case presented later.

Chapters 9 and 10 deal with the concepts of norm-referenced reliability and validity, respectively. Some topics receiving special attention are the difference score reliability paradox and the Campbell-Fiske multitrait-multimethod construct validity methodology.

Chapter 11 focuses on norms and their role in test score interpretation. Special attention is given to considerations in developing norms and in the use of existing normative data for interpreting test scores.

Chapter 12 presents some standard item analysis techniques for norm-referenced tests. The relationship between item difficulty level and item discrimination power is examined, and procedures are described for using item difficulty and discrimination index values in identifying items that do not perform satisfactorily in a norm-referenced testing application.

Chapters 13 through 16 deal with topics more relevant to test design and production. Chapter 13 is a rather severely abridged version of Bloom's *Taxonomy*; some knowledge of which seems essential to an understanding of the traditional test construction procedures presented in Chapter 14.

Chapter 14 presents the traditional approach to achievement test construction, including selected aspects of test planning and item writing. With respect to the latter, emphasis is on the essay and multiple-choice formats. Some alternative scoring methods (e.g., confidence weighting) also are considered briefly.

Chapter 15 deals with the writing of instructional objectives. Together with the Airasian and Madaus article, "Criterion-Referenced Testing in the Classroom" (reprinted in Chapter 18), it provides a useful methodology for classroom lesson planning and test construction.

Chapter 16 presents some newer extensions and alternatives to the methodology presented in Chapter 15. In addition to the consideration of a number of content domain definition/item generation strategies, attention is paid to item selection, establishment of a criterion score (or cut score), and the types of decision errors that are possible, and how they might be taken into account in a criterion-referenced testing situation.

In Chapter 17, selected approaches to the assessment reliability and validity of domain-referenced tests (including the criterion-referenced case) are described. The development in this and the previous chapter draws heavily on the relatively recent work of Melvin Novick and his colleagues, Jason Millman, and Ron Hambleton and his colleagues.

Chapter 18 contains reprints of three articles that either amplify or extend the content of selected sections of the first 17 chapters. The Airasian and Madaus article, "Criterion-Referenced Testing in the Classroom," presents a fairly comprehensive treatment of the origins of the criterion-referenced testing movement, and is probably best studied in conjunction with Chapter 15 of this text.

The Gardner article, "Interpreting Achievement Profiles – Uses and Warnings," points out a number of factors that must be considered when using profile data to compare performance of a single student (or a group of students) across different tests or subject matter areas. It is most appropriately read in conjunction with Chapter 11, which deals with norm-referenced test score interpretation.

The Deutsch et al. article, "Guidelines for Testing Minority Group Children," aptly describes a number of problems frequently encountered in testing "culturally different" students, and suggests steps that can be taken to minimize possible negative consequences in such testing situations. It is an appropriate sequel to Chapters 8–12.

In the preparation of any text, numerous individuals contribute in varying amounts and ways to the final product. I would like to acknowledge the very useful critiques of various early draft segments of this text provided by Jon Magoon, Irwin Kirsch, and Stan Jacobs; and especially thank Mary Wolfe, who provided a great deal of assistance at the various stages of manuscript development and, in addition, contributed many examples and exercises to Chapter 13. In addition, I would like to acknowledge the support provided by the faculty and secretarial staff of the Department of Educational Foundations and by the Graduate School of the University of Delaware. Finally, I would like to express my appreciation to those who permitted me to reprint excerpts of their work. Of course, any and all shortcomings of this text, whatever their nature, are the sole responsibility of this author.

Victor Martuza

1

Measurement: An Overview

The purposes of this chapter are (a) to define the terms "measurement" and "test," (b) to present a system for classifying measurement rules, (c) to distinguish between the norm-referenced and criterion-referenced approaches to testing, and (d) to introduce the concepts "test validity" and "test reliability."

DEFINITIONS OF MEASUREMENT AND TEST

Measurement may be defined as the process of assigning numerals to objects, events, or people using a rule.[1] Ideally, the rule assigns the numerals to represent the amounts of a specific attribute possessed by the objects, events, or people being measured. This is not always the case, however, as will be seen shortly.

A *test* is a particular kind of measurement rule which consists, at a minimum, of (a) a set of items (e.g., statements to be verified or completed, questions to be answered), (b) a set of directions telling the examinee how to respond to the items, and (c) a scoring procedure for converting the collection of item responses for each examinee to a numeral. The application (i.e., administration and scoring) of a test

---

1. In certain situations, symbols other than numerals may be used in the measurement process. For example, classroom teachers frequently assign the letters A, B, C, D, and F to indicate student standing in a course, or verbal labels such as "excellent," "good", and "poor" to indicate their assessment of a student's performance on a particular task. Since a meaningful correspondence between these symbolic systems and the set of numerals can easily be established, their use is justifiable. However, the definition, as stated, is preferred because it emphasizes the quantitative aspect of measurement and, in addition, stresses the use of a symbolic system which can be manipulated mathematically.

to one or more examinees is just one kind of measurement and is, in fact, not very different from applying a tape measure to quantify height.

LEVELS OF MEASUREMENT

Measurement rules may be classified in terms of the amount and kind of information retrievable from the numerals assigned by a particular rule. One such classification system, developed by Stevens (1946), enjoys widespread usage, and it is to the explanation and application of this system that we now turn our attention.

In Stevens' system, measurement rules are classified into one of four hierarchical categories or levels: nominal, ordinal, interval, and ratio. Rather than attempting to explain the nature of the hierarchy at this point, we shall define and illustrate each level of this classification system, revealing the nature of the hierarchy in the process.[2]

Nominal Measurement Rules

Suppose a rule assigns numerals to objects simply to represent membership in one of a set of *mutually exclusive* and *exhaustive, unorderable* categories.[3] Then given the numerals assigned to two or more objects, the best we can do is tell which objects are in the same category and which ones are in different categories. Consider the following two examples of nominal measurement:

1. RULE: In coding your answer sheet, pencil in answer position 1 if you are male, position 2 if you are female.

   COMMENT: Knowing the rule, it then becomes quite easy to separate a set of answer sheets into two stacks: one turned in by males, the other by females.

2. RULE: Assign blue-eyed people the numeral 1; brown-eyed people, 2; gray-eyed people, 3; all others, 4.

   COMMENT: Knowing the rule and the numerals assigned to various people, one can easily tell whether any two people belong to the same eye-color category by checking to see if the numerals they were assigned are identical.

2. Actually, some rules seem impossible to classify in this system, and as a result, more elaborate classification schemes have been advanced; however, the Stevens' system is quite adequate for our purposes and, hence, is the only one described and used in this text.

3. A set of categories is *exhaustive* if every element to be classified belongs to at least one category; the set is *mutually exclusive* if each element belongs to no more than one category. A set of categories is called *unorderable* here if the manner in which they differ is one of quality rather than quantity. For example, "religious preference" is the name for a set of categories (Protestant, Catholic, Jewish, Moslem, etc.) which differ qualitatively, while "weight in pounds" is the name for a set of categories (0 lb, 1 lb, 2 lb, etc.) which differ quantitatively.

Some variables (e.g., eye color, occupation, hand preference) are only measureable with nominal level rules, but most variables of interest in education (e.g., achievement, attitude, intelligence) are measureable using more informative rules. Whenever a variable can be measured by more than one rule, factors like (a) the amount of information desired, (b) rule complexity, (c) time constraints, and (d) cost enter into the decision as to the type of rule which should be used. In most instances, it is good practice to use the most informative (or highest level) measurement rule available from among those which are not excluded by factors such as those cited above. The reason for this is quite simple. If too much information is obtained initially, the excessive information can be ignored; however, if too little information is obtained initially, and subsequently, more information is required, the resulting dilemma is obvious.

Ordinal Measurement Rules

Variables consisting of a mutually exclusive and exhaustive set of *orderable* categories can be measured using an ordinal level rule. Given the rule and the numerals assigned to the objects of interest, we can not only tell which objects occupy the same or different categories, but we can also order the objects according to the amount of the measured attribute they possess. Consider the following:

EXAMPLE
RULE: Order the objects in the set from tallest to shortest. Assign the numeral 1 to the tallest; 2 to the next tallest; etc. If two objects are equally tall, assign to each the average of the numerals they would be assigned if one were taller than the other. Be sure the sum of all numerals assigned equals $1 + 2 + 3 + \cdots + n$, where n is the number of objects measured.

COMMENT: Given this rule and two randomly selected numerals, we can not only tell whether the objects they represent differ in height, but we can also indicate which one is taller (or shorter) than the other. Our ability to make *greater than* (and *less than*) judgments is due to the increase in information inherent in ordinal level measurements.

Interval Measurement Rules

Numerals assigned by an interval measurement rule represent a mutually exclusive and exhaustive set of *equally spaced, ordered* categories. Note, this means that knowledge of the rule not only enables one to rank-order objects using the numerals assigned but, in addition, permits one to rank-order the relative sizes of the differences existing between pairs of objects. For example, suppose the 1:00 A.M. Fahrenheit temperatures in New York City on three particular days were as follows: January 1 – 27°; March 1 – 42°; August 1 – 93°. We are not only able to rank-order these days on a cold to hot continuum, but since the categories involved (i.e., $0°$, $1°$, $2°$, $3°$, etc.) are equally spaced, we can also rank-order the differences between categories, e.g., the temperature difference between August 1 and March 1 was greater than the difference between March 1 and January 1. Furthermore, we know that the August 1–March 1 difference is $36°$ more than the March 1–January 1 difference. This is not possible using ordinal level measurement procedures. A very important limitation of interval level measurement is that the numerals are not indicative of the absolute amount of the attribute possessed by the objects to which they are assigned. The reason for this is the arbitrary nature of the zero point on the measurement scale. For example, a temperature of $0°F$ does not represent the complete absence of heat. As a result, an $80°F$ temperature does not represent a condition twice as warm as a $40°F$ temperature. This problem will be discussed a bit more after the properties of ratio scales have been introduced.

Ratio Measurement Rules

The numerals assigned to objects using a ratio level measurement rule provide all the information inherent in interval measurement plus information concerning the absolute amount of the measured characteristic possessed by an object. For example, suppose we use a tape measure to determine the heights of three people, and the results are as follows: John – 60 in., Mary – 50 in., and Sue – 30 in. These numerals convey the following kinds of information: (a) John, Mary, and Sue are not equally tall (nominal information); (b) John is taller than Mary and Sue, and Mary is taller than Sue (ordinal information); and (c) the difference in height between John and Mary is 10 in. less than the difference between Mary and Sue (interval information). Notice that we have not exhausted the available information. We can make meaningful statements like "John is twice as tall as Sue" and "Mary is 5/6 as tall as John." The reason for this is that each numeral represents the absolute quantity of the attribute possessed by the measured object, a condition possible only when the scale used has a natural zero point (i.e., the numeral zero represents the complete absence of the attribute in question).

Table 1-1 summarizes the salient differences in the levels of the Stevens system.

Suppose we now consider the problem of classifying educational and psychological tests using this system. For example, suppose we have the scores of three students on the math portion of the Scholastic Aptitude Test (SAT)[4] – John's score is 600, Mary's is 500, and Sam's is 300. What do these scores tell us about the math ability of these three people? First, the unequal scores imply differences in math ability; therefore, the scores certainly convey nominal infor-

---

4. The Scholastic Aptitude Test (SAT), designed by the College Entrance Examination Board, is the admissions or entrance examination used by colleges and universities participating in the College Board program. For a brief description of this test and a comparison of it with its chief competitor, the ACT, see L. J. Cronbach, *Essentials of Psychological Testing*, 3rd ed. New York: Harper and Row, 1970, pp. 274–276.

TABLE 1-1. *Summary of the Stevens System.*

Level of Measurement	Salient Properties	Sample Objects and their Assigned Numerals	Some Permissible Statements
Nominal	1. mutually exclusive/ exhaustive/ unorderable categories	$a = 1$ $b = 2$ $c = 6$	1. $a \neq b \neq c$
Ordinal	1. mutually exclusive/ exhaustive/ orderable categoris	$a = 1$ $b = 2$ $c = 6$	1. $a \neq b \neq c$ 2. $a < b < c$
Interval	1. all ordinal properties 2. equidistant categories	$a = 1$ $b = 2$ $c = 6$	1. $a \neq b \neq c$ 2. $a < b < c$ 3. $(c - b) - (b - a) = 3$
Ratio	1. all interval properties 2. natural zero point	$a = 1$ $b = 2$ $c = 6$	1. $a \neq b \neq c$ 2. $a < b < c$ 3. $(c - b) - (b - a) = 3$ 4. $c = 6$ times a

mation. Additionally, we can order these students on a math continuum (see Figure 1-1); thus the scores also convey ordinal information. If we then obtain

Low Aptitude ——— **Sam** ——— **Mary** **John** ——— *High Aptitude*

FIGURE 1-1. *Position of three hypothetical students on an ability continuum.*

the pairwise score differences, we find that John's score is 100 points more than Mary's and Mary's is 200 more points than Sam's. Does this mean that the ability difference between John and Mary is less than that between Mary and Sam? It would seem that most people would reach this conclusion, and hence, SAT-math scores are usually treated as interval level measurements. However, even with a test of this caliber, there is no assurance that a fixed difference in test scores means the same thing all along the scale, i.e., there is no reason to believe that the difference in math ability between individuals scoring 200 and 300, respectively, on SAT-math is necessarily the same as the difference in math ability between individuals scoring 600 and 700, respectively, on the same test. In addition, educational and psychological test scales constructed by traditional methods, the SAT included, typically lack a natural zero (i.e., a zero point which signals the complete absence of the attribute being measured), and hence, ratio statements like "John is twice as bright (or twice as knowledgeable) as Sam" are meaningless. Because test scores of this type clearly convey more than ordinal information but do not quite satisfy (in a strict sense) the requirements of an interval scale, some individuals prefer to label them *quasi-interval* to emphasize this fact.

Because most educational and psychological test score scales are not characterized by equal units and a natural zero, the argument is sometimes made that the statistical procedures clearly suitable for use with interval and ratio measurements are not appropriate for use in summarizing the information contained in, or making statistical inferences based on, sets of test scores.[5] Following Lord (1953), our position is that the statistical treatment of any set of numerals (test scores included) should be determined by the nature of the question one is trying to answer and not by the level of measurement attained. If the question makes sense, then the best statistical technique available for finding the answer should be used. For example, if one wants to know whether the average numeral assigned to Delaware football players is greater than the average numeral assigned to Notre Dame football players, the obvious procedure is to compare appropriate measures of averageness. Even though football numerals are assigned using a nominal-level rule (i.e., they do no more than indicate the position played by the bearer), statistics like the arithmetic mean (defined in the next chapter), which find their greatest utility with interval and ratio measurement, can be used sensibly in answering this question. As a result, the distinction between quasi-interval and interval measurements is not maintained beyond this chapter.

NORM-REFERENCED VERSUS CRITERION-REFERENCED MEASUREMENT

In a *norm-referenced* measurement framework, an examinee's performance is evaluated relative to the performance of others in some well-defined comparison or norm group. Most standardized tests of achievement, aptitude, and specific personality factors are interpreted in a normative fashion and, hence, are called norm-referenced tests. In addition, many teachers use norm-referenced grade assignment policies, i.e., the grade assigned to each student is determined by comparing his academic performance to that of his classmates. Students usually refer to such norm-referenced grading policies as "grading on the curve."

In recent years, educators have become increasingly aware of the limitations of norm-referenced measurement procedures for (a) diagnosing student achievement deficiencies, (b) assessing the level of a student's knowledge within a well-defined content area, (c) evaluating the effects of a curriculum change on student achievement, (d) assessing the strengths and weaknesses of school programs within a particular school district, etc.[6] In instances like these, how well a particular student's performance compares to the performance of others in some well-defined comparison (or norm) group is really irrelevant. What is required is a set of tests

5. Perhaps the discussion of this issue will be more meaningful after Chapters 2 through 8 have been read. If it does not seem clear at the moment, make a mental note to reread this paragraph later.

6. See, for example, the Arasian and Madaus article entitled "Criterion-Referenced Testing in the Classroom" reprinted in Chapter 18 of this text, and Millman (1974) or Hambleton *et al.* (1975) for additional discussion relative to these limitations.

(in some cases, just one), each measuring the achievement of a specific objective (or mastery of a well-defined content domain) and each yielding a score interpretable in an *absolute* rather than a *relative* sense.

For example, if one is interested in, or must make a decision regarding, a particular student's ability to calculate the square root of whole numbers from 0 to 1000, inclusive, just finding out that this student does better than 50, 75, or 90% of his classmates is not completely satisfactory. What is of interest is the percentage (or proportion) of problems in this set that the student is capable of solving. Given this type of information, a decision can be made regarding the advisability of remedial work for this student on problems of the type described.

A test consisting of a representative sample of items from a well-defined content domain similar to the one just described is said to be *domain-referenced*. With tests of this type, it is perfectly reasonable to use the percentage-correct score on the test (or some refinement of it) as an estimate of the examinee's status in that content domain. Whenever a decision about an examinee's mastery of the content in such a domain or about his achievement with respect to an explicit instructional objective is made by comparing his test score to some preset standard or *criterion* for success, his test score is said to be given a *criterion-referenced*, as opposed to a *norm-referenced*, interpretation. Since criterion-referenced test score interpretations are most meaningful when based on domain-referenced tests, it should be understood that in the remainder of this text the term "criterion-referenced test" refers to a domain-referenced test subject to a criterion-referenced interpretation.[7]

While special aptitudes, personality variables, etc., are defined normatively and, hence, are meaningful only within a norm-referenced framework, the measurement of achievement can frequently be conducted within either a norm-referenced or criterion-referenced framework. When there is a choice available regarding test score interpretation (e.g., percent mastery vs "grading on the curve"), the use to which the scores are to be put should be the primary factor in deciding which of the two frameworks ought to be adopted for test construction and test score interpretation.[8] If, for example, the purpose for testing is simply to rank-order the examinees along some achievement continuum (as in competitive scholarship exams), a norm-referenced orientation seems most appropriate; on the other hand, if the test scores are to be used as a basis for deciding whether to prescribe remedial work in a given content or skill area, or to pass the student along to the next unit in an instructional sequence, a criterion-referenced orientation would appear to be more appropriate.

---

7. Millman (1974) uses the term "criterion-referenced" in a more general sense. In his usage, any absolute (as opposed to normative) interpretation of a domain-referenced test is called "criterion-referenced." Notice that this includes cases where no explicit criterion for success is specified, – e.g., where domain-referenced test scores are used for purely descriptive purposes. For both historical and semantic reasons, it seems better to reserve the term "criterion-referenced" for cases where an explicit criterion (for success or mastery) is stated.

8. The term "percent mastery" refers to the percentage of items or tasks in some *well-defined domain* to which the examinee can respond correctly. This is not the same as the traditional "percentage score" or "percentage grade" which has a long tradition of usage in American school systems. For more on this point, see the Airasian and Madaus article, "Criterion-Referenced Testing in the Classroom," reprinted in Chapter 18 of this text.

The type of measurement framework (i.e., norm-referenced vs criterion-referenced) one chooses to work within has important implications for item writing, test construction, and test selection. Within a norm-referenced framework, the test constructor not only wants to build tests which measure a specific characteristic, but he also wants to build tests which maximally discriminate among different individuals possessing different amounts of that characteristic. If successful, the test will be moderately difficult and the resulting distribution of examinee scores will exhibit a considerable amount of variability (i.e., the scores will be spread out rather than bunched). Within a criterion-referenced framework, the test constructor is usually interested in assessing examinee mastery in a well-defined content domain. When such a test is administered, especially if it follows an instructional treatment known to produce a high level of mastery in most individuals given that treatment, the distribution of test scores will tend to cluster near the high end of the score scale and to display little, if any, variability. Because traditional procedures for assessing the quality of tests and test items depend heavily on the existence of test score variability, they tend to have limited utility within a criterion-referenced testing context. This problem and its resolution will be examined in detail subsequently.

TWO IMPORTANT CHARACTERISTICS OF EVERY TEST: RELIABILITY AND VALIDITY

Regardless of the measurement framework chosen for a particular testing situation, the quality of the test used in that situation is assessed in terms of two characteristics: *reliability* and *validity*. Let us examine what is meant by each of these terms.

Reliability

A test is *reliable* in a particular examinee population to the extent that the scores it assigns to the examinees in that population are free of *variable* or *random* errors. These kinds of errors are caused by factors which influence test performance in an unpredictable fashion, sometimes causing a score to he higher than it ought to be and other times causing it to be lower. If *many* independent measurements were made on any one examinee and averaged, the effects of such errors would cancel each other out. Hence, variable errors do not directly affect the meaning of the measurements, but do affect their precision. The following illustrations should help clarify this point. First, suppose five individuals are given a task of measuring the length of a relatively long room (say 25 ft long) using a 3-ft cloth tape measure. Even if these individuals conscientiously carry out this task, as long as they are unaware of each others results, they will probably obtain noticeably different measurements. Since the object being measured has a length which obviously is fixed, the discrepancies between their results must be due to measurement errors.

One can speculate on factors which might contribute to these discrepancies, for example, (a) different degrees of tension on the tape measure, (b) mismatching the starting point of some of the successive 3-ft measurements with the endpoints of the previous ones, and (c) momentary lapses in attention. You can probably think of a number of others.

Similarly, if one repeatedly weighs oneself using a standard bathroom scale, the successive weighings (between which the individual steps off the scale and moves it to a different location) will probably produce weight values which vary somewhat. Some of the factors contributing to this variation are (a) changes in location of the individual's position on the scale platform (causing the internal mechanism to react differently), (b) variations in the amount of friction between the moving parts of the scale, (c) small, random fluctuations in the initial adjustment of the zero point which may occur from one weighing to the next, and (d) changes in floor slope or evenness as the scale is repositioned.

In both of these illustrations, certain factors (which are largely uncontrollable or controllable only up to a point) cause the observed measurements (or scores) to differ from the single value we would expect in each case if an error-free (or perfectly reliable) measurement procedure were available. Since the influence of factors like these fluctuates in an unpredictable fashion from one measurement application to the next, and since their effects tend to cancel each other out if many similar measurements are taken *independently* (i.e., in such a way that no one measurement affects any other) and averaged, they are examples of *random errors* (also called *variable, unsystematic,* or *chance* errors). Note, they do not directly influence the meaning of the measurement but do directly affect the *precision* with which the characteristic of interest is being measured. While highly reliable (or precise) instruments can be constructed to measure most physical characteristics of people, objects, or events, the task is much more difficult in the measurement of inferred characteristics such as achievement, intelligence, and anxiety. In such cases, random errors are introduced into the measurement process by factors associated with the examinee, the general testing conditions, and the scoring procedures, in addition to those associated with the instrument (test). Some examples of *examinee characteristics* which tend to fluctuate from one occasion to the next are (a) state of health, (b) level of motivation, (c) level of interest, (d) mood, (e) ability to concentrate, and (f) luck in choosing correct answers when forced to guess. Some examples of *testing conditions* which do not remain constant and, hence, are potential sources of random error are (a) disruptive noises (e.g., coughing, dropped books and pencils), (b) lighting, temperature, and humidity variations, and (c) observance of time limits (when such limits are specified). Some examples of *test characteristics* which tend to result in random errors are (a) ambiguous instructions to the examinee, (b) ambiguous items (or items which are too difficult for the examinees and, hence, encourage guessing), and (c) an insufficient number of items in the test.

In general, variable measurement errors tend to be quite sizable in educational test scores (or, equivalently, educational tests tend to be unreliable) unless a deliberate effort is made to insure an acceptable level of reliability. The need to be concerned about test reliability should be obvious. It is just as absurd to make important instructional or administrative decisions based on test scores heavily laden with random error as it is to base a decision concerning whether to shed five pounds using the weight score obtained from a scale which is accurate only to the nearest ten pounds.

Validity

A test is *valid* for supporting a particular type of inference to the extent that it is free of the effects of biasing factors which result in *constant* or *systematic errors.* Errors of this sort cause independent measurements obtained using the same test with the same examinee to be consistently *higher or lower* than they ought to be. If many independent measurements were taken of each examinee and, for each examinee, the scores were averaged, the constant errors would *not* cancel each other out because they consistently tend to occur in the same direction.

To illustrate this, reconsider the first example described above. If the five individuals in that situation were allowed to use a finely calibrated, 50-ft steel-tape measure to assess room length, their results might vary somewhat but probably much less than the results obtained using the short, cloth tape. The reason is the steel tape eliminates errors due to stretching of the measuring device, matching endpoints and starting points of successive measurements, etc. Thus, the steel tape would be a more *reliable* device than the cloth tape. However, if unbeknown to our five individuals, a 3 1/2-ft segment had been inadvertently broken off the lead end of the tape, they would all obtain room length measurements approximately 3 1/2 ft greater than the actual length of the room. In other words, all measurements would be biased upward (or in the positive direction). If the room were 25 ft long, then the obtained measurements would be equal to or near 28 1/2 ft, leading one to make an incorrect inference about the length of the room. Notice, the introduction of this positive bias does not affect the reliability of the measurements, but does affect *validity.*

Similarly, in the weighing example a positive or negative bias would be introduced if one forgot to set the scale dial at zero before stepping on the platform. The effect would be to add (subtract) a constant to (from) the value which would be obtained if the scale were properly adjusted. No matter how many independent weighings were conducted and averaged, the bias would not go away. The result is a weight score which does not present a truthful picture of the absolute weight of the individual being weighed. In other words, an inference about the absolute weight of the individual based on such data would be invalid. Please note that in this and the preceding example, scores (for room length and weight) containing such biases could be used to correctly infer the *relative* lengths of different rooms or the relative weights of different persons, but they would lead to incorrect inferences about absolute amounts. This illustrates the fact that validity determinations can be made only in light of the type of inference (or test score interpretation) one intends to make. Any measuring device (tests included) may be quite valid for making some types of inferences and less valid (or, perhaps, invalid) for making other types.

Your reaction may be that both random and constant errors are easily minimized in physical measurement situations like those described above. This is usually true in instances where the characteristic of interest is directly observable or has some directly observable effects (e.g., the effect of temperature on the expansion of mercury in a thermometer tube). However, when the characteristics are not directly observable, such as human cognitive, emotional, or attitudinal factors, the problem of minimizing the effects of constant errors is more complicated. For example, paper and pencil tests of mathematical achievement typically require a certain minimal level of reading comprehension on the part of the examinee. To the extent that the examinee's score depends on, or is influenced by, factors like these, the measurements will be biased (i.e., contain constant errors), and hence, inferences about mathematics achievement based on them may be subject to question. In fact, if the bias is appreciable, one may not be justified in concluding anything about the examinee's level of mathematics achievement given his score on the test.

There are numerous potential biasing factors one must consider within an educational testing context. Unlike the sources of random error whose effects tend to fluctuate from one testing situation to the next, the sources of constant error are associated with more lasting characteristics of the *examinee, test,* and/or *testing process* and exert the same influence on test performance regardless of the circumstance. Examples of the first type include (a) chronic illness, (b) testwiseness, (c) negative attitude toward test taking, and (d) incomplete comprehension of the language used in the test items or instructions. Some *test characteristics* which tend to bias measurements are (a) the inclusion of items measuring knowledge, skills, and abilities irrelevant to the test and/or (b) the use of instructions which bring personality factors into play (e.g., stringent penalty-for-guessing instructions which result in scores reflecting the examinee's "willingness to gamble"). Finally, some examples of *testing process characteristics* which result in constant measurement errors are (a) substandard testing environment factors like inadequate lighting, heating, etc., which remain constant over long periods of time (as in many schools located in areas of extreme poverty) and (b) scorer biases (such as the teacher's tendency to assign scores to essay responses which are influenced by the examinee's penmanship, spelling and grammar).

By now it should be clear that the reliability and validity problems in educational measurement are quite complex — much more so than in the tape measure and scale examples given earlier. A more complete picture of this complexity will be had when we deal with reliability and validity later in this text. Before closing the present discussion, however, it is worth noting two facts: (a) a measurement procedure (tests included) can be highly reliable but of questionable validity (e.g., the steel tape measure with the missing piece and the scale with the incorrect initial setting are cases in point), and (b) if a measurement procedure has low reliability (i.e., the scores it assigns contain large random errors), it cannot have an acceptable degree of validity for any type of inference. The following analogy to the reliability—validity distinction which concerns the tuning of a radio may help clarify this latter point.

In this analogy, the term *validity* corresponds to the success in obtaining certain information from a particular radio station; *reliability* corresponds to the absence of noise (or static) which might distort the signal and, hence, obscure the message. Within this framework, a clear signal from the desired station would allow the listener to acquire the desired information and, hence, is like a highly reliable, highly valid test. A clear signal from the wrong station would allow one to acquire the information that station is broadcasting; however, the information obtained may not be relevant to the listener's purpose or may only be partially relevant. This would correspond to a highly reliable test of low or moderate validity. Finally, if one is successful in tuning the desired station, but there is an appreciable amount of noise or static, fragments (or perhaps all) of the message will be obscured. This, in effect, is what happens when a test has low reliability. The errors of measurement or noise obscure the signal or message the test scores are supposed to convey, and hence, inferences made using such scores may be questionable, i.e., lack validity.

As a final note to this introduction, the concepts of reliability and validity are equally important in all testing contexts and with all types of tests. However, for a variety of reasons, which will become clear as we proceed, the technical procedures for assessing reliability and validity of tests constructed in the traditional manner (currently referred to as norm-referenced) and those constructed using domain-referenced technologies differ. In order to understand these techniques and to appreciate the necessity for different approaches, certain prerequisite statistical knowledge is necessary. Much of this information is contained in Chapters 2 through 7. This material should be studied carefully before proceeding to the more detailed treatment of test reliability and validity contained in the subsequent chapters.

SUMMARY

In this chapter, we defined some basic measurement terminology and introduced certain fundamental measurement concepts. In addition, an attempt was made to provide a framework within which the subsequent discussions in this text are comprehensible. In the next several chapters, we examine statistical concepts and techniques essential to understanding the theory and principles of measurement presented later and to appreciating both the power and limitations embodied in them. Before moving on, test your understanding of the contents of this chapter using the self-evaluation exercise provided for this purpose.

SELF-EVALUATION

1. Define each of the following terms:
    a. measurement
    b. mutually exclusive
    c. exhaustive
    d. unorderable categories
    e. nominal measurement rule
    f. ordinal measurement rule

g. interval measurement rule

h. ratio measurement rule

i. test

j. test validity

k. test reliability

l. norm-referenced measurement

m. criterion-referenced measurement

2. Classify each of the following variables according to the level of measurement with which they are most typically associated:

   a. years of education completed

   b. college entrance exam score

   c. Wechsler Intelligence score

   d. eye color

   e. posted speed limit

   f. running speed

   g. finishing position in the Boston marathon

   h. sex

   i. length of index finger

   j. grade point average

   k. temperature at noon [on the Centigrade (Celsius) scale]

   l. reading speed.

3. Generate at least two examples of each type of measurement rule. Do not use any of the examples from item 2.

4. What are the properties of ratio level measurement?

5. What is the property which distinguishes ratio from interval level measurement?

6. What is the principle difference between ordinal and nominal measurement?

7. Indicate whether each of the following is a potential source of *random* or *constant* measurement errors in a standardized achievement testing situation.

   a. Amount of prior experience in taking standardized achievement or aptitude tests.

   b. Instructions to the examinee which do not indicate how the examinee ought to respond to multiple-choice questions to which he/she does not know the correct answers.

   c. Temporary shifts in attention span.

   d. General rate of work on tests (assuming a stringent time limit).

8. If a random sample of 30 words from the most recent edition of *The American College Dictionary* were used as a spelling test, the test would most properly be called _____ .

   a. norm-referenced   b. criterion-referenced   c. domain-referenced

9. If pass/fail status in the test described in item 8 depends upon whether one responds correctly to at least 80% of the spelling items, the type of test score interpretation being used is most properly called _____ .

   a. norm-referenced   b. criterion-referenced   c. domain-referenced

10. A student learns that he scored at the 70th percentile (i.e., he scored better than 70% of the individuals in some well-defined comparison or norm group) on the SAT. This type of test score interpretation is most properly called _____ .

    a. norm-referenced   b. criterion-referenced   c. domain-referenced

REFERENCES

American Psychological Association (1966). *Standards for Educational and Psychological Tests and Manuals.* Washington, D.C.: American Psychological Association.

Hambleton, R. K., H. Swaminathan, J. Algina, and D. Coulson (1975). Criterion-Referenced Testing and Measurement: Review of Technical Issues and Developments. An invited symposium presented at the annual meeting of the American Educational Research Association (mimeo). Washington, D.C.

Lord, F. M. (1953). On the Statistical Treatment of Football Numbers. *American Psychologist*, 8, 750−751.

Millman, J. (1974). Criterion-Referenced Measurement, *Evaluation in Education, Current Applications*, (W. J. Popham, ed.). Berkeley, California: McCutchan.

Stevens, S. S. (1946). On the Theory of Scales of Measurement. *Science*, 103, 677−680.

2

Three Important Characteristics of a Distribution of Test Scores: Central Tendency, Dispersion, and Shape

A number of questions constantly recur among test constructors, examiners, and examinees. Some examples are: (a) What is the class average on this test? (b) Was the test too easy (or too difficult) for this group? (c) Do the test results indicate that Mr. Jones' class is homogeneous in mathematical ability? The purpose of this chapter is to introduce the concepts and techniques necessary for answering questions like these. We begin by defining and illustrating two important terms: *raw score* and *distribution.*

A *raw score* is usually the number of points earned by the examinee. When the test items are each worth 1 point (as in the case of most multiple-choice tests), the raw score is simply the number of correct responses made by the examinee. Geometrically, a raw score is the distance from the zero point on the number line to the numerical value representing the examinee's test performance. To illustrate, a score of 7 on a 10-item quiz is shown in Figure 2-1.

FIGURE 2-1. *Geometric representation of a raw score.*

A *distribution* of raw scores is a set of raw scores and is perhaps best thought of as a table or graph in which each score is paired with its frequency of occurrence. To illustrate, the distribution for the set (2, 4, 4, 6, 1, 3, 3, 3) is shown in tabular and graphical form in Figure 2-2. The type of table shown in Figure 2-2a is

a. Table

Raw Score	Number of Individuals
6	1
5	0
4	2
3	3
2	1
1	1

b. Histogram

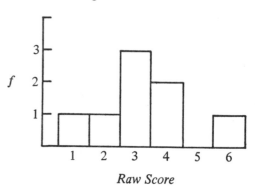

FIGURE 2-2. *Tabular and graphical representations of a hypothetical raw score distribution. (The symbol f on the vertical axis of the histogram indicates the axis is scaled in terms of frequency of occurrence. For example, this distribution contains the raw score of 2 just one time.)*

called a *frequency distribution.* Notice, it clearly shows how many examinees obtained each score. The type of graph shown in Figure 2-2b is called a *histogram.* It neatly displays all of the information contained in the frequency distribution and has one added advantage, namely, it makes information regarding the shape of the distribution more accessible to the reader. As a result, we will make frequent use of the histogram method for displaying test data in subsequent units.

EXERCISE SET 2-1[0]

1. How many examinees obtained a score of 3 in Figure 2-2?
2. How many examinees obtained a score of 5 in Figure 2-2?

___

CENTRAL TENDENCY, VARIABILITY, AND SHAPE OF A DISTRIBUTION

___

Every distribution of scores has three characteristics in which examiners are usually interested, namely, (a) location or central tendency, (b) dispersion or variability, and (c) general shape. Each of these characteristics will be discussed in turn. In addition, procedures for measuring the first two characteristics will be

___

0. Answers to exercise sets appear in boxes at the end of each chapter.

presented and geometric representations used for illustrative purposes wherever it seems advantageous to do so.

When a student first learns his test score, he may very well ask, "What was the average?" The term "average" is a generic name for a family of quantitative indexes used, in some sense, to represent a large set of scores. Some members of this family are: (a) the arithmetic mean, (b) the median, and (c) the mode. Each has its unique advantages and disadvantages in particular situations, and the relative merits of each ought to be considered whenever an index of "averageness" is selected.

Mode. The *mode* (or *modal interval*) is simply the score (or interval of scores) in a distribution obtained by the largest number of examinees. Graphically, it is the score (or interval of scores) straddled by the tallest column in a histogram. The mode of the distribution in Figure 2-2 is 3. Be sure you see why.

Median. The *median* of a distribution of scores is the score value which separates the upper 50% of the scores in the distribution from the lower 50% of the scores. The median can be estimated by locating the value on the raw score scale which divides the area in the histogram into two equal portions. In Figure 2-3 the shaded area and unshaded area each represent 50% of the total area in the histogram. Therefore, the point on the baseline marked with an X (i.e., the point having a raw score value of 3.5) is the median of the distribution. (*Note:* This is a very cumbersome procedure for determining the median of a distribution and is not recommended for general use. It is used here only for illustrative purposes.) A more practical procedure for determining the value of the median is to

1. Arrange the scores in the distribution from the lowest to the highest values.
2. Count the number of scores in the distribution.
3. If the count is an *odd* number, the value of the median is taken to be the central score in this ordered arrangement; if the count is *even*, the value of the median is taken to be the average of the two adjacent central values.
   For example, the median of (1, 3, 15, 70, 103) is 15; the median of (1, 2, 50, 53, 70, 92) is (1/2)(50 + 53), or 51.5.

Note: If there are duplicate numbers in the central region of the ordered sets of scores (for example, 1, 2, 5, 5, 6, 6, 6, 7) or if the distribution of scores is presented in grouped form (see, for example, the two distributions in question 2 of Exercise Set 2-2), this procedure provides an approximate (rather than an exact) value for the median. Since the approximation arrived at in this way is adequate for most purposes, an exact procedure is not presented in this text.[1]

---

1. Exact procedures for calculating the median of grouped data can be found in most elementary statistics texts [see, for example, Edwards, A. L., *Statistical Analysis* (4th ed.). New York: Holt, Rinehart, and Winston, 1974].

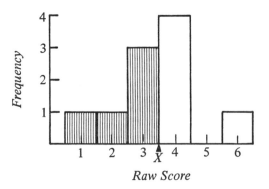

FIGURE 2-3. *Histogram showing the median of a hypothetical distribution of raw scores.*

Arithmetic Mean.[2] The *arithmetic mean* is the sum of the scores in a distribution divided by the number of scores entering into the sum. The formula is

$$M = \frac{\Sigma X}{N} \qquad (2\text{-}1)$$

Where M represents the arithmetic mean
         Σ means "the sum of"
         X represents the variable whose values are to be summed
         N represents the number of scores summed

For example, to calculate the mean of the scores 1, 4, and 10, we use the formula as shown below:

$$M = \frac{\Sigma X}{N} = \frac{1 + 4 + 10}{3} = \frac{15}{3} = 5$$

By locating these values on a number line (see Figure 2-4), we can see that the mean is the fulcrum or balancing point of the distribution. That is, if the line were thought of as a ruler and objects of equal weight were placed at points X_1,

```
1              4                              10
├──┴──┴──┴──┴──┴──┴──┴──┴──┴──┤
  X₁         X₂   M                        X₃
```

Data: John had 1 item correct.
       Sue had 4 items correct.
       Sam had 10 items correct.

FIGURE 2-4. *Geometric representation of an arithmetic mean.*

---

2. In most statistics and measurement texts, the Greek letter μ is used to represent the mean of a population (i.e., the mean of the entire collection of scores in which one is interested), while $\hat{\mu}$ or $\bar{X}$ are typically used to represent the mean of a sample (subset) of scores from the population. Throughout this text, we confine our attention to population data and consistently use the letter M to represent the mean.

X_2, and X_3, the balancing point would be at the position associated with the scale value of 5. The median, on the other hand, divides the distribution into two equal-sized sets of scores or frequencies; therefore, the median for this distribution is equivalent to the value 4 on the raw score scale.

EXERCISE SET 2-2

1. What is the mode of the distribution in Figure 2-3?
2. What are the modes of the distributions shown below?

Distribution A		Distribution B	
Raw Score	Number of Examinees	Raw Score	Number of Examinees
5	1	20–24	3
4	17	15–19	7
3	12	10–14	12
2	3	5–9	19
1	6	0–4	2
0	2		

3. Using the histogram method illustrated in Figure 2-3, or the approximation procedure outlined in this section, determine the value of the median for each of the following data sets:
   a. 1, 2, 2, 2, 3   b. 1, 2, 2, 2, 6
   c. 1, 2, 3, 4   d. 1, 2, 4, 5
   e. 1, 2, 4, 7
4. a. What is the mean of the following set of scores: 1, 5, 7, 27?
   b. What is the median of the same set of scores?

Dispersion or Variability

A second question, raised more frequently by the teacher than the student, is "How spread out are the scores in the distribution?" In order to quantify the amount of *variability* or *dispersion* when the arithmetic mean is chosen as the measure of "averageness," any one of the following three indices may be used: (a) the sum of the squared deviation scores (*sum of squares*, for short), (b) the *variance*, and (c) the *standard deviation*. Before explaining and illustrating each of these measures of variability, the *deviation score* must be explained since each of these dispersion measures is calculated using deviation scores.

As shown previously, a raw score represents the distance between an examinee's test performance and the zero point on the scale; i.e., individual scores take on their meaning by virtue of their distance from the scale origin. *Deviation scores*, on the other hand, represent the distances of individual performances from the arithmetic mean of the distribution and are obtained by subtracting the mean of the raw score distribution from each raw score contained in the distribution.

For example, the illustrations in Figure 2-5 represent the performances of three individuals on a 10-item multiple-choice quiz in raw and deviation score form, respectively. Examine and compare them.

a. **Raw Scores**

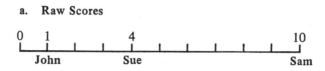

b. **Deviation Scores**

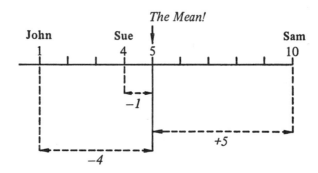

FIGURE 2-5. *Geometric representation of three hypothetical raw scores and the corresponding deviation scores.*

The following three facts about deviation scores should be noted and verified by the reader at this time:

1. Although deviation scores and raw scores represent distances from different origins, they are expressed in the same units, e.g., test score points.
2. The *sign* of a deviation score indicates whether the performance it represents is below (−) or above (+) the mean. The numerical portion of the deviation score indicates the distance between "average" performance and that represented by the raw score under consideration.
3. The sum and arithmetic mean of any complete distribution of deviation scores are both equal to zero. For example, the sum of the deviation scores shown in Figure 2-5 is $(-4) + (-1) + (+5) = 0$.

EXERCISE SET 2-3

1. The following raw scores were obtained in a 10-item quiz administered to 4 examinees: 1, 5, 8, and 6.
   a. Convert these to deviation scores.
   b. Represent the deviation score distribution using the number line.
   c. Calculate the sum of these deviation scores.

Let us now consider three indexes used to measure the *variation* or *dispersion* inherent in a set of scores. (A set of scores which displays very little variation or dispersion looks bunched, while a set which displays considerable variation or dispersion is spread out.) As stated earlier, the indexes which are especially useful when the mean is the appropriate measure of location or "averageness" are

1. The sum of squared deviation scores (more commonly called the *sum of squares*), designated by the symbol SS(X).
2. The *variance*, designated Var(X).
3. The *standard deviation*, designated SD(X).

Sum of Squares.[3] The *sum of squares*, SS(X), is simply the sum of the squared deviation scores. Using the scores (1, 4, 10), we have

$$SS(X) = \Sigma(X - M)^2$$
$$= (X_1 - M)^2 + (X_2 - M)^2 + (X_3 - M)^2$$
$$= (-4 \text{ points})^2 + (-1 \text{ point})^2 + (+5 \text{ points})^2$$
$$= 16 \text{ (points)}^2 + 1 \text{ (point)}^2 + 25 \text{ (points)}^2$$
$$= 42 \text{ (points)}^2 \quad \text{(Read: 42 square points)}$$

There are two problems with using the SS(X) as the measure of dispersion:

1. The SS(X) is expressed in square units, e.g., square points. Although we are quite comfortable in dealing with other kinds of square units, e.g., square yards of carpet and square miles of territory, the square point proves discomforting for most people.
2. In comparing the variability of two distributions of test scores, the set having the larger number of scores will probably have the larger SS(X) value whether or not it displays the greatest amount of variability. In other words, the size of SS(X) depends not only on the amount of variability but also on the number of scores in the set. For example, the set of scores (1, 5) is more spread out than the set (2, 2, 2, 2, 2, 3, 4, 4, 4, 4, 4), yet it has a smaller sum of squares.

---

3. Through elementary algebra, the definitional formula for the sum of squares discussed can be transformed to

$$SS(X) = \Sigma X^2 - \frac{(\Sigma X)^2}{N}$$

where ΣX^2 is the sum of the squared raw scores and $(\Sigma X)^2$ is the squared raw score total.

The primary advantage of this formula is computational convenience, particularly when the number of scores in the distribution is large and/or the value of the mean is not a whole number. Applying this formula to the example in this section, we get

$$SS(X) = (1^2 + 4^2 + 10^2) - \frac{(1 + 4 + 10)^2}{3}$$

$$= (1 + 16 + 100) - \frac{(15)^2}{3}$$

$$= 117 - 75$$

$$= 42 \text{ square points}$$

We can eliminate the second of these problems by defining a statistic called the *variance.*

Variance.   The *variance* is simply the sum of squares, SS(X), divided by the number of deviation scores involved in the calculation.   Once again, using the scores (1, 4, 10), we find:

$$\mathrm{Var}(X) = \frac{\mathrm{SS}(X)}{N} = \frac{42 \text{ square points}}{3} = 14 \text{ square points}$$

Notice that the variance is plagued by the same interpretive difficulty as the "sum of squares," namely, the square point unit.   However, because the variance is an average, it is not affected by the number of scores in the set.

Standard Deviation.   To return to the original scale (which is linear rather than square measure), we simply calculate the positive square root of the variance.   This result is called the *standard deviation,* designated SD(X).   For our illustration,

$$\mathrm{SD}(X) = \sqrt{14 \text{ square points}} = 3.74 \text{ points}$$

Notice that we are now back to linear units and the interpretation problem vanishes.   For this reason, the standard deviation is the preferred measure of variation for many measurement applications, particularly where test score interpretation is involved.

EXERCISE SET 2-4

1. a. Calculate the sum of squares for the distribution of raw scores: 1, 5, 8, and 6.
   b. Calculate the sum of squares for the distribution of raw scores: 1, 5, 7, and 27.
   c. Which distribution, a or b, displays the greatest dispersion?
2. a. Calculate the variance for the distributions given in questions 1a and b.
   b. Does the variance provide any more information about the relative amount of dispersion in these two distributions than was provided by SS(X)?
   c. Under what circumstance might SS(X) and Var(X) provide conflicting information in comparing the amount of variability in two sets of test scores?
3. a. Calculate the SD(X) for the distributions given in questions 1a and b.
   b. Does SD(X) provide more information about the amount of dispersion in a distribution than is provided by Var(X)?
   c. What is the principal advantage of using SD(X) as the measure of variation?

Distribution Shape

The third characteristic of interest is the general shape of the distribution. Although distributions of educational measurements may assume almost any shape, many of the distributions actually obtained tend to assume one of the shapes shown in Figure 2-6.   By this we mean that the histograms of many

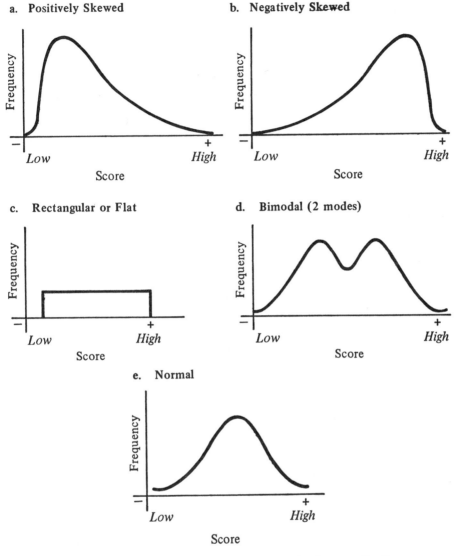

FIGURE 2-6. *Illustrations of several idealized score distribution shapes.*

distributions of test scores and other educational measurements conform *approximately* to one of the shapes shown here. A number of remarks about these several kinds of distributions are in order at this point:

1. The *normal* and *flat* distributions are symmetrical; the *skewed* distributions are asymmetrical; the *bimodal* distribution may be either. (Symmetrical means that the left half of the distribution is a perfect mirror image of the right half.)

2. Easy, moderately difficult, and very difficult tests usually yield negatively skewed, approximately normal, and positively skewed distributions, respectively.
3. Measuring two distinctly different populations (e.g., men and women) on selected variables (e.g., physical weight) may yield a bimodal distribution.
4. For theoretical reasons to be discussed later, a normal distribution is desirable in norm-referenced testing. In addition, examinees are most spread out at the ends of such a distribution which is where the most crucial decisions are made, e.g., who gets the grades of A and F.
5. Anything but a negatively skewed distribution following instruction within a criterion-referenced instruction/measurement context is a sign of trouble. (Think about it.)
6. In a normal distribution, the value of the mean, median, and mode are identical. In a positively skewed distribution, the mean has the largest value the median has the next largest value, and the mode is the smallest. In a negatively skewed distribution, the order of magnitude (i.e., absolute size) of these three statistics is reversed. In some unusual cases, the value of the median may equal the value of the mode.

EXERCISE SET 2-5

1. What are the relative sizes of the arithmetic mean (M), the median (Md) and the mode (Mo) in the following:
   a. positively skewed distribution
   b. normal distribution
   c. negatively skewed distribution
   d. flat distribution
2. What kind (shape) of score distribution should you expect if you administered:
   a. a college level calculus test to a random sample of 12th grade students?
   b. a reading readiness test to a random sample of middle class third grade students?
   c. the Wechsler Adult Intelligence Scale (WAIS) to a random sample of American adults?
3. Suppose 100 examinees randomly guessed at the answer to a four-alternative multiple-choice item. What would you expect the distribution of preferences for the four alternatives to look like?

THREE KINDS OF TEST SCORES

We began by defining and geometrically illustrating the meaning of a raw score. Repeating, the *raw score* obtained on a test is simply the number of points accumulated by an examinee. Geometrically, a raw score is the distance on the number line from zero to the value which represents the exam performance of one examinee.

Later, we derived a new set of scores by subtracting the mean of the test score distribution from the raw score of each examinee and called these deviation scores. Geometrically, deviation scores show where each examinee's performance is located on the number line relative to the mean performance of the group to which he belongs. Deviation scores, like the raw scores from which they are derived, are expressed in the original measurement units (in this case, test points).

In many instances, it is desirable to go one step further and convert the deviation scores to Z scores (e.g., whenever it is advantageous to have scores which directly indicate the relative, as opposed to absolute, standing of an individual in some well-defined group or population). (One advantage of the Z score over the deviation score is that it not only tells at a glance whether the individual obtaining it is above or below the group mean, but it also tells how far he is from the mean in standard deviation units. This latter feature is especially useful when the distribution has a *normal* shape, a point we will explore more fully in Chapters 4 and 5.) This is accomplished by dividing each deviation score in the distribution by the standard deviation of the distribution. In mathematical form,

$$Z = \frac{X - M}{SD(X)}$$

Where X is an examinee's raw score on a test

M is the arithmetic mean of the test score distribution with which his score is being compared

$SD(X)$ is the standard deviation of the distribution

If an examinee obtains a raw score of 8 in a distribution with $M = 5$ and $SD(X) = 2$, his deviation score would be $8 - 5 = 3$ and his Z score would be $3/2$ or $+1.50$.

This tells us that his performance is 1.5 standard deviation units above the arithmetic mean of this group. If an individual's raw score were below the mean, his Z score would have a negative sign. Unlike the deviation score, which represents the examinee's distance from the mean in raw score points, the Z score represents his distance from the mean in standard deviation units. In subsequent chapters, we will examine the usefulness of the Z score, particularly within the norm-referenced measurement framework.

EXERCISE SET 2-6

1. a. Suppose an examinee obtains a quiz score of 15. The mean and standard deviation of the quiz score distribution for his class are 12 and 3, respectively. What is this examinee's Z score?
   b. Suppose a second examinee has a quiz score of 9 in the same distribution. What is his Z score?
2. What Z score corresponds to a raw score of 15 in a distribution having a mean of 9 and a standard deviation of 4?

SUMMARY

In this chapter, we have considered the three most important characteristics of test score distributions as well as selected procedures for quantifying two of them (central tendency and dispersion). In addition, we defined and illustrated three kinds of test score scales (the raw, deviation, and Z score scales). Mastery of the information in this chapter will facilitate comprehension of the material in subsequent chapters. Before proceeding to Chapter 3, "Percentage Scores, Percentile Ranks, and Percentiles," check your comprehension of the material in this chapter using the self-evaluation forms provided.

SELF-EVALUATION

Form A

1. The _____ is the score in a distribution obtained by the largest number of examinees.
   a. arithmetic mean   c. mode
   b. median   d. standard

2. John's raw score on a 10-item French test was 9. The mean for the test was 6. What was John's deviation score?
   a. 7.5   b. 15   c. 1   d. 3

3. In a negatively skewed test score distribution, the value of the arithmetic mean is _____ the value of the median.
   a. less than   b. equal to   c. greater than

4. A group of 20 students took a test in human geography. The mean score of the group was 60. The sum of squares was 500. What was the standard deviation?
   a. 2   b. 5   c. 10   d. 20

5. What is the mode of the following distribution?

Score	Number of Examinees
5	3
4	12
3	10
2	7
1	3
0	1

   a. 3   b. 7   c. 4   d. 5

6. What is the arithmetic mean of the scores (2, 2, 3, 6, 7)?
   a. 3   b. 4   c. 2   d. 6

7. Which of the following measures is *not* expressed in the same units as the other three?
   a. variance   c. arithmetic mean
   b. median   d. standard deviation

8. Distribution A has a mean of 110 and a *variance* of 144, distribution B a mean of 50 and a *standard deviation* of 15. Which of the following statements about these distributions is true?
   a. A is more variable than B.
   b. A and B display equal amounts of variability.
   c. B is more variable than A.

9. A class of 25 students was given a 15-item test. If the mean of this distribution is 10, the sum of the raw scores must be _____ .
   a. 225   b. 250   c. 300   d. 375

10. If a ninth grade test was administered to a random sample of college students, the distribution would probably be _____ .
   a. positively skewed   c. negatively skewed
   b. normal   d. symmetrical

Form B

1. Geometrically, the distance from the zero point on the number line to the numerical value representing the examinee's test performance is called a _____ score.
   a. deviation   b. raw   c. standard   d. Z

2. The sum of raw scores in a distribution divided by the number of scores entering into the sum is called the _____ .
   a. mean   b. mode   c. median

3. What is the arithmetic mean of the scores (3, 6, 1, 1, 4)?
   a. 1   b. 4   c. 5   d. 3

4. Determine the value of the median for the data set (2, 2, 3, 4, 5).
   a. 2   b. 5   c. 3   d. 2.5

5. What is the sum of squares, SS(X), for the scores (2, 1, 2, 3, 2, 2, 3, 1)?
   a. 2   b. 8   c. 4   d. 6

6. The variance of the set of scores (1, 4, 10) is _____ .
   a. 3   b. 14   c. 27   d. 42

7. Distribution A has a mean of 100 and a *variance* of 225, distribution B a mean of 80 and a *standard deviation* of 15. Which of the following statements about these distributions is true?
   a. A is more variable than B.
   b. A and B display equal amounts of variability.
   c. B is more variable than A.

8. In a norm-referenced context, a negatively skewed test distribution usually means the test was _____ .
   a. too easy   b. of moderate difficulty   c. too difficult

9. Teacher X gave a 10-item quiz to three students and immediately converted the individual scores to deviation form. His results were (−5, 1, 3). Were Teacher X's calculations correct?
   a. yes   b. no

10. Which one of the following is *not* a measure of the dispersion in a test score distribution?
   a. sum of squares   c. standard deviation
   b. variance   d. arithmetic mean

EXERCISE SET 2-1: ANSWERS

1. three
2. none

EXERCISE SET 2-2: ANSWERS

1. Four points
2. The mode for distribution *A* is 4 points since there are more scores of 4 in the set than any other score.

   In distribution *B*, the scores have been grouped into equal-sized intervals. Three examinees scored in the interval 20–24; seven had scores in the interval 15–19; etc. In this distribution, the largest number of examinees obtained scores in the interval 5–9. Therefore, it is correct to say that the *modal interval* in this distribution is 5–9.

   Since the mode has relatively few applications of interest in a measurement context, most of our attention is henceforth focused on the median and arithmetic mean.
3. a. 2.0
   b. 2.0
   c. 2.5 (Unlike the mode, the median may be a value which is not a member of the set of scores in the distribution. For example, the median in this distribution is 2.5; this value is not a member of the set.)
   d. 3.0
   e. 3.0 [*Remark*: The value of the median is not influenced by extreme scores. For example, the median of the set (1, 2, 3) and the set (1, 2, 100) is 2. As we will see later, this is not true of the arithmetic mean.]
4. a. $M = \Sigma X/N = (1 + 5 + 7 + 27)/4 = 10$ points
   b. 6 points

1. a. The mean is 5. Therefore, the deviation scores are −4, 0, +3, and +1.
   b.

   c. zero

---

1. a. $SS(X) = (1 − 5)^2 + (5 − 5)^2 + (8 − 5)^2 + (6 − 5)^2$
      $= (−4)^2 + (0)^2 + (3)^2 + (1)^2$
      $= 16 + 0 + 9 + 1$
      $= 26$ square points
   b. $SS(X) = (1 − 10)^2 + (5 − 10)^2 + (7 − 10)^2 + (27 − 10)^2$
      $= 81 + 25 + 9 + 289$
      $= 404$ square points
   c. b

2. a. 6.5 square points; 101 square points
   b. Not in this case. Although the values of $Var(X)$ and $SS(X)$ differ for each distribution, the relative sizes of the $Var(X)$ measures and the $SS(X)$ measures do, in fact, reflect the amounts of variability in each distribution equally well. In cases like this one where the number of scores in each distribution is the same, it does not matter whether $Var(X)$ or $SS(X)$ is used; the conclusion will be the same.
   c. When the two sets of scores have different numbers of elements. For example, the set of scores (0, 5) is more variable than the set (0, 0, 4, 4). The $SS(X)$ values for these distributions are 12.50 and 16, respectively, suggesting the latter is more variable. The $Var(X)$ values are 12.50/2 = 6.25 and 16/4 = 4, respectively, indicating the former is more variable. Since $Var(X)$ is not distorted by the number of observations in the set, it is the preferred measure in most cases.

3. a. 2.55 points; 10.05 points
   b. No, not about the amount of dispersion. Interpretability is another matter.
   c. $SD(X)$ is easier to interpret. Unlike $SS(X)$ and $Var(X)$, it is not expressed in square units.

EXERCISE SET 2-5: ANSWERS

1. a. Mo has the lowest value; Md is intermediate in value; M has the highest value.
   b. Md = Mo = M, because of the symmetry of the distribution.
   c. The opposite of (a).
   d. Md = M because of the symmetry of the distribution. Notice, however, there is no uniquely defined mode.

   [*Note:* The following illustration may be of help in comprehending the answers to parts (a) and (c). In the symmetrical distribution (2, 3, 3, 4), the mean, median, and mode all equal 3. If, however, the distribution were made assymetrical (or skew) by increasing the value of the right-hand value in this set to 10, the resulting distribution (2, 3, 3, 10) would still have a mode and median equal to 3, but the mean would now be 4.5. If, instead of 10, the right-most value were 52, the mode and median would remain unchanged while the mean would now be 10. Notice how the value of the mean is affected by extreme scores that "pull" it towards the tail of the skewed distribution. In most situations the value of the median tends to be somewhere between the values of the mode and mean.]

2. a. positively skewed (too tough!)
   b. negatively skewed (too easy!)
   c. normal (because research shows that that is the way Wechsler IQ scores distribute in randomly selected test samples).

3. Flat (or nearly so) since each alternative has an equal chance of selection in a random process. In the real world, however, there is very little random guessing.

EXERCISE SET 2-6: ANSWERS

1. a. $Z = \dfrac{X - M}{SD(X)} = \dfrac{15 - 12}{3} = +1.00$

   That is, this examinee's performance is one standard deviation unit above the mean.

   b. −1.00

2. $Z = \dfrac{15 - 9}{4} = \dfrac{6}{4} = +1.50$

3

Percentage Scores, Percentile Ranks, and Percentiles

In Chapter 2 we defined three types of test scores: raw, deviation, and Z scores. The first type of score, i.e., the raw score, most directly reflects the amount of the measured attribute possessed by an individual (e.g., points on a test, pounds on a scale). The other two scores, obtained from a raw score distribution using specific arithmetical operations, are sometimes referred to as *derived scores*. In the present chapter, we shall (a) define two additional types of derived scores, namely, percentage scores and percentile ranks, (b) examine procedures for deriving these kinds of scores from a distribution of raw scores, (c) examine the utility of each within criterion- and norm-referenced measurement contexts, and (d) differentiate between the terms percentile and percentile rank. In the process, it should become clear that the percentage score (which reflects an individual's absolute level of performance) has some utility within a criterion-referenced context, while the percentile rank (which reflects an individual's standing relative to some well-defined group) is more appropriate for use in norm-referenced applications. Let us begin with percentage scores.

PERCENTAGE SCORES

A *percentage score* is simply the percentage of the total number of points available which have been earned by the examinee. The rule for converting a raw score to a percentage score can be stated as follows:

1. Divide the examinee's raw score by the maximum possible raw score obtainable on the test.
2. Multiply the result by 100 and round off to the nearest whole number.

For example, a raw score of 12 on a 20-item quiz is equivalent to a percentage score of 60. Recall, the raw score is a measure of an individual's absolute distance from the scale origin or zero point; the percentage score, on the other hand, tells us where the individual's performance is in relation to the minimum and maximum possible values on the raw score scale.

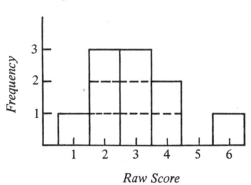

a   Table

Raw Score	Frequency
6	1
5	0
4	2
3	3
2	3
1	1

b   Histogram

FIGURE 3-1.   *Tabular and histogram displays of a hypothetical test score distribution.*

Before moving on, consider the data displayed in Figure 3-1. If these scores were the result of a 6-item multiple-choice quiz, it is easy to see that a raw score of 6 would be equivalent to a percentage score of $(6/6) \times 100 = 100$. Similarly, a raw score of 3 would be equivalent to a percentage score of $(3/6) \times 100 = 50$. On the other hand, if these scores were the result of a 10-item quiz, raw scores of 6 and 3 would be equivalent to percentage scores of 60 and 30, respectively.

PERCENTILE RANKS AND PERCENTILES

In this segment of the discussion, we will examine the difference between percentiles and percentile ranks. We begin by defining the term *percentile rank*.

Percentile Ranks

The *percentile rank* of a particular raw score in a specific score distribution is the percentage of area in the histogram located to the left of the raw score in question. For example, the percentile rank of the raw score 2.5 in the distribution shown in

Figure 3-1 is 40 since 4/10 or 40% of the histogram area (i.e., 4 out of 10 blocks of area) is located to the left of the value 2.5 on the raw score scale. Similarly, the raw score 3.0 has a percentile rank of 55 because 55% of the histogram area is located to the left of 3.0 on the raw score scale. (*Note:* If we construct a vertical line perpendicular to the point labeled 3 on the raw score scale, we will find exactly 5.5 blocks to the left of the line and 4.5 blocks to the right of the line.)

Percentiles

The Xth *percentile* is the point or value on the raw score scale which separates the left-most $X\%$ of the histogram area from the remainder of the graph. For example, the raw score 3 in the distribution shown in Figure 3-1 is the 55th percentile since 55% of the histogram area is located to the left of the value 3 on the raw score scale, i.e., the percentile rank of the raw score 3 is 55. Similarly, the raw score 6 is the 95th percentile point in this distribution.

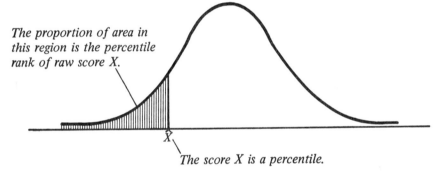

The proportion of area in this region is the percentile rank of raw score X.

The score X is a percentile.

FIGURE 3-2. *Illustration of the concepts* percentile rank *and* percentile.

Geometrically, a *percentile rank* is an area, while a *percentile* is a point on the raw score scale. The percentage of the area which is in the shaded region of Figure 3-2 is the percentile rank of the raw score X shown on the baseline. Therefore, if the shaded area is 20%, a person obtaining a raw score of X is said to be the 20th percentile of the distribution.

EXERCISE SET 3-1

1. What would the percentage-score equivalent of the raw score 6 be if the distribution shown in Figure 3-1 had been the result of:
   a. a 10-item quiz?
   b. a 20-item quiz

2. a. What is the percentile rank of the raw score 6 in the distribution shown in Figure 3-1?
   b. In Figure 3-1, the raw score 6 is called the _____ percentile.

3. What is the 70th percentile in the distribution shown in Figure 3-1?

4. a. Suppose that John had a raw score of 75 on his geography test and that this score equaled or surpassed the scores earned by 37% of his classmates. John's percentile rank would be _____ .

   b. Suppose Sue's score on the same test was 85 and this equaled or surpassed the scores obtained by 91% of her classmates. The 91st percentile in this distribution must be _____ .

   c. Suppose student X scored at the 45th percentile point on an arithmetic final exam. This means he has:
      (1) Correctly answered 45 items on the test.
      (2) Correctly answered 45% of the items on the test.
      (3) Performed as well as or better than 45% of his classmates.
      (4) Performed as well as or better than 55% of his classmates.

Recapitulation and Some Measurement Implications

1. Before we look at procedures for calculating and/or estimating percentile ranks, let us consider one more test score distribution. Suppose we administered a 5-item True-False quiz to a group of 10 examinees and obtained the data shown in Figure 3-3. Notice the following:

a. Table

Raw Score	Frequency
5	1
4	5
3	1
2	2
1	1

b. Histogram

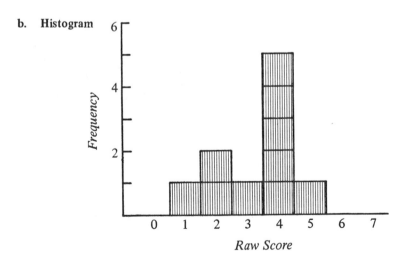

FIGURE 3-3.   *Hypothetical test score data.*

(a) The raw score 4 is the absolute distance from the zero point to the point labeled 4 on the raw score scale. Geometrically, it may be represented as a line segment extending from 0 to 4 (see Figure 3-4).

Raw Score

FIGURE 3-4. *Geometric representation of a raw score.*

(b) The *percentage score* equivalent of this raw score is 80 because the raw score of 4 is geometrically equivalent to 80% of the line segment extending from 0 to 5.
(c) The *percentile rank* of the raw score 4 is the histogram area to the left of the point labeled 4 on the raw score scale (see the shaded area in Figure 3-5). In this example, the percentile rank of 4 is 65.

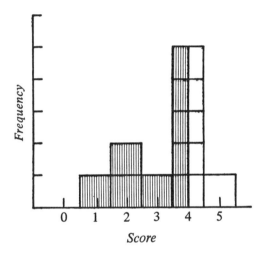

Score

FIGURE 3-5. *Histogram of a hypothetical raw score distribution with the percentile rank of the raw score 4 shown by the shaded area.*

(d) Since 65% of the area in this histogram is located to the left of the raw score 4, the point labeled 4 on the raw score scale is called the 65th *percentile point* or the 65th *percentile.*
2. Like the raw score, the *percentage score* is a measure of absolute performance; i.e., the percentage score of one examinee is completely independent of the percentage scores of all other examinees. Therefore, it is an excellent measure of performance in a criterion-referenced context.
3. The *percentile rank* is a measure of relative performance; i.e., the percentile rank of an examinee is totally dependent on the quality of his performance as compared to the performances of the others in the group of examinees with which he is being compared. It is totally independent of test length (i.e., the

number of points available). Therefore, it is an excellent measure of performance in a norm-referenced measurement context.

4. A *percentile* is simply a value or point on the raw score continuum. Since it is a point and points are dimensionless, it is incorrect to say, "Mr. X scored *in* the 90th percentile." The correct statement is, "Mr. X scored *at* the 90th percentile," that is, provided Mr. X's performance was better than or equal to exactly 90% of the performances in the reference group.

Calculating Percentile Ranks

In the earlier discussion of percentile ranks, we used a block-counting or area estimation technique to determine the percentile rank equivalent of a selected raw score in a specific test score distribution. That procedure was useful because it helped focus our attention on what the term *percentile rank* really means. From a practical standpoint, a much better procedure exists for transforming raw scores to percentile ranks. The procedure and an illustration of it are given below.

PROBLEM: Suppose a 5-item quiz were administered by Teacher Q to his class of 10 students and the test score distribution shown in Table 3-1 resulted. What is the percentile rank of the raw score 3 in this distribution?

TABLE 3-1. *Distribution of Scores on Quiz Given by Teacher Q.*

Raw Score	Frequency
4	1
3	4
2	2
1	2
0	1

PROCEDURE: Given a raw score x and the distribution to which it belongs,

1. Determine how many examinees obtained quiz scores equal to x in value; take 1/2 of this number.
2. Count the number of examinees who obtained scores less than x on this quiz.
3. Add the results of steps 1 and 2.
4. Divide the result of step 3 by the total number of scores in the distribution.
5. Multiply this value by 100 and round off to the nearest whole number.

EXAMPLE
Find the percentile rank of the raw score 3 in the distribution shown above.

1. Four examinees obtained quiz scores equal to 3. Taking 1/2 of this number, the result is 2.

2. Exactly 5 examinees had raw scores less than 3.
3. Add the results of the first two steps, 5 + 2 = 7.
4. Since there are 10 scores in the distribution, we have 7/10 = 0.70.
5. 0.70 x 100 = 70. Since this result is exact, no rounding is necessary. (*Note*: The student may easily confirm this result by sketching a histogram and observing that, indeed, 70% of its area is located to the left of the raw score value of 3.)

EXERCISE SET 3-2

1. Find the percentile rank of each of the following raw score values in the distribution given in Table 3-1 using the procedure just illustrated.
   a. 0
   b. 1
   c. 2

Some Remarks

1. Certain percentiles have special names. For example, the 75th percentile point may be called the *third quartile* (or quartile point); the 50th percentile may be called the *second quartile*; and the 25th percentile may be called the *first quartile*. These are sometimes designated Q_3, Q_2, and Q_1, respectively.
2. The second quartile, Q_2, is also known as the *median* of the distribution.
3. A percentile value can be a value which is not in the set of scores actually obtained by the examinees represented in a particular distribution. For example, the 50th percentile (or median) of a test score distribution frequently equals a value like 3.50, 43.72, or some similar result.

   Hence, the median or 50th percentile, like the arithmetic mean, may have a score value not actually obtained by any examinees represented in the distribution; in contrast, the mode always equals a value represented in the distribution.

SUMMARY

We have compared and contrasted *percentage scores, percentile ranks,* and *percentiles.* In the process, we transformed selected raw scores to percentages and percentile ranks, and discussed the meanings of these transformed or derived scores in both norm-referenced and criterion-referenced measurement contexts. We also examined the meaning of the term *percentile.* Since teachers, administrators, and counselors are hardly ever called on to calculate percentiles, procedures for doing so were not included in this discussion.

Before proceeding to the next chapter which deals with characteristics and uses of the theoretical *normal* model, check your comprehension of the material in this chapter using the self-evaluation forms provided for this purpose.

Form A

1. Of the following, the most meaningful measure of student performance in a norm-referenced measurement situation is the _____ .
   a. percentage score   b. percentile rank   c. raw score

2. The value on the raw score scale which divides a distribution in half is called

   _____ .
   a. the 50th percentile   b. the second quartile
   c. the median   d. a, b, or c

3. Percentage scores and percentile ranks are sometimes referred to as _____ scores.
   a. raw   b. derived

   Use the data displayed in the table below to answer questions 4–6, which follow.

Quiz Scores for a Class of 10 Students

Raw Score	Frequency
4	1
3	4
2	2
1	2
0	1

4. The raw score 2 is the _____ percentile in this distribution.

5. Assume the maximum possible score for this quiz is 10 points.
   a. A raw score of 4 is equivalent to a percentage score of _____ .
   b. A raw score of 4 is equivalent to a percentile rank of _____ .
   c. A percentage score of 30 is equivalent to a percentile rank of _____ .
      (*Hint*: Begin by determining the raw score equivalent of this percentage score.)

6. Assume the maximum possible score for this quiz is 5 points.
   a. A raw score of 4 is equivalent to a percentage score of _____ .
   b. A raw score of 4 is equivalent to a percentile rank _____ .
   c. A percentage score of 40 is equivalent to a percentile rank of _____ .

Form B

1. Percentile ranks are more meaningful than percentage scores in a _____ measurement context.
   a. criterion-referenced   b. norm-referenced

2. The 25th percentile is sometimes referred to as the _____ quartile.
   a. first   b. second   c. third

3. What is wrong with the statement, "John's cumulative grade point average is in the third quartile of his class"?

4. Student X's cumulative grade point average was exceeded by exactly 10% of his classmates. Therefore, we can say that student X's percentile rank within class is _____ .

Use the data displayed in the table below to answer questions 5–7, which follow.

Quiz Scores for a Class of 40 Students

Raw Score	Frequency
10	4
9	6
8	10
7	12
6	8

5. Assume the maximum possible score for the quiz that yielded the distribution shown above is 10 points.
   a. A raw score of 10 is equivalent to a percentage score of _____ .
   b. A raw score of 10 is equivalent to a percentile rank of _____ .
   c. A percentage score of 70 is equivalent to a percentile rank of _____ .

6. Assume the maximum possible score for the quiz is 20 points.
   a. A raw score of 10 is equivalent to a percentage score of _____ .
   b. A raw score of 10 is equivalent to a percentile rank of _____ .

7. Questions 5 and 6 illustrate the fact that percentage scores (are/are not) independent of test length while percentile ranks (are/are not) independent of test length.

4

The Normal Distribution

The term "normal distribution" is the name of a family of theoretical distributions which can be generated using the same mathematical equation and which, as a result, share a number of defining characteristics. The term "a normal distribution" is used usually when referring to one member of this family of theoretical distributions.

The normal distribution is especially important in measurement and statistics because much of the theoretical work in each of these areas is based on it. (This will be especially noticeable in Chapters 8 through 12.) Consequently, in preparing to study either measurement or statistics, one must study the properties of this distribution so its relevance and utility within both contexts can be fully understood and appreciated. The purpose of the present chapter is to provide the means for acquiring this important prerequisite knowledge.

In this chapter, we (a) briefly examine the difference between theoretical and empirical distributions, (b) note the salient characteristics of the normal distribution (i.e., the family of all normal distributions), (c) look at several examples of empirical distributions which can be approximated reasonably well using one of the theoretical normal distributions, (d) learn to use the theoretical normal distribution for making Z-score/percentile rank transformations where appropriate, (e) lay the foundation for certain statistical prediction procedures and test score interpretation techniques to be treated later, and (f) note the relevance of the normal distribution model (or *normal model,* for short) within norm-referenced and criterion-referenced measurement contexts.

THE DIFFERENCE BETWEEN THEORETICAL AND EMPIRICAL DISTRIBUTIONS

An *empirical distribution* is a distribution of values obtained through the actual measurement of a sample or population of objects on a particular characteristic or dimension. A *theoretical distribution,* on the other hand, is one which is deduced from theory, be it mathematical or otherwise. For example, if you were asked what you would expect in the event that a single "unbiased," or "fair," coin were tossed a million times in such a way that each toss was completely independent of those preceding it, you would probably reply "about 500,000 outcomes would be *heads* and the remainder *tails.*" Note, you would do this despite the fact that you personally have never carried out such an experiment and you know of no one else who has. This distribution of 500,000 *heads* and 500,000 *tails* is theoretical in nature, being deduced from the relevant property of the coin, namely, its lack of bias. If you now actually conducted this experiment and tabulated the results, you would observe an *empirical* distribution similar in shape to the theoretical distribution just mentioned (provided, of course, your coin is unbiased).

The principal point here is that distributions which are deduced from theory and are not dependent on obtaining measures in the real world are called *theoretical* distributions, while those obtained by real world measurements are called *empirical* distributions. There are a number of theoretical distributions of interest to measurement specialists, but we will restrict our attention to just one at this time: the normal distribution.

CHARACTERISTICS OF THE NORMAL DISTRIBUTION

At this point, we simply note the salient characteristics of the normal distribution and provide illustrations or examples where doing so seems to purchase a measure of clarification.

1. All normal distributions are generated by the same mathematical equation. Since the equation is a bit complex and because knowledge of it is not crucial at this point, it is not presented here.
2. A normal distribution can be derived for every conceivable pair of values representing the mean and standard deviation of a set of scores. Therefore, there are an infinite number of curves which collectively comprise *the normal distribution.*
3. All normal distributions are (a) continuous, (b) symmetrical, and (c) unbounded. The unbounded property implies that regardless of the mean and standard deviation specifying a particular normal distribution, the curve extends infinitely far in both the positive and negative directions.

     In contrast, actual distributions of test scores are (a) never continuous (i.e., scores like $\sqrt{7}$ or 1.35896 are not attainable), (b) hardly ever symmetrical in the strict sense, and (c) always bounded by maximum and minimum scores. Therefore, test score distributions can never be normal, only approximately normal.
4. In a normal distribution, the values of the mean, median, and mode are equal.
5. In every normal distribution (regardless of the mean and standard deviation values), *approximately* 68% of the area between the curve and the baseline is within 1 SD of the mean, approximately 95% of the area is within 2 SD's of the mean, and approximately 99% of the area is within 3 SD's of the mean (see Figure 4-1). Therefore, if we know that a particular distribution of 1,000

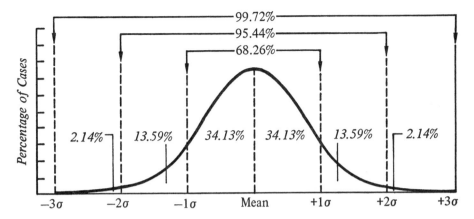

FIGURE 4-1. *Percentage distribution of cases in a normal curve. (Reproduced by permission of Anne Anastasi.)*

scores is approximately normal, we can conclude that about 680 examinees scored within 1 SD of the mean and almost all scored within 3 SD's of the mean. (*NOTE:* The σ symbol in Figure 4-1 means *standard deviation*.)

6. There is a very useful relationship existing between Z scores and percentile ranks (i.e., percentages of area under the curve located to the left of the various Z-score values) in the normal distribution. For example, 50% of the area is located to the left of $Z = 0.00$; therefore, $Z = 0.00$ has a percentile rank of 50 (see Figure 4-2a). Similarly, about 85% of the area is located to the left of

a. Percentile rank = 50   b. Percentile rank = 85

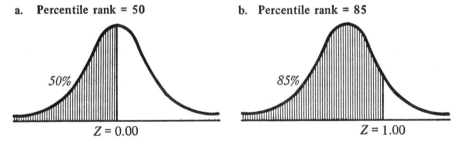

FIGURE 4-2. *Percentile ranks corresponding to Z scores equal to 0.00 and +1.00, respectively, in the normal distribution.*

$Z = +1.00$, therefore, $Z = +1.00$ has a percentile rank of 85 (see Figure 4-2b). The procedure for making conversions like these using the cumulative unit normal table[1] will be examined shortly. For now, it is most important to

1. Whenever a normal distribution (regardless of the values of its mean and standard deviation) is transformed using $Z = (X - M)/SD$, the resulting normal distribution has $M = 0$ and SD = 1. The name for this resulting standardized or linearly transformed normal distribution is the *unit normal distribution* or *standard normal distribution*. A table which shows the percentile rank associated with selected Z scores in the unit normal distribution is called a *cumulative* unit normal table.

realize that approximate Z to percentile rank and percentile rank to Z transformations are quite easy to make when the scores are normally distributed. (*Note:* This neat correspondence between observed scores and percentile ranks holds only in a normal distribution. If the distribution is reasonably close to normal, good percentile rank approximations can be obtained this way. For decidedly nonnormal distributions, this procedure must be abandoned in favor of arithmetic conversion procedures.)

SOME EXAMPLES OF EMPIRICAL DISTRIBUTIONS WHICH APPROXIMATE NORMALITY

In this section, we describe several kinds of empirical distributions which tend to be normal in form.

1. A very large number of independent observations of the length of a fence post obtained using the same measuring device, e.g., a tape measure.
2. The number of *heads* obtained in a large number of repetitions of an experiment which consists of tossing 100 presumably unbiased coins into the air and observing the number of coins with the *heads* side up on each repetition.
3. Scores on a test of general intelligence obtained from a large, random sample of the population of this country. (*Note:* Intelligence is usually assumed to distribute normally, and hence, tests of intelligence are designed to produce score distributions having this shape.)
4. Scores on many well-constructed, norm-referenced tests of achievement, ability, etc. As in item 3, every attempt is made to produce tests which generate normal distributions of test scores. Reasons for this are discussed elsewhere (see Chapter 9, for example).

SOME EXAMPLES OF DISTRIBUTIONS WHICH DO NOT APPROXIMATE NORMALITY

Some examples of decidedly nonnormal empirical distributions are:

1. The weight (in pounds) of the current student population of the University of Delaware. (*Note:* The fact that men tend to have a considerably higher mean weight than women would probably result in a bimodal distribution.)
2. The distribution of scores obtained with a test too easy (or too hard) for the group of examinees to which it was administered. (*Note:* The first instance would produce a negatively skewed distribution; the latter, a positively skewed distribution.)
3. The distribution of values observed in a large number of throws of a single "fair" die. (*Note:* The expected distribution of values 1 through 6 would be rectangular or flat.)
4. The distribution of scores on the final achievement test of a criterion-referenced instructional module. (*Note:* If the module is effective, the final test should be relatively easy for most of the students.)

Table 4-1 shows the proportion of area under the unit normal curve below (or to the left of) selected Z score values. For example, 0.1587 of the total area is below (or to the left of) $Z = -1.00$, 0.5000 of the area is below $Z = 0.00$ (see, also, Figure 4-2a), 0.8413 of the area is below $Z = +1.00$ (see, also, Figure 4-2b), and 0.9946 of the area is below $Z = +2.55$.

Given the unit normal distribution (i.e., the normal distribution having $M = 0$ and SD $= 1.00$), the percentile rank equivalent of a particular Z score can be obtained by (a) reading the area value in Table 4-1 corresponding to the Z score of interest, (b) rounding this value off to two decimal places, and (c) dropping the decimal point (or, if you prefer, multiplying by 100). For example, the proportion of area to the left of $Z = -1.00$ is 0.1587; therefore, the percentile rank of $Z = -1.00$ is 16. This means that approximately 16% of the scores in a normal distribution are more than 1 SD below the distribution mean.

Given a distribution of raw scores which is approximately normal in form, the approximate percentile rank of a particular score may be obtained by (a) transforming the raw score to the Z scale and (b) applying the procedure just described. For example, if $X = 70$ in a normal distribution having $M = 50$ and SD $= 10$, then $Z = (70 - 50)/10 = +2.00$ and the percentile rank equivalent is 98. That is, approximately 98% of the scores in a normal distribution are less than 2 SD's above the mean; equivalently, 2% of the scores are more than 2 SD's above the mean.

**FINDING NORMAL DISTRIBUTION Z-SCORE EQUIVALENTS OF
PARTICULAR PERCENTILE RANKS**

Occasionally, it is necessary to find the Z score corresponding to a particular percentile rank. If the distribution is approximately normal in form, an estimate can be obtained directly from Table 4-1 by (a) converting the percentile rank to a proportion, (b) finding the area value in Table 4-1 closest numerically to the one of interest, and (c) reading the corresponding Z score. For example, the percentile rank 58 is equal to 0.5800 in proportion form and, hence, approximately equal to +0.20 on the Z scale. Similarly, the percentile rank 37 is approximately equivalent to −0.33 on the Z scale.

FINDING THE PERCENTAGE OF AREA BETWEEN TWO Z SCORES

In subsequent chapters, it will be necessary on occasion to find the percentage or proportion of area in a normal distribution between two specific values of Z. This can be done using Table 4-1 by (a) reading the area to the left of each Z score and (b) calculating the difference between these two area values. For example, the proportion of area in a normal distribution between $Z = -1.00$ and $Z = +1.00$ is $0.8413 - 0.1587 = 0.6826$. Similarly, the area between $Z = +2.00$ and $Z = -2.00$ is $0.9772 - 0.0228 = 0.9544$.

TABLE 4-1. *Cumulative Unit Normal Distribution.*

z	0.00	0.01	0.02	0.03	0.04	0.05	0.06	0.07	0.08	0.09
−3.0	0.0014									
−2.9	0.0019	0.0018	0.0018	0.0017	0.0016	0.0016	0.0015	0.0015	0.0014	0.0014
−2.8	0.0026	0.0025	0.0024	0.0023	0.0023	0.0022	0.0021	0.0021	0.0020	0.0019
−2.7	0.0035	0.0034	0.0033	0.0032	0.0031	0.0030	0.0029	0.0028	0.0027	0.0026
−2.6	0.0047	0.0045	0.0044	0.0043	0.0041	0.0040	0.0039	0.0038	0.0037	0.0036
−2.5	0.0062	0.0060	0.0059	0.0057	0.0055	0.0054	0.0052	0.0051	0.0049	0.0048
−2.4	0.0082	0.0080	0.0078	0.0075	0.0073	0.0071	0.0069	0.0068	0.0066	0.0064
−2.3	0.0107	0.0104	0.0102	0.0099	0.0096	0.0094	0.0091	0.0089	0.0087	0.0084
−2.2	0.0139	0.0136	0.0132	0.0129	0.0125	0.0122	0.0119	0.0116	0.0113	0.0110
−2.1	0.0179	0.0174	0.0170	0.0166	0.0162	0.0158	0.0154	0.0150	0.0146	0.0143
−2.0	0.0228	0.0222	0.0217	0.0212	0.0207	0.0202	0.0197	0.0192	0.0188	0.0183
−1.9	0.0287	0.0281	0.0274	0.0268	0.0262	0.0256	0.0250	0.0244	0.0239	0.0233
−1.8	0.0359	0.0351	0.0344	0.0336	0.0329	0.0322	0.0314	0.0307	0.0301	0.0294
−1.7	0.0446	0.0436	0.0427	0.0418	0.0409	0.0401	0.0392	0.0384	0.0375	0.0367
−1.6	0.0548	0.0537	0.0526	0.0516	0.0505	0.0495	0.0485	0.0475	0.0465	0.0455
−1.5	0.0668	0.0655	0.0643	0.0630	0.0618	0.0606	0.0594	0.0582	0.0571	0.0559
−1.4	0.0808	0.0793	0.0778	0.0764	0.0749	0.0735	0.0721	0.0708	0.0694	0.0681
−1.3	0.0968	0.0951	0.0934	0.0918	0.0901	0.0885	0.0869	0.0853	0.0838	0.0823
−1.2	0.1151	0.1131	0.1112	0.1093	0.1075	0.1056	0.1038	0.1020	0.1003	0.0985
−1.1	0.1357	0.1335	0.1314	0.1292	0.1271	0.1251	0.1230	0.1210	0.1190	0.1170
−1.0	0.1587	0.1562	0.1539	0.1515	0.1492	0.1469	0.1446	0.1423	0.1401	0.1379
−0.9	0.1841	0.1814	0.1788	0.1762	0.1736	0.1711	0.1685	0.1660	0.1635	0.1611
−0.8	0.2119	0.2090	0.2061	0.2033	0.2005	0.1977	0.1949	0.1922	0.1894	0.1867
−0.7	0.2420	0.2388	0.2358	0.2327	0.2296	0.2266	0.2236	0.2206	0.2177	0.2148
−0.6	0.2743	0.2709	0.2676	0.2643	0.2611	0.2578	0.2546	0.2514	0.2482	0.2451
−0.5	0.3085	0.3050	0.3015	0.2981	0.2946	0.2912	0.2877	0.2843	0.2810	0.2776
−0.4	0.3446	0.3409	0.3372	0.3336	0.3230	0.3264	0.3228	0.3192	0.3156	0.3121
−0.3	0.3821	0.3783	0.3745	0.3707	0.3669	0.3632	0.3594	0.3557	0.3520	0.3483
−0.2	0.4207	0.4168	0.4129	0.4090	0.4052	0.4013	0.3974	0.3936	0.3897	0.3859
−0.1	0.4602	0.4562	0.4522	0.4483	0.4443	0.4404	0.4364	0.4325	0.4286	0.4247
−0.0	0.5000	0.4960	0.4920	0.4880	0.4840	0.4801	0.4761	0.4721	0.4681	0.4641
0.0	0.5000	0.504	0.5080	0.5120	0.5160	0.5199	0.5239	0.5279	0.5319	0.5359
0.1	0.5398	0.5438	0.5478	0.5517	0.5557	0.5596	0.5636	0.5675	0.5714	0.5753
0.2	0.5793	0.5832	0.5871	0.5910	0.5948	0.5987	0.6026	0.6064	0.6103	0.6141
0.3	0.6179	0.6217	0.6255	0.6293	0.6331	0.6368	0.6406	0.6443	0.6480	0.6517
0.4	0.6554	0.6591	0.6628	0.6664	0.6770	0.6736	0.6772	0.6808	0.6844	0.6879
0.5	0.6915	0.6950	0.6985	0.7019	0.7054	0.7088	0.7123	0.7157	0.719	0.7224
0.6	0.7257	0.7291	0.7324	0.7357	0.7389	0.7422	0.7454	0.7486	0.7518	0.7549
0.7	0.7580	0.7612	0.7642	0.7673	0.7704	0.7734	0.7764	0.7794	0.7823	0.7852
0.8	0.7881	0.7910	0.7939	0.7967	0.7995	0.8023	0.8051	0.8078	0.8106	0.8133
0.9	0.8159	0.8186	0.8212	0.8238	0.8264	0.8289	0.8315	0.834	0.8365	0.8389
1.0	0.8413	0.8438	0.8461	0.8485	0.8508	0.8531	0.8554	0.8577	0.8599	0.8621
1.1	0.8643	0.8665	0.8686	0.8708	0.8729	0.8749	0.8770	0.8790	0.8810	0.8830
1.2	0.8849	0.8869	0.8888	0.8907	0.8925	0.8944	0.8962	0.8980	0.8997	0.9015
1.3	0.9032	0.9049	0.9066	0.9082	0.9099	0.9115	0.9131	0.9147	0.9162	0.9177
1.4	0.9192	0.9207	0.9222	0.9236	0.9251	0.9265	0.9279	0.9292	0.9306	0.9319

TABLE 4-1. *(Continued)*

Z	0.00	0.01	0.02	0.03	0.04	0.05	0.06	0.07	0.08	0.09
1.5	0.9332	0.9345	0.9357	0.9370	0.9382	0.9394	0.9406	0.9418	0.9429	0.9441
1.6	0.9452	0.9463	0.9474	0.9484	0.9495	0.9505	0.9515	0.9525	0.9535	0.9545
1.7	0.9554	0.9564	0.9573	0.9582	0.9591	0.9599	0.9608	0.9616	0.9625	0.9633
1.8	0.9641	0.9649	0.9656	0.9664	0.9671	0.9678	0.9686	0.9693	0.9699	0.9706
1.9	0.9713	0.9719	0.9726	0.9732	0.9738	0.9744	0.9750	0.9756	0.9761	0.9767
2.0	0.9772	0.9778	0.9783	0.9788	0.9793	0.9798	0.9803	0.9808	0.9812	0.9817
2.1	0.9821	0.9826	0.9830	0.9834	0.9838	0.9842	0.9846	0.9850	0.9854	0.9857
2.2	0.9861	0.9864	0.9868	0.9871	0.9875	0.9878	0.9881	0.9884	0.9887	0.9890
2.3	0.9893	0.9896	0.9898	0.9901	0.9904	0.9906	0.9909	0.9911	0.9913	0.9916
2.4	0.9918	0.9920	0.9922	0.9925	0.9927	0.9929	0.9931	0.9932	0.9934	0.9936
2.5	0.9938	0.9940	0.9941	0.9943	0.9945	0.9946	0.9948	0.9949	0.9951	0.9952
2.6	0.9953	0.9955	0.9956	0.9957	0.9959	0.9960	0.9961	0.9962	0.9963	0.9964
2.7	0.9965	0.9966	0.9967	0.9968	0.9969	0.9970	0.9971	0.9972	0.9973	0.9974
2.8	0.9974	0.9975	0.9976	0.9977	0.9977	0.9978	0.9979	0.9979	0.9980	0.9981
2.9	0.9981	0.9982	0.9982	0.9983	0.9984	0.9984	0.9985	0.9985	0.9986	0.9986
3.0	0.9986									

Examples: (1) The proportion of area to the left of $Z = -2.56$ is 0.0052.
(2) The proportion of area to the left of $Z = -0.08$ is 0.4681.
(3) The proportion of area to the left of $Z = +1.00$ is 0.8413.
(4) The proportion of area to the left of $Z = +2.09$ is 0.9817.

EXERCISE SET 4-1

1. Find the percentile ranks of the following normal distribution Z scores:
   a. -1.40
   b. -0.05
   c. $+2.16$
2. Find the normal distribution Z scores which correspond approximately to the following percentile ranks:
   a. 12
   b. 43
   c. 68
3. What proportion of the area in a unit normal distribution is located between:
   a. $Z = -1.50$ and $Z = +1.50$
   b. $Z = -1.50$ and $Z = -2.00$
   c. $Z = +0.20$ and $Z = +2.80$

SOME NOTES ON THE UTILITY OF THE NORMAL DISTRIBUTION

The normal distribution is a simplifier. That is, when test scores or measurement errors distribute in a normal fashion, everything is much simpler than would otherwise be the case. For example, when test scores are normally distributed (or approximately so), Z score/percentile rank transformations are a trivial matter. In addition, test score interpretation (within a norm-referenced context) and grade assignments (e.g., "grading on the curve") are much easier. But most importantly, the assumption that measurement errors distribute normally is a cornerstone of the mathematical edifice called classical measurement theory (see Chapter 8) which, until recently, has been the gospel of many measurement specialists. In fact, measurement texts (like this one) are full of formulas handed to us by classical measurement theory (e.g., item analysis and reliability estimation procedures).

As a result, norm-referenced measures of intelligence, achievement, mathematical aptitude, etc., are deliberately constructed to generate normal test score distributions in heterogenous examinee populations. Once this is done, classical measurement theory (sometimes called normal test theory) becomes applicable and all of the fringe benefits (e.g., the simplicity in interpreting individual scores and differences between individual scores) accrue. When the test fails to behave in this fashion, it is usually refined (by techniques to be discussed later, e.g., Chapter 12) or the shape of the obtained distribution is altered using a rule called a transformation (see Chapter 5). Whether the latter technique is justifiable varies from case to case and some comments concerning the indiscriminate use of this technique are made later.

In a criterion-referenced measurement framework, especially in an instructional context, tests are frequently designed to measure the achievement of prestated objectives before, during, and after the application of an appropriate instructional treatment. If the test is primarily sensitive to changes in student behavior due to the instructional treatment and relatively insensitive to changes in student behavior which are a natural consequence of extratreatment environment, pre- and post-administrations will probably result in oppositely skewed test score distributions. As a consequence, the distributions typically display little variability, and hence, the results of classical measurement theory are inapplicable. The principal point to be made is that the normal model, which occupies a lofty position within the norm-referenced measurement framework, is of little value in the criterion-referenced framework.

SUMMARY AND A LOOK AHEAD

In this chapter we have examined the normal model and explored its application within the norm- and criterion-referenced measurement frameworks. In subsequent chapters it will be employed in a variety of ways. For example, in the next chapter its utility in test-score interpretation is partially explained. In Chapter 8, its critical role in the formulation of the classical theory of measurement errors is revealed. Before continuing, check your comprehension of the ideas and procedures in this unit by taking one of the self-evaluation tests provided for this purpose.

Form A
1. A distribution of values obtained through the actual measurement of a collection of objects on a specific dimension or characteristic is called a(n) _____ distribution.
   a. empirical   b. theoretical
2. Which one of the following is an example of a theoretical distribution?
   a. The expected distribution of the values 1, 2, 3, 4, 5, and 6 resulting from an infinite number of rolls of an "unbiased" die.
   b. The observed distribution of the values 1, 2, 3, 4, 5, and 6 resulting from 1,000 rolls of an "unbiased" die.
3. Identify each of the adjectives below which describes a characteristic of the normal distribution.
   a. symmetrical   b. empirical   c. continuous   d. unbounded
4. What percentage of the area in a normal distribution is located within one standard deviation of the mean?
   a. 16%   b. 34%   c. 68%   d. 95%
5. What percentage of the area in the unit normal distribution is located between $Z = -0.5$ and $Z = +0.5$?
6. What percentage of the area in the unit normal distribution is located below (to the left of) $Z = +1.5$?
7. In the unit normal distribution, $Z = +0.37$ is equivalent to a percentile rank of
   _____ .
8. What percentage of the scores in a normal distribution *exceed* a score located exactly one standard deviation below the mean?
9. Suppose a distribution of 1,000 test scores is approximately normal with mean 50 and standard deviation 10. About how many of those scores are between the values of 40 and 50?
   a. 340   b. 680   c. 950   d. more information is needed
10. The normal distribution is most useful in a _____ testing context.
    a. criterion-referenced   b. norm-referenced.

Form B
1. What is a theoretical distribution?
2. Which one of the following is an example of an empirical distribution?
   a. The expected distribution of *heads* and *tails* resulting from an infinite number of tosses of an "unbiased" coin.
   b. The observed distribution of *heads* and *tails* resulting from one million tosses of an "unbiased" coin.
3. Sketch a normal distribution and indicate the approximate locations of the mean, median, and mode.
4. What percentage of the area in a normal distribution is located within two standard deviations of the mean?
   a. 16%   b. 34%   c. 68%   d. 95%
5. What percentage of the area in the unit normal distribution is located between $Z = -1.2$ and $Z = +1.2$?

6. What percentage of the area in the unit normal distribution is located below (to the left of) $Z = -0.75$?

7. In the unit normal distribution, $Z = -2.3$ is equivalent to a percentile rank of _____ .

8. A raw score of 40 in a normal distribution having mean 50 and standard deviation 10 corresponds approximately to the _____ percentile.
   a. 15th   b. 30th   c. 45th   d. 60th

9. Mr. X obtained a raw score of 80 on his history final exam. The distribution of scores for his class was approximately normal with mean 75 and standard deviation 5. What is Mr. X's percentile rank in this distribution?
   a. 50   b. 68   c. 84   d. 95

10. Identify the most likely shape of each of the distributions described below.
    a. The per capita income in a West Virginia coal-mining community.
    b. The physical height of the freshman women attending the University of Delaware.

ANSWER KEY

Form A
1. a
2. a
3. a, c, and d
4. c
5. 38% (approximately)
6. 93% (approximately)
7. 64 (approximately)
8. 84% (approximately)
9. a
10. b

Form B
1. See p. 42

2. b
3. Compare your results with Figure 4-1. The mean, median, and mode are equal in value and located at the center of the distribution.
4. d
5. 77% (approximately)
6. 23% (approximately)
7. 1 (approximately)
8. a
9. c
10. a. positively skewed
    b. approximately normal

EXERCISE SET 4-1: ANSWERS

1. a. 8   b. 48   c. 98
2. a. −1.175 or −1.18
   b. −0.18
   c. +0.47
3. a. 0.9332 − 0.0668 = 0.8664
   b. 0.0668 − 0.0228 = 0.0440
   c. 0.9974 − 0.5793 = 0.4181

5

Derived Scores and Their Interrelationships

In norm-referenced measurement, the individual score is meaningful only in relation to the other scores in some well-defined examinee group, called a norm group. The norm group may be the class to which the student belongs, a group to which he aspires, etc. To facilitate the interpretation of scores in a norm-referenced context, various sorts of *transformed* or *derived* scores have been invented. Some of these have already been introduced in Chapters 2 and 3, e.g., deviation, Z, and percentage scores; others, e.g., T scores, are first encountered in the present chapter.

Knowledge of these various types of scores and how they are related is useful to laymen and professional educators alike. For the former, such knowledge may facilitate understanding of news media items related to current topics of public interest, e.g., the value of standardized testing, the declining trend in college entrance examination scores. For the latter, such knowledge also facilitates interpretation of standardized test data as it exists in school records. Rather than examining the various types of score scales as separate, discrete entities, the general approach taken here is to explain what is meant by the process of score transformation and then to show how this notion can be used to translate scores from one scale to a variety of other related scales.

The subsequent sections have the following goals: (a) to formalize the treatment of transformations, (b) to describe and illustrate some of the more commonly encountered transformed score scales (e.g., Z, T, and stanine scales), and (c) to show the relationships which exist among selected transformed score scales. Let us begin by defining and illustrating several important terms.

A *transformation* is a rule (or set of rules) for converting scores from one scale (e.g., the raw score scale) to another scale (e.g., the deviation score scale). All transformations can be categorized as being either linear or nonlinear.

A *linear transformation* converts the scores from one scale to another in such a way that the distribution shape is not changed. For example, the transformation from the raw score scale to the deviation score scale, and vice versa, is linear (see Figure 5-1).

a. Raw Score Distribution   **b. Deviation Score Distribution**

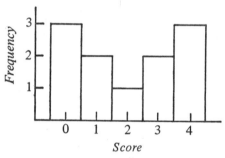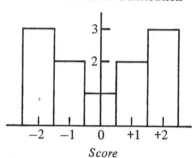

FIGURE 5-1. *Hypothetical raw score and deviation score distributions related by the rule:* Deviation Score = Raw Score − Mean.

a. Raw Score Distribution

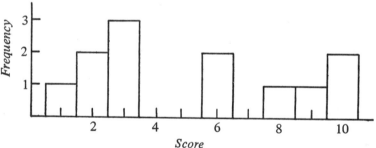

b. Transformed Score Distribution

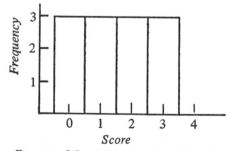

FIGURE 5-2. *An example of the effect of applying a particular nonlinear transformation to a hypothetical raw score distribution.*

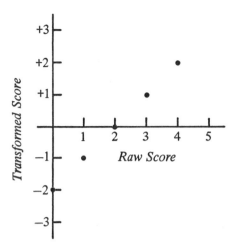

FIGURE 5-3. *Plot of the raw scores and corresponding linearly transformed scores.*

A *nonlinear transformation* converts the scores from one scale to another in such a way that the shape of the distribution is altered. Consider the following example in which a "jagged" appearing raw score distribution is transformed by a rule which produces a rectangular or flat distribution.

RULE: Given a set of scores, (a) arrange them in order from the highest to the lowest and (b) assign all scores in the highest 25% of the distribution a transformed score of 3; the next 25%, a score of 2, etc.

The effect of applying this rule to the raw score distribution (1, 2, 6, 2, 6, 8, 9, 10, 10, 3, 3, 3) is shown in Figure 5-2.

One way of finding out whether a transformation is linear or not is to plot the original and transformed scores as shown in Figures 5-3 and 5-4. If all points

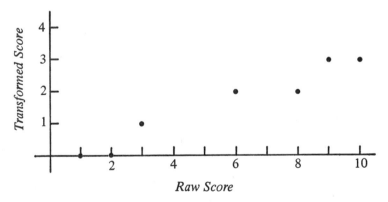

FIGURE 5-4. *Plot of the raw scores and corresponding non-linearly transformed scores.*

in the plot fall exactly on a straight line as in Figure 5-3, you can be sure the transformation is linear; if the points do not fall on a straight line, as in Figure 5-4, the transformation is nonlinear.

The important fact is that linear transformations preserve the shape of a test score distribution (i.e., a histogram based on linearly transformed scores has the identical shape characteristics as the histogram based on the original set of scores). Nonlinear transformations, on the other hand, always alter the shape of the test score distribution.

EXERCISE SET 5-1

1. A rule for deriving scores on one scale given a set of scores on another scale is called a(n) _____.

2. A linear transformation _____ changes the shape of the score distribution.
   a. never
   b. sometimes
   c. always

3. Nonlinear transformations _____ change the shape of the score distribution.
   a. never
   b. sometimes
   c. always

4. Examine the transformations listed below and tell whether each is linear or nonlinear. Given a set of raw scores,
   a. Add 10 points to each raw score.
   b. Take the square root of each raw score.
   c. Multiply each raw score by 5.

Z SCORES

In this section of the chapter, we consider two fundamental types of Z scores: linear and normalized. First, let us review and add to what we know about linear Z scores.

Linear Z Scores

Linear Z scores are obtained by applying the linear transformation $Z = (X - M)/SD$ to the elements of a raw score distribution. For example, a raw score of 140 in a distribution having $M = 100$ and $SD = 20$ would correspond to $Z = (140 - 100)/20 = 40/20 = +2.00$. This indicates that an examinee obtaining a score of 140 is two standard deviations above the mean performance of the group of examinees represented in this distribution. If the distribution was really normal in form, the percentile rank of this examinee in this distribution could be determined using Table 4-1.

Occasionally a raw score distribution is obtained which is decidedly non-normal in shape (e.g., positively skewed), but the measured attribute is known to distribute normally in the population of interest. In order to use *normal* test theory procedures in interpreting individual scores, empirically obtained distributions of this type are sometimes *normalized*, i.e., nonlinearly transformed to normality. (*Comment*: This is a questionable practice. When measuring a normally distributed variable, a non-normal score distribution may reflect inadequacies in the test or nonrepresentativeness in the examinee sample. Forcing the distribution into a normal form is not the answer.)

The procedure for transforming a raw score distribution to a normalized *Z* score scale is as follows:

1. Transform all raw scores to percentile ranks.
2. Using the cumulative unit normal distribution (Table 4-1), convert the percentile ranks to *Z* scores.

The application of this transformation to a hypothetical raw score distribution is shown in Table 5-1.

TABLE 5-1. *Example of the Normal Z Score Transformation.*

Raw Score	Frequency	Percentile Rank	Normalized Z score
5	1	98	+2.05*
4	2	92	+1.41
3	4	80	+0.84
2	6	60	+0.25
1	10	28	−0.58
0	2	4	−1.75
	25		

* A percentile rank of 98 in a normal distribution is equivalent to the *Z* score that cuts off the lower .9800 of the area under the curve. According to Table 4-1, this value is $Z = +2.05$.

Some Remarks About *Z* Scores

The following characteristics about *Z* scores are worth remembering:

1. Whether the linear or normalizing transformation is used, the resulting *Z* score distribution will have a mean of zero and a standard deviation of one.
2. *Z* scores provide normative information about an examinee's performance, and hence, an individual's *Z* score provides a meaningful summary of his norm-referenced test performance. In particular, the sign of the *Z* score tells you

whether the performance is below (−) or above (+) the mean of the norm distribution; the numerical portion tells how many standard deviations away from the mean it is located (e.g., $Z = +1.3$ means the person's raw score is 1.3 standard deviation units above the mean).

3. The sign and decimal aspects of the Z score result in record-keeping inconveniences. However, such inconveniences can be avoided by transforming the Z score to other scales which do not share these drawbacks. Selected transformations of this type are the subject of the next section.

EXERCISE SET 5-2

1. A raw score of 50 in a distribution having a mean of 60 and a standard deviation of 10 corresponds to a linear Z score of _____.

2. A raw score of 50 in a distribution having a mean of 40 and a standard deviation of 5 corresponds to a linear Z score of _____ .

3. Transform the raw scores in the distribution displayed below to normalized Z scores.

Raw Score	3	2	1	0
Frequency	4	8	6	2

TRANSFORMING LINEAR AND NORMALIZED Z SCORES TO OTHER STANDARD SCALES

As suggested above, a number of transformations have been devised to ameliorate the record-keeping inconveniences inherent in the Z score. The general form of all such transformations is

$$Z' = SD'(Z) + M'$$

Where Z represents the examinee's original linear or normalized Z score
Z' represents his examinee's score on the new scale
SD' represents the standard deviation of the new distribution
M' represents the mean of the new distribution

Whether the Z' scores are related to the raw scores in a linear or nonlinear fashion depends only on the nature of the rule used to obtain the original Z scores.

In the next several sections, we examine several useful standard score scales related to the Z scale by the formula $Z' = SD'(Z) + M'$, namely, T, CEEB, and Deviation IQ. A pictorial representation of the relationship which exists among these and several other scales is presented in Figure 5-5.

The *T*-Score Scale

The equation $T = 10\,Z + 50$ transforms a distribution of Z scores from a scale having $M = 0$ and $SD = 1$ to a scale having $M' = 50$ and $SD' = 10$. Thus, $Z = +1.00$

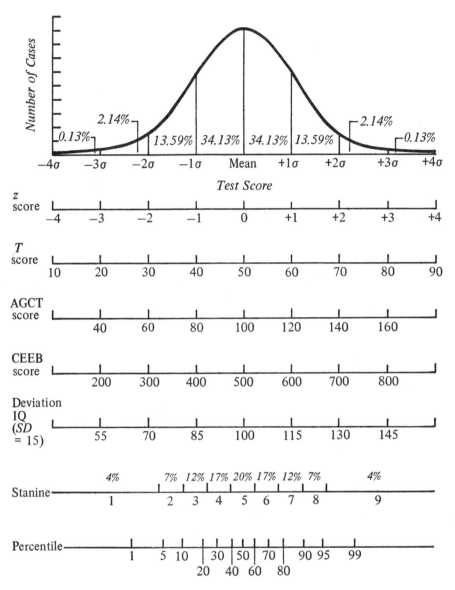

FIGURE 5-5. *Relationships among different types of test scores in a normal distribution. (Reproduced by permission of Anne Anastasi.)*

corresponds to $T = 60$; $Z = +2.00$ corresponds to $T = 70$; $Z = -1.50$ corresponds to $T = 35$; etc. Whenever the application of this formula yields a decimal result (e.g., $Z = -1.23$ corresponds to $T = 37.7$), the T value is recorded after rounding to the nearest whole number (here, $T = 38$).

Since T scores are (a) reported to the nearest whole number and (b) positive in sign, they are preferred over Z scores by many individuals.

The CEEB Scale

In order to minimize the loss of information due to the rounding off process used above, the College Entrance Examination Board (CEEB) transformation, CEEB = $100\,Z + 500$, may be used. Notice, this equation converts Z scores with $M = 0$ and SD = 1 to CEEB scores with $M' = 500$ and $SD' = 100$. Thus, $Z = -2.00$ corresponds to a score of 300 on the CEEB scale; $Z = +1.50$ corresponds to 650 on the CEEB scale, etc.

As you may have noticed, the CEEB scale values are exactly ten times corresponding T scale values. Thus, "CEEB/T" and "T/CEEB" transformations are relatively simple. For example, a score of 650 on the verbal subtest of the Scholastic Aptitude Test (which uses the CEEB scale), corresponds to a T score of 65 (and, incidentally, to a Z score of +1.50).

The Deviation IQ Scale

The Wechsler Intelligence Tests (WISC, WAIS, and WPPSI) use a scale related to Z by the equation $Z' = 15\,Z + 100$. Thus, an examinee scoring 1 standard deviation below the mean ($Z = -1.00$) on the WAIS (Wechsler Adult Intelligence Scale) would be assigned an IQ score of 85. Similarly, a WAIS score of 130 would indicate an examinee performance 2 standard deviations above the mean of the norm group.

In like fashion, the deviation IQ transformation used with the Stanford-Binet Intelligence Test is $Z' = 16\,Z + 100$. Thus, a score one standard deviation below the mean ($Z = -1.00$) of the Stanford-Binet norm group corresponds to a Stanford-Binet IQ of 84.

SUMMARY

In this section, we have examined procedures which transform raw scores to various kinds of standard score scales. The first step in each procedure required us to transform the raw scores to Z scores using either a linear or a normalizing transformation. The rule $Z' = SD'(Z) + M'$ was then used to transform the Z scores to several other standard score scales. In the final section of this discussion, we examine two nonlinear transformations which enjoy considerable use by test publishers and are not dependent on the Z score scale in any fashion.

EXERCISE SET 5-3

1. What does $Z = -1.30$ correspond to on
   a. the T scale
   b. the CEEB scale
   c. the Wechsler IQ scale
   d. the Stanford-Binet IQ scale

2. What does a Wechsler IQ of 145 correspond to on
   a. the Z scale
   b. the T scale
   c. the CEEB scale
   d. the Stanford-Binet scale
3. A Wechsler IQ of 145 means the examinee scored as well or better than _____% of the individuals in the norm group.

TWO MORE NONLINEAR TRANSFORMATIONS

Because of their popularity with test publishers and test users, a brief description of the stanine and grade equivalent score scales and some pertinent comments regarding them are appropriate at this time.

The Stanine Scale

The word stanine is an abbreviation of the phrase "standard nine". The scale itself consists of only 9 score values, i.e., the counting numbers 1 through 9. Notice, this is a normalizing transformation which generates a set of scores having mean 5 and standard deviation 2. Where measurements of test data must be recorded in compact form, this scale is especially convenient since each test score requires only one column on a standard 80-column computer data card.

To transform a distribution of raw scores to the stanine scale, convert each raw score value to a percentile rank and then refer the results to Table 5-2. For example, percentile ranks of 85 and 3 are equivalent to the stanine scores 7 and 1, respectively.

TABLE 5-2. *Percentile Rank to Stanine Conversion Table.**

If the Percentile Rank (PR) is _____ .		Assign a Stanine score of _____.
4 or less		1
more than 4, but less than or equal to 11		2
11	23	3
23	40	4
40	60	5
60	77	6
77	89	7
89	96	8
more than 96		9

* *Note*: Since Percentile Ranks are rounded values, this table provides only approximate conversions near the category boundaries (e.g., 4, 11, 23). The accuracy of these conversions can be improved by referring the unrounded values (i.e., the proportions of examinees at or below each score value multiplied by 100) to this table.

While the stanine scale is easily understood by most laymen, the price which must be paid for this convenience is a significant loss of information about examinee performance. (For example, the stanine score of 5 represents a relatively broad range of performance — the percentile ranks in the interval 40 to 60.)

The Grade Equivalent Scale

Over the years, it has been common practice to base the interpretation of standardized educational achievement test[1] performance on grade equivalent (GE) scores. The construction of a GE scale is relatively straightforward. Briefly, if a test which sampled the vocabulary content taught in a particular elementary school (grades 1–6) were administered to all of the students in the school during the first month of a particular academic year, the mean score earned by the first grade students would be set equal to a grade equivalent score of 1.0; the mean score of the second grade group would be set equal to a grade equivalent score of 2.0, and so on. To illustrate, if the first grade class answered 8 vocabulary items correctly (on the average) while the sixth graders averaged 37 items correct, the scores of 8 and 37 could correspond to GE scores of 1.0 and 6.0, respectively. If the tests were administered during the fourth month of the school year and these same raw score averages were obtained, the equivalent GE scores would be 1.4 and 6.4, respectively.

There are a number of major problems associated with GE scores, in particular their susceptibility to misinterpretation. For example, if a fourth grade student earns a GE score of 6.7 on a math test, this *does not* mean that his math achievement is equivalent to that of the average sixth grader in the seventh month of school. Obviously, there is a great deal of content the average sixth grade student has had which the fourth grade student has not. All it means is that he has performed better than the average fourth grader, i.e., his score was above the fourth grade average. For this reason, GE scores are not recommended for routine use, and any attempt to interpret them should be made with a great deal of caution.

---

1. A standardized test is any test for which the administrative, scoring, and interpretation procedures have been completely specified (as far as is practically possible). The purpose of standardization is to insure comparability of score meaning regardless of the time, place, or examinee population involved in a particular application of the test. Of course, this presumes that the test is used only with appropriate examinee populations.

While most tests marketed for use in educational situations are standardized, one should not assume that all are. Also, the quality of standardization varies considerably across tests commonly referred to as standardized tests.

Clearly, the responsibility for test selection, appropriate usage, and test results interpretation rests squarely on the shoulders of the consumer — *caveat emptor.*

A useful first step in assessing the quality of standardization and the appropriateness of any published test for a specific application is consulting the relevant entry in O. K. Buros, (ed.) (1972) *The Seventh Mental Measurements Yearbook.* Gryphon Press, Highland Park, New Jersey.

This completes our discussion of transformed or derived scores. We have looked at (a) procedures for converting raw scores to selected standard score scales using linear transformations (i.e., transformations which preserve the shape of the test score distributions), and normalizing transformations (i.e., transformations which change distributions of any shape into normal distributions), and (b) the nonlinear grade equivalent transformation. Many of the transformations discussed involve converting raw scores to either linear or normalized Z scores and using the rule $Z' = SD'(Z) + M'$ to create a set of scores having the desired mean M' and standard deviation SD'. The stanine and grade equivalent transformations were not of this type.

In the development of norms (the subject of Chapter 11), commercial producers of standardized tests attempt to maximize user convenience by providing relatively easy to use transformation tables for a number of different norm groups. For example, nationally distributed intelligence tests have separate norm groups for the various age levels, while nationally distributed achievement tests may have separate norm groups for different grade levels. Within each of these groups, tables are prepared which allow one to easily transform raw scores obtained on the test to some of the derived scales we have examined in this unit. While some of the scales are used with just a few tests or test batteries (e.g., the CEEB scale), others are used by many test producers (e.g., percentile ranks). The ease with which stanines are interpreted seems to be increasing the popularity of this scale among many test users, and hence, this transformation is being utilized ever more frequently.

Before proceeding to the next chapter, check your comprehension of this unit using the self-evaluation forms provided for this purpose.

SELF-EVALUATION

Form A
1. Define *linear transformation.*
2. Which one of the following equations for transforming scores on scale X to scores on scale Y is nonlinear?
    a. $Y = 2X$ b. $Y = X - 3$ c. $Y = X^2$
3. The equation $Z' = 7Z + 3$ will transform any distribution of Z scores to a scale having $M = $ _____ and $SD = $ _____ .
4. Suppose the mean and standard deviation of a particular test score distribution are 50 and 7, respectively. Write the equation for transforming the raw test scores to linear Z scores.
5. The value of the mean on the College Board scale is exactly_____ times the value of the mean on the T scale.
    a. 2   b. 5   c. 10   d. 100

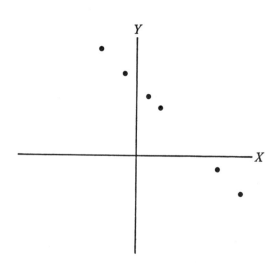

6. Suppose the test scores on one scale are transformed to a second scale and the pairs of scores for each examinee are then plotted in 2-space as shown above. Is the transformation linear or nonlinear?

7. A raw score of 45 in a distribution having $M = 60$ and SD = 5 corresponds to a score of_____ on the T scale.

8. A T score of 60 corresponds to a_____ on the Z scale and_____ on the CEEB scale.

9. If an individual obtains a linear Z score of +2.00 on Test X which has $M = 50$ and SD = 5, we know his raw score is _____ .

10. If a distribution of raw scores is transformed to the stanine scale, the new distribution will have a_____ shape with $M = 5$ and SD = 2.
   a. rectangular   b. bimodal   c. skewed   d. normal

Form B

1. Define *normalizing transformation.*

2. Which one of the following equations for transforming scores on the X scale to scores on the Y scale is linear?
   a. $Y = 3X - 7$ b. $Y = \sqrt{X}$ c. $Y = X^2 + 2$

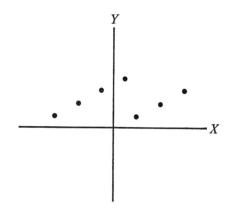

3. Suppose the test scores on one scale are transformed to a second scale and the pairs of scores for each examinee are then plotted in 2-space as shown on the previous page. Is the transformation linear or nonlinear?

4. Suppose an individual has a raw score of 130 in a distribution of test scores having a mean of 100 and a standard deviation of 15. What is his Z score in this distribution?

5. Match the score scales in the left column with the appropriate mean (M) and standard deviation (SD) values in the right column.

   1. Z a. $M = 50$ SD = 10
   2. T b. $M = 50$ SD = 1
   3. CEEB   c. $M = 100$ SD = 50
                      d. $M = 500$ SD = 100
                      e. $M = 0$ SD = 1
                      f. $M = 100$ SD = 15

6. Write the equation for transforming a distribution of Z scores to a scale so that the mean and standard deviation of the transformed distribution will be 30 and 8, respectively.

7. A CEEB score of 420 corresponds to a score of_____ on the T scale.

8. A Wechsler IQ of 85 corresponds to scores of_____ on the CEEB scale and_____ on the T scale.

9. To get a linear Z score of -2.5, the examinee must obtain a raw score 2.5 standard deviations_____ the mean of the examinee group with which his performance is being compared.

   a. above   b. below

10. Examinee X earns a stanine score of 9 on the ABC measure of achievement. This means that examinee X's performance placed him in the:

    a. Top 4% of the norm group.
    b. Middle 20% of the norm group.
    c. Lowest 4% of the norm group.

ANSWER KEY

Form A
1. See definition, p. 52
2. c
3. 3, 7
4. $Z = (X - 50)/7$
5. c
6. linear
7. 20
8. +1.00; 600
9. 60
10. d

Form B
1. See definition, p. 55
2. a
3. nonlinear
4. +2.00
5. 1. e   2. a   3. d
6. $Z' = 8Z + 30$
7. 42
8. 400; 40₁
9. b
10. a

```
EXERCISE SET 5-1: ANSWERS

1. transformation
2. a
3. c
4. a. linear      b. nonlinear      c. linear
```

```
EXERCISE SET 5-2: ANSWERS

1. $Z = (50 - 60)/10 = -10/10 = -1.00$
2. $Z = (50 - 40)/5 = +2.00$
3.
```

Raw Score	Percentile Rank	Normalized Z Score
3	90	+1.28
2	60	+0.25
1	25	−0.67
0	5	−1.64

```
EXERCISE SET 5-3: ANSWERS

1. a. 37          b. 370          c. 80          d. 79
2. a. +3.00       b. 80           c. 800         d. 148
3. 99 (approximately)
```

6

Measuring the Linear Relationship Between Two Variables

Many procedures have been developed for measuring the quality of norm-referenced tests and test items, and evaluating the appropriateness of each for specific purposes. A significant number of these procedures involve the use of the Pearson correlation coefficient. The purposes of this chapter are (a) to develop some of the concepts and tools necessary for understanding norm-referenced reliability and validity theory and (b) to provide the knowledge and skills necessary for the sensible application and proper interpretation of the Pearson correlation coefficient (or, for short, Pearson r) in a variety of norm-referenced measurement contexts.[1] To accomplish this, we begin with a nonmathematical discussion of the concept of linear association. In subsequent sections we deal with the calculation and inter-pretation of three measures of linear association and the effects of *restricted variance* and *measurement error* on the magnitude (i.e., absolute size) of the Pearson r. Finally, we examine several special cases of the Pearson r, namely, the point biserial, phi, and Spearman rank-order correlation coefficients.

---

1. In most statistics and measurement texts, the Greek letter ρ is used to represent the linear correlation between two variables in a population and the Roman letter r is typically used to represent the linear correlation in a sample. In this text, the symbol r is used throughout. Unless otherwise indicated, population data are assumed.

TABLE 6-1. *Scores of 30 Hypothetical Students on Two Forms of an Achievement Test.*

		Test Form	
		A	B
Student	1	8	6
	2	3	4
	3	6	8
	.	.	.
	.	.	.
	.	.	.
	29	4	7
	30	7	5

THE CONCEPT OF LINEAR ASSOCIATION

Suppose alternate forms of a 10-item achievement test were given to a group of 30 students and the data shown in Table 6-1 obtained. The 30 scores in distribution A may be presented graphically using a histogram; the scores in distribution B may be presented in a similar fashion. However, in assessing the equivalence of two forms of a test, we are interested in the joint performances of the 30 students on both variables. We can begin to examine joint performance by constructing a 2-*space* or 2-dimensional representation, called a *scatterplot,* as shown in Figure 6-1.

First, we construct the reference axes as shown in Figure 6-1a. Once this is done, we can then locate any individual's joint performance on test forms A and B by (1) finding his location on each reference axis separately, (2) drawing perpendicular lines through these points, and (3) locating the intersection of the newly drawn lines. The intersection of these lines is the person's location in 2-space. As an example, the location of person 3 in 2-space is shown in Figure 6-1b. Similarly, the joint performances of persons 1 and 2 can be added to the plot as shown in Figure 6-1c. Finally, the remaining 27 individuals (represented by data points) can be added with a result like that shown in Figure 6-1d.

While scatterplots like this help one determine the nature of the relationship between two variables, it is often desirable to summarize the scatterplot information using a single numerical index. Recall that most of the information in a single test score distribution is summarized by the arithmetic mean, M, and the standard deviation, SD. In the two-variable case, as shown here, the correlation coefficient performs a similar summary function. A general notion of the relationship between the value of the Pearson r and the configuration of points in a scatterplot may be obtained from the following comments:

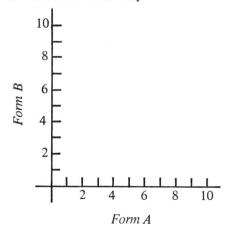

a. Reference Axes Only

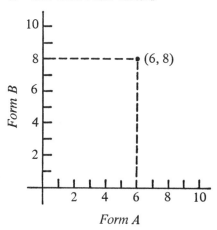

b. One Data Point Plotted

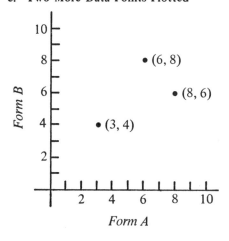

c. Two More Data Points Plotted

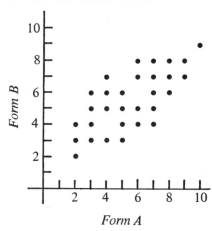

d. All Data Points Plotted

FIGURE 6-1. *Construction of a scatterplot.*

1. If the points in a scatterplot fall in a straight line (absolutely no deviation), the Pearson *r* value will be 1.00. If the line slopes upward from left to right, $r = +1.00$ (see Figure 6-2a); if it slopes downward from left to right, $r = -1.00$ (see Figure 6-2b).
2. If the points in a scatterplot do not lie in a straight line but still appear to exhibit a linear or straight line trend (as shown in Figures 6-2c and 6-2d), the absolute value of the Pearson *r* will be somewhere between 0 and 1. The closer the points are to a straight line, the closer the absolute value of *r* is to 1.00; the greater the scatter among the points, the closer *r* is to 0.00. Figures 6-2c and 6-2d are typical scatterplots and are based on variables having fairly strong positive and negative linear relationships, respectively.

a. Example of a Perfect Positive
   Linear Relationship,
   $r = +1.00$

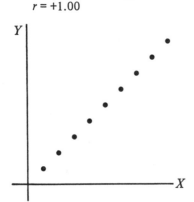

b. Example of a Perfect Negative
   Linear Relationship,
   $r = -1.00$

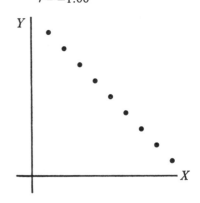

c. Example of a Positive Linear
   Relationship, $0 < r < +1.00$

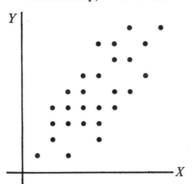

d. Example of a Negative Linear
   Relationship, $-1.00 < r < 0$

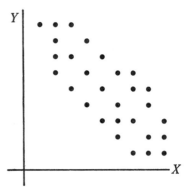

FIGURE 6-2.   *Scatterplot examples of several types of linear trend.*

3. There are two general classes of scattergram patterns which lead to a Pearson r of zero (or a value very close to zero). Remember, the Pearson r only measures the extent to which the trend in a scatterplot is summarized by a straight line. If the pattern does not have a straight-line (or linear) shape, either because it looks like an amorphous glob, or it seems to follow a well-defined curve (e.g., a parabola), the value of the Pearson r will be 0 (or close to 0). In the first instance (i.e., where the configuration is an amorphous glob), there is no useful relationship between the variables and this is accurately reflected in the Pearson r value of 0. In the latter instance, however, a meaningful relationship may exist. In this case, the Pearson r value will be quite misleading. For example, consider the relationship between scholastic achievement and anxiety. Numerous studies show that relatively poor achievement tends to be associated with both very low and very high anxiety levels, while relatively high achieve-

FIGURE 6-3. *Scatterplot example of two variables having a curvilinear relationship.*

ment tends to be associated with moderate anxiety levels. The typical scatterplot relating anxiety and achievement tends to look something like Figure 6-3. If one were to attempt to fit a straight line to this set of points, there would be considerable scatter about it. Therefore, the value of r would be 0 (or a value close to 0). There are statistical indices which are appropriate for measuring the degree of curvilinear association between variables, e.g., the correlation ratio. Since we are at present concerned only with measuring linear relationships, we will not further discuss curvilinear relationships or their quantification. However, be sure that in using r to measure the degree of linear association, you keep in mind the possibility that an r of 0 may result either when two variables are unrelated or when two variables are related, but in a curvilinear manner.

To summarize briefly, the Pearson r measures the extent to which a set of data points in 2-dimensional space follows a linear (straight-line) trend. Its value, if computationally correct, must be in the interval -1.00 to $+1.00$, inclusive. The extreme values represent perfect negative and perfect positive relationships respectively; i.e., knowledge of a person's score on one variable allows us to predict perfectly his score on the other variable. The midpoint of this interval, 0.00, represents the complete absence of a linear association between the variables. Values between 0 and 1 (either positive or negative) indicate varying degrees of linear association.

EXERCISE SET 6-1

1. If the points in a scatterplot seem to cluster about a straight line, the two variables represented in the plot are said to have a _____ relationship.
2. The statistic used to measure the extent to which two variables are linearly related is _____ .

3. The value of r is positive only when the points in the scatterplot cluster about a line sloping ―――――― .
4. Under what two circumstances can r = 0.00?
5. Describe the general nature of the relationship which exists between the following among the population of 21—25 year old American males:
   a. Height and weight.
   b. Height and intelligence.
   c. Weight and running speed.

STATISTICS FOR MEASURING THE LINEAR RELATIONSHIP BETWEEN TWO VARIABLES

We now examine three statistics which can be used to measure the extent to which the points in a scatterplot exhibit a linear trend. They are (1) the *sum of products*, SP(X, Y), (2) the *covariance*, Cov(X, Y), and (3) the *Pearson correlation coefficient*, $r(X, Y)$. We begin with a small two-variable, or bivariate, distribution of test scores representing the performances of three students on each of two quizzes. Their scores are shown in Table 6.2. A scatterplot constructed from these data would show that the three data points fall in a straight line, indicating a perfect-positive linear relationship.

The Sum of Products[2]

To calculate the *sum of products* SP(X, Y), we do the following:

1. Convert the raw scores on each variable to deviation scores.

―――――――

2. The procedure described in this section for calculating SP(X, Y) translates into the following mathematical form:

$$SP(X, Y) = \Sigma(X - M_X)(Y - M_Y)$$

Where $(X - M_X)$ = individual's deviation score on variable X
   $(Y - M_Y)$ = same individual's deviation score on variable Y

Through some elementary algebraic manipulations, the following more computationally convenient formula can be derived:

$$SP(X, Y) = \Sigma XY - \frac{(\Sigma X)(\Sigma Y)}{N}$$

Where ΣXY = sum of the raw score products
   $(\Sigma X)(\Sigma Y)$ = product of the X score total and the Y score total

Applying this computational formula to the example of Table 6-3, we have

$$SP(X, Y) = (0 \cdot 0 + 1 \cdot 2 + 2 \cdot 4) - \frac{(0 + 1 + 2)(0 + 2 + 4)}{3}$$

$$= (0 + 2 + 8) - \frac{3(6)}{3}$$

$$= 10 - 6$$

$$= 4$$

TABLE 6-2. *Scores of 3 Hypothetical Students on Two Quizzes.*

		Quiz	
		X	Y
Student	A	0	0
	B	1	2
	C	2	4

2. Take the product of two deviation scores for each person.
3. Find the sum of these deviation score products.

This is illustrated in Table 6-3, where we find SP(X, Y) = +4.

The sum of products has two serious shortcomings:

1. Since the raw scores obtained on each quiz are expressed in terms of points, the deviation scores are also expressed in point units. The result is that the *sum of products* is, like the *sum of squares,* expressed in a rather unusual type of unit. Therefore, the problems of interpretation here are similar to those encountered when using the *sum of squares* to measure the amount of dispersion in a single-variable (univariate) distribution.
2. Adding another pair of test scores to the set shown in Table 6-3 may change the value of SP(X, Y) even if the perfect relationship between Quiz X and Quiz Y is preserved. An example is shown in Table 6-4 where student D has been added. Notice the nature of the relationship has not changed; we still have a perfect-positive relationship. However, the value of SP(X, Y) has changed and, therefore, is of little use to us because knowing the value of SP(X, Y) does not tell us much about the nature of the relationship. What we need is an index which is sensitive to changes in the nature of the relationship between two variables while it remains unaffected by the number of data points in the plot. This leads us to a measure of linear association called the *covariance.*

TABLE 6-3. *Calculation of SP(X,Y) for the Data of Table 6-2.*

		Raw Score		Deviation Score		Deviation Score Products
		Quiz		Quiz		
		X	Y	X	Y	
Student	A	0	0	−1	−2	+2
	B	1	2	0	0	0
	C	2	4	+1	+2	+2

SP(X, Y) = +4

TABLE 6-4. *Illustration of the Effect of the Number of Data Points on SP(X,Y).*

		Raw Scores		Deviation Scores		Deviation Score Products
		Quiz		Quiz		
		X	Y	X	Y	
	A	0	0	−1.5	−3	+4.5
	B	1	2	−0.5	−1	+0.5
Student	C	2	4	+0.5	+1	+0.5
	D	3	6	+1.5	+3	+4.5

$$SP(X, Y) = 10.0$$

THE COVARIANCE

The *covariance* of two variables, Cov(X,Y), is simply SP(X,Y) divided by the number of products contributing to SP(X,Y). Using the data of Table 6-3, we find

$$\text{Cov}(X, Y) = \frac{SP(X, Y)}{N} = \frac{4}{3} = 1\frac{1}{3}$$

Similarly, using the data of Table 6-4, we find

$$\text{Cov}(X, Y) = \frac{10}{4} = 2.5$$

The covariance has not solved either the uniqueness or interpretation problems. However, using either SP(X,Y) or Cov(X,Y) and some other easily obtainable information, we are not able to resolve both of these problems simultaneously. The result is the Pearson correlation coefficient.

THE PEARSON CORRELATION COEFFICIENT

To calculate the value of a Pearson correlation coefficient, r(X,Y), simply divide Cov(X,Y) by the product of the standard deviations of distributions X and Y.[3]

$$r(X, Y) = \frac{\text{COV}(X, Y)}{\text{SD}(X) \cdot \text{SD}(Y)} \tag{6-1}$$

---

3. If the data are available in Z score form, then a more convenient formula for computing r(X, Y) is

$$r(X, Y) = \frac{1}{N} \Sigma (Z_X \cdot Z_Y)$$

In words, this formula tells us to
(a) Find the product of Z_X and Z_Y for each individual.

An equivalent formula which is frequently easier to use is

$$r(X, Y) = \frac{SP(X, Y)}{\sqrt{SS(X) \cdot SS(Y)}} \qquad (6\text{-}2)$$

To illustrate the use of Eq. (6-2), consider the data in Table 6-2. First, calculate the statistics $SP(X, Y)$, $SS(X)$, and $SS(Y)$ for these data. The results are as follows:

1. $SP(X, Y) = 4$

2. $SS(X) = (0 - 1)^2 + (1 - 1)^2 + (2 - 1)^2 = +2$

3. $SS(Y) = (0 - 2)^2 + (2 - 2)^2 + (4 - 2)^2 = +8$

Substituting these values in Eq. (6-2), we have

$$r(X, Y) = \frac{4}{\sqrt{(2)(8)}} = 1.00$$

First of all, the units cancel, and hence, the statistic $r(X, Y)$ is an index number, i.e., a number not dependent on the unit of measurement. In addition, we now have the value we typically associate with a perfect positive relationship, i.e., $r(X, Y) = 1.00$.

Besides solving the uniqueness and interpretation (unit) problems, the correlation coefficient has one other valuable feature: its value does not change when either or both variables under consideration are subjected to a linear transformation, i.e., the Pearson r is *invariant* under linear scale transformations. For example, if we add +1 to the values in column X of Table 6-2, multiply each value in column Y by 2, and recalculate the Pearson r, we get the result shown in Table 6-5. In a similar fashion, r is unaffected by transforming raw scores to the Z, T, or CEEB sales. This is not true for either the *sum of products* or the *covariance*.

(b) Sum these products.
(c) Multiply by $1/N$, where N is the number of products entering into the sum. For example, $r(X, Y)$ for the data shown below is $(1/3) (-0.40) = -0.13$.

Remember, the value of r is unaffected by linear transformations of the data. Because Z scores are linearly transformed raw scores, $r(X, Y)$ has the same value as $r(Z_X, Z_Y)$.

Person	Z_X	Z_Y	$Z_X \cdot Z_Y$
A	−1.00	0.50	−0.50
B	0.00	−0.60	0.00
C	+1.00	+0.10	+0.10

$$\Sigma (Z_X \cdot Z_Y) = -0.40$$

TABLE 6-5. *Illustration of the Invariance of the Pearson r under Linear Scale Transformations.*

		$X + 1$	$2Y$	New $(X + 1)$ Deviations	New $2Y$ Deviations	Deviation Products
	A	1	0	−1	−4	+4
Student	B	2	4	0	0	0
	C	3	8	+1	+4	+4

$$SP(X + 1, 2Y) = +8$$

$$r(X + 1, 2Y) = \frac{SP(X + 1, 2Y)}{\sqrt{SS(X + 1) \cdot SS(2Y)}}$$

$$SS(X + 1) = (-1)^2 + (0)^2 + (+1)^2 = 2$$

$$SS(2Y) = (-4)^2 + (0)^2 + (+4)^2 = 32$$

$$r(X + 1, 2Y) = \frac{+8}{\sqrt{(2)(32)}} = \frac{+8}{\sqrt{64}} = +1.00$$

EXERCISE SET 6-2

1. Calculate $SP(X, Y)$, $Cov(X, Y)$ and $r(X, Y)$ using the two data sets shown below.

a.

	X	Y
1	1	4
2	2	3
3	3	2
4	4	1

b.

	X	Y
1	0	0
2	0	6
3	6	0
4	6	6

2. If $Cov(X, Y) = 0.00$, $r(X, Y) = $ _____ .

3. If $SD(X) = 2$, $SD(Y) = 3$, and $r(X, Y) = 1.00$, then $Cov(X, Y) = $ _____ .

4. Which one of the following statistics can *never* have a value less than 0?
   a. $SD(X)$ ⁕b. $Cov(X, Y)$ c. $r(X, Y)$

5. If $Cov(X, Y) = -3.00$, $SD(X) = 4$ and $SD(Y) = 6$, then $r(X, Y) = $ _____ .

6. *True or False.*   For every bivariate distribution, the sign of $Cov(X, Y)$ is the same as the sign of $r(X, Y)$.

7. The Pearson r is a "better" measure of linear relationship than the sum of products and covariance statistics because:
   a. It is invariant with respect to linear scale transformations.
   b. It is the easiest to interpret.
   c. a and b

At this point, some attention must be paid to the interpretation of $r(X,Y)$. For the moment, we restrict our attention to the form of the statement typically made given a specific value of $r(X,Y)$. Justification for this statement form will be postponed until the next chapter.

To interpret $r(X,Y)$, square it and change the result to a percentage. The resulting value is interpretable as the *percentage of explained variance*. For example, if $r(X,Y) = -0.80$, then the square of $r(X,Y) = (-0.80)^2 = 0.64$, or 64%. This represents the amount of variation in the X distribution explained by variable Y, and vice versa. Similarly, $r(A,B) = 0.90$ would mean that $(0.90)^2$, or 81%, of the variance in distribution A would be explained by variable B, and vice versa. Now, let us look at a more realistic example.

Suppose one hundred applicants for a job on the Chrysler assembly line are given the Manual Dexterity Test (MDT). After one week on the job they are rated by their supervisor on the Job Proficiency Scale (JPS). The MDT–JPS correlation obtained is 0.50. How should this coefficient be interpreted?

The square of this value, $(0.50)^2$, indicates that 25% of the variation in JPS ratings can be explained in terms of examinee performances on the MDT. This also means that 75% of the variation in JPS ratings cannot be explained using the information provided by the MDT, and hence, suggests that skills, knowledges, and personality traits (e.g., tolerance of boredom) not measured by the MDT may be required by assembly line work. Note, we have not provided a rational basis for such an interpretation; this will be done later. Note also, this type of statement does not imply a cause-effect relationship. All we have said is that we can account for, or explain, 25% of the variation in the JPS distribution using the information we have on MDT performance.

To take still another example, suppose the correlation between reading ability and average annual income among the population of American adults is +0.60. This would mean that $(0.60)^2$, or 36%, of the variability in income among American adults can be explained on the basis of measured differences in reading ability, and vice versa.

EXERCISE SET 6-3

1. a. The linear correlation between performances on the Miller Analogies Test (MAT) and the Graduate Record Exam (GRE) for a select group of graduate students at University XYZ is found to be +0.40. This means that _____ % of the variability in GRE scores in this group is predictable from (or explainable given) their scores on the MAT.
   b. What percentage of the variability in the MAT distribution is explainable in terms of GRE score differences?
2. Suppose the linear correlation between a particular measure of socioeconomic status (SES) and high school grade point average (GPA) were +0.30. This would mean that _____ % of the variability in the GPA distribution could be accounted for in terms of this particular measure of SES.

Early in the discussion, we said that the Pearson r is the preferred measure of the strength of the linear trend because of its uniqueness, invariance, and "ease-of-interpretation" properties. However, there are factors which may, and frequently do, distort the value of this correlation coefficient, such as *variance restriction* and *measurement error*.

Effects of Variance Restriction on $r(X, Y)$

In general, reducing the variability in distribution X or Y or both tends to reduce the absolute size of $r(X, Y)$. Two ways in which this may happen are: (1) through loss of measurement information (e.g., substituting a nominal measurement rule for an ordinal one or the use of a 3-point rather than a 5-point rating scale), and (2) by restricting the calculation to a homogeneous subset of data points in the scatterplot. The latter, called *restriction of range*, merits some additional discussion.

Suppose the association between variables X and Y in population Z were as depicted in Figure 6-4. Because the data points exhibit a fairly strong positive linear trend, the value of $r(X, Y)$ would be fairly close to +1.00. However, if we were to calculate $r(X, Y)$ using only the individuals having scores of 80 or higher on the variable X, the value we obtain will be close to zero. The reason for this is that the data points in that portion of the plot do not exhibit a strong linear trend.

The effect of restricting the range does not always reduce the absolute size of $r(X, Y)$. For example, in the achievement–anxiety plot of Figure 6-3, calculating r on the whole plot would yield a coefficient close to zero, while calculating r on only the data points in the low–medium range would yield a value considerably higher than zero. The reason for this is that achievement and anxiety exhibit a positive linear trend in this restricted segment of the population. The main idea here is that the restriction of range on either variable can alter the value of $r(X, Y)$ appreciably. Although restriction of range may either increase or decrease the absolute value of $r(X, Y)$, the latter effect is the most frequent.

Values of $r(X, Y)$ obtained in reliability and validity studies are frequently distorted by variance restrictions (e.g., using a test too difficult for the group or measuring the validity of a predictor on a preselected group or subpopulation as shown in the example above) and should be remembered when interpreting correlation coefficients, regardless of the context in which they are calculated.

Effects of Measurement Error on $r(X, Y)$

While we are not yet in a position to provide a rigorous treatment of this topic, a simple illustration may be used to demonstrate the effects of measurement error on the magnitude of $r(X, Y)$. Suppose we have two variables which correlate 1.00 (see Figure 6-5a). If the measurement of either variable is contaminated by random or

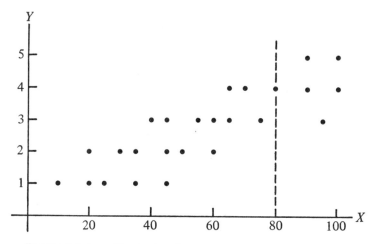

FIGURE 6-4.   *Illustration for restriction of range example.*

nonsystematic error, the true nature of the relationship, and hence, the value of $r(X, Y)$ will be distorted.   In Figure 6-5b, we see the results of adding an error component of +1 or −1 to each measure of X using a coin flip procedure.   Notice that the value of $r(X, Y)$ in Figure 6-5b is less than that in Figure 6-5a.   While this illustration shows how random error can distort the value of $r(X, Y)$, it may mislead one into believing that measurement error always lowers the magnitude of $r(X, Y)$. This is not so.   Measurement error may either increase or decrease the value of $r(X, Y)$; however, when dealing with real data, especially where more than just a few cases are involved, a reduction in magnitude of $r(X, Y)$ almost always occurs.

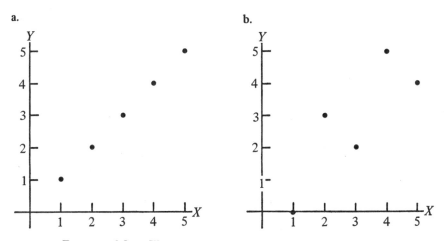

FIGURE 6-5.   *Illustration of a perfect-positive linear relationship (a), and the same relationship distorted by random error (b).*

1. In each of the following examples, tell whether the absolute size of the linear correlation between intelligence and scholastic grade point average would probably be lower in Population I or Population II.
   a. I. The entire group of applicants for admission to Harvard University for the 1970–1971 academic year.
      II. The members of this applicant population actually admitted to Harvard for the 1970–1971 academic year.
   b. I. All fourth grade students enrolled in the Newark city schools.
      II. All "underprivileged" fourth grade students enrolled in the Newark city schools.
2. Name two kinds of factors which may mask the true value of a correlation coefficient in a particular population.

THE FAMILY OF PEARSON CORRELATION COEFFICIENTS

The Pearson correlation coefficient has a number of different names, or aliases, depending on the kinds of data entered into the formula. In Table 6-6, which summarizes this information, the right-hand column indicates that the Pearson r has three aliases, namely, the point biserial coefficient, the phi coefficient, and Spearman's rank-order correlation coefficient (or rho). The formula

$$r(X, Y) = \frac{\text{Cov}(X, Y)}{\text{SD}(X) \cdot \text{SD}(Y)}$$

TABLE 6-6. *The Family of Pearson Correlation Coefficients.*

Nature of Variables	Name of Coefficient
a. both are interval or ratio level (e.g., height and weight)	Pearson r
b. one is an interval or ratio variable (e.g., total test score) one is a dichotomous variable* (e.g., score on one multiple-choice test item)	Point biserial correlation
c. both are dichotomous variables (e.g., score on each of two multiple-choice items)	Phi coefficient
d. both are ordinal variables (where scores are ranks)	Spearman rank order correlation (rho)

* A dichotomous variable is a variable that can assume only two values, typically 1 and 0.

may be used to calculate each of these correlational indexes; the name of the result being determined solely by the kinds of data upon which the computation is based.

In examining standardized test manuals and research articles, one frequently encounters the terms point biserial coefficient, phi coefficient, etc. The coefficient name tells the reader what kinds of data were entered into the Pearson formula. For example, if a test manual contains phi coefficients, one can be sure that only dichotomous data were used. Similarly, if rho coefficients are reported, the variables in question must have been measured using a ranking procedure. Since short cut computational formulas for these special cases of the Pearson r are given in most elementary statistics texts, they are not presented here.

EXERCISE SET 6-5

The entries in Column A below describe data sets to which the Pearson r formula might be applied. The entries in Column B are the names of the various Pearson correlation coefficients. Match the most appropriate coefficient name from Column B with each entry in Column A.

Column A	Column B
1. Height (in inches) and weight (in pounds) among New York City adults.	a. Pearson r b. Point biserial r c. phi d. rho
2. Height (in feet) and weight (in ounces) among Kansas farmers.	
3. Order of finish in the pie eating contest and order of finish in the subsequent potato sack race at the Widgit Company annual picnic.	
4. Performance on item 1 and performance on item 20 of a multiple-choice final exam.	
5. Scores on the Scholastic Aptitude Test and grade point average among Foggy Bottom University freshman.	

SUMMARY

This completes the discussion of correlation. We have examined the general notion of linear correlation, calculated the linear correlation between two variables, discussed the interpretation of $r(X,Y)$, examined the effects of variance restrictions and measurement error on the magnitude of a correlation coefficient, and briefly considered the Pearson r family of coefficients. A more rigorous treatment of this material and the discussion of other kinds of correlation coefficients can be found in many intermediate level statistics tests.[4]

---

4. See, for example, W. L. Hays and R. L. Winkler, *Statistics; Probability, Inference, and Decision* (Volume II), New York: Holt, Rinehart, and Winston, 1970, Chapter 10.

Before proceeding to the unit on linear statistical regression, check your comprehension of the material in this chapter using the self-evaluation forms provided for this purpose.

Form A

1. What is a scatterplot?
2. If one were to calculate the value of $r(X,Y)$ for the data displayed below, the obtained value would be in the interval from _____ .
   a. −1.00 to −0.30   b. −0.30 to +0.30   c. +0.30 to +1.00

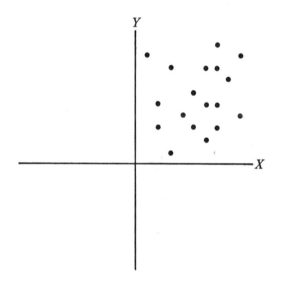

3. Calculate the sum of products for the following set of data:

	Raw Scores	
Examinee	Quiz 1	Quiz 2
A	0	2
B	2	4
C	4	6

4. The sum of products for variables X and Y for a group of 30 examinees is −60. The value of $Cov(X, Y)$ must be _____ .
5. If Cov (IQ, achievement) = 500, SD(IQ) = 20, and SD(achievement) = 50 in a particular student population, then r(IQ, achievement) = _____ in this population.

6. If the value of $r(X, Y)$ is negative, then one can be sure that
   a. The value of $Cov(X, Y)$ is negative.
   b. The value of $SD(X)$ is negative.
   c. The value of $SD(Y)$ is negative.
   d. a, b, and c.

7. Which of the following values of $r(X, Y)$ is indicative of the strongest linear relationship between X and Y?
   a. 0.86   b. −0.93   c. 1.34

8. If the Pearson r formula is used to calculate the correlation between a multiple-choice item (scored 1 for a correct response and 0 otherwise) and total test score, the obtained value is most appropriately called a_____ coefficient.

9. If the sum of Z-score products (or cross products) on variables X and Y for 30 individuals is −15.00, the value of $r(X, Y)$ for this group must be _____.
   (*Hint:* Use the formula in footnote 2.)

10. Suppose the value of r(IQ, socioeconomic status) = +0.30 for the 20 year old students at Braintrust University. The value of r(IQ, socioeconomic status) among the entire population of 20 year olds would most likely be _____ +0.30.
    a. less than   b. about equal to   c. greater than

Form B

1. Which of the following procedures is the best for revealing the nature of the relationship between two variables?
   a. Constructing a scatterplot.
   b. Calculating a measure of linear association.
   c. Calculating the square of $r(X, Y)$.

2. If one were to calculate the value of $r(X, Y)$ for the data displayed below, the result would be in the interval from _____.
   a. −1.00 to −0.30   b. −0.30 to +0.30   c. +0.30 to +1.00

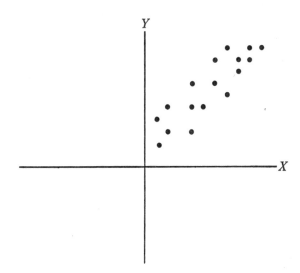

3. Calculate the sum of products for the 5 pairs of scores plotted below.

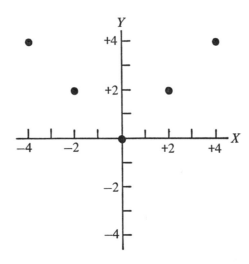

4. The sum of products for variables A and D in a group of 100 examinees is +650. The value of the covariance must be _____ .
5. If Cov(IQ, shoe size) = −2, SD(IQ) = 20, and SD(shoe size) = 2 among a population of athletes, then r(IQ, shoe size) = _____ in this population.
6. If the value of Cov(X,Y) is 0, and the values of SD(X) and SD(Y) are greater than 0, then one can be sure that:
   a. The value of $r(X,Y)$ is 0.
   b. X and Y are linearly related.
   c. A computational error has been made.
7. If one calculates the value for $r(X,Y)$ and obtains a value of +1.34, he can be sure that
   a. Performances on X and Y are not related.
   b. High scores on X tend to be associated with high scores on Y.
   c. The $X-Y$ relationship is probably nonlinear.
   d. A computational error has been made.
8. If the Pearson r formula is used to measure the degree of linear association between performance on two multiple-choice test items (each scored 1 if correct and 0 otherwise), the obtained value is most appropriately called a _____ coefficient.
   a. point biserial   b. phi   c. Spearman rho   d. Pearson r
9. Achievement and IQ measures are obtained for 100 students attending Clearthink University. A linear transformation is used to convert each of these distributions to the Z scale. The sum of the Z-score products turns out to be +78. The value of r(achievement, IQ) for this set of data must be _____ .
10. Suppose the value of r(math aptitude, math achievement) in the population at large is +0.70. One can be quite sure that the value of r(math aptitude, math achievement) for the population of Harvard engineering students is _____ +0.70.
    a. less than   b. about equal to   c. greater than

Form A
1. A scatterplot is a graphical representation of a set of ordered pairs of measurements in 2-dimensional space.
2. b
3. +8.00 (test points)^2
4. −2.00
5. +0.50
6. a
7. b
8. point biserial
9. $r(X, Y) = (1/30)(-15) = -0.50$

10. c

Form B
1. a
2. c
3. 0
4. +6.50
5. −0.05
6. a
7. d
8. b
9. +0.78
10. a

EXERCISE SET 6-1: ANSWERS

1. linear
2. the Pearson correlation coefficient r
3. upward from left to right
4. When the two variables are completely unrelated or when they are related in a curvilinear fashion.
5. a. positive linear   b. near zero   c. negative linear

EXERCISE SET 6-2: ANSWERS

1. a. $r(X, Y) = -1.00$ b. $r(X, Y) = 0.00$
2. 0.00
3. 6.00
4. a
5. −0.125
6. True
7. c

1. a. 16
   b. 16%.   The linear correlation coefficient has a symmetrical interpretation. If $r(X,Y) = +0.40$, this means that 16% of the dispersion in distribution X is predictable using information on variable Y, and vice versa.   Since the reason for this can be most easily explained in a linear prediction context, further discussion of this subject is delayed until the latter part of Chapter 7.

2. 9

---

1. a. II
   b. II
   Comment: In each case Population II represents a restricted segment of a much larger population of students, and the restriction has an adverse effect on the absolute size of r(IQ, GPA).   A common, but erroneous, belief held by many is that the correlation between IQ and GPA would be high for the portion of the applicant population actually admitted to Harvard, while the correlation between the same two variables would be low for the applicant population refused admission.   You may convince yourself that this is not so by constructing a scatterplot which represents the entire Harvard applicant population and identifying the two subsets of points which represent the subpopulations of admitted and nonadmitted applicants, respectively.   The linear trend of the entire plot should be much more clearly defined than it is in either restricted subpopulation.   This clearly shows that $r(X,Y)$ computed using the entire data set is greater than it is when computed using either of the subsets of points alone.

2. variance restriction, measurement error

---

1. a
2. a
3. d
4. c
5. a

7

An Introduction to Linear Statistical Regression

There are many situations in which tests and other measures are used to predict or forecast how an individual or group of individuals will perform on some important task or set of tasks. For example, test scores and other measurements (e.g., indexes of past academic success) are frequently used as the basis for predicting how well applicants will perform academically if admitted to a particular university and, hence, provide important input into admissions and scholarship award decisions. Similarly, to insure employment of the most suitable individual for a particular job, industrial personnel officers frequently make use of tests and other measures (e.g., performance on a work sample, background data) to predict how well the various applicants will perform on the jobs for which they are being considered.

One procedure which has demonstrated utility for predicting the score of an individual on one task (called the *criterion*)[1] given his score on another (called the

---

1. A *criterion* variable is any variable on which performance is to be predicted or estimated. A *predictor* variable is the variable being used as a basis for predicting or estimating performance on the criterion. Consider the following examples:

a. The *number of years of school completed* is used in predicting the *annual income* of an individual.
b. In many graduate schools, an applicant's admission depends, at least in part, on an estimate of his *grade point average* given his *score on the Miller Analogies Test*.
c. The best predictor of an individual's *future performance in mathematics* is his *past mathematics performance*.

The criterion variables in these examples are *annual income, grade point average*, and *future performance in mathematics*; the predictor variables are the *number of years of school completed, score on the Miller Analogies Test*, and *past mathematics performance*.

predictor) is *least-squares linear prediction* (or *least-squares linear regression*).[2] The purpose of this chapter is to examine the logic and method of least-squares linear prediction in the simplest case, i.e., the case in which performance on a single criterion variable is being predicted or estimated using an individual's score on just one predictor variable. The more general case, involving one criterion variable and two or more predictor variables, called *multiple linear prediction* (or *multiple linear regression*), is not covered here.

In succeeding sections of this chapter, we examine (a) the logic of linear least-squares prediction, (b) the equations appropriate for use with raw score and Z score data, (c) procedures for assessing the usefulness of a particular predictor variable for one or several criterion variables and comparing the relative predictive power of several potential predictor variables for one or more criterion variables, and (d) the recipes for making both single-value and interval estimates of criterion performance given either raw score or Z score data. (Interval estimation is especially important in the interpretation of individual scores obtained using norm-referenced tests.) In the process, the rationale for interpreting $r^2(X,Y)$ as the proportion of explained criterion variance is discussed, and the foundation for subsequent norm-referenced reliability and validity discussions (see Chapters 9 and 10) is established. We begin with the logic of least-squares regression.

THE LOGIC OF LINEAR STATISTICAL REGRESSION

In the last chapter, it was pointed out that a perfect, positive (or negative) linear relationship means that the Pearson r value is +1.00 (or −1.00) and that given a person's score on X, we could perfectly predict his score on Y. This is illustrated in Figure 7-1a. Notice that for each value of X there is one, and only one, value for Y.

In practice, however, such relationships are rarely, if ever, observed. For example, one typically finds a high positive relationship between student performances on math aptitude and math achievement tests when the examinee population is heterogeneous with respect to each variable. The relationship is by no means perfect, however, because numerous other factors affect test performance, e.g., motivation and test anxiety. Therefore, a typical scatterplot involving these variables tends to look something like the one shown in Fig. 7-1b.

Given such a plot, we can use the information it contains to predict individual math achievement scores. As you will see, the quality of the prediction process depends only on (a) knowledge of an individual's score on the math aptitude variable and (b) the strength of the relationship between the *predictor* variable (in this case, math aptitude) and the *criterion* variable (here, math achievement). Consider the following two possibilities:

---

2. A "least-squares" prediction procedure is one which minimizes the average squared error of the predictions made in repeated applications of the procedure. For both practical and mathematical reasons, least-squares prediction procedures are employed in many situations. (The terms *prediction* and *regression* are synonomous and, hence, may be used interchangeably.)

a.

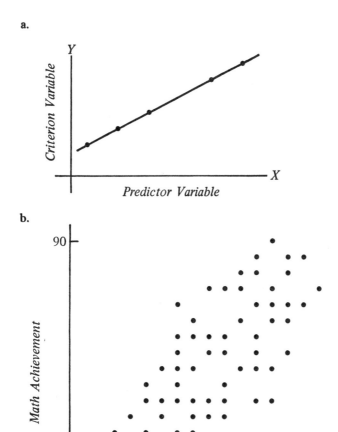

FIGURE 7-1. *Examples of (a) a perfect linear relationship and (b) a more typical linear relationship.*

1. Suppose we have the scatterplot shown in Figure 7-1b and know Mr. Q, whose math achievement score is to be predicted, is represented in the plot. We do not know his math aptitude score. How shall we estimate his criterion score? First of all, we see that the minimum and maximum math achievement scores represented in the plot are 10 and 90, respectively. Therefore, Mr. Q must have a math achievement score somewhere in that 10–90 range. One reasonable strategy or policy involves calculating the arithmetic mean of the distribution of criterion scores (i.e., math achievement scores) represented in the entire plot and

using that value as our estimate of Mr. Q's criterion performance. This procedure obviously results in many errors of prediction (or errors of estimate) if repeatedly applied. It can be shown, however, that the squared errors resulting from this procedure are, on the average, smaller than those made by consistently assigning some arbitrary value or making the estimate using a random procedure.

2. Suppose we have the information given above and, in addition, we know Mr. Q's score on the math aptitude test. Suppose his aptitude score is the one shown by the arrow in Figure 7-2a. Notice how this supplementary information allows us to improve our estimate of his score. Before, we only knew that his criterion score was some value between 10 and 90. Now we know that his criterion score is restricted to the much narrower interval 20–70 bounded by the dashed lines in Figure 7-2b.

Given this additional information about Mr. Q (i.e., his math aptitude score), we can use the same prediction policy as before. Now, however, we restrict our attention to the subset of scatterplot points located directly above the arrow in Figure 7-2b. That set of points represents the distribution of scores on the math achievement test for all of the individuals who obtained exactly the same math aptitude score as Mr. Q. Since an individual's criterion score is included in this distribution conditional upon his having the same aptitude score as Mr. Q, this is called a *conditional* (or, equivalently, *contingent*) distribution. Notice that a separate conditional distribution of criterion scores exists for each distinct predictor score.

Our final step is to calculate the arithmetic mean of the math achievement scores in the conditional distribution to which Mr. Q belongs. The value we obtained is a "least-squares" estimate of Mr. Q's criterion performance.[3]

Obviously, this procedure, which involves constructing a scatterplot and determining the mean of the various conditional distributions, is not very practical. Fortunately, if the criterion and predictor variables are linearly related, the means of the conditional distributions fall in a straight line, as shown in Figure 7-3. If we can find the equation of the line which passes through the conditional distribution means, we can use it to predict scores on the criterion variable from individual scores on the predictor variable. In the present context, such an equation would allow us to predict Mr. Q's math achievement score from his math aptitude score.[4]

---

3. Estimates made using a least-squares procedure are called least-squares estimates. As stated previously, the average squared error of estimate (or prediction) is minimized when least-squares procedures are used. If one's goal is to minimize the average absolute size of the error or the number of estimation errors made, different procedures would be employed. Because the various procedures tend to be in agreement in a wide variety of situations and least-squares theory is (for mathematical reasons) most fully developed, least-squares estimation is widely used.

4. The least-squares procedure as described, i.e., locating an individual's conditional distribution and using its mean as the estimate of his criterion variable score, is quite general. In fact, it can be used regardless of the nature of the relationship between two variables. However, the mathematical difficulties encountered in attempting to determine the equation of the line passing through the conditional distribution means may be quite formidable at times and provide strong motivation for assuming linearity whenever it seems reasonable to do so.

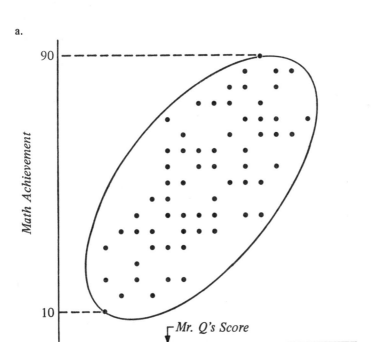

a.

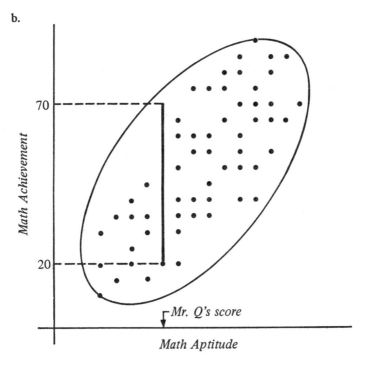

b.

FIGURE 7-2. *Illustration of the subset of data points, (i.e., the conditional distribution) to which Mr. Q belongs.*

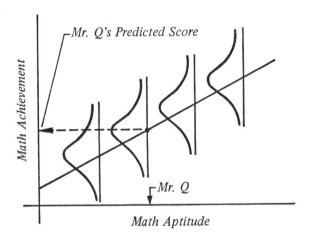

FIGURE 7-3.   *Illustration of several conditional distributions in a scatterplot exhibiting a linear relationship. (The curved lines provide an indication of the shape of each conditional distribution. Here, the shapes are shown to be normal – a condition which must be met, at least approximately, when interval estimates of individual criterion scores are being made.)*

By way of summary, when (a) the correlation between predictor variable *P* and criterion variable *C* is zero or (b) the correlation between *P* and *C* is known but the score of a particular individual (Mr. Q) on *P* is not known, the best estimate of his performance on *C* which we can make is the mean of the *C* distribution. If the correlation between *P* and *C* is nonzero and we know Mr. Q's score on *P*, then a more precise estimate of his performance on *C* is possible. That estimate is the mean of the *C* score conditional distribution which consists of all other individuals exhibiting the same level of performance on *P* as Mr. Q. The linear least-squares regression procedure illustrated in this chapter greatly facilitates this process.

THE LINEAR PREDICTION EQUATION FOR Z-SCORE DATA

When criterion and predictor scores are each separately standardized, i.e., transformed to the Z scale, formulas tend to simplify considerably. In Chapter 6, footnote 2, we saw that the Pearson *r* could be calculated using the formula

$$r(C,P) = \frac{1}{N} \sum (Z_P \cdot Z_C)$$

(with *C* and *P* replacing *Y* and *X*, respectively).

As it turns out, the equation for predicting an individual's standardized score on the criterion variable ($\hat{Z}_C$) given his standardized score on the predictor variable, Z_P, is

$$\hat{Z}_C = r(C,P) \cdot Z_P \qquad (7\text{-}1)$$

Where $\quad \hat{Z}_C$ = individual's predicted Z score on the criterion variable
$\qquad Z_P$ = same individual's Z score on the predictor variable

To illustrate the use of Eq. (7-1), suppose Mr. Q is a member of a population in which the linear correlation between math aptitude and math achievement is +0.85. Further, suppose Mr. Q's Z score on the math aptitude test is +2.00. Then his predicted score on the math achievement scale in this population must be

$$\hat{Z}_C = r(C,P) \cdot Z_P = +0.85(+2.00) = +1.70$$

This result is interpreted to mean that our best estimate (in the least-squares sense) of Mr. Q's criterion performance is 1.7 standard deviations *above* the mean of the criterion distribution.

Since $r(C,P)$ is always in the interval −1.00 to +1.00, inclusive, $\hat{Z}_C$ must always be less than or equal to the value of Z_P in absolute size (i.e., ignoring the sign). For example, an individual located 2 SD's above the mean in the predictor distribution would be estimated at exactly 2 SD's above the criterion-distribution mean only if $r(C,P) = +1.00$; 1 SD above the criterion mean if $r(C,P) = +0.50$; at the criterion mean if $r(C,P) = 0.00$; 1 SD below the criterion mean if $r(C,P) = -0.50$; and 2 SD's below the criterion mean if $r(C,P) = -1.00$. *For a fixed value of Z_P, as the value of $r(C,P)$ gets closer to zero, the value of $\hat{Z}_P$ tends (or regresses) towards zero — the mean of the criterion distribution when Z scores are used.*

If one were to construct a scatterplot following the standardization of both C and P, the least-squares regression line would be placed roughly as shown in Figures 7-4a through f depending on the value of $r(C,P)$. Notice the following about Figure 7-4:

1. $r(C,P)$ is the slope of the regression line. That is, if the value of Z_C is divided by the corresponding value of Z_P for any point on the regression line, the result is $r(C,P)$. (*Note*: The concept of slope is illustrated on page 93.)
2. When $r(C,P)$ equals +1.00 or −1.00, (a) all of the data points fall exactly on the regression line, and (b) the regression line forms a 45° angle with the Z_P axis (see Figures 7-4a and 7-4f).
3. As the value of $r(C,P)$ approaches zero, (a) the data points exhibit increasing amounts of scatter about the regression line, and (b) the slope of the regression line approaches zero. (Compare drawings of Figures 7-4a through d.)
4. When $r(C,P)$ equals zero, (a) there is no semblance of a linear trend, and (b) the regression line is coincident with the Z_P axis (see Figure 7-4d).
5. As the value of $r(C,P)$ moves from +1.00 toward 0.00, the estimated criterion score for a particular individual (say Mr. Q, whose $Z_P = +2.00$) regresses from $\hat{Z}_C = Z_P$ to $\hat{Z}_C = 0.00$; the latter being the mean of the criterion distribution when all scores are expressed in SD units (i.e., in Z-score form).

a. $r(C,P) = +1.00$

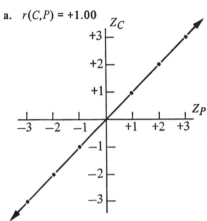

b. $r(C,P) = +0.50$

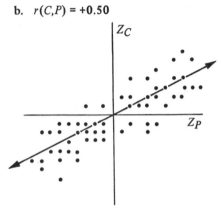

c. $r(C,P) = +0.20$

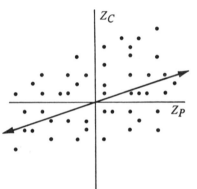

d. $r(C,P) = 0.00$

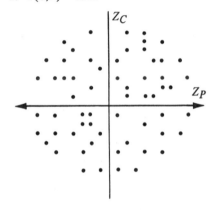

e. $r(C,P) = -0.50$

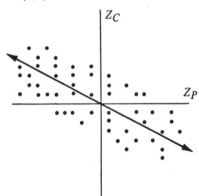

f. $r(C,P) = -1.00$

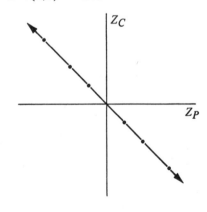

FIGURE 7-4.   *Illustration of regression lines for selected values of r(C,P).*

Frequently, we are confronted with data in raw rather than Z score form, and hence, it would be most convenient if a raw score equivalent of Eq. (7-1) was available. Using some relatively straightforward algebraic manipulation, it can be shown that Eqs. (7-2) and (7-3) are appropriate for use with raw score data.

$$\hat{C} = M_C + B \cdot (P - M_P) \qquad (7\text{-}2)$$

or, equivalently,

$$\hat{C} = B \cdot P + (M_C - B \cdot M_P) \qquad (7\text{-}3)$$

Where　$\hat{C}$　= estimated raw criterion score for an individual
　　　M_C = mean of the criterion score distribution
　　　M_P = mean of the predictor score distribution
　　　P　= individual's raw score in the predictor distribution
　　　B　= slope of the regression line and is numerically equal to $r(C,P)$ times $SD(C)/SD(P)$. The term *slope* is defined below.

Pictorially, a raw score regression line for a moderate, positive criterion-predictor correlation would appear as shown in Figure 7-5. Notice the following characteristics of linear regression lines in general as exemplified by the line in Figure 7-5:

1. The prediction line passes through the point (M_P, M_C), i.e., the point whose coordinates are the means of the criterion and predictor variables in this data set.
2. B is the slope of the line, i.e., the vertical distance between points (2) and (1), called the *rise*, divided by the horizontal distance between the same two points, called the *run*. Please note that the slope of a straight line can be determined using any two arbitrarily selected points since the ratio rise/run is constant for

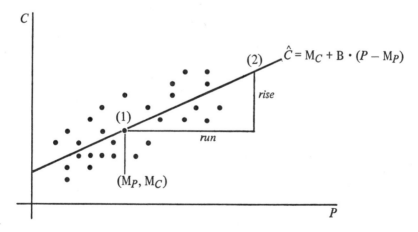

FIGURE 7-5.　*Example of a raw score regression line.*

any particular linear regression line. Also, note that the rise and run are measured in the units of the vertical and horizontal axes, respectively.

3. The C intercept (i.e., the point on the C axis cut by the prediction line) can be calculated directly using the term $(M_C - B \cdot M_P)$ taken from Eq. (7-3).

Also, notice the following facts about the relationship between B and $r(C,P)$: Since $B = r(C,P) \cdot SD(C)/SD(P)$, then

1. $B = 0.00$ whenever $r(C,P) = 0.00$.
2. $r(C,P)$ and B always have the same sign.
3. $B = r(C,P)$ whenever $SD(C) = SD(P)$; B and $r(C,P)$ have different values whenever $SD(C) \neq SD(P)$.

EXERCISE SET 7-1

1. Assuming $r(C,P) = -0.30$ in population T and all scores have been standardized, write the linear equation for estimating criterion performance given individual scores on the predictor variable.
2. If $r(C,P) = +0.27$, the slope of the Z score regression line is _____.
3. If $r(C,P) = 0.27$ and Mr. Q scored exactly 3 SD's above the mean in the predictor distribution, his estimated criterion performance $\dot{Z}_C$ is _____.
4. Suppose the following information exists concerning the performances of the members of population T on the predictor variable P and criterion variable C: $M_P = 100, M_C = 25$, and $B = 0.20$.
   a. Write the equation for estimating performance on the criterion C given information about performance on variable P.
   b. Suppose Mr. Q, a member of this population, has a score of 80 on variable P. What is his estimated score on the criterion?
5. The distribution of scores on C associated with a score of 80 on P is called a _____ distribution.

ERRORS OF ESTIMATE

Once an individual's score has been predicted, the discrepancy between his actual criterion score C and his predicted criterion score $\hat{C}$ is called an *error of estimate*, designated by the symbol E. The result of predicting a single score using a linear prediction policy is illustrated in Figure 7-6. In this illustration, Mr. Q's predictor score is designated P; his criterion score, C; his predicted criterion score, $\hat{C}$; and the error in estimating his criterion score, $E = C - \hat{C}$. Looking at it another way, this prediction policy effectively partitions (or divides) each criterion score C into an estimated criterion score $\hat{C}$ and an error of estimate $E = C - \hat{C}$. Such a partition is illustrated in Figure 7-7, where it is easy to see that $C = \hat{C} + E$.

If the criterion score were similarly estimated for each person in the population, three distributions of scores would be generated: (1) the distribution of *observed criterion scores C*, (2) the distribution of *predicted criterion scores $\hat{C}$*, and

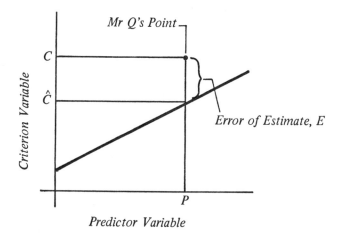

FIGURE 7-6.   *Illustration of the error of estimate associated with Mr. Q.*

(3) the distribution of *error scores E.* An example is shown in the last three columns of Table 7-1.

If we assume that the prediction line passes through the mean value of *C* in each conditional distribution and that the conditional distributions are all normal and display the same amount of variation, it can be shown that

$$\text{Var}(C) = \text{Var}(\hat{C}) + \text{Var}(E) \qquad (7\text{-}4)$$

In words, the variance of the criterion score distribution is the simple sum of the

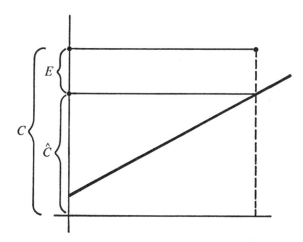

FIGURE 7-7.   *Partition of Mr. Q's criterion score (C) into predicted (Ĉ) and error (E) components.*

TABLE 7-1. *Illustration of the Relationship* $\text{Var}(C) = \text{Var}(\hat{C}) + \text{Var}(E)$, *Using a Simple Data Set.*

Person	Score on P	Score on C	$\hat{C}$	$E = C - \hat{C}$
A	1	7	8.37	−1.37
B	3	10	11.17	−1.17
C	2	11	9.77	1.23
D	3	12	11.17	0.83
E	5	12	13.97	−1.97
F	4	15	12.57	2.43

1. For these data, $B = 1.40$, $M_C = 11.17$, $M_P = 3$.
2. To calculate $\hat{C}$ for each person, one may use the equation

$$\hat{C} = 11.17 + 1.40\,(P - M_P)$$

3. As a result, $\text{Var}(C) = 6.97$, $\text{Var}(\hat{C}) = 3.92$, and $\text{Var}(E) = 3.05$, which provides an example of $\text{Var}(C) = \text{Var}(\hat{C}) + \text{Var}(E)$.

variance of the $\hat{C}$ distribution and the variance of the error score distribution. Dividing each term in this equation by $\text{Var}(C)$, we have

$$\frac{\text{Var}(C)}{\text{Var}(C)} = \frac{\text{Var}(\hat{C})}{\text{Var}(C)} + \frac{\text{Var}(E)}{\text{Var}(C)}$$

$$1.00 = \frac{\text{Var}(\hat{C})}{\text{Var}(C)} + \frac{\text{Var}(E)}{\text{Var}(C)}$$

Where $\dfrac{\text{Var}(\hat{C})}{\text{Var}(C)}$ = proportion of criterion variance predictable (or explainable) using the scores on variable P.

$\dfrac{\text{Var}(E)}{\text{Var}(C)}$ = proportion of criterion variance unpredictable (or unexplainable) using the scores on P. Furthermore, it can be shown that the proportion of explainable variance, $\text{Var}(\hat{C})/\text{Var}(C)$, is equal to the square of the linear correlation coefficient, $r^2(C,P)$. This provides the basis for the interpretation of the Pearson r presented in the previous chapter.

EXERCISE SET 7-2

1. The difference between an individual's actual criterion score and his estimated criterion score is called a(n) _____ .
2. Suppose $r(C,P) = -0.80$, $SD(C) = 20$, $SD(P) = 5$, $M_C = 100$, and $M_P = 50$.
   a. What is the slope of the prediction line?
   b. What is the prediction equation?

c. Suppose Mr. Q, a member of this population, has a score of 40 on the predictor measure. What is his estimated score on the criterion?

d. Suppose Mr. Q's actual criterion score turns out to be 120. What is his error of estimate (or error score)?

THE QUALITY OF PREDICTION

Regardless of whether one is using raw or Z-score data, the quality or goodness of a particular predictor for estimating performance on a specific criterion variable depends only on the value of $r(C,P)$. The higher the value of $r(C,P)$, the closer the data points in the scatterplot follow or cluster about the straight line running through the means of the various conditional distributions. The closer the data points within these conditional distributions are to the straight line (and hence, to the means of their respective conditional distributions), the smaller the value of the standard deviation of each of these distributions. Since each conditional distribution is really a distribution of prediction or estimation errors, the standard deviation of each conditional distribution is called the *standard error of estimate* for that particular distribution. Therefore, the larger the value of $r(C,P)$, the smaller the standard errors of estimate conditional upon the various values of the predictor variable tend to be.

In Figure 7-8, we see an illustration of three conditional distributions. Notice that the first distribution consists of all values of the criterion variable obtained by individuals having the score 100 on the predictor variable. Since the mean criterion score for this distribution is 35, the linear regression equation assigns the value 35 as the criterion variable estimate for each person scoring 100 on the predictor. Notice, however, that the actual criterion scores are quite variable. If

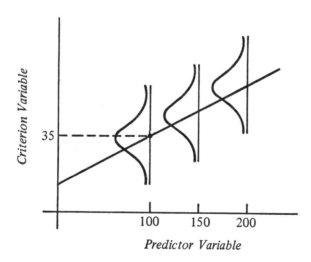

FIGURE 7-8. *Illustration of three conditional distributions having the same shape and variability.*

we subtract 35 from each of these scores, the result is a set of deviation scores representing the estimation errors resulting from our prediction policy. The standard deviation of this error score distribution is the standard error of estimate associated with (or conditional upon) the predictor score of 100. Similarly, a separate standard error of estimate can be computed for each of the remaining conditional distributions. In practice, however, we can usually avoid this tedious task. If all of the conditional distributions are approximately normal in shape and equally variable, the following formula provides a good estimate of these standard deviations:

$$SD(E) = SD(C) \cdot \sqrt{1 - r^2(C,P)}$$

In this formula, $SD(C)$ and $r(C,P)$ are used as previously defined: $SD(E)$ represents the standard deviation of the distribution of errors which occur in estimating performances on C given scores on variable P. Because it represents the *standard deviation* of a distribution of *errors of estimate*, it is most frequently referred to as the *standard error of estimate*. The value of $SD(E)$ in any particular situation can be used both as a measure of the "goodness" of the prediction and to construct interval (as opposed to single-value) estimates of criterion performance. To illustrate the use of this formula, suppose $SD(C) = 10$ points and $r(C,P) = +0.80$. Then, $SD(E) = 10\sqrt{1 - 0.64} = 10\sqrt{0.36} = 10(0.6) = 6$ points.

In the Exercise Set 7-3, we will see that the value of $SD(E)$ and the value of $r^2(C,P)$ are related in a rather straightforward manner; the larger the value of $r^2(C,P)$ becomes for a particular predictor, the smaller the value of $SD(E)$ becomes. Conversely, the less dispersion there is among the criterion scores in the various conditional distributions, the larger the value of $r^2(C,P)$. Since $r^2(C,P)$ is an index number (i.e., it has no units) and because it always has a value between 0 and 1, inclusive, it seems like the better of the two measures to use in assessing the quality of a particular predictor for estimating performance on a specific criterion variable. Although $SD(E)$ can also be used for this purpose, the value of this statistic ranges between 0 and the value of $SD(C)$; hence, the bounds for this statistic, unlike those for $r^2(C,P)$, fluctuate from situation to situation, making interpretation quite difficult. While we will not further discuss the use of $SD(E)$ as a measure of predictor quality, we will subsequently discuss its use in making interval estimates of individual criterion performances. Before entering into that discussion, however, further examination of the utility of $r^2(C,P)$ as a measure of predictor quality is in order.

Suppose that the entering body of graduate students at Foggy Bottom University is given the Miller Analogies Test (MAT) and the correlation between performance on this test and grade point average (GPA) after twelve credit hours of graduate work is found to be +0.40. Is the Miller Analogies Test worth using as a predictor of graduate school grade point average? One way of evaluating the utility of the MAT for predicting GPA in this population is to square the value of $r(C,P)$. In this case, we find that $r^2(C,P) = (+0.40)^2 = 0.16$. This means that 16% of the variation in the actual GPA distribution in this population is attributable to or explainable by measured individual differences on the MAT. In other words, performance on the MAT and performance in the graduate program (as quantified in the form of the GPA) are affected by certain common influences (e.g., intelligence). Performance on each variable is also affected by a conglomeration of unique influences (i.e., some factors affecting performance on the MAT do not affect GPA, and some factors affecting GPA do not influence performance on the MAT). The value of $r^2(C,P)$ tells what proportion of the dispersion in the predictor and criterion distributions is due to common influences. Therefore, the larger the value of $r^2(C,P)$, the more both measures (that is, C and P) are functioning in a similar fashion.

Be sure to note that $r(C,P)$ and $r^2(C,P)$ are related in a curvilinear fashion. Values of $r^2(C,P)$ are always smaller in absolute size than corresponding values of $r(C,P)$, except when $r(C,P)$ equals -1.00, 0.00, or $+1.00$. For example, $r(C,P) = 0.80$ indicates that $(0.80)^2$ or 64% of the criterion variance is explainable by measured individual differences in performance on the predictor. This means that 36% of the criterion variance cannot be explained by predictor performances and, hence, must be due to skills, knowledge, abilities, etc., not measured by the predictor test. Similarly, a correlation of -0.20 between predictor and criterion indicates that $(-0.20)^2$ or 4% of the criterion variance is explainable using the information provided by the predictor variable and 96% is not.

To summarize, $SD(E)$ and $r^2(C,P)$ are both usable as measures of the goodness of any variable as a predictor of performance on a specific criterion task. However, $r^2(C,P)$ has several characteristics which tend to make it the preferred index: (a) its value is always in the interval zero to positive one, (b) it is an index number and therefore is independent of the unit of measurement, and (c) it is directly interpretable as the proportion of criterion variance attributable to measured individual differences in performance on the predictor variable. While there are special situations where $SD(E)$ provides a more appropriate comparison of several potential predictors relative to a specific criterion variable, they lie outside the mainstream of this presentation and are not discussed in this chapter.

EXERCISE SET 7-3

1. If $SD(C) = 10$ and $r(C,P) = 0.00$, $SD(E) =$ _____ .
2. If $SD(C) = 10$ and $r(C,P) = 0.50$, $SD(E) =$ _____ .
3. If $SD(C) = 10$ and $r(C,P) = +1.00$, $SD(E) =$ _____ .
4. For a fixed value of $SD(C)$, what happens to the magnitude of the standard error of estimate as $r(C,P)$ goes from 0 to 1.00?
5. What value does $SD(E)$ approach as $r(C,P)$ is allowed to decrease from 1.00 to 0.00?

MAKING INTERVAL ESTIMATES OF CRITERION PERFORMANCE

In interpreting estimates of criterion scores for individuals, it is usually good policy to use interval rather than single-value estimates because the former permit the predictions to be tempered by the strength of the relationship which exists between the predictor and criterion variables. If the correlation between these variables is very high, the interval estimates will be relatively tight and, hence, quite useful; if the correlation is low, the intervals will be relatively wide and, hence, of dubious value. This is a desirable characteristic because it prevents us from attributing a high degree of precision to predictions where we are not justified in doing so.

To construct an interval estimate of an individual's criterion score:

1. Calculate the single-valued estimate $\hat{C}$ (for raw score data) or $\hat{Z}_C$ (for Z score data).
2. Calculate SD(E), the standard error of estimate.
3. Substitute these values into the formula:

$$\text{Lower bound of interval} = \text{estimated score} - k \cdot \text{SD}(E)$$
$$\text{Upper bound of interval} = \text{estimated score} + k \cdot \text{SD}(E)$$

Where $k = 1$ (for an approximate 68% interval estimate)
$= 2$ (for an approximate 95% interval estimate)
$= 3$ (for an approximate 99% interval estimate)

Be sure to note the fact that the value of SD(E) will usually differ for raw and Z score data simply because SD(C) always equals 1.00 in the Z score case and rarely equals that value in the raw score case.

For example, suppose Mr. Q's estimated score is 68, SD(C) = 20, $r(C,P)$ = 0.80, and M_C = 100. To find a 95% interval estimate of his actual criterion score, we follow the recipe outlined above:

1. $\hat{C} = 68$
2. $\text{SD}(E) = \text{SD}(C)\sqrt{1 - r^2(C,P)} = 20\sqrt{0.36} = 12$
3. Lower bound = $68 - 2(12) = 44$
   Upper bound = $68 + 2(12) = 92$

As a result, we would say that we are 95% confident that Mr. Q's actual criterion score is between 44 and 92. This is roughly equivalent to saying that we would be willing to bet 95–5 (or 19–1) that his actual criterion score is between these values. Please remember, this procedure for constructing and interpreting interval estimates is based on the assumption that the conditional distributions are normal and equally variable.

If we wished to look at the interval in Z-score form, we follow the same recipe:

1. $\hat{Z}_C = (\hat{C} - M_C)/\text{SD}(C) = (68 - 100)/20 = -1.60$
2. $\text{SD}(E) = 1\sqrt{1 - r^2(C,P)} = 1\sqrt{0.36} = 0.60$
3. Lower bound = $-1.60 - 2(0.60) = -2.80$
   Upper bound = $-1.60 + 2(0.60) = -0.40$

Just as in the raw score case, we see that the 95% interval estimate falls entirely below the mean of the criterion distribution and we may be quite confident (i.e., 95% confident) in the prediction that Mr. Q is (or will be) a below average performer on the criterion variable of interest here. In order to consolidate all of the operations considered in this unit, we will now review the entire discussion by example.

Suppose we have the following information about the math aptitude subtest of the Scholastic Aptitude Test (SAT-math) and the freshman GPA for the current student population of Foggy Bottom University. Using the given data, answer the following questions:

	SAT-Math	Freshman GPA
Mean	500	2.80
SD	100	0.50
r(SAT-Math, Frosh GPA) = +0.40		

(a) What is the raw score equation for predicting freshman GPA from SAT-math scores? What is the corresponding Z score equations?

(b) If Mr. Q's SAT-math raw score is 300, what is the single-value estimate of his freshman GPA in raw score units? What is the corresponding estimate in Z score units?

(c) Calculate the value of SD(E) to be used in constructing raw score and Z score interval estimates of criterion performance.

(d) Calculate the 95% interval estimate of Mr. Q's criterion performance in raw score units. Determine the corresponding Z score interval.

(e) If a passing GPA is 2.00, would it seem reasonable to counsel Mr. Q to enter Foggy Bottom University if he wishes to do so?

ANSWERS:

(a) $\hat{C} = M_C + B \cdot (P - M_P)$ $\hat{Z}_C = r(C,P) \cdot Z_P$

$\quad = 2.80 + 0.40 \left(\dfrac{0.50}{100}\right)(P - 500)$ $= 0.40 \, Z_P$

(b) $C = 2.80 + 0.002\,(300 - 500)$ $\hat{Z}_C = 0.40\,(-2.00)$

$\quad = 2.80 - 0.40$ $= -0.80$

$\quad = 2.40$

(c) $SD(E) = SD(C)\sqrt{1 - r^2(C,P)}$ $SD(E) = SD(C)\sqrt{1 - r^2(C,P)}$

$\quad = 0.50\sqrt{1 - (0.40)^2}$ $= 1.00\sqrt{1 - (0.40)^2}$

$\quad = 0.50\sqrt{0.84}$ $= 1.00\sqrt{0.84}$

$\quad = 0.46$ $= 0.92$

(d) Upper limit $= 2.40 + 2(0.46)$ Upper limit $= -0.80 + 2(0.92)$

$\quad = 3.32$ $= 1.04$

Lower limit $= 2.40 - 2(0.46)$ Lower limit $= -0.80 - 2(0.92)$

$\quad = 1.48$ $= -2.64$

We are 95% sure that Mr. X's GPA will be between 1.48 (a solid D) and 3.32 (a grade of B).

We are 95% sure that his performance will be between 2.64 SD's below the mean and 1.04 SD's above the mean of the GPA distribution.

(e) If a passing grade is 2.00, the single value estimate, taken alone would lead us to unequivocally counsel Mr. Q to enter the program. However, because the interval estimate contains values less than 2.00 in its range, the best strategy would probably be to interpret the meaning of this interval to Mr. X and withhold any advice until additional relevant information is obtained.

EXERCISE SET 7-4

Suppose we have the following information about the Manual Dexterity Test (MDT) and performance in an automobile repair course (ARC) for a particular population of trainees. Mr. Q applies for admission to the course and is immediately given the MDT. His MDT score turns out to be 60.

	MDT	ARC
Mean	50	10
SD	10	2
$r(C,P) = +0.80$		

1. Make raw and Z-score single-valued estimates of this ARC performance rating.
2. Calculate $SD(E)$ for the raw and Z-score cases.
3. Make 99% raw and Z-score interval estimates of his ARC performance rating.

SUMMARY

In this chapter we examined the least-squares regression procedures for the simplest case (i.e., one criterion and one predictor) using raw and Z score data, discussed the relative utility of $r(C,P)$ and $SD(E)$ as measures of the quality of a particular prediction equation, and used $SD(E)$ to construct interval estimates of criterion scores given individual scores on the predictor. These concepts and techniques, along with those of the prior chapters, provide an adequate base for dealing with the norm-referenced reliability and validity discussions which are to follow. Before moving to Chapter 8, which deals with classical measurement theory, check your comprehension of the present chapter using one of the self-evaluations provided for this purpose.

Form A

1. If scores on Test A are being used to estimate performance on Test B, then Test B is called the _____ variable.

2. The equation $\hat{Y} = M_Y + B \cdot (X - M_X)$ is the _____ score equation for estimating performance on variable _____ given information on variable _____ .

3. The symbol B represents the _____ of the prediction line. In the figure shown below, the value of B is _____ .

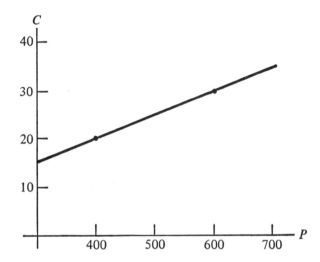

4. Suppose Mr. Q's actual criterion score is 25 and his predicted criterion score is 30. The difference between these scores is called an _____ .

5. If $r(X, Y) = -0.40$, $M_X = 100$, $SD(X) = 10$, $M_Y = 50$, and $SD(Y) = 3$, then $B =$ _____ . (Assume Y is the criterion variable.)

6. Using the information of problem 5, write the equations for determining $\hat{Y}$ and $\hat{Z}_Y$.

7. Using the information of problem 5, calculate the value of $SD(E)$ for (a) the raw score case, and (b) the Z score case.

8. Using the results of problem 6, calculate $\hat{Y}$ and $\hat{Z}_Y$ for an individual whose score on X equals 80.

9. Using the results of problem 7 and 8, determine the approximate 95% interval estimates of Y and Z_Y.

10. Correct interval estimates will be obtained using the methods of this chapter only if
   a. C and P are linearly related.
   b. The distribution of C for each value of P is normal.
   c. The variance of the conditional C score distributions are equal.
   d. All of the above are true.
   e. None of the above are true.

1. If performance on the Stanford-Binet Intelligence Test is being estimated using performance on the Peabody Picture Vocabulary Test, the Stanford-Binet is the _____ variable.
   a. predictor   b. criterion

2. In the equation $\hat{Y} = 2.50(X - 10) + 500$, the slope of the regression line is _____ and the mean of the criterion distribution is _____ .

3. Suppose Mr. Q's estimated criterion score in a particular situation is 30 and the error of estimate is +5. His actual criterion score must be _____ .

4. If $r(C,P) = -0.30$, then the value of B must be _____ .
   a. negative   b. equal to zero   c. positive

In questions 5 to 7 suppose $r(C,P) = +0.60$, $M_C = 100$, $SD(C) = 10$, $M_P = 20$, and $SD(P) = 4$, and C is the criterion variable.

5. $B =$ _____ .

6. $SD(E) =$ _____ .

7. The value of $\hat{C}$ for an individual obtaining a score of 16 on P is _____;
   the 95% interval estimate of C is _____ .

8. In general, the greater the value of $r(C,P)$, the _____ the value of $SD(E)$.
   a. larger   b. smaller

9. When we state a 68% confidence interval, we are essentially saying that we are willing to bet at _____ odds that the actual criterion score is in the interval.

10. If $r(C,P) = +0.60$, the equation for calculating $\hat{Z}_C$ is _____ and the standard error associated with the use of this equation is _____ .

ANSWER KEY

Form A
1. criterion
2. raw; Y; X
3. slope; $10/200 = 1/20 = .05$
4. error of estimate
5. -0.12
6. $\hat{Y} = M_Y + B \cdot (X - M_X)$ $\hat{Z}_Y = -0.40\,(Z_X)$
   $\quad = 50 + (-0.12)(X - 100)$

7. *Raw score case*   *Z-score case*
   $SD(E) = SD(Y)\sqrt{1 - r^2(X, Y)}$ $SD(E) = SD(Y)\sqrt{1 - r^2(X, Y)}$
   $\quad\quad = 3\sqrt{1 - (-0.40)^2}$ $\quad\quad = 1.00\sqrt{0.84}$
   $\quad\quad = 3\sqrt{0.84}$ $\quad\quad = 0.92$
   $\quad\quad = 2.76$

8. $\hat{Y} = 50 + (-0.12)(80 - 100)$ $\hat{Z}_Y = -0.40\,(-2)$
   $\quad = 52.4$ $\quad\quad = 0.8$

9. $52.4 + 2(2.76) = 57.9$ $0.8 + 2(0.92) = 2.6$
   $52.4 - 2(2.76) = 46.9$ $0.8 - 2(0.92) = -1.0$

10. d

ANSWER KEY (Cont.)

Form B

1. b
2. 2.50, 500
3. 35
4. a
5. $B = 0.60\,(10/4) = 1.50$
6. $\text{SD}(E) = 10\sqrt{1 - (0.60)^2} = 10\sqrt{0.64} = 8$
7. $\hat{C} = M_C + B(P - M_P) = 100 + 1.50(16 - 20) = 100 - 6 = 94;\ 78-110$
8. b
9. 68 to 32 or about 2 to 1
10. $\hat{Z}_C = +0.60\,Z_P;\ \text{SD}(E) = 1.00\sqrt{1 - (0.60)^2} = \sqrt{0.64} = 0.80$

EXERCISE SET 7-1: ANSWERS

1. $\hat{Z}_C = -0.30\,Z_P$
2. $+0.27$
3. $3(+0.27) = +0.81$
4. a. $\hat{C} = M_C + B(P - M_P)$ or $\hat{C} = B \cdot (P) + (M_C - B \cdot M_P)$
   $\phantom{\hat{C}} = 25 + 0.20\,(P - 100)$ $\phantom{\hat{C}} = 0.20\,P + (25 - 0.20 \cdot 100)$
                                               $\phantom{\hat{C}} = 0.20\,P + 5$

   b. $\hat{C} = 25 + 0.20\,(80 - 100)$ or $\hat{C} = 0.20\,(80) + 5$
   $\phantom{\hat{C}} = 21$ $\phantom{\hat{C}} = 21$

5. conditional

EXERCISE SET 7-2: ANSWERS

1. error of estimate
2. a. $B = r(C,P) \cdot \dfrac{\text{SD}(C)}{\text{SD}(P)} = -0.80 \left(\dfrac{20}{5}\right) = -3.20$

   b. $C = M_C + B \cdot (P - M_P) = 100 + (-3.20)(P - 50) = 100 - 3.20(P - 50)$
   c. $\hat{C}Q = 100 - 3.20(40 - 50) = 100 - 3.20(-10) = 100 + 32 = 132$
   d. $E = C - \hat{C} = 120 - 132 = -12$

EXERCISE SET 7-4: ANSWERS

Raw score case   *Z-score case*

1. $C = M_C + B(P - M_P)$ $\dot{Z}_C = r(C,P) \cdot Z_P$

$= 10 + 0.80 \dfrac{2}{10}(60 - 50)$ $= 0.80 \left(\dfrac{60 - 50}{10} \right)$

$= 10 + 1.6$ $= 0.80(1.00)$

$= 11.6$ $= 0.80$

2. *Raw score case*   *Z-score case*

$SD(E) = SD(C)\sqrt{1 - r^2(C,P)}$ $SD(E) = SD(C)\sqrt{1 - r^2(C,P)}$

$= 2\sqrt{1 - (0.80)^2}$ $= 1\sqrt{1 - (0.80)^2}$

$= 2\sqrt{1 - 0.64}$ $= 1\sqrt{0.36}$

$= 1.2$ $= 0.60$

Raw score case   *Z-score case*

3. Upper limit $= 11.6 + 3(1.2)$ Upper limit $= 0.80 + 3(0.60)$

$= 15.2$ $= 2.60$

Lower limit $= 11.6 - 3(1.2)$ Lower limit $= 0.80 - 3(0.60)$

$= 8.0$ $= -1.00$

8

An Introduction to Classical Measurement Theory

In Chapter 1, the concept "test reliability" was introduced and its importance discussed. In the present unit, we examine one theory of measurement error (i.e., the classical measurement theory) and show in a more rigorous manner the meaning of reliability. We begin with the basic tenet of this theory, namely, every observed score is the simple sum of a true score (which reflects the true amount of the attribute possessed by the person being measured) and an error score (which reflects the effects of extraneous influences on the measurement process). We then develop, in a rather straightforward way, the fundamental notion of classical measurement theory and apply the important results (or formulas) we obtain in interpreting individual test scores and laying the groundwork for estimating test reliability.

This chapter is not intended to be a comprehensive treatment of classical test theory, but it is designed to provide (a) an adequate introduction to the theory for those students intending to pursue the study of measurement at a more rigorous level and (b) an intuitive exposition for the nonmeasurement specialists in order that they may better understand the meaning and importance of test reliability.

THE CLASSICAL MEASUREMENT MODEL

The fundamental equation of classical measurement theory is

$$X = T + E \qquad (8\text{-}1)$$

Where X = observed score (e.g., the weight of an individual obtained from a platform scale)

T = true score (i.e., the individual's true weight at the time X is obtained)

E = error score (i.e., the discrepancy between X and T due to a myriad of extraneous influences which just happen to be present at the time of the measurement)

This equation simply says that the observed score is the sum of two independent components: (a) a *true score* component, which represents the precise quantity of the measured characteristic possessed by the person at the time of measurement, and (b) an *error score* component, which reflects the influence on X, of the myriad of extraneous influences which happen to be present at the time the measurement is taken. In other words, the error score (E) reflects the extent to which the observed score (X) misses the mark as an estimate of the true score (T).

To clarify the notion of true and error score, consider the following example:

EXAMPLE

Suppose person A has a true weight of 150 lb. at the precise moment he reads the indicator on the platform scale on which he is standing. Furthermore, suppose the value he reads is 150.5 lb. Then, according to Eq. (8-1), his error score (or the size of the discrepancy between his true and observed weights) is +0.5 pounds.

$$X_2 = T + E_1$$

$$150.5 = 150 + {+}0.5$$

Had the conditions at the time of weighing been different (e.g., had he stood in a different position on the scale platform or had the distribution of dust in the scale mechanism been different), the observed weight might have been 149.3 lb. In that case, the error score (E_2) would have been −0.7 lb. That is

$$X_1 = T + E_2$$

$$149.3 = 150.0 + (-0.7)$$

In summary, the person or object being measured is assumed to possess a specific amount of the attribute of interest at the time the measurement is taken. The exact amount is obscured or distorted, however, by numerous factors which are not controlled either because (a) the effect of each is presumed to be so small that it is not worth the effort, (b) their effect is appreciable, but we do not have the wherewithal to control them, or (c) they are not known to us. The total impact of these transient, random influences on the observed measurement is what we call the error of measurement. The true score and the error of measurement are assumed to combine additively to produce the value we observe when the measurement is taken.

1. Write the statement $X = T + E$ in words.

2. If an individual's true height is 57 in. and his measured height at a particular time is 56.31 in., the error score associated with that measurement is _____ .

3. If the measuring device used in item 2 were perfectly reliable, his error score would have been _____ .

4. If the measuring device used in item 2 were completely unreliable his observed score would have been approximately equal in value to his _____ score.
   a. true   b. error

5. Suppose person A weighs exactly 150 lb. at the time he measures his weight using a standard bathroom scale.
   a. What is his error score if the scale registers 150 lb.?
   b. What would his observed score be if his error score equaled −1.3 lb.?
   c. Which one of the following factors is a potential source of measurement error in this situation?
      (1) Person A's socioeconomic status
      (2) Person A's position on the scale
      (3) The diet person A's wife happens to be on

6. Suppose an individual knew the answers to exactly 7 items on a 10-item multiple-choice geography quiz. In recording his response to one of the items, however, he mistakenly marked the wrong alternative. This inadvertent mismark affects the value of his

   _____ .

   a. true score
   b. error score
   c. observed score
   d. true and observed scores
   e. error and observed scores

THE HYPOTHETICAL DISTRIBUTION OF POTENTIAL OBSERVED SCORES

At the precise time an individual is measured, his true score (T) is assumed to be fixed. His error score (E), however, is just one of a large set of possible values – each associated with a unique combination of chance factors which contribute to the true score-observed score discrepancy. If it were possible to hold T constant, manipulate the extraneous error-producing factors at will, and obtain independent measurements under each set of conditions, a distribution of observed scores (X) could be generated. Furthermore, if the observations were made under a representative sample of all possible measurement circumstances, the shape of the observed distribution would probably be *normal* in shape and the arithmetic mean of the scores in this distribution would, by definition (see Lord and Novick, 1968), be the individual's true score (T).[1]

---

1. Notice, according to this definition *constant errors* or biases like those described in Chapter 1 become part of (or are absorbed into) the true score. As a result, they affect validity, but not reliability. This should be clearer after Chapters 8 through 10 have been completed.

For example, suppose it were possible to repeatedly administer the same multiple-choice test to one examinee under essentially the same conditions and in such a manner that his performance on any one administration was not affected by previous exposures to the test. Assuming the examinee does not have perfect knowledge of the content being tested, his observed score would randomly fluctuate across administrations of the test due to factors like differential guessing success and changes in test taking disposition (e.g., motivation to do well, degree of comfort and well-being, mood, carelessness). If scores (X) were obtained for all possible combinations of such random error producing factors, their mean would, by definition, be the examinee's true score (T). Such a hypothetical, observed score distribution is shown in Figure 8-1.

To summarize the relevant points made earlier:

1. The classical score model, $X = T + E$, asserts that an observed score (X) is the simple sum of two components: a true score component (T) and an error score component (E).
2. The potential distribution of observed scores is assumed *normal* and centers about the individual's true score at the time the measurement is taken.

THE STANDARD ERROR OF MEASUREMENT

If the individual's true score (T) is subtracted from each observed score value (X) in the hypothetical distribution shown in Figure 8-1, the resulting set of deviation scores are the *errors of measurement*. Therefore, by rescaling the baseline of Figure 8-1 in deviation score units, we transform this hypothetical observed score distribution to a hypothetical error score distribution (see Figure 8-2).

The amount of variation in this distribution can be measured a number of ways; the most common being the standard deviation. Because this hypothetical distribution is a distribution of error scores, its standard deviation is called the *standard error of measurement*, designated SEM or SD(E). (The term *standard error of measurement* is short for *standard* deviation of the distribution of *error* scores obtained in *measurement*.)

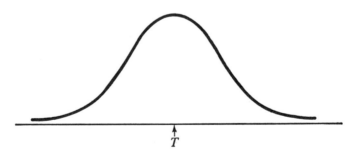

FIGURE 8-1. *Hypothetical distribution of potential raw scores for one person at a specific point in time.*

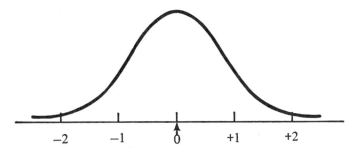

FIGURE 8-2. *Hypothetical distribution of potential error scores for one person at a specific point in time.*

If our measurement procedure or instrument were perfectly reliable, the observed score (X) would exactly equal T regardless of the extraneous conditions present at the time of measurement. In that case, SEM would equal zero. The less reliable an instrument is, the larger SEM turns out to be. Therefore, SEM can be used to indicate the quality of X as an estimate of T.

INTERPRETING THE INDIVIDUAL TEST SCORE

If a particular observed score is just an estimate of the individual true score at the time of measurement, it seems reasonable to determine how good an estimate it is and to incorporate this information into our statement about the amount of the measured attribute possessed by the examinee. Since the hypothetical distribution of potential observed (or error) scores is assumed to be distributed *normally*, a brief review of some characteristics of normal distributions may be in order. Use Exercise Set 8-2 to see whether a review of Chapter 4 is necessary before continuing.

EXERCISE SET 8-2

1. In every normal distribution, approximately _____% of the observations are located within ±1 SD's of the mean.
   a. 34   b. 68   c. 85   d. 95
2. In every normal distribution, approximately _____% of the observations are located within ±2 SD's of the mean.
   a. 34   b. 68   c. 85   d. 95
3. In every normal distribution, approximately _____% of the observations are located more than 1 SD away from the mean.
   a. 68   b. 32   c. 15   d. 5

Whenever a measurement is taken, primary interest is in the true score of the individual being measured. The problem, as previously stated, is we have no way of observing the true score. If we did, this discussion would be unnecessary. Therefore, we use the information at hand to make the best estimate of his true score that we can. This involves measuring the individual, determining the standard error of measurement, and using these two bits of information to make an interval or band estimate of his true score. The procedure is exactly the same as the one used in Chapter 7 for constructing interval estimates of criterion scores. The logic is as follows:

1. Since the potential error scores for any measurement are assumed to distribute normally, approximately 68% of the potential observed scores are within ±1 SEM of the individual's true score. For example, suppose a particular test has an SEM of approximately 5 points. Then approximately 68% of the potential observed scores for an individual having a true score of 105 at the time of testing are located in the interval 100–110. Notice that the interval is 10 points wide and centers about his true score 105.

2. If the same size interval (10 points wide) were centered around any observed score located between 100 and 110, the interval would contain the true score. For example, the interval around an observed score of 107 is 102–112. This interval contains the true score.

3. *Conclusion:* If an interval this size (±1 SEM) were constructed around every potential observed score in this hypothetical distribution, 68% of the intervals would contain T and 32% would not. Therefore, armed with a single observed score and the standard error of measurement, we would say that we are 68% sure (or certain) that the true score is in the interval $X \pm 1$ SEM whatever the value of X we observe.

EXERCISE SET 8-3

After examining examples A through D in the following table, complete lines 1 and 2.

Raw Score (X)	SD(E)	Interval Estimation Procedure	Interval Estimate	Interpretation
A. 101	5	$X \pm 1$ SEM	96–106	"...68% sure that T is between 96 and 106"
B. 101	5	$X \pm 2$ SEM	91–111	"...95% sure that T is between 91 and 111"
C. 53	8	$X \pm 1$ SEM	45–61	"...68% sure that T is between 45 and 61"
D. 53	8	$X \pm 3$ SEM	29–77	"...99% sure that T is between 29 and 77"
1. 115	5	$X \pm 1$ *SEM*	⸻	⸻
2. 87	3.2	⸻	⸻	"...95% sure that T is in the interval 80.6–93.4"

Similar reasoning can be applied in constructing 95% and 99% interval estimates. To save time and space, several examples are presented in Exercise Set 8-3, with lines 1 and 2 to be completed by the reader.

Since, in practice, we cannot possibly measure an individual under all possible error-producing conditions to generate his distribution of potential observed scores, we measure a large number of individuals on the attribute in question just once or twice and use these data to estimate an average standard error of measurement. Before this procedure is introduced, its rationale must be explained and the concept "test reliability" more precisely defined. We begin by partitioning the observed score variance. (*Note: To partition means to divide into disjoint or mutually exclusive components.*) In the next segment of this discussion, we see how the observed score variance can be partitioned in a way which eventually leads to a precise definition of the term "reliability."

PARTITIONING THE OBSERVED SCORE VARIANCE

If we measure a large number of persons with respect to the same attribute (e.g., achievement of the objectives on an item writing unit), the observed scores will probably not all be the same numerical value. This is because (a) there are *true* differences in achievement among the examinees (i.e., there is variance in the distribution of true scores) and (b) there are differences in the effects of extraneous error-producing factors on the various examinees (e.g., some examinees are "luckier" in guessing than others, some make more mismarks on the answer sheet than others). As a result, we really have *three* different score distributions: (a) the observed sco. distribution, (b) the distribution of true scores, and (c) the distribution of error scores. The first of these is observable; the latter two are not. It turns out, however, that if the linear correlation between the true and error scores is zero, i.e., $r(T,E) = 0$, then the following relationship holds:

$$\text{Var}(X) = \text{Var}(T) + \text{Var}(E) \tag{8-2}$$

Where $\text{Var}(X)$ = variance of *observed* score distribution
  $\text{Var}(T)$ = variance of *true* score distribution
  $\text{Var}(E)$ = variance of *error* score distribution

This is the *basic variance equation.* It must be clearly understood that this simple relationship holds precisely only if the true scores and error scores are uncorrelated, i.e., knowledge of a person's error score does not help in the prediction of his true score, and vice versa. This is an important *assumption.* The following example may help to clarify its meaning.

EXAMPLE
Suppose the quiz scores of four individuals are 5, 7, 6, and 8. Furthermore, suppose that the true and error components of each observed score are as follows:

Person	X	=	T	+	E
A	5	=	6	+	(−1)
B	7	=	6	+	(+1)
C	6	=	7	+	(−1)
D	8	=	7	+	(+1)

Notice that persons A and B have the same true score, but because of the susceptibility of our measurement procedure to error, they have different observed scores. Similarly, persons C and D have the same true score, but different observed scores. In this hypothetical example, knowing a person's true score (6 or 7) would not help in the prediction of his error score (+1 or −1), and vice versa. This lack of predictive power implies that $r(T,E) = 0$, i.e., the linear correlation between the set of true scores and the set of error scores is zero. Computing the variance of these three distributions, we find $\text{Var}(X) = 1.25$, $\text{Var}(T) = 0.25$, and $\text{Var}(E) = 1.00$ showing that the relationship expressed in Eq. (8-2) holds.

Summarizing, we have shown by example that the variance of the observed score distribution can be *partitioned* into true variance (i.e., variance caused by true achievement differences among examinees) and error variance (i.e., variance caused by extraneous factors). We can now use the resulting basic variance equation to give the term "reliability" a more precise meaning.

RELIABILITY REDEFINED

We begin with the basic variance equation:

$$\text{Var}(X) = \text{Var}(T) + \text{Var}(E)$$

If we divide each term by $\text{Var}(X)$, the result is

$$\frac{\text{Var}(X)}{\text{Var}(X)} = \frac{\text{Var}(T)}{\text{Var}(X)} + \frac{\text{Var}(E)}{\text{Var}(X)} \qquad (8\text{-}3)$$

$$1.00 = \frac{\text{Var}(T)}{\text{Var}(X)} + \frac{\text{Var}(E)}{\text{Var}(X)}$$

The first ratio, $\text{Var}(T)/\text{Var}(X)$, is a precise definition of *reliability*. In words, it represents the proportion of variation in the observed score distribution due to true score differences among examinees. In the correlational notation of Chapter 7, a variance ratio is equivalent to a squared Pearson r, and hence, $\text{Var}(T)/\text{Var}(X)$ may be thought of as $r^2(X,T)$, i.e., the squared observed score-true score correlation. The second ratio, $\text{Var}(E)/\text{Var}(X)$, is a precise definition of unreliability. In words, it represents the proportion of variation in the X score distribution due to errors of measurement. In correlational notation, it may be equivalently written as $r^2(X,E)$.

Using one of the methods to be presented in Chapter 9, suppose we estimate the reliability of an achievement test to be 0.80. This would tell us that approximately 80% of the variance in the X distribution is due to true differences in knowledge levels among the examinees tested and the remaining 20% is due to random errors of measurement, i.e., differential effects of guessing, mismarks, ambiguity in test instructions and items, etc.

EXERCISE SET 8-4

1. The reliability of test XYZ for the undergraduate-student population of the University of Delaware is 0.85.
   a. This means that _____% of the variation in the XYZ test scores in this population is due to true differences among the students on the attribute measured by XYZ.
   b. What percent of the variation is due to error?

DERIVATION OF A FORMULA FOR CALCULATING SEM

We are now in a position to derive a formula which can be used to calculate an estimate of SEM (the standard error of measurement). Beginning with Eq. (8-3), we may write

$$1.00 = r^2(X,T) + \frac{\text{Var}(E)}{\text{Var}(X)}$$

where $r^2(X,T)$ represents the reliability ratio $\text{Var}(T)/\text{Var}(X)$. If we multiply each term by $\text{Var}(X)$, the result is

$$\text{Var}(X) = r^2(X,T) \cdot \text{Var}(X) + \text{Var}(E)$$

Solving for $\text{Var}(E)$, we have

$$\text{Var}(E) = \text{Var}(X) - r^2(X,T) \cdot \text{Var}(X)$$

Factoring $\text{Var}(X)$ out of both terms on the right side of this equation produces

$$\text{Var}(E) = \text{Var}(X) \cdot [1 - r^2(X,T)]$$

Taking the square root of both members of this equation yields

$$SD(E) = SD(X) \cdot \sqrt{1 - r^2(X,T)} \tag{8-4}$$

Where $SD(E) = \text{SEM} = $ standard deviation of error score distribution

To illustrate the use of Eq. (8-4), suppose the administration of a test to a population of examinees produced the following information: reliability = 0.84, mean = 50, and standard deviation = 10. The average standard error of measurement in that population would be

$$\text{SEM} = SD(X) \cdot \sqrt{1 - r^2(X,T)} = 10\sqrt{1 - 0.84} = 4 \text{ points}$$

As a result, the approximate 68% interval estimate of the true score for an examinee having a raw score of 63 would be 59–67.

If formula (8-4) looks familiar, it should. It is the formula for the standard error of estimate presented in Chapter 7 with X replacing C and T replacing P. In the next section, we recast the notions presented thus far in the linear regression framework of Chapter 7.

EXERCISE SET 8-5

1. For the example just concluded, the 68% interval estimate for a score of 63 was found to be 59–67. What does this mean?
2. a. Suppose the administration of a test to a group of examinees yields the following data: reliability = 0.64, M = 50, and SD(X) = 10. The average standard error of measurement is _____ .
   b. If the reliability of this test were 1.00 while M and SD(X) were 50 and 10, respectively, what would the value of SEM be?
   c. If the reliability were 0.00 while M and SD(X) had values as reported above, what would SEM be?
3. Can the reliability of a test theoretically be less than 0.00 or more than 1.00? Explain your answer.

CLASSICAL MEASUREMENT THEORY IN A LINEAR REGRESSION FRAMEWORK

In Chapters 6 and 7, we examined procedures for measuring the linear relationship between two variables and for using this knowledge to estimate individuals' scores on one variable (the criterion) given their scores on another variable (the predictor). Using these procedures, we will now reexamine classical measurement theory in order to accomplish two ends: (a) to further clarify the interpretation of a reliability coefficient and (b) to show the rationale for using the standard error of measurement obtained from group data to interpret individual test scores.

Recall the following facts from Chapter 7:

1. If a criterion (C) and predictor (P) score is obtained for each of a large number of individuals and if these scores are linearly related, a scatterplot of these data points will resemble the one shown in Figure 8-3.
2. Associated with each value of P is a distribution of C values. These are called conditional distributions.
3. If C and P are linearly related, the mathematical equation for the line of best fit passes through the arithmetic mean value of C in each conditional distribution and, hence, can be used to predict criterion scores given specific predictor scores.
4. The standard deviation of each contingent distribution is the standard error of estimate associated with a particular value of P. The average of the standard errors of estimate associated with all of the conditional distributions in this plot can be obtained using the formula $SD(E) = SD(C) \cdot \sqrt{1 - r^2(C,P)}$.

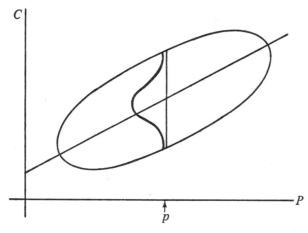

FIGURE 8-3. *The distribution of C conditional on the specific score p on the predictor.*

If a norm-referenced test was given to a large number of people and a scatterplot was constructed using their observed and true scores, treating the observed score as the criterion variable and the true score as the predictor, the plot would probably look like the one shown in Figure 8-4.[2] The standard deviation of each conditional distribution is a standard error of estimate, i.e., it is a measure of

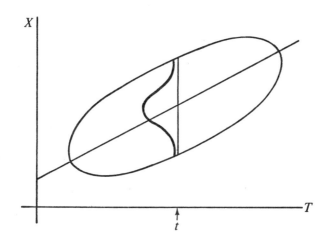

FIGURE 8-4. *The distribution of observed scores (X) conditional on a specific true score (t).*

---

2. The reason we are treating the observed score as the criterion variable and the true score as the predictor is that we are attempting to explain observed score variance in terms of individual true score differences. One can, in fact, reverse the role of T and X in a regression framework and obtain more precise interval estimates of individual true scores than we can obtain using the procedures of this chapter. To avoid needless complexity at this time, we choose not to consider that development.

the amount of error involved in the process of estimating the observed score given an individual's true score. If measurement error were completely absent, the conditional distributions would display no variability. Since all of the errors in estimating X from T are due to the extraneous influences affecting the measurement process, these standard errors of estimate are called standard errors of measurement (SEM). Since for most practical purposes, we require only a rough estimate of these standard errors of measurement, we can compute the average SEM using the formula $\text{SEM} = \text{SD}(X) \cdot \sqrt{1 - r^2(X,T)}$. Notice that this is exactly the formula shown in item 4 above with X and T replacing C and P, respectively.

Since errors of measurement are assumed to operate in a random fashion, it seems quite reasonable to assert that the SEM conditional on a particular true score will have approximately the same value whether obtained (a) with repeated testings of one individual under the "idealized" measurement conditions described earlier or (b) with single measurements on a large number of individuals having the same true score on the attribute in question. While the idealized repetitive measurements are not possible, the latter procedure is. Since we have no way of knowing the values of T and E for each individual, the problem of estimating $r^2(X,T)$, i.e., test reliability, still remains and is the subject of the next chapter.

The standard error of measurement is a neat index of precision. All other things remaining equal, the smaller the standard error for a particular test, the more precisely an individual's true score can be estimated using his observed score. An interesting fact is that while factors like restriction of range (see Chapter 6) seriously distort reliability estimates, they have practically no effect on the standard error of measurement. In fact, for tests having 20 to 200 moderately difficult items, Lord (1959) found that the formula $3\sqrt{k}/7$ (where k is the number of items in the test) provides a good approximation to the standard error regardless of group homogeneity or range restriction.

An intuitive grasp of this can be had if one realizes that SD(X) and reliability tend to increase or decrease together as a function of observed score variability. As a result, the relatively low value of SD(X) obtained in a very homogeneous examinee population tends to be offset by a relatively high value of $\sqrt{1 - \text{reliability}}$; the opposite being true in a very heterogeneous population.

A second way of thinking about this phenomenon is aided by looking at a scatterplot. Restricting the range of X and T for a particular test by deleting the high and low scoring groups reduces the correlation between X and T, but does not increase the scatter in the distributions of X conditional on specific values of T. For example, cutting off the high and low groups along the true score dimension in Figure 8-4 would certainly reduce the correlation of X and T, but it would have no effect on the amount of variability of X for the remaining specific values of T, i.e., the conditional distributions shown in the figure would not be at all affected.

SUMMARY

We began with three assumptions: (1) $X = T + E$ is an adequate representation of the scores obtained in a norm-referenced testing situation, (2) every examinee possesses a true score on the attribute being measured at the time the measurement is obtained, and (3) the linear correlation between these true scores and the errors of measurement is zero, that is, $r(T,E) = 0$.[3] Using an "idealized" repetitive measurement model we developed the notion of a personal standard error of measurement and showed how such a standard error is used to provide an interval estimate of an individual's true score given the reliability of the test and the individual's observed score. In this regard, we noted that the average standard error of measurement (i.e., the average of the personal standard errors) is typically estimated and used in constructing such interval estimates. Next, we partitioned observed score variance into true and error variance, thereby enabling us to redefine reliability in a fairly precise manner. Finally, we looked at the classical measurement model as a simple linear prediction problem and showed that the standard error of measurement is a special case of the standard error of estimate. The next unit deals with some practical procedures for estimating test reliability. Before moving to that discussion, check your comprehension of the material in this unit by using the self-evaluation form provided for this purpose.

SELF-EVALUATION

1. The classical score model, $X = T + E$, asserts that an observed score (X) is the simple sum of two components (T and E). What do these symbols represent?
2. The classical test score model ($X = T + E$) assumes
   a. The error scores are normally distributed.
   b. The error and true scores are uncorrelated.
   c. a and b.
   d. neither a nor b.
3. Identify the terms in the equation $Var(X) = Var(T) + Var(E)$.
4. If a reliability coefficient is 0.80, what proportion of the variability in test scores is error variance?
   a. 0.20   b. 0.36   c. 0.64   d. 0.80
5. Suppose a teacher calculates a reliability estimate for a classroom achievement test and obtains a value of −0.31. How should this be interpreted?
6. The standard error of measurement is the standard deviation of the _____ distribution.
   a. true score   b. error score   c. observed score

---

3. Classical measurement theory also assumes that the measurement rule used has at least interval level measurement properties (see Chapter 1 to refresh your mind on these properties, if necessary). Although norm-referenced educational tests typically come up short in this regard, the formulas derived from this theory tend to work reasonably well in practice and, hence, are used routinely by many experienced testers. Lord and Novick (1968, p. 215) point out, however, that whenever interest in a set of test scores is limited to just the ordinal information they carry (e.g., "grading on the curve"), a more appropriate definition of true score is in terms of examinee ranks, rather than raw scores. In such a case, an examinee's true score may be conceived as the mean of his rankings across a large number of independent repeated testings and his error of measurement on any one testing as the difference between his rank on that occasion and his true score.

7. a. If a test were perfectly reliable, SEM would equal _____ .
   b. If a test were completely unreliable, SEM would equal _____ .

8. Suppose the administration of a test to a group of examinees yields the following data: reliability = 0.84, mean = 50, SD(X) = 10.   The estimated standard error of measurement is _____ .

9. Suppose the administration of test X to the members of population Y yields the following data: reliability = 0.64, mean = 100, SD(X) = 15.   The average standard error of measurement is _____ .

10. The average standard error of measurement for test X in population Y is 4.5 points.   What is the 68% interval estimate of the true score for any person in population Y having an observed score of 36 points?

ANSWER KEY

1. T represents the true score component of X. E represents the error component, or the error of measurement.

2. c

3. Observed score variance = true score variance + error score variance.

4. a

5. 0 (Since, in theory, the lower bound of reliability is zero [i.e., Var(T)/Var(X) cannot be less than zero since both Var(T) and Var(X) can never be negative], this value is probably best interpreted as indicating a completely unreliable test.)

6. b

7. a. 0
   b. SD(X)

8. SD(E) = $10\sqrt{1 - 0.84}$ = 10(0.4) = 4 points

9. 9 points

10. 31.5–40.5

EXERCISE SET 8-1 ANSWERS

1. An observed score is equal to the sum of the true score and an error score.
2. −0.69
3. zero
4. b
5. a. zero, b. 148.7 lb., c. 2
6. e

EXERCISE SET 8-2: ANSWERS

1. b
2. d
3. b

EXERCISE SET 8-3: ANSWERS

1. 110—120; I am 68% sure that the examinee's true score is between 110 and 120.
2. $X \pm 2$ SEM; 80.6—93.4

COMMENT: Instead of saying I am 68% sure, 95% sure, or 99% sure that the true score is within a certain band of values, the terms *fairly certain, quite certain,* and *very certain* are sometimes used.   For example, one could say, "I am fairly certain (or reasonably certain) that the examinee's true score is between 110 and 120."   Similarly, the interpretation of line 2 could be, "I am quite sure that the examinee would score between 80.6 and 93.4 on a retest."   However, because the connotations of terms like *fairly certain,* etc., differ from one person to the next, their use is not recommended.

EXERCISE SET 8-4: ANSWERS

1. a. 85
   b. 15

EXERCISE SET 8-5: ANSWERS

1. We can be 68% sure that this individual's true score is between 59 and 67.
2. a. SEM = $10\sqrt{1 - 0.64} = 10\sqrt{0.36} = 6$ points
   b. 0 points
   c. 10 points
3. No. Reliability is a ratio of two variances. Since a variance, by definition, cannot be negative, $\text{Var}(T)/\text{Var}(X) = r^2(X,T)$ cannot be negative. Also, since $\text{Var}(X) = \text{Var}(T) + \text{Var}(E)$ and $\text{Var}(E)$ cannot be negative by definition, $\text{Var}(T)$ can never be larger than $\text{Var}(X)$. Therefore, the reliability ratio, $\text{Var}(T)/\text{Var}(X)$, cannot be greater than one.

REFERENCES

Lord, F. M.   (1959).   Tests of the Same Length Do Have the Same Standard Error of Measurement.   *Educational and Psychological Measurement,* *19,* 233—239.

Lord, F. M. and M. R. Novick.   (1968).   *Statistical Theories of Mental Test Scores.*   Reading, Massachusetts: Addison-Wesley.

9

Norm-Referenced Test Reliability

In Chapter 1, we said that the reliability of a test in a particular examinee population depends on the extent to which the scores it assigns to examinees in that population are free of the effects of random or variable errors. In Chapter 8, we defined reliability more precisely as $r^2(X,T)$ or $\text{Var}(T)/\text{Var}(X)$, i.e., the proportion of observed score variance due to true differences among examinees. However, because true scores are unobservable, the definitional formulas $r^2(X,T)$ and $\text{Var}(T)/\text{Var}(X)$ are of no practical value when one wants to estimate the reliability of a particular test. In the present chapter, we examine three approaches to assessing norm-referenced test reliability, in particular, the test-retest, parallel forms, and internal analysis approaches. As you will see, the sources of variability in the observed scores which are treated as random error by each of these three approaches differ considerably, and hence, the coefficients they produce reflect slightly different kinds of test reliability. Following the discussion of these procedures, we consider two techniques which are useful in determining the extent to which essay item responses (as well as other types of constructed response items, e.g., short answer completion) are affected by a particular type of random error, i.e., rater (or scorer) inconsistency. Then, we examine the relationships between test length and test reliability, and between the amount of variability in the observed scores and test reliability. Finally, we consider the problem of unreliability of difference scores and the implications of this for assessing individual pupil progress in school.

In this section, we examine three approaches to the assessment of test reliability: the test-retest, parallel forms, and internal analysis techniques. We begin with the test-retest approach.

The Test-Retest Approach

The test-retest procedure for assessing the reliability of a test in a particular examinee population requires two administrations of the same test to all examinees in that population.[1] If we let X_1 represent the set of scores obtained on the first test administration and X_2 represent the set of scores obtained on the second, the linear correlation between these two sets of scores, $r(X_1, X_2)$, is a test-retest reliability coefficient and is interpretable as $r^2(X,T)$ or, equivalently, $\text{Var}(T)/\text{Var}(X)$.

To see what the value of $r(X_1, X_2)$ tells us, let us first consider the application of this procedure in a nontesting situation, e.g., in assessing the reliability of a common bathroom scale. Assuming we have available a population of individuals who vary considerably with respect to weight, all we have to do to obtain a value of $r(X_1, X_2)$ is to weigh each individual in the population twice and compute the linear correlation between these two sets of measurements. However, first we must decide what the time interval should be between the successive measurements for each person. If, for example, the measurements on each person were separated by a two-week interval, the weight values for each individual obtained on the separate measurement occasions would probably differ due to inadequacies of the measurement process (e.g., imprecision of the scale, random errors in observing and/or recording weight values), as well as true changes in individual weights. Hence, one would not know whether a low value for $r(X_1, X_2)$ is indicative of scale imprecision, observer/recorder errors, fluctuations in individual true weights, or a combination of these factors. It is clear, however, that in this type of application,

---

1. The reliability formulas presented in this chapter assume that test data are available on all examinees in the population of interest. If data are available only for a representative sample of examinees, the application of these formulas provides *estimates* of the actual reliability coefficients. Furthermore, if the sample is quite small, a variance components approach to reliability estimation presented by Lord and Novick (1968, Chapters 7 and 9) can be used to obtain better estimates than those obtainable using the formulas in the present chapter.

A note on sampling variability: When, as is usually the case, the reliability of a test is assessed using a sample rather than the entire population of examinees, the quality of the reliability estimate is directly related to the representativeness and size of the sample. Lack of representativeness may result in a severely biased estimate while sample size is directly related to the precision of the estimate. To elaborate a bit on the latter point, large (representative) samples tend to yield estimates close in value to the true population reliability coefficient, and hence, large sample estimates tend to vary very little from one sample to the next. On the other hand, small (representative) samples produce estimates which vary more in their degree of closeness to the true population reliability coefficient. The practical implication of this is that two small random samples from the same population may provide reliability estimates which differ considerably. Hence, small sample estimates should be interpreted cautiously.

an interval of two weeks between measurements would probably result in a value of $r(X_1,X_2)$ which underestimates the reliability of the measurement process in question. A more appropriate tack in this situation would be to obtain the pair of measurements for each individual in fairly rapid succession, thereby preventing (or at least minimizing) the distorting effects of true changes in weights on $r(X_1,X_2)$. The net result is a coefficient which more accurately reflects the reliability of the measurement process being scrutinized. Whenever the sources of random error affecting the magnitude of $r(X_1,X_2)$ are due solely to inadequacies of the measurement procedure, the resulting value is referred to as a *coefficient of precision*.

Next, let us consider what happens when the procedure just described is used to assess the reliability of an aptitude test. (We assume that the same test is administered twice under essentially the same conditions to a population of examinees who vary considerably on the aptitude of concern.) If the test were administered twice in rapid succession, the two sets of scores would probably agree quite well (i.e., their correlation would be close to +1.00) suggesting a high degree of reliability. However, a more plausible explanation for this outcome might be that the examinees remembered how they responded to most of the items on the initial testing and simply responded in the same way on the second testing; the result being a *spurious* consistency in test scores and a value of $r(X_1,X_2)$ which overestimates the reliability of the test under consideration. The cure for this problem seems obvious: choose a longer intertest (between test) interval to minimize the effects of memory on the value of $r(X_1,X_2)$. This is an appropriate strategy, but one must avoid choosing an interval which is long enough to permit true score changes to occur. This is relatively easy to accomplish with tests designed to measure relatively stable characteristics (i.e., characteristics which remain constant or change very slowly over relatively long time periods — for example, general intelligence, specific aptitudes, certain personality characteristics). Since the value of $r(X_1,X_2)$ obtained in such a context (with an appropriate interval) reflects the absence of measurement errors caused not only by inadequacies of the measurement process but also by those due to temporal changes in the examinee [e.g., fluctuations in (a) ability to concentrate, (b) mood, (c) health status, and (d) level of motivation], it is usually referred to as a *coefficient of stability*. Like the coefficient of precision, the coefficient of stability can be interpreted as $r^2(X,T)$ or $\mathrm{Var}(T)/\mathrm{Var}(X)$; however the sources of random error affecting the two coefficients are different, and this should be kept in mind.

In the case of achievement tests, the problems associated with this approach can be quite troublesome. In particular, individual differences in (a) the acquisition of new knowledge between testings, (b) the rate and amount of forgetting of previously acquired knowledge, and (c) memory tend to distort the test-retest reliability coefficient. For example, if the interval between tests is short, true scores will probably not change much; however, recall of the specific items and the answers given to them on the first occasion will probably influence performance on the second occasion, resulting in an unduly high value of $r(X_1,X_2)$ and, hence, in an overestimate of $r^2(X,T)$. On the other hand, if the interval is too long, specific item recall will probably not be a factor; however, differential occurrence of new learning and forgetting among examinees will probably have a considerable effect on examinee true scores. The result is an unduly low value of $r(X_1,X_2)$ and, hence, an underestimate of $r^2(X,T)$. To complicate matters, one can never be sure of the extent to which memory and new learning (or forgetting) interact and contribute to the distortion of a test-retest reliability coefficient. Therefore the use of this technique with achievement tests should only be undertaken with extreme caution.

Finally, a fact which merits reemphasis is that any test-retest correlation coefficient is a measure of *stability* specific to (a) the particular time interval between measurement occasions and (b) the particular population of examinees involved. If a different time interval is used between testings (say two months instead of two weeks), or if the test is used with a different examinee population, the value of $r(X_1,X_2)$ will almost surely be different.

The Parallel Forms Approach

The parallel form procedure for assessing the reliability of a test in a particular examinee population requires the administration of two parallel forms of the same test to all examinees in that population. If we let X_A represent the set of scores obtained with Form A and X_B represent the scores on Form B, then the linear correlation between them, $r(X_A,X_B)$, is a parallel form reliability coefficient and is interpretable as $\text{Var}(T)/\text{Var}(X)$.

Two forms of a test are considered parallel in the strict sense only if they have been constructed using the same recipe and if, in addition, the true score and personal standard error of measurement for each examinee in the population of interest is the same with respect to both forms. An immediate and observable consequence of parallelism is that forms meeting these requirements with respect to a particular population of examinees will generate distributions of scores having (a) equal means, (b) equal standard deviations, (c) equal reliabilities, and (d) equal correlations with any other variable in that population. These parallelism criteria are very difficult to satisfy, and hence, the terms *alternate forms* or *equivalent forms* are frequently used as labels for "nearly parallel" tests. Examples of these can be found among the available standardized test batteries, e.g., the Metropolitan Achievement Test.

To implement the parallel forms approach, one would (a) administer two parallel (or nearly parallel) forms (e.g., Forms A and B) of the test to all examinees in the population of interest and (b) compute the linear correlation, $r(X_A,X_B)$. This is the desired reliability coefficient and, hence, may be interpreted as $r^2(X,T)$.

In contrast to the test-retest procedure, this approach can be used with a *very short time interval* between administrations of the alternate forms because examinee recall of the items on Form A (and how he answered them) should not affect his performance on Form B. When this technique is used, the resulting correlation coefficient, $r(X_A,X_B)$, is called a *coefficient of equivalence*. Since both forms are administered at about the same time, random errors due to temporal factors tend to be minimal; the primary sources of measurement error being (a) inadequacies of the measurement process, i.e., imprecision, *and* (b) nonequivalence of the forms used.

If the time interval between testings allows temporal factors to become sources of random error (but is not long enough to allow true score changes), the resulting correlation, $r(X_A, X_B)$, is referred to as a *coefficient of equivalence and stability.*

As in the test-retest case, use of this procedure requires some wisdom in the specification of an intertest (i.e., between test) interval. If two relatively long forms of a test are administered in succession, fatigue will take its toll on the examinees; on the other hand, if the intertest interval is too long, examinee true scores may change differentially. In either case, the reliability coefficient will be of questionable value.

The parallel forms (or, realistically speaking, the equivalent forms) approach is especially useful in assessing the quality of achievement tests because (a) the memory factor is not a problem, (b) the effects of new learning and/or differential forgetting on the reliability coefficient can be minimized by choosing the size of the intertest interval judiciously, and (c) several measures of the same characteristic are frequently desirable or necessary. The primary drawback of this approach is the need to construct two parallel (or nearly parallel) forms of the same test.

In evaluating a standardized test or test battery which offers alternate forms for use in pupil or program evaluation, attention should be paid to parallel form reliability estimates reported in the test manual and the existing measurement literature (e.g., the validity section of the *Journal of Educational and Psychological Measurement* and the *Mental Measurements Yearbooks* edited by O. K. Buros). Reliability estimates obtained using this general approach which are considerably less than +1.00 in value (say, less than +0.80), suggest that measurement imprecision and/or nonparallelism may be a serious problem.

EXERCISE SET 9-1

1. Outline the procedures for implementing the (a) test-retest and (b) parallel forms approaches to reliability assessment.

2. Identify the sources of observed score variation treated as random error by each approach cited in question one above.

3. The procedures described in this chapter assume that data are available on _____ of the examinees in the population of interest.
   a. all   b. a random sample

4. *True or False.* The statistics $r(X_1, X_2)$ and $r(X_A, X_B)$ provide estimates of $r^2(X, T)$, i.e., the proportion of observed variance due to true score differences among examinees.

5. If the standard deviation of a set of test scores is 10 and the test-retest reliability is estimated to be 0.84, what would the estimated standard error of measurement be? (This formula is in Chapter 8.)

The Internal Analysis Approach

A test is said to be internally consistent if all of its items measure "the same thing." For example, tests consisting either of 10 vocabulary items or 20 addition problems are examples of internally consistent tests; on the other hand, a test containing several items of each type would not be internally consistent. The two most frequently used techniques for measuring the internal consistency of a test are (a) the split-half procedure and (b) coefficient alpha and its specialized versions, Kuder-Richardson formulas 20 (KR20) and 21 (KR21).

The Split-Half Procedure.   To estimate the internal consistency of a test using the split-half procedure, one would proceed as follows:

1. Administer the test under suitable conditions to all examinees in the population of interest on one occasion.
2. Divide the test into two subtests having equal numbers of items. This can be done in many ways; the most convenient and, hence, most commonly used strategy being the inclusion of all odd numbered items in one subtest and all even numbered items in a second subtest. The result is that each examinee now can be assigned two subtest scores — one on the subtest containing the even numbered items, X_E, and one on the subtest containing the odd numbered items, X_O.
3. If we calculate the correlation between these two subtests, $r(X_E,X_O)$, the result is a *coefficient of equivalence* (as in the parallel forms approach). Since both forms are integral parts of the same test, this qualifies as a gross measure of the internal consistency of that test, i.e., it tells how well performance on the even item subtest predicts performance on the odd item subtest, and vice versa. However, all other things being equal, reliability is directly related to test length (i.e., the longer the test, the more reliable it tends to be).[2] Since $r(X_E,X_O)$ is based on forms which are each one-half as long as the test whose reliability concerns us, it is an underestimate of the reliability of the whole test, and therefore, must be adjusted.
4. Adjust the value of $r(X_E,X_O)$ using the Spearman-Brown prophecy formula, a simplified version of which is

$$\text{Split-half reliability} = \frac{2 \cdot r(X_E,X_O)}{1 + r(X_E,X_O)}$$

For example, if the correlation between the odd and even subtest scores is 0.60, the split-half reliability estimate equals 2(0.60)/(1.00 + 0.60), or 0.75.

While this approach is quite useful in many situations, it does have several limitations with which one ought to be familiar, namely, (a) any test can be split into subtests in a variety of ways (e.g., odd-even, first half-second half, randomly), and each possible split results in a different reliability estimate; and (b) if the half-tests are not parallel (or nearly so), the Spearman-Brown adjustment tends to undercorrect, resulting in a reliability coefficient which is too low. The alpha coefficient, to which we now turn our attention, provides a useful alternative approach.

The Alpha Coefficient.   Like the split-half coefficient, *alpha* also provides a measure of internal consistency. Rather than being based on a division of the test

---

2. For more on this point see pp. 136–138.

into two subtests of equal length, *alpha* effectively treats each item as a mini-test, e.g., a 10-item test is viewed as 10 one-item tests. If all of the items in a test are measuring "the same thing," the correlations among the items will be relatively high and alpha will be relatively close to 1.00. If subsets of test items are measuring different things, some of the interitem (i.e., between item) correlations will tend to be relatively low, and hence, alpha will be appreciably less than +1.00.

Given a choice between the split-half and alpha coefficients for measuring the internal consistency of a test, alpha seems preferable because its application to any particular set of test data results in an unique value. One formula for computing alpha is the following:

$$\text{alpha} = \frac{k}{k-1}\left(1.00 - \frac{\Sigma \text{ Var}(i)}{\text{Var}(X)}\right) \tag{9-1}$$

Where k = number of items in the test
         $\Sigma \text{ Var}(i)$ = sum of the variances of the various item score distributions
         $\text{Var}(X)$ = variance of the distribution of test scores

To illustrate the necessary computations, suppose a five-item essay test were given to each of four students and the test scores shown in Table 9-1 were obtained. The value of alpha for this test is 0.90. This value indicates that the test is quite consistent internally, i.e., the average correlation between items is quite high. As a result, performance on any one item (or subset of items) is a fairly good predictor of performance on any other item (or subset of items). A high value of alpha like this one is usually taken to mean that the test as a whole is measuring just one attribute, like verbal fluency, arithmetic computation skill, etc., in addition to assigning scores to examinees which have relatively small random error components. Values of alpha which depart appreciably from +1.00 suggest the presence of relatively large measurement errors and/or clusters of test items which measure distinctly different examinee attributes.[3]

When each item in a test is scored 1 if correct and 0 otherwise, the coefficient obtained using the alpha formula is called KR20.[4] Whenever such a scoring rule is

---

3. Actually, coefficient alpha is much more useful than indicated in this section. For example, if the scores in Table 9-1 represented examinee performances on five 10-item subtests in a particular test battery and the reliability of the total (or composite) scores was of interest, formula (9-1) would be applied exactly as shown in Table 9-1 to obtain the desired result. In other words, alpha provides a general method for assessing the reliability of a composite test using information on the component parts of that test. In our discussion, we simply regarded each item as a subtest.

4. The formulas KR20 and KR21 are so named because they represent equations number 20 and 21 in the original derivation by Kuder and Richardson (1937). Subsequently, Cronbach (1951) derived the more general formula alpha, of which KR20 is a special case. The popular form of the KR20 formula is

$$\text{KR20} = \frac{k}{k-1}\left(1.00 - \frac{\Sigma p \cdot q}{\text{Var}(X)}\right)$$

Where p = proportion of correct responses to an item
         q = proportion of incorrect responses
         $p \cdot q$ = variance of a particular item distribution
         $\Sigma p \cdot q$ = sum of the item variances

TABLE 9-1.   *Illustration of Alpha Coefficient Calculations.*

a. Data:

		Item					Total Test Score
		1	2	3	4	5	
	A	6	8	9	1	7	31
	B	8	8	8	2	4	30
Student	C	0	3	6	1	3	13
	D	2	1	1	0	2	6
	Total	16	20	24	4	16	80
	Mean	4	5	6	1	4	20

b. Computations:

1. $K = 5$, since there are 5 items.

2. $\text{Var}(X) = \dfrac{SS(X)}{n} = \dfrac{(31-20)^2 + (30-20)^2 + (13-20)^2 + (6-20)^2}{4} = 116.5.$

3. $\text{Var(item 1)} = \dfrac{SS(\text{item 1})}{n} = \dfrac{(6-4)^2 + (8-4)^2 + (0-4)^2 + (2-4)^2}{4} = 10.0.$

4. Similarly, the variances for items 2 through 5 are 9.5, 9.5, 0.5 and 3.5, respectively.

5. Therefore, $\Sigma\text{Var}(i) = 10.0 + 9.5 + 9.5 + 0.5 + 3.5 = 33.0.$

6. Substituting this information in the alpha formula yields

$$\text{alpha} = \frac{5}{4}\left(1.00 - \frac{33.0}{116.5}\right) = 0.90.$$

in effect, the calculation of item variances is especially easy — the variance of an item is simply the proportion of 1's in the distribution times the proportion of 0's in the same distribution. For example, if 30 examinees answered an item correctly and 10 examinees answered it incorrectly, the variance of the scores in that item distribution would be the proportion of correct responses (30/40) times the proportion of incorrect responses (10/40), or 3/16. Similarly, if the proportion of correct responses (or scores equal to one) were 0.80 and the proportion of incorrect responses (or zeros) were 0.20, the item variance would be 0.80 (0.20), or 0.16.

Let us now examine the use of the KR20 formula with a sample data set. Suppose in the quiz group described earlier, examinee responses rated 5 or higher were called correct and awarded one test score point, while responses rated less than 5 were called incorrect and awarded 0 test score points. The data matrix would appear as shown in Table 9-2 where the value of alpha is seen to be 0.81. In changing from a 0–9 to a 0–1 scale we have lost a considerable amount of information about the relative standings of individuals as well as experiencing a

TABLE 9-2. *Illustration of KR20 Calculations.*

a. Data:

		Item					Quiz Score
		1	2	3	4	5	
Student	A	1	1	1	0	1	4
	B	1	1	1	0	0	3
	C	0	0	1	0	0	1
	D	0	0	0	0	0	0

b. Calculations:
   1. $k = 5$, since there are 5 items in the quiz.

   2. $\mathrm{Var}(X) = \dfrac{(4-2)^2 + (3-2)^2 + (1-2)^2 + (0-2)^2}{4} = \dfrac{10}{4}$

   3. Since the variance of any distribution of 1's (representing correct responses) and 0's (representing incorrect responses) is simply the proportion of 1's times the proportion of 0's, the variance of item 1 is $(2/4)(2/4)$ or $4/16$.
   4. Similary, the variances of items 2 through 5 are $4/16$, $3/16$, 0 and $3/16$, respectively.
   5. Therefore, $\Sigma\mathrm{Var}(\text{items}) = 4/16 + 4/16 + 3/16 + 0/16 + 3/16 = 14/16$.
   6. Substituting in the alpha formula yields

$$\mathrm{KR20} = \frac{5}{4}\left(1.00 - \frac{14/16}{10/4}\right) = 0.81$$

reduction in score variance, thus, the drop in the value of alpha from 0.90 to 0.81 is not surprising. In general, score scale restrictions tend to reduce correlations of all types (even those among items, as in the present case).

KR21. If one makes the simplifying assumption that all of the items are equally difficult (i.e., the proportion of ones is the same for every item), then KR20 can be rewritten as follows:

$$\mathrm{KR21} = \frac{k}{k-1}\left(1 - \frac{M(1 - M/k)}{\mathrm{Var}(X)}\right) \qquad (9.2)$$

where M is the mean of the test scores and the remaining symbols are defined as above.

To illustrate, we use the data of the KR20 example shown in Table 9-2, where the mean of the quiz score distribution is $(4 + 3 + 1 + 0)/4 = 2$. (Remember, this formula, like the KR20 version discussed above, can only be used when all items are scored 1 or 0. If it were applied to the data in the original alpha example, an absurd result would be obtained.) In this example, we find

$$KR21 = \frac{5}{4} \left(1 - \frac{2(1 - 2/5)}{2.5}\right) = \frac{5}{4} \left(1 - \frac{6/5}{2.5}\right) = 0.65$$

The value of KR21 is always less than or equal to the value of KR20 and, because it is so easy to calculate, is frequently used as a lower bound estimate of KR20. In addition, if a test is known to be homogeneous, i.e., to be measuring a single attribute, KR20 and KR21 provide useful lower bound estimates of the coefficients discussed previously.

Some Comments About Internal Consistency Statistics. The following factors must be kept in mind when using (or considering the use of) one of these measures of internal consistency:

1. The indexes discussed in this section not only measure internal consistency, but test length as well. All other things being equal, the longer a test, the more reliable it tends to be. More is said about this in a subsequent section of this chapter.
2. Administering a test under speeded conditions (i.e., conditions which make it impossible for most of the examinees to attempt all of the items) spuriously raises the value of these indexes. For example, shorthand and typing tests are typically administered under stringent time deadlines, i.e., they are, by nature, highly speeded tests. In addition, achievement and other types of paper and pencil tests are typically speeded to some extent for practical reasons. Deadlines for completion of achievement tests are quite common. Whether or not the element of speed in a particular situation is important depends on the proportion of examinees finishing the test. As a rule, if less than 85% of the examinees have the opportunity to respond to all of the items in a test, it should be regarded as a speeded test. In such instances, the internal consistency estimates tend to be spuriously high and, therefore, should not be used.
3. Like all other reliability coefficients, a measure of internal consistency obtained in any one situation is not generalizable. If we give the same quiz to a different examinee population, the value of the index may change drastically.
4. The values of these indexes are directly related to the total test variance. In general, the greater the value of $Var(X)$, the greater the value of the internal consistency estimate. In a criterion-referenced framework, a highly skewed test score distribution frequently results. The amount of variability in such a distribution is typically quite modest. As a result, an internally consistent test used in such a situation may yield a relatively low internal consistency coefficient. Hence, the internal consistency statistics discussed in this chapter should only be used in criterion-referenced applications with extreme caution, if at all.

EXERCISE SET 9-2

1. *True or False.* A test of achievement which includes arithmetic, reading, and history items would be an example of an internally consistent test.

2. In calculating the split-half reliability for a classroom achievement test, the odd-even correlation is found to be 0.70. What is the split-half reliability estimate for this test?

3. Suppose a 5-item quiz were given to each of four students and the items were scored 1 if correct and 0 otherwise. Calculate alpha for the data matrix shown below.

Student	Item Number					Quiz Score
	1	2	3	4	5	
A	1	1	1	1	1	5
B	1	1	1	1	1	5
C	0	0	0	0	0	0
D	0	0	0	0	0	0

4. *True or False.* The application of alpha to the type of data matrix shown in Exercise 3 produces a coefficient commonly referred to as KR20.

5. *True or False.* KR21 is always a good estimate of KR20.

Some General Remarks

In this section, we examined a number of approaches to reliability assessment within a norm-referenced measurement context. Each approach, if used with care, can provide a reasonable approximation to the *precision* of the measurement process (i.e., the relative absence of random errors due to inadequacies of the measurement process.) For example, if two equivalent forms of a test are administered at the same time and the resulting coefficient of equivalence is equal to 0.90, an obvious conclusion would be that 10% of all observed score variance is due to imprecision and/or nonequivalence of the forms; 90% is due to true differences among examinees. Hence, the two forms appear to be nearly equivalent and each appears to be providing reasonably reliable measurements. If the forms are parallel, in the strict sense, all error must be attributed to imprecision.

Each type of coefficient examined in this section, i.e., stability, equivalence, and internal consistency, may also be of interest in its own right – not just as an approximation to the coefficient of precision. For example, if a particular test is designed to measure an ability (e.g., mathematical ability) or trait (e.g., general hostility) believed (for theoretical reasons) to be stable over a particular period of time, one would expect the coefficient of stability for that test and time interval to be reasonably close to +1.00. If the obtained value departs appreciably from +1.00, either the test, the testing process, or the theory on which the test is based needs reexamination. (This assumes, of course, that the data were collected from a suitable examinee population.) Similarly, if one wants to know whether two forms of a test can be used interchangeably, the coefficient of equivalence would provide useful information. Finally, if one wants to know whether all of the items in the same test measure "the same thing," coefficient alpha would be of interest. The choice of approach depends on the type of information one is seeking. In some situations, a combination of these may be of interest. For convenience, some of the important characteristics of each of these techniques are summarized in Table 9-3.

We now turn our attention to selected approaches to assessing the impact of one particular source of random error which tends to be especially troublesome in essay testing, namely, scorer inconsistency.

Reliability of Essay Tests

One source of random error which is of special concern whenever subjective rating or scoring procedures are used (as in the case of essay testing) is rater inconsistency, i.e., (a) the tendency of different, equally qualified, independent raters to assign different scores to the same item response and (b) the tendency of a single rater to assign different ratings to an item response at different times. If scorer inconsistency is appreciable, then the random error component of each examinee's score will tend to be large and, hence, reduce test reliability. Two methods for assessing rater consistency (i.e., the absence of random scoring errors) are the *interrater* (between rater) and *intrarater* (within rater) reliability procedures. Let us consider each in turn.

Interrater Reliability

Interrater reliability refers to the extent to which the scores or ratings assigned to a stimulus (e.g., an essay test item response, a work of art, a class term paper) by two (or more) independent raters (or judges) are in agreement. This approach is especially useful in determining whether the criteria for rating essay items are unambiguous.

The two most common approaches to the scoring of essay item responses are the global and analytical methods [see Coffman (1971) for an extensive discussion of these methods]. The global method involves the assignment of a rating or score based on one's overall impression of the quality of the response. The analytical method, on the other hand, involves the advance preparation of a scoring key containing a list of important points expected in a good response, and a system of assigning credit and/or penalties for different aspects of the response. Regardless of the approach used, interrater reliability can be assessed as follows:

1. Have two or more competent raters independently rate the stimuli of interest using the appropriate criteria.
2. Measure the degree of agreement among them using a suitable index. If there are only two raters, the Pearson correlation coefficient may be used. If more than two raters are used, one can compute the correlation for each possible pair of raters and use the distribution or, alternatively, the mean of these correlations in making any final judgments about scorer reliability. If the raters are asked to rank order or categorize the responses instead of assigning scores to them or if one only intends to use the ordinal or nominal information contained in a set of

TABLE 9-3. *Summary of Test Reliability Assessment Procedures*

Approach	Type of Coefficient	Number of Forms	Number of Occasions	Statistics Used	Sources of Random Error	Some Potential Problems
Test-Retest	Stability	1	2	$r(X_1, X_2)$	(a) Imprecision (b) Temporal Factors	(a) Memory (b) Practice (c) New Learning (or Forgetting)
Parallel (equivalent) Forms	(a) Equivalence	2	1	$r(X_A, X_B)$	(a) Imprecision (b) Nonequivalence	(a) Fatigue (b) Practice or Warm-up
	(b) Equivalence and Stability	2	2	$r(X_A, X_B)$	(a) Imprecision (b) Nonequivalence (c) Temporal Factors	(a) New Learning (or Forgetting)
Internal Analysis (a) Split-Half	Internal Consistency	1	1	$r(X_O, X_E)$ plus Spearman-Brown	(a) Imprecision (b) Nonequivalence of Half-tests	(a) Fatigue (b) Restrictive Time Limit
(b) Alpha	Internal Consistency	1	1	alpha KR20 KR21	(a) Imprecision (b) Items Measure Different Things	(a) Restrictive Time Limit

Note: Keep in mind that factors like test length, homogeneity of the examinee group and the characteristic being measured, and amount of variance in the test scores affect all correlationally based reliability statistics.

ratings, then measures of ordinal agreement (e.g., the coefficient of concordance, as described in S. Siegel, *Nonparametric Statistics*, New York: McGraw-Hill, 1956, 229–338) or nominal agreement (e.g., the kappa coefficient, as described in Chapter 17 of this text) should be considered.[5]

If the Pearson correlation coefficient is the statistic used, then values close to +1.00 would signify a high degree of agreement or interrater reliability. (Please note, the Pearson correlation coefficient only measures relative, not absolute, agreement. For example, if one rater assigns scores of 3, 6, 2, and 5 to a set of four essay item responses while the second rater assigns scores of 5, 8, 4, and 7, the Pearson *r* value would be 1.00.) Low interrater reliability usually means that either the criteria upon which the ratings are based are ambiguous, or at least one judge is not applying the criteria properly.

Tests which require the examinee to choose the correct response (e.g., multiple-choice, true-false) rather than to construct a response (e.g., essay) permit the use of a scoring key which, in fact, is a completely unambiguous specification of the scoring criteria. Whether the rater applying these criteria is the instructor, a computer, or a file clerk, interrater reliability will always be extremely close to +1.00. For this reason, such tests are said to be *objective*. The kinds of tests which do not consistently yield such high interrater reliability estimates (e.g., essay tests) are said to be *subjective*. The interrater reliability factor is the sole basis for the objective-subjective distinction as it is used in describing tests.

One way of improving interrater reliability in a test-like situation is to have independent raters assign scores to the items of concern and then, through discussion, determine the reasons for whatever discrepancies appear in the ratings. One or more exercises like this will usually help clarify the scoring criteria and make them easier to apply. The end result is an increase in interrater reliability. Obviously, this is somewhat easier to do when using the analytical method described above.

Intrarater Reliability

Whenever an individual rater wants to assess his own rating consistency, the concept of *intrarater reliability* is relevant. To estimate one's own ability to apply the scoring criteria for an essay item consistently, the following procedure may be used:

1. Have a reasonably large number of examinees respond to the item.
2. Using your rating procedure, assign scores to the items on some fixed scale, for example, a 10-point scale. Do not record the answers on the examinees' response sheets.
3. Some time later (say two weeks), shuffle the response sheets and rescore them using the same procedure as before.

---

5. A neat visual method for examining interrater or intrarater variability is presented in W. E. Coffman's monograph "On the Reliability of Ratings of Essay Examinations in English" which is reproduced in Chapter 15 of this book.

4. Use the Pearson correlation coefficient as the measure of relative agreement between the sets of scores assigned on the two different occasions.

Again, a coefficient of 0.00 would mean total disagreement and +1.00, perfect agreement.

This technique is analagous to the test-retest procedure described earlier but focusses on scorer inconsistency, ignoring the factors which result in examinee response inconsistency (e.g., mood, luck, situational factors). In using it, suitable precautions should be taken to prevent knowledge of the ratings assigned on the first occasion from influencing the ratings assigned on the second occasion.

THE RELATIONSHIP BETWEEN TEST LENGTH AND TEST RELIABILITY

As indicated earlier, the magnitude of the test-retest, parallel form and internal consistency indices tends to increase as the number of items in the test is increased. The Spearman-Brown prophecy formula, which specifies the relationship between test reliability and test length, may be written as follows:

$$r_l = \frac{nr_s}{1 + (n-1)r_s} \tag{9-3}$$

Where r_l = reliability of the long test
            r_s = reliability of the short test
            n = factor by which the number of items in the short test must be multiplied to equal the number of items in the long test

Several examples should help clarify the relationship expressed by this formula. First, suppose the test-retest reliability estimate for a 20-item test is 0.60. What would the reliability of the test be if 40 more items of comparable quality were added to the test? *Solution*: Here, $r_s = 0.60$ and $n = 3$ (i.e., the lengthened test would be 3 times as long as the original short test). Therefore,

$$r_l = \frac{3(0.60)}{1 + (3-1)(0.60)} = \frac{1.80}{2.20} = 0.82$$

The reliability of the lengthened test should be 0.82. Of course, this is predicated on the assumption that the new items added to the test are comparable in quality to the items included in the original short version.

Next, suppose the problem were reversed — we had a 60-item test with the reliability coefficient equal to the 0.82 and wanted to estimate the probable effect of randomly deleting two thirds of the items. What would the reliability of such a shortened test be? *Solution*: Here, $r_l = 0.82$ and $n = 3$. Therefore,

$$0.82 = \frac{3r_s}{1 + (3-1)r_s}$$

Multiplying both sides of the equation by $1 + 2r_s$ yields

$$0.82(1 + 2r_s) = 3r_s$$

Multiplying through the left member of the equation results in

$$0.82 + 1.64r_s = 3r_s$$

Subtracting $1.64r_s$ from both sides of the equation yields

$$0.82 = 1.36r_s$$

Dividing both sides of the equation by 1.36 results in

$$0.60 = r_s$$

For a second example of the same type, suppose we had a 300-item test having a reliability coefficient equal to 0.90. What would be the projected reliability for a shorter test obtained by randomly deleting 250 items? *Solution*: In this case, $r_l = 0.90$ and $n = 6$. Therefore,

$$0.90 = \frac{6r_s}{1 + (6 - 1)r_s}$$

Solving for r_s, we obtain a reliability estimate of 0.60 for the shortened test.

As you can see, the reliability coefficient for the shorter test is predicted to be much lower than for the long test in each case. It must be kept in mind, however, that the procedure for adding or deleting items is very important. The accuracy of the estimate one obtains using the Spearman-Brown formula depends upon the comparability of the items added or deleted to those in the original set. The less comparable they are, the more erroneous this estimate will be. In most situations, items added to a test for the purpose of increasing test length are usually no better than, and frequently are much worse than, the items in the original set. Hence, the Spearman-Brown estimate is almost always an overestimate of the increase in reliability one can expect using a test lengthening procedure. Similarly, when tests are shortened, the less discriminating items are typically deleted leaving a short test of better overall quality than the original long test. If such a procedure is used, the Spearman-Brown estimate, r_s, will tend to be an underestimate of the reliability of the shortened test. The point being made here is that the accuracy of the Spearman-Brown estimate is heavily dependent on the quality of the items added to or deleted from a test. Unless this is kept in mind, the effect of changing test length on test reliability may be grossly misperceived.

The reliability of ratings (i.e., ratings of essay item responses, responses to inkblots, etc.) can generally be increased by having two or more judges independently rate each response, using the sum or average of their ratings of each response as the score for that response. This increase in reliability can also be estimated using the Spearman-Brown Formula. In this case, r_l equals the reliability of the mean ratings based on the larger number of raters, r_s represents the reliability of the mean ratings based on the smaller number of raters, and n is the factor by which the number of raters in the smaller set must be multiplied to equal the number of raters in the larger set.

For example, suppose an art expert is asked to assign scores on a 10-point scale to indicate the relative quality of 20 paintings on two separate occasions and the correlation between the two sets of measurements turns out to be 0.70. If two *equally competent* judges had performed the ratings independently on each occasion and either their total or average scores for each painting used instead, the correlation between the scores on the first and second occasions should be approximately

$$r_l = \frac{2r_s}{1 + (2 - 1)r_s} = \frac{2(0.70)}{1 + 0.70} = 0.82$$

EXERCISE SET 9-3

1. The Spearman-Brown prophecy formula is a mathematical statement of the relationship between norm-referenced test reliability and _____ .

2. According to the Spearman-Brown formula, an increase in test length produces a(n) _____ in test reliability.

3. Accuracy of the Spearman-Brown prediction in any particular application depends upon _____ .

4. Suppose the test-retest reliability estimate for a 100-item vocabulary test is 0.80. Assuming the Spearman-Brown assumptions are satisfied, what would be the effect of
   a. doubling test length?
   b. halving test length?

THE RELATIONSHIP BETWEEN TEST SCORE VARIANCE AND TEST RELIABILITY

In general, the more variance in a test score distribution, the higher the reliability estimate tends to be. The easiest way to explain this is through the use of the formula for alpha. Recall,

$$\text{Alpha} = \frac{k}{k - 1} \left(1 - \frac{\Sigma \, \text{Var}(i)}{\text{Var}(X)} \right)$$

To keep matters simple, let us assume that the values of k and $\Sigma \, \text{Var}(i)$ are fixed. By assuming different values for $\text{Var}(X)$, we can see what the effect is on the value of alpha.[6] Notice, the constant $k/(k - 1)$ is just an adjustment for test length and, except in cases of very short tests, has little effect on the magnitude of alpha. The dominant influence is really the quantity in parentheses. If the fraction

---

6. It can be shown that total test score variance $\text{Var}(X)$ equals the sum of the item variances, $\Sigma \, \text{Var}(i)$, *plus* twice the sum of the interitem covariances. Therefore, it is possible for two tests of equal length (i.e., two tests having the same number of items) to have equal values for $\Sigma \, \text{Var}(i)$, but different interitem covariance sums and, hence, different total score variances.

Σ Var(i)/Var(X) is small, the value alpha will be relatively close to 1.00; if this fraction is large, the value of alpha will be close to zero. Notice, the size of the fraction depends on Var(X), the amount of variation in the distribution of test scores. The larger the value of Var(X), i.e., the greater the variance in the test score distribution, the smaller the fraction Σ Var(i)/Var(X) and, hence, the closer alpha is to 1.00; the smaller the value of Var(X), the closer the value of alpha is to zero.

A second way of looking at this relationship is to reconsider the effect of restriction of variance (see Chapter 6 for a refresher, if necessary) on the magnitude of a correlation coefficient. Since all forms of norm-referenced reliability estimation are based on the concept of correlation (recall that the magnitude of alpha depends on the sizes of the interitem correlations), restriction of variance reduces the magnitude of the reliability estimate. For example, if one attempted to estimate the test-retest reliability of the Stanford-Binet Intelligence Test administered to highly selected (i.e., restricted) groups like (a) the low SES children typical of a ghetto environment or a Head Start class, or (b) a group of intellectually gifted children, the estimate obtained would tend to be quite low. The point is that any norm-referenced test which is highly reliable when used in a heterogeneous population of individuals, may be quite unreliable when used within a very homogeneous subset of that same population. Needless to say, if a test is used with a population of examinees different than the one for which it was designed, there is no basis for predicting its reliability in that situation unless one knows a great deal about the ways in which these two populations are similar and the ways in which they differ, a very unlikely state of affairs.

THE RELIABILITY OF DIFFERENCE SCORES: A PARADOX

Frequently, pretests and posttests are administered and difference scores calculated for the purpose of assessing pupil growth, evaluating the effect of a curricular innovation, etc. In such cases, the reliability of these difference scores is extremely important. Since the pretest and posttest measures are usually obtained using the same or equivalent forms of a test, they tend to be highly correlated. The paradox is that the more highly correlated the pretest and posttest measures are, the lower the reliability of their difference scores will be. The formula which specifies this relationship is as follows:

$$r_{\text{diff}} = \frac{r_B + r_A - 2 \cdot r(A,B)}{2 \cdot [1 - r(A,B)]} \tag{9-4}$$

Where r_A = pretest reliability
r_B = posttest reliability
r_{diff} = reliability of the differences between posttest and pretest performances
$r(A,B)$ = correlation between the pretest and posttest performances

Consider the following examples:

1. Suppose the reliability of the pretest is 0.80, the reliability of the posttest is 0.90, and the correlation between the pretest and posttest scores is zero. Here we have the unlikely situation in which difference scores are based on two highly reliable, but uncorrelated measures. What is the reliability of the difference scores in this situation?

$$r_{diff} = \frac{0.90 + 0.80 - 2(0)}{2(1 - 0)} = 0.85$$

Notice, the difference score reliability in this case turns out to be the simple average of the pre- and posttest reliabilities. This is always the case when $r(A,B) = 0.00$.

2. Next, suppose the pre- and posttest reliabilities are the same as above, but $r(A,B) = 0.50$. What is the reliability of the difference scores in this case?

$$r_{diff} = \frac{0.90 + 0.80 - 2(0.50)}{2(1 - 0.50)} = 0.70$$

Notice, as the correlation between A and B increased, the reliability of the difference scores was reduced. Let us consider one more example before attempting to find out just what is causing this result.

3. Finally, suppose we consider a more typical case in which the reliabilities are as indicated above, but where $r(A,B) = 0.80$. What is the difference score reliability in this case?

$$r_{diff} = \frac{0.90 + 0.80 - 2(0.80)}{2(1 - 0.80)} = 0.25$$

The basic principles illustrated in these three examples are

1. The maximum reliability a set of difference scores can have is the simple average of the reliabilities of the two sets of scores used to calculate these differences. This occurs only when $r(A,B) = 0.00$.
2. The higher the value of $r(A,B)$, the lower the reliability of the difference scores.
3. When the value $r(A,B)$ equals the average reliability of the two tests, r_{diff} equals zero.

An insight into this paradox can be gained by considering the two sets of pre- and posttest scores shown in Table 9-4. The first set is uncorrelated while the second set has a perfect, positive correlation. Notice what happens to the variance of the difference scores in each case. In case 1 where the scores have 0.00 correlation, there is a considerable amount of variability in the distribution of difference scores. In case 2 however, where the correlation between pre- and posttest measures is 1.00, there is absolutely no variance in the distribution of difference scores. Recalling the earlier discussion of the relationship between reliability and the amount of variance in a test score distribution, the basis for this paradox should be apparent.

TABLE 9-4. *The Effect of the Correlation Between Two Measures on the Variance in the Distribution of Their Difference Scores.*

Case 1: $r(A,B) = 0.00$			Case 2: $r(A,B) = 1.00$		
Pretest Score	Posttest Score	Difference Score	Pretest Score	Posttest Score	Difference Score
1	9	8	1	7	6
2	10	8	2	8	6
3	9	6	3	9	6
4	9	5	4	10	6
5	10	5	5	11	6
6	9	3	6	12	6

The problem of measuring change in a school environment is a particularly important one. To be meaningful, difference (or gain) scores must be based on highly correlated measures. This is precisely the case which results in difference (or gain) scores having low reliability. Since low reliabilities and large standard errors of measurement tend to go hand-in-hand, the interpretation of individual gain scores as measures of pupil progress is an especially risky business.[7]

EXERCISE SET 9-4

1. In general, as the correlation between two tests increases, the reliability of the difference scores calculated using these measures _____ .

2. The maximum difference score reliability occurs when the correlation between the two measures upon which the differences are based equals _____ . In this case the reliability of the difference scores equals the _____ of the reliabilities of the scores used in computing the differences.

3. a. If the reliabilities of the scores using tests *A* and *B* are 0.90 and 0.60, respectively, and $r(A,B) = 0.50$, then $r_{diff} = $ _____ .

   b. If $r(A,B)$ were 0.00, then r_{diff} would be _____ .

SUMMARY AND CONCLUSIONS

In this chapter we examined several approaches to assessing norm-referenced test reliability. In addition, we considered in some detail the relationship between

---

7. Keep in mind that the discussion in this section pertains to unreliability of individual, not group, difference scores. If a group of 30 students are tested before and after a unit of instruction and the mean pretest score is subtracted from the mean posttest score, the resulting group difference score will probably be quite reliable. The pretest-posttest difference scores for any particular student in this group, however, will probably be quite unreliable as shown in this section's illustrative examples.

test reliability and test score variance. The following points are especially important and, hence, merit restatement at this time:

1. There are several different kinds of test reliability. The type of test and the use to which it will be put determine which type(s) of reliability which ought to be considered in a given situation.
2. Measures of internal consistency tend to be distorted in speed test situations and, hence, must be used with extreme caution (or not at all) when a test is administered under highly restrictive time limits.
3. All of the reliability coefficients considered in this chapter are affected by a number of factors including (a) test length, (b) homogeneity of the examinee group with respect to the characteristic being measured, and (c) item difficulty. Hence, the relative influence of each of these factors must be considered in the interpretation of a particular reliability estimate.
4. The reliability of a set of examinee difference (or gain) scores will always be less than or equal to the average reliability of the two sets of scores used in calculating the differences.
5. Though not previously discussed, the upper bound on test validity is fixed by test reliability. In fact, the theoretical maximum for the validity of any test (i.e., the linear correlation of it with any other measure) is the square root of its reliability. So, if the reliability of a test is 0.00, the maximum validity for that test is $\sqrt{0.00}$, or 0.00; if the reliability is 0.50, the maximum validity is $\sqrt{0.50}$, or 0.70; etc. An unreliable test cannot possibly be valid for any purpose.
6. Though not previously discussed, the relationship between the average standard error of measurement and reliability can be used to help one decide what degree of reliability is desirable in a particular testing situation. In Chapter 8, we encountered the formula

$$SD(E) = SD(X)\sqrt{1 - \text{reliability}}$$

Solved in terms of reliability, we have

$$\text{Reliability} = 1.00 - \frac{\text{VAR}(E)}{\text{VAR}(X)}$$

which is the required formula. For example, if one wants to be 68% sure that an observed score is no more than 3 points away from its true score component (i.e., the individual error score is 3 points or less), then the desired standard error of measurement, $SD(E)$, equals 3 and the corresponding reliability is $1.00 - 3^2/\text{VAR}(X)$. If we know (on the basis of past usage), or can confidently estimate, the observed score standard deviation of the test in the population of interest, we can solve for the desired reliability. To illustrate, suppose $SD(X) = 5$. Then

$$\text{Reliability} = 1.00 - \frac{3^2}{5^2} = 0.64$$

That is, the test reliability must be 0.64 or greater for us to be 68% sure that X differs from T by no more than 3 points in *this application*. Similarly, if one wants to be 68% sure that X differs from T by no more than 1 point, then

$$\text{Reliability} = 1.00 - \frac{1^2}{5^2} = 0.96$$

is the minimum desired reliability in this application.

7. As indicated earlier, the phrase, "test X is highly reliable in population Q", means that the measurements produced by test X correlate highly with examinee true scores in that population. To emphasize this, some writers speak of the reliability of the test scores rather than the reliability of the test.

SELF-EVALUATION

1. All other things being equal, short tests tend to be _____ long tests.
   a. more reliable than
   b. as reliable as
   c. less reliable than

2. All other things being equal, test reliability is _____ to the amount of variation in the test score distribution.
   a. positively related
   b. unrelated
   c. negatively related

3. Suppose a 50-item multiple-choice test reliability estimate in population X is found to be 0.75. If 50 items of comparable quality are added to the test, what would the approximate reliability of this lengthened test in population X be?

4. Which type of reliability estimate(s) is(are) probably most relevant in each of the following situations?
   a. A new test has been developed which presumably measures tendency to gamble.
   b. The XYZ school district is using two forms of the Metropolitan Achievement Test in the evaluation of a curriculum change involving a pretest-posttest design.
   c. A social studies teacher wants to assess the quality of a "home-made" test of student ability to critically analyze the content of political speeches.

5. Suppose the alpha coefficient for a 50-item achievement test, which takes one hour to administer, turns out to be 0.40. Can the reliability of this test be raised to an acceptable level by increasing the number of items it contains?

6. Suppose a 5-item true-false quiz were given to a group of four students and the following results were obtained. Assuming the numeral 1 represents a correct response and 0 represents an incorrect response, calculate the value of alpha for these data.

Student	Item Number					Quiz Score
	1	2	3	4	5	
A	1	1	1	1	0	4
B	1	1	1	0	0	3
C	1	0	0	0	0	1
D	0	0	0	0	0	0

7. Suppose a large representative sample is used to estimate the reliability of Test X in population P and the result is a coefficient of stability equal to 0.93. This may be interpreted to mean that _____% of variance in the observed scores, $\text{Var}(X)$, is due to true differences among examinees and _____% is due to random measurement errors.

8. If one administered the Stanford-Binet Intelligence Test to a group of students on two occasions separated by a one-month interval and calculated the difference score for each student, the reliability of these difference scores would probably be _____ .
   a. high   b. moderate   c. low

9. Which one of the following coefficients would treat the effects of 24-hour flu on test performance as random error?
   a. Precision
   b. Stability
   c. Equivalence
   d. Internal consistency

10. KR21 provides a meaningful measure of internal consistency when
    a. All items are scored either one or zero.
    b. All items are approximately equal in difficulty.
    c. a and b.
    d. Neither a nor b.

ANSWER KEY

1. c

2. a

3. Reliability of longer test

$$= \frac{2(0.75)}{1 + (0.75)} = \frac{1.50}{1.75} = 0.86$$

4. a. internal consistency and, perhaps, stability (i.e., test-retest)
   b. equivalence
   c. internal consistency

5. Probably not. According to the Spearman-Brown formula, tripling test length by adding items of comparable quality only raises reliability to 0.67. This probably does not justify the additional time which would be required to administer the test.

6. 0.81

7. 93, 7

8. c. Although the reliabilities of the two administrations may be high, the correlation between the two administrations would be high also. In such cases, the difference score reliability tends to be quite low.

9. b

10. c

EXERCISE SET 9-1: ANSWERS

1. See pp. 123–126.
2. See pp. 123–126.
3. a
4. True
5. SEM $= 10\sqrt{1 - 0.84} = 10\sqrt{0.16} = 4$ points

EXERCISE SET 9-2: ANSWERS

1. False
2. Using Spearman-Brown, we estimate the reliability to be

$$\frac{2(0.70)}{1.00 + 0.70} = \frac{1.40}{1.70} = 0.82$$

3. Alpha $= 1.00$. The quiz is totally consistent. Notice, the five items correlate perfectly with each other in this case.
4. True
5. False. (It is a lower bound estimate which provides a good approximation only when all items are approximately equal in difficulty.)

EXERCISE SET 9-3: ANSWERS

1. test length
2. increase
3. item or judge comparability (The set of items (or judges) added to or deleted from the original set are assumed comparable to those constituting the original set.)
4. a. $r_l = \dfrac{n r_s}{1 + (n - 1)r_s} = \dfrac{2(0.80)}{1 + (2 - 1)(0.80)} = \dfrac{1.60}{1.80} = 0.89$

   b. $0.80 = \dfrac{2r_s}{1 + r_s}$; $0.80(1 + r_s) = 2r_s$; $0.80 = 1.20r_s$; $r_s = \dfrac{0.80}{1.20} = 0.67$

EXERCISE SET 9-4: ANSWERS

1. decreases
2. zero, arithmetic mean
3. a. $r_{\text{diff}} = \dfrac{0.90 + 0.60 - 2(.50)}{2(1 - 0.50)} = \dfrac{1.50 - 1.00}{1.00} = 0.50$
3. b. 0.75

REFERENCES

Buros, O. K. (ed.) (1972). *The Seventh Mental Measurements Yearbook.* Highland Park, New Jersey: Gryphon Press.

Coffman, W. E. (1971). Essay Examinations. in *Educational Measurement* (R. L. Thorndike, ed.), 2nd ed., Washington: American Council on Testing.

Cronbach, L. J. (1951). Coefficient Alpha and the Internal Structure of Tests. *Psychometrika*, 16, 297–334.

Kuder, G. F. and M. W. Richardson (1937). The Theory of the Estimation of Reliability. *Psychometrika*, 2, 151–160.

Lord, F. M. and M. R. Novick (1968). *Statistical Theories of Mental Test Scores.* Reading, Massachusetts: Addison-Wesley.

10

Norm-Referenced Test Validity

The score an examinee obtains on a test may reflect the influence of systematic, as well as random, error. Since systematic error is constant for an individual across various testings, it becomes part of the true score in the model $X = T + E$. Therefore, it does not affect test reliability, but does affect the meaning of the observed score and, hence, test validity.

Some sources of systematic error are easily detected and their influence on measurements easily assessed (e.g., the scale and tape measure examples discussed in chapter one). However, the sources of systematic error in educational and psychological testing more often than not tend to be quite complex and subtle and, as a result, necessitate considerable care on the part of the test constructor and test user.

Test scores are generally used as a basis for inferring (a) how well an examinee would do on a population of test items (or tasks) the test is presumed to represent, (b) an examinee's relative standing on some hypothetical continuum presumed to be the primary determinant of performance on the test, or (c) an examinee's present or future standing on some other important test or task (called the criterion or criterion variable). Tests deliberately constructed to provide maximally valid inferences of one type do not necessarily provide maximally valid inferences of the remaining two types. Hence, the type of inference to be made tends to have considerable impact on the way a test is constructed for a particular application and, also, on the type of evidence one seeks to check on the validity of the inferences (or test score interpretations) to be made. For the first type of inference listed above, evidence of *content validity* is most important; for the second type, evidence of *construct validity* is essential; and for the third type, evidence of *criterion-related validity* is the paramount concern. Please note, the type of validity evidence required for a given testing application is not dictated by the nature of the test; rather, both the type of test constructed (or selected) and the relevant type of validity evidence are dictated by the type of inference to be made. We now turn our attention to a rather detailed examination of these three types of validity within a norm-referenced measurement context. We begin with content validity.

CONTENT VALIDITY[1]

In this section, we examine the definition of content validity and the criteria by which the content validity of a test is determined. Since content validity is especially important in the measurement of achievement, the discussion of it is developed within that context.

The term *content domain* (or *content universe*) refers to a population of tasks or test items. A *test* is a sample of tasks or items from a particular content domain. The problem of determining the extent to which a test has *content validity* is essentially one of determining whether or not the test contains a representative sample of tasks which define the content domain of interest. To accomplish this, one must have (a) a clear definition or description of the content domain and (b) knowledge of the procedures used to select the sample of items which consititute the test in question. For the moment, let us focus on the problem of domain definition or description.

Some content domains are very simple and can be described by enumeration, i.e., the set of tasks which constitute the domain can be listed. Some examples of enumerable content domains can be found in areas like elementary arithmetic, elementary science, etc. Most content domains, however, consist of such a wide variety of tasks that enumeration is out of the question. In such instances, one must be satisfied with a description rather than a complete listing of the content contained in the domain. As a result, the practice of listing the objectives of instruction has found increasing usage in this regard. (See Chapter 16 for a discussion of several approaches to the problem of domain definition.) The manner in which the content domain is defined or described is not of paramount importance. The important thing is the provision of a definition or description of the content domain that is sufficient for determining whether or not the sample of items contained in a test is a subset of that domain. Unless informed judgments can be made about whether a particular item is contained in the content domain of interest, the determination of content validity is impossible.

Once the domain definition problem has been resolved, the relation of the test to the domain must be determined. The question to be answered is whether

---

1. Content validity, as described in this section, is an ideal which is seldom, if ever, fully realized by the *traditional* test construction procedures employed in the construction of standardized and teacher made achievement tests. The traditional approaches to domain definition, test design, and item writing described in Chapter 15 tend to produce tests which at best may approximately satisfy the content validity requirements described in this section. The newer approaches to domain definition, item writing, and item selection discussed in Chapter 16 appear to be an improvement in this regard.

the test items constitute a representative sample from the domain of interest. This is, for the most part, a judgmental process. Given an adequate domain definition or description, content area specialists may then be used to subjectively assess the relationship of the sample of items in the test to the population of items in the domain through an examination of the process used to select items for inclusion in the test. Since a universally accepted, easy-to-interpret, quantitative measure of representativeness has not yet been invented, the conclusion of such a judgmental process tend to be a statement like "the test appears to be content valid." (Several approaches to measuring content validity of domain-referenced tests are discussed in Chapter 17.) Let us now examine a simple, hypothetical content validation problem.

In this illustration we limit our attention to a very simple case. Suppose we want to know whether a young child has mastered the addition facts (i.e., the sums of the numbers 0 through 9 taken two at a time). The domain of tasks here is well-defined. In fact, it would be a simple matter to enumerate or list the entire set of problems which comprise or define this domain. If we were given a subset of these items, called a test, purported to measure mastery of the items in this domain, we would examine the collection of items in the test to determine two things: (a) whether all of the test items are, in fact, contained in the domain of interest, and (b) whether the sample of tasks contained in the test is representative of the set of tasks which constitute the domain of interest. If we found the following item in the test "27 − 13 = ?," we would immediately begin to raise a content validity question because this item is clearly not in the domain of tasks as defined. On the other hand, if all of the test items were clearly in the domain, we would still have the problem of determining whether the test sample was representative of the domain from which it was taken. At this point, our attention would turn to the sampling procedure used. If the set of test items were a random sample of the items in the domain, content validity would be assumed because random sampling assures representativeness within the limits of sampling variability. If, as is the more common practice, the test consisted of the first 20 items which came to the test constructor's mind, we would be quite unwilling to concede representativeness. At a minimum, we would insist on a careful examination of the test item set to be sure that the sample of items covered the full range of difficulty associated with the items which make up the entire universe or domain.

It would indeed be convenient if all content validation studies were as simple as the one just described. However, most content domains of interest are very difficult to define. Nonetheless, the content validation paradigm remains the same: (a) define or describe the domain of interest; (b) determine whether the test items are a representative sample of the domain.

Please note, content validity judgments require subject matter expertise; in contrast, the term *face validity* refers to the appearance of the test to the layman. If a test, upon cursory inspection, appears to measure what the test constructor claims it measures, it is said to have face validity. All standardized achievement tests are face valid (e.g., arithmetic tests look like they measure arithmetic skills, reading tests appear to measure reading skills); the content validity of many, however, has not been adequately established.

Let us conclude this section by briefly considering two frequently occurring situations in which content validity considerations are of particular interest: (a) evaluation of a standardized test for use in a particular situation and (b) construction of a classroom achievement test.

Frequently, persons charged with the responsibility for selecting and/or developing measures to use in evaluating the effectiveness of a particular school program or curricular innovation choose a well-known, published, standardized test. However, in doing this, one runs the risk of using a measure that suffers from the lack of content validity; i.e., some test items may measure the achievement of objectives not included in the curriculum being evaluated, while there may be no items to measure the achievement of some domain objectives which are deemed important in this particular situation. The only way one can tell whether this is so is to clearly state the objectives of the curriculum under evaluation and then to evaluate the test being considered with respect to these objectives, the criteria being those previously stated, namely, inclusion in the domain of interest and representativeness.

In the construction of a classroom test (or any new measure of achievement, however it may be used), the best strategy one can adopt is to use a procedure which maximizes content validity. A popular way of doing this is to state the objectives to be achieved by the students in the course (or program) as unambiguously as possible and then to design the test to measure all of the objectives, if that is feasible, or a representative sample of them, otherwise. In this case, the list of objectives constitutes the domain definition and serves not only as a boundary between relevant and irrelevant content, but also as a basis for generating the tasks or items to be included in the test. In addition, if specified at the outset (prior to instruction), the objectives will help insure that the instructional activities will also be content valid. More will be said about instructional objectives and item generation in subsequent chapters.

In conclusion, it should be clear by now that the assessment of content validity is, by and large, a subjective process. Whether a particular test has an acceptable degree of content validity for use in a given situation can only be determined by having individuals who are knowledgeable about that particular universe of tasks make judgments concerning the adequacy of the domain or universe definition and the representativeness of (or the procedure for selecting) the sample of test items.

CONSTRUCT VALIDITY

In this discussion we (a) define the term "construct validity," (b) briefly examine the contrasted groups and experimental manipulation construct validation procedures, (c) state the convergent and discriminant construct validity principles, and (d) explain the Campbell and Fiske multitrait-multimethod approach to collecting and displaying construct validity evidence. The discussion is intended to provide an overview of the several construct validity techniques mentioned above with primary emphasis on the multitrait-multimethod approach. Let us begin with two brief excerpts from the American Psychological Association's *Standards for Educational and Psychological Tests* dealing with the meaning of the term "construct validity."

> A psychological construct is an idea developed or "constructed" as a work of informed, scientific imagination; that is, it is a theoretical idea developed to explain and to organize some aspects of existing knowledge. Terms such as "anxiety," "clerical aptitude," or "reading readiness" refer to such constructs, but the construct is much more than the label; it is a dimension understood or inferred from its network of interrelationships. It may be necessary to postulate several different constructs to account for the variance in any given set of test scores. Moreover, different constructs may be required to account for the variance in different tests of the same general type, or a given test may provide evidence relating to several constructs. For example, given proper evidence, scores on vocabulary tests might be used to infer (a) the level of present vocabulary; (b) the existence of pathology, interests, or values; or (c) intellectual capacity. (American Psychological Association, 1974, p. 29.)
>
> *Construct validity* is evaluated by investigating what qualities a test measures, that is, by determining the degree to which certain explanatory concepts or constructs account for performance on the test. To examine construct validity requires a combination of logical and empirical attack. Essentially, studies of construct validity check on the theory underlying the test. The procedure involves three steps. First, the investigator inquires: From this theory, what hypotheses may we make regarding the behavior of persons with high and low scores? Second, he gathers data to test these hypotheses. Third, in light of the evidence, he makes an inference as to whether the theory is adequate to explain the data collected. If the theory fails to account for the data, he should revise the test interpretation, reformulate the theory, or reject the theory altogether. Fresh evidence would be required to demonstrate construct validity for the revised interpretation. (American Psychological Association, 1966, p. 13.)

We will now examine three procedures for collecting evidence of construct validity, namely, the contrasted groups procedure, experimental manipulation techniques, and the multitrait-multimethod approach.

The Contrasted Groups Approach

The contrasted groups procedure for collecting construct validity evidence involves the following kind of reasoning. If, for example, we have a test presumed to measure individual differences in "willingness to gamble," we attempt to identify groups of individuals *known* to occupy the extremes on this hypothesized "willingness to gamble" continuum. That is, we attempt to constitute a group of examinees known to gamble at nearly every opportunity and a second group consisting of examinees who consistently refrain from gambling. If our "willingness to gamble" test is sensitive to individual "willingness to gamble" differences, then the mean performance of these two groups on our test should differ significantly.[2]

Having predicted the relative order of the mean performances of these contrasted groups, we administer the test to each and compare their average or mean performances. If the data are consistent with our prediction, we have some evidence to support our claim that the test measures "willingness to gamble." (Note, however, that such evidence is not absolute proof that our test measures this characteristic. Since the two groups probably differ in many ways, the mean difference in test score performance might be due to group noncomparability on some other variable.) If the data we collect are not consistent with our prediction, we will probably conclude that either (a) our test is unreliable (we can check this), (b) our test is reliable, but not a valid measure of the "willingness to gamble" construct, or (c) our conception of the construct "willingness to gamble" is faulty and needs to be reformulated. In any event, we have no basis for claiming that our test is sensitive to individual differences on the hypothesized "willingness to gamble" continuum.

The Experimental Manipulation Approach

In this approach, one must use the theory of which the construct in question is a component to predict how a group of individuals (or examinees) will perform on the test under a variety of experimentally induced conditions. The individuals are then placed in these conditions and measured using the test in question. If the individuals (as a group) perform on the test as predicted, we can offer this as evidence of construct validity. If the individuals behave in a manner inconsistent with our prediction, we face the same alternatives listed in our Contrasted Groups discussion above with one additional possibility, i.e., the experimental design may not have provided an adequate test of the hypothesis in question. Consider the following example.

Spielberger et al. (1970) developed two 20-item self-report instruments designed to measure trait and state anxiety, respectively. State anxiety refers to an individual's emotional response to the threat he perceives in a particular stimulus situation (e.g., immediately before and perhaps during a final exam). Trait anxiety, on the other hand, refers to an individual's tendency to perceive threatening elements across a broad spectrum of stimulus conditions (i.e., low trait anxious individuals remain calm regardless of the situation they are in, while extremely high trait anxious individuals experience heightened anxiety feelings in many different kinds of situations, e.g., when taking a test, when making a speech). Before those instruments are used for diagnostic purposes, evidence must be collected which supports the contention that they measure the constructs *state anxiety* and *trait anxiety*, respectively. An impressive body of evidence has been accumulated thus far which provides this support.

---

2. Whether a difference between means is significant is determined by using an appropriate statistical test.

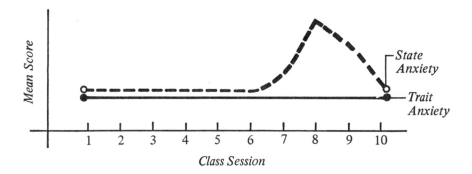

FIGURE 10-1. *Illustration of the effects of test anxiety on student performance as measured by the Spielberger et al. measures of State and Trait Anxiety.*

For example, in an unpublished study conducted for instructional purposes by this author, these instruments were administered to an introductory tests and measurements class at the beginning of each of the first 10 class meetings. The first seven sessions were ordinary class meetings, while sessions eight and nine were testing periods. Session number 10 was again an ordinary class discussion period. The mean trait and state anxiety scores using each instrument were calculated for each class session and plotted as shown in Figure 10-1. The trait anxiety means were approximately the same regardless of the class conditions (i.e., test vs nontest conditions) which existed at the time the trait measures were obtained. Since trait anxiety is presumed to be stable across time, these data support the contention that this instrument does, in fact, measure trait anxiety. The state anxiety means, on the other hand, remained relatively constant for the first several sessions and then began to increase as the first achievement test approached. The highest state anxiety mean occurred on the day of the first achievement test, decreased slightly on the day of the second achievement test (possibly because the first test gave the students an idea of what sort of items to expect on the second test), and dropped to nearly the pretest level on the last measurement occasion. Since achievement tests are known to be anxiety arousing stimuli for many individuals, these data support the claim that the Spielberger *et al.* state anxiety measure is sensitive to individual differences in the level of state anxiety experienced under changes in academic stress.

The Multitrait-Multimethod Approach

This approach is based on two principles: (a) the convergent validity principle and (b) the discriminant validity principle. The *convergent validity principle* asserts that any two different measures of the same construct should have a relatively high linear correlation, i.e., tests designed to measure the same characteristic should rank a group of examinees in approximately the same order. The *discriminant validity principle* asserts that any two measures of different constructs should have a low linear correlation. How low these correlations are depends on the extent to which the constructs are related. For example, two measures of intelligence should have a relatively high correlation, while a measure of intelligence and a measure of trait anxiety should have a relatively low correlation. One advantage of the Campbell and Fiske technique is the accent placed on the use of these two principles in collecting and displaying construct validity evidence.

A second significant feature of their approach is it allows the separation of trait and method variance. Trait variance is the variability in a set of test scores due to individual differences in the trait being measured. Method variance refers to the variability in a set of test scores due to individual differences in examinee ability to respond appropriately to the particular item form used, the structure of the items used, etc. For example, some students tend to get higher scores on objective tests than they do on essay tests, while for others, the reverse is true. The form of the item appreciably affects the score the student obtains. As a result, one can easily see that the size of the correlation between two tests is determined partly by the extent to which these tests measure the same trait and partly by the extent to which performance on the item form used in one test is correlated with performance on the item form used in the second test. This notion is discussed further following an introduction to the Campbell and Fiske multitrait-multimethod procedure.

Suppose we had two instruments designed to measure trait anxiety, two instruments designed to measure state anxiety, and two instruments designed to measure hostility. Further, suppose that one measure of each construct consists of a series of statements which each examinee rates on a 5-point scale to indicate the extent to which a particular statement describes how he feels. The second measure of each construct is cast in the form of an adjective checklist, i.e., the examinee checks all of the adjectives in a standard list which describe his feelings. In using the Campbell and Fiske approach, each of these six instruments is administered to every member of the validation sample. Because state anxiety fluctuates from one occasion to another, these measures would have to be obtained during the same testing session. The following statistical analyses are then performed: (a) the reliability of each form is determined using one of the procedures discussed in Chapter 9, and (b) the correlation between each pair of forms is calculated. These results are then displayed in a multitrait-multimethod matrix. The procedure for constructing a matrix of this type is illustrated in Table 10-1. First, we enter the reliability estimate for each form as shown in Table 10-1a. The sets of three reliability estimates in the upper left and lower right blocks of the matrix are called the *reliability diagonals*. If these estimates are acceptably high, we continue to the next step; if they are too low, we stop because reliability is a prerequisite for validity. Since the hypothetical reliability estimates shown in Table 10-1a are acceptable, we continue.

Next, we enter the correlations between the two measures of each trait cast in different forms in the lower left block of the matrix (see Table 10-1b). This is called the *validity diagonal*. These coefficients indicate the degree of relationship between two measures of the same trait obtained by different methods and, therefore, provide evidence of *convergent validity* (provided, of course, the coefficients are sufficiently large).

Then, we enter the correlations between the various pairs of different trait measures cast in rating scale form in the upper left block, and the correlations between the different pairs of trait measures cast in checklist form in the lower right block of the matrix (see Table 10-1c). All of these coefficients are indicators of the relationships between measures of different traits presented using the same item form or method. Therefore, these values are partly determined by the relationships existing among these three traits and partly by the common item forms they employ. These are called the *heterotrait-monomethod triangles*. The values in these triangles should be lower than the values in the validity diagonal. Two measures of different constructs cast in the same form should have a lower linear correlation than two measures of the same construct cast in different forms unless the test score variation is primarily due to method rather than trait variance. To claim evidence of construct validity, one must be able to show that the larger portion of the test score variability is the result of trait variance. This is one implication of the discriminant validity principle.

Finally, the remaining correlation coefficients calculated using sets of scores obtained by measures of different traits cast in different forms (e.g., state anxiety in rating scale form and hostility in checklist form) are entered in the triangles in the lower left block of the matrix (see Table 10-1d). These are called the heterotrait-heteromethod triangles. Since each of these correlations involves measures of different traits cast in different forms, their values should be lower than the corresponding values in the validity diagonal and in the heterotrait-monomethod triangles. A comparison of these correlations with those in the heterotrait-monomethod triangles provides information concerning the relative contribution of the methods used to the covariation existing in the data. If the values in these triangles are as expected, further evidence of discriminant validity is provided.

To summarize briefly, evidence of convergent validity resides in the validity diagonal of the matrix, while evidence of discriminant validity is found by comparing the relative magnitudes of the validity diagonal entries with the elements of the heterotrait-monomethod triangles and the entries in the heterotrait-heteromethod triangles. One additional characteristic of the matrix dictated by the logic of the procedure is that the pattern of relative coefficient sizes should be approximately the same in all of the triangles. Note, this does not mean that the values in one triangle should be nearly equal to the corresponding values in the other triangles. It does mean that the largest and smallest coefficients (regardless of their absolute size) in each triangle should be located in the same position in each triangle. The fictitious data displayed in Table 10-1d provide an illustration of this multitrait-multimethod matrix characteristic.

If the matrix in Table 10-1d were the result of an actual study like that described above, it could be offered as evidence that the instruments involved measure the constructs in question. Note, these data are not proof positive that these tests have construct validity. Like the techniques discussed in the previous sections of this paper, multitrait-multimethod matrix information merely supports

TABLE 10-1. *Illustration of a Multitrait-Multimethod Matrix Constructed in a Step-By-Step Fashion.*

a. Basic Matrix Showing Reliability Diagonals.

	Traits	Method 1 (Rating Scale)			Method 2 (Adjective Checklist)		
		State Anxiety	Trait Anxiety	Hostility	State Anxiety	Trait Anxiety	Hostility
Rating Scale	State Anxiety	(.80)					
	Trait Anxiety		(.91)				
	Hostility			(.85)			
Adjective Checklist	State Anxiety				(.75)		
	Trait Anxiety					(.87)	
	Hostility						(.84)

b. Validity Diagonal Added.

	Traits	Method 1 (Rating Scale)			Method 2 (Adjective Checklist)		
		State Anxiety	Trait Anxiety	Hostility	State Anxiety	Trait Anxiety	Hostility
Rating Scale	State Anxiety	(.80)					
	Trait Anxiety		(.91)				
	Hostility			(.85)			
Adjective Checklist	State Anxiety	[.63]			(.75)		
	Trait Anxiety		[.60]			(.87)	
	Hostility			[.55]			(.84)

c. Heterotrait-Monomethod Triangles Added.

	Traits	Method 1 (Rating Scale)			Method 2 (Adjective Checklist)		
		State Anxiety	Trait Anxiety	Hostility	State Anxiety	Trait Anxiety	Hostility
Rating Scale	State Anxiety	(.80)					
	Trait Anxiety	.45	(.91)				
	Hostility	.33	.27	(.85)			
Adjective Checklist	State Anxiety	[.63]			(.75)		
	Trait Anxiety		[.60]		.47	(.87)	
	Hostility			[.55]	.38	.32	(.84)

d. Heterotrait-Heteromethod Triangles Added to Complete the Matrix.

	Traits	Method 1 (Rating Scale)			Method 2 (Adjective Checklist)		
		State Anxiety	Trait Anxiety	Hostility	State Anxiety	Trait Anxiety	Hostility
Rating Scale	State Anxiety	(.80)					
	Trait Anxiety	.45	(.91)				
	Hostility	.33	.27	(.85)			
Adjective Checklist	State Anxiety	[.63]	.20	.15	(.75)		
	Trait Anxiety	.18	[.60]	.09	.47	(.87)	
	Hostility	.13	.11	[.55]	.38	.32	(.84)

or fails to support the hypothesis that these instruments measure the constructs they were designed to measure.[3]

SUMMARY

In this section we examined the meaning of the term "construct validity" and discussed several procedures typically used to collect construct validity evidence. Examples of the application of each technique were presented. A more complete treatment of the Campbell and Fiske procedure can be found in their initial paper on the subject (Campbell and Fiske, 1959).

EXERCISE SET 10-1

1. When two traits are measured using a common method, the correlation between them is placed in _____ of the multitrait-multimethod matrix.
   a. the reliability diagonal
   b. the validity diagonal
   c. a heterotrait-monomethod triangle
   d. a heterotrait-heteromethod triangle

2. All of the correlations in a validity diagonal of a multitrait-multimethod matrix are based on _____ measured by _____ .
   a. one trait . . . two different methods
   b. two traits . . . a common method
   c. two traits . . . different methods

3. Indicate whether each of the numerals in the multitrait-multimethod matrix shown below is located in a (a) reliability diagonal, (b) validity diagonal, (c) heterotrait-monomethod triangle, or (d) heterotrait-heteromethod triangle.

		Method 1			Method 2			Method 3		
		Trait 1	Trait 2	Trait 3	Trait 1	Trait 2	Trait 3	Trait 1	Trait 2	Trait 3
Method 1	Trait 1									
	Trait 2									
	Trait 3		3							
Method 2	Trait 1	7			1					
	Trait 2									
	Trait 3									
Method 3	Trait 1	2				4				
	Trait 2					6				
	Trait 3							5		

---

3. When matrices like this are constructed using actual data, more often than not the patterns among the correlation coefficients are not as clear as they are in this contrived

In the following sections, we focus in turn on (a) definitions of two types of criterion-related validity, (b) the procedures appropriate for assessing each type of criterion-related validity, and (c) a number of problems which must be considered in planning or evaluating the results of a criterion-related validity study vis-à-vis the assumptions underlying criterion-related test validation.

Some Terminology

Criterion-related validities apply when one wishes to infer from a test score an individual's most probable standing on some other variable called a criterion. Statements of predictive validity indicate the extent to which an individual's future level [of performance] on the criterion can be predicted from a knowledge of prior test performance; statements of concurrent validity indicate the extent to which the test may be used to estimate an individual's present standing on the criterion. The distinction is important. Predictive validity involves a time interval during which something may happen (e.g., people are trained, or gain experience, or are subjected to some treatment). Concurrent validity reflects only the status quo at a particular time. Under appropriate circumstances, data obtained in a concurrent [validity] study may be used to estimate the predictive validity of a test. However, concurrent validity should not be used as a substitute for predictive validity without an appropriate supporting rationale. (American Psychological Association, 1974, p. 26.)

Procedures and Some Examples

Consider the following questions: (a) Is the Scholastic Aptitude Test (SAT) a good predictor of academic performance in college? (b) Is the "Hand-Is-Quicker-Than-The-Eye" test of visual perception a good predictor of performance on the Stanford-Binet? (c) Is the Manual Dexterity Test a good predictor of performance on an automobile assembly line? These are all questions of criterion-related validity. In each case, we want to know the extent to which performance on an important criterion variable (e.g., academic performance in college) can be estimated using information on a more economical, more accessible measure. The mathematics for accomplishing this has been covered in the units on linear correlation and prediction. The procedure entailed by a criterion-related validity study is as follows: (a) measure the performance of a target population, or a representative sample of that population, on both the predictor and criterion

---

example. As a result, sophisticated statistical techniques for separating and measuring the relative contributions of trait and method variance to the variability found in the data have been developed. These procedures are beyond the scope of this discussion, and are therefore not pursued in this book.

variables and (b) compute the linear correlation, i.e., Pearson r, using those data. The value of r calculated in this way is a measure of the goodness of that predictor for estimating performance on that particular criterion in, and only in, that target population. For example, the validity of the SAT for predicting freshman grade point average (GPA) may differ considerably in the population of Harvard applicants and the population of community college applicants. Additionally, the SAT can be used to estimate performance on many different criteria within the same target population, e.g., freshman GPA, cumulative GPA, success in the College of Engineering, wealth ten years following graduation, current socioeconomic status (SES). Since a particular test can be used to estimate performance on many criteria (with varying degrees of goodness) and in many different target populations, it is well to keep these factors in mind when planning a validity study or selecting a test to be used as a predictor of some important criterion variable.

To further sharpen the distinction between concurrent and predictive validity consider the following examples. First, suppose we had to measure the IQ's of many children in a relatively short period of time. Since the preferred measures of IQ (i.e., the Stanford-Binet and Wechsler scales) must be administered to each child separately and require a great deal of administration and scoring time, we may wish to substitute a pencil-and-paper measure which can be administered to a large group of examinees simultaneously and scored rather quickly. To check the wisdom of such a substitution, we may select a sample of students from a target population, test them using the preferred criterion measure and the potential pencil-and-paper substitute, and calculate the correlation based on these data. If it is acceptably high, say above 0.85, we may decide that the more economical measure is quite acceptable for our purposes. Since both sets of data in such a situation are obtained concurrently, the index is interpreted as a measure of concurrent validity.

By way of contrast, suppose we have the task of selecting students for admission to Foggy Bottom University. If we have fewer applicants than slots to be filled, there would be no problem. We simply admit all applicants. However, it is more often the case that the number of applicants exceeds the number of slots to be filled. In such cases, the standard practice is to use at least one test to identify those members of the applicant population having the best chance to excel academically at Foggy Bottom. What is required is a test (typically referred to as an entrance exam) which is a good predictor of success (typically defined in terms of grade point average) at Foggy Bottom. To determine whether a particular test is suitable, the ideal procedure would involve: (a) obtaining a representative sample of the applicant population, (b) administering the entrance exam (e.g., the SAT) to them, (c) admitting the entire sample to the University, (d) calculating the end-of-freshman-year grade point average, and (e) computing the predictor – GPA correlation coefficient. This yields an estimate of predictive validity. If this correlation coefficient is acceptably high (determined with an appropriate statistical test), the entrance test under consideration may subsequently be used in making admission decisions regarding members of that applicant population; if not, some other measure will probably be sought for this purpose. It should be noted that predictors having moderate to low validities for specific criteria are frequently used. This may be justifiable in specific situations either because no better predictors are available at the time, or the selection ratio is very favorable, i.e., there are many more applicants than there are positions to be filled. Unlike the previous example where substitutability is in question and always requires a very high correlation between measures, the merits of each predictive validity coefficient must be judged separately considering factors like those just mentioned, namely, availability of better measures and the selection ratio.

Some Frequently Encountered Problems

We conclude the discussion of criterion-related validity by considering several factors which must be considered in planning or evaluating the results of such studies. These include the changing nature of the target population, the nature of the validation sample, criterion validity, measurement unreliability, and the need for cross-validation.

The Changing Nature of the Target Population. Criterion-related validation assumes that the nature of the target population is essentially an unchanging one. That is, the validity of test X as an indicator of performance on criterion Y in some population Q is assumed to remain constant over time. However, important characteristics of many populations are changing continuously and rapidly, especially in these times. Therefore, it is much more reasonable to believe that the relationship between any two variables, say X and Y, within a particular population Q is more apt to change than remain constant, even over relatively short time spans. The practical implication of this phenomenon is that the useful life span of many criterion-related validity coefficients is relatively short. One cannot place much confidence in "old" validity data.

The Nature of the Validation Sample. Criterion-related validation requires that the examination of the relationship between variables X and Y in population Q be carried out using the entire population or a representative sample of that population. Frequently, validation studies are based on samples which are not representative because of sloppy sampling procedures, selection, attrition, or a combination of these factors. While the effects of sloppy sampling are easily seen, the effects of selection and attrition are somewhat more subtle. To illustrate the effects of these factors, suppose we consider the following alternative solution to the college admission problem discussed previously. Since the SAT and freshman grade point average data are currently on file for last year's group of applicants who were admitted and actually completed their freshman studies, one may be tempted to estimate predictive validity using these data. If the SAT (or some measure highly correlated with the SAT) were used in admitting those freshmen in the first place, then the portion of the applicant population scoring low on the SAT was not admitted and, hence, is not represented in our validation sample. In addition, applicants who were admitted and, for one reason or another, failed to complete their freshman year are not represented in this sample. Since both of these factors tend to reduce score variability on both the predictor and criterion measures, the coefficient obtained usually underestimates the true validity of the predictor in question.

Criterion Validity. Criterion-related validation is predicated on the assumption that the criterion measure is valid. Occasionally, the selection of a criterion measure is influenced more by convenience than by appropriateness or quality. Two facets of this problem are *criterion definition* and *criterion relevance*. In addition, whenever rating procedures are used in collecting criterion data, the threat of *criterion contamination* must be considered. Let us consider briefly each of these criterion validity problems in turn.

Criterion Definition. Many socially important criteria are difficult to measure principally because they are difficult to define to everyone's satisfaction. As a case in point, consider the variable socioeconomic status (SES). Although there are many variables which may serve as indicators of SES, like annual income, level of education, father's occupation, etc., there is no single universally accepted SES measure. As a result, the quality of variable X (say Stanford-Binet intelligence measured at age 10) as a predictor of adult SES (measured at age 35) may vary considerably depending upon how SES is defined and, hence, measured. Thus, it is important to realize that a particular criterion-related validity coefficient is interpretable only in terms of how the criterion is defined in that instance.

Criterion Relevance. Frequently, one wants to know whether variable X is a good predictor of some criterion (say professional productivity 10 years after obtaining a college degree). When the criterion data of interest are not available, it is tempting to use some substitute criterion (like cumulative college GPA) rather than wait 10 years until the criterion data become available. Such a procedure would be justifiable if it could be demonstrated that a very high correlation existed between GPA and professional productivity. However, such data do not typically exist and, in fact, the suspicion is harbored by many that if they did exist, the story they tell would be quite different than the one presumed to be true. This is the basis used by many for questioning the merit of a variety of college admissions tests and college course final exams, i.e., many such exams are believed to bear little relation to professional productivity following graduation. Here, the relevance of the criterion used (GPA) to the criterion of interest (professional productivity) must be seriously considered. Expediency should not always rule the day.

Criterion Contamination. Frequently, criteria are quantified using some sort of rating procedure. For example, on-the-job performance in an industrial setting is typically quantified using supervisory ratings. Similarly, measures of teacher effectiveness are frequently quantified in the form of student, peer, and supervisory ratings. Whenever criterion performance is quantified using a rating procedure, criterion contamination can be a problem. If the rater or judge knows how the members of the validity sample performed on the predictor, this knowledge will probably influence his rating on the criterion, i.e., low scorers on the predictor tend to be rated low on the criterion, and high scorers on the predictor tend, more often than not, to be rated high on the criterion. Obviously, the result of such contamination is a spurious increase in the predictor-criterion correlation coefficient. When this happens, the predictor appears to be more effective than it actually is. Since there is no known procedure to correct a correlation coefficient for criterion contamination, all one can do is to procedurally guarantee that such contamination does not occur.

Measurement Unreliability. Unreliability of both predictor and criterion measures is always a problem. Only if one had error-free or perfectly reliable measures of both variables would the true correlation between predictor and criterion be determinable. The effect of measurement error is to reduce or attenuate the correlation between predictor and criterion. As a result, the correlation obtained using fallible measures (measures containing measurement error) always underestimates the true correlation which would be obtained if error-free measurement techniques were available. Fortunately, there exists a mathematical procedure for correcting a correlation for attenuation. The formula is very simple (although the rationale is a bit complicated) and may be presented as follows:

$$r'(C,P) = \frac{r(C,P)}{\sqrt{r_C \cdot r_P}}$$

Where $r'(C,P)$ = correlation corrected for unreliability (i.e., the correlation which one would obtain if the measures used were perfectly reliable)

$r(C,P)$ = predictor-criterion correlation actually obtained using the measures C and P.

r_P = reliability of the predictor

r_C = reliability of the criterion

Consider the following example. Suppose the linear correlation between predictor X and criterion Y is 0.40 and the estimated reliabilities of these measures are 0.70 and 0.80, respectively. What is the correlation corrected for unreliability?

$$r'(X,Y) = \frac{0.40}{\sqrt{0.70(0.80)}} = 0.53$$

In this example, it seems quite clear that X and Y probably correlate about 0.53 in the population of interest. Note that if both tests were prefectly reliable, then $r'(X,Y)$ would equal $r(X,Y)$.

Although there are situations in which the correlation for attenuation is applicable, its general use is not recommended. In most practical situations, we choose the most reliable predictor and criterion measures we can and live with the results obtained in that way. In multitrait-multimethod studies, its use in correcting the correlations may be justifiable because the focal points of such studies typically are the true interrelationships among constructs. In such cases, internal consistency statistics (e.g., split-half and alpha coefficients) are not recommended because they more often than not provide underestimates of reliability and, hence, overcorrect for attenuation in the present procedure. See Lord and Novick (1968) for more on this point.

EXERCISE SET 10-2

Suppose an estimate of the correlation between two constructs obtained using measures having estimated reliabilities of 0.80 and 0.40, respectively, was found to be 0.40. What is the correlation after correction for attenuation?

Cross-Validation.   It must be apparent at this point that the validity of variable X for predicting performance on criterion Y in population Q is simply the linear correlation between the predictor and the criterion in that population. In real prediction problems, the total membership of the target population is not usually available, and hence, most studies (if not all) involve a subset or a sample of the members of that population. Even if the sample used in the validation study is selected using a random process, the least-squares equation for predicting criterion performance given predictor information tends to be somewhat misleading. The reason for this is that the least-squares procedure produces a line which minimizes the average squared error of prediction. As a result, both sampling variability (or sampling error) and measurement error affect the orientation of the line. One consequence of this is that the correlation coefficient, which is also based on the least-squares principle, tends to overestimate the magnitude of the predictor-criterion relationship. Therefore, a procedure called cross-validation should be used to obtain a more realistic estimate of the relationship between the predictor and criterion variables.

A cross-validation study involves the use of two samples and the following procedure: (a) derive a prediction equation using data generated by the first sample, (b) administer the predictor test to the second sample drawn from the same population, (c) use the prediction equation obtained from the first sample (called the *validity sample*) to estimate criterion performance for each of the individuals in the second sample (called the *cross-validation sample*), (d) measure the actual criterion performance for each individual in the cross-validation sample, and (e) calculate the linear correlation between the predicted and actual criterion scores for this cross-validation sample. This correlation is a better estimate of the true worth of predictor X for estimating performance on criterion Y in this particular population. Since it is usually quite difficult to draw two random samples from a population for the purpose of cross validating a predictor, a standard technique involves randomly splitting the available validation sample, using one of these subgroups in the validation phase of the study and the other subgroup in the cross-validation phase. Needless to say, if the original validation sample was chosen by a nonrandom procedure from the population in question, the validity coefficient obtained using data generated by that sample would probably be quite different from the correlation which actually exists in the population. In such a case cross-validation is even more important and must be carried out using a fresh sample from the population in question. The split-sample technique is not appropriate in such a situation.

Summary

In this section, we examined the logic and assumptions of criterion-related validity, as well as a number of factors which must be considered in planning a criterion-related validity study or evaluating the results of such a study. It should be obvious by the definition of this concept that every test has an infinite number of criterion-related validities in any given population — one for each criterion with which it can be paired. Some tests allow moderately valid inferences to be made relative to many criteria while others support highly valid inferences relative to a very small class of criteria. Examples of the first type would be well-constructed measures of general intelligence; examples of the latter type, measures of specific aptitudes or personality traits.

In closing, it should be noted that criterion-related validity does not require evidence of either content or construct validity though such evidence is usually informative as well as comforting. By its definition, the most valid predictor of criterion C in population Q is that predictor variable which has the largest absolute Pearson r with the criterion in population Q. Thus, if mean daily pulse rate correlated more highly than any other variable with socioeconomic status (SES) in population Q, it would be the most valid predictor of SES in that population. If one began to question what factors were responsible for this unexpected relationship, one would then be in the realm of construct validity.

SUMMARY

In this chapter, we saw that an answer to the question "Is test X valid?" can be obtained only if the intended use of test X is known. For example, if test X consists of a sample of 50 words taken from a dictionary of the English language and is going to be used to estimate the size of an examinee's reading vocabulary, content validity is most important. On the other hand, if performance on test X is going to be used as the basis for inferring an examinee's general intelligence level, construct validity is of paramount importance. Finally, if test X is going to be used as a means of predicting success in a particular scholastic program, then criterion-related validity is of prime concern. In many testing situations, a combination of these validation procedures is of interest.

The discussions in this chapter should be helpful in deciding how to go about the task of doing a validity study and how to evaluate a test's utility for a particular purpose.

Now, check your comprehension of the material in this chapter using the self-evaluation form provided for this purpose.

1. Content validity is primarily a question of —————— .
   a. domain definition
   b. item sampling procedures
   c. both a and b
   d. neither a nor b

2. If a 100-item vocabulary list were used to estimate the size of an individual's vocabulary, one would be most interested in —————— validity.
   a. content
   b. construct
   c. criterion-related
   d. face

3. *True or False.* One favorable construct validity study is sufficient to establish the existence of a construct.

4. Which one of the following is an example of a construct?
   a. Political party affiliation
   b. Attitude towards religion
   c. Reaction time in an emergency situation

5. The correlation between performance on a college entrance exam and cumulative grade index at graduation is most frequently a measure of —————— validity.
   a. face   b. content   c. construct   d. predictive

6. *True or False.* The difference between concurrent and predictive validity is based on a subtle distinction related to how the instruments involved were constructed.

7. The procedure used to estimate the true correlation between two constructs (i.e., without measurement error) is called —————— . Its routine use (is/is not) recommended.

8. If the correlation between two traits measured by a common method is appreciably higher than the correlation between the same two traits measured by different methods, the difference in correlations would signify the presence of —————— .
   a. trait variance
   b. method variance

9. *True or False.* The true worth of a potential predictor can be assessed using a procedure called cross-validation.

10. Referring to Table 10-1d, identify each of the following:
    a. The most reliable measure
    b. The highest validity coefficient
    c. The location of the information bearing directly on the convergent validity question.

EXERCISE SET 10-1: ANSWERS

1. c
2. a
3. 1—a, 2—b, 3—c, 4—d, 5—c, 6—b, 7—b

EXERCISE SET 10-2: ANSWER

$$r'(X,Y) = \frac{0.40}{\sqrt{0.80(0.40)}} = 0.71$$

REFERENCES

American Psychological Association (1966). *Standards for Educational and Psychological Tests and Manuals.* Washington, D. C.: American Psychological Association.

Ibid. (1974). *Standards for Educational and Psychological Tests.* Washington, D. C.: American Psychological Association.

Campbell, D. T. and D. W. Fiske, (1959). Convergent and Discriminant Validation by the Multitrait-Multimethod Matrix. *Psychological Bulletin,* 56, 81–105.

Lord, F. M. and M. R. Novick (1968). *Statistical Theories of Mental Test Scores.* Reading, Massachusetts: Addison-Wesley.

Spielberger, C. D., R. Gorsuch, and R. E. Lushene (1970). *Manual for the State-Trait Anxiety Inventory.* Palo Alto, California: Consulating Psychologists Press.

11

Norms: Definition, Types, and Uses

Before making any decisions based on norm-referenced test scores, one must be sure that (a) the test has an acceptable degree of reliability and validity, (b) examinee performance is quantified or scaled in a manner suitable to norm-referenced interpretation (see Chapters 3 and 5), and (c) appropriate normative data are available or readily obtainable.[1] The last of these is essential if one wants to assess the quality of performance of an examinee (or of the mean performance of a collection of examinees like a class, school, school district, etc.) and is the focus of the present chapter. In turn, we define the term *norms*, briefly discuss several important characteristics of norms, briefly describe several useful classes of norms, and examine several fairly typical norms tables appearing in the technical manual of a standardized test.

DEFINITION OF NORMS

At the outset, we must agree on the meaning of the term *norms*. According to Angoff (1971, p. 534):

> In general, there are two kinds of meaning that have been attached to the term *norms*. One of these is associated with notions of acceptable,

---

1. The reader should be aware of the existence of procedures for developing norm-free scales (see, for example, Angoff, 1971, pp. 527–533). Because such scales have enjoyed rather limited use in educational measurement to date, the present discussion focuses on the manner in which scales are given normative meaning and related topics.

desired, or required *standards* or *clinical ideals.* Thus it may be said that Mr. Jones is 15 pounds overweight, meaning that he is 15 pounds heavier than *he should be.* The determination of what he should be may have been made previously on some independent basis, related to medical or athletic considerations, to the work that Mr. Jones does or is applying to do, or to some other consideration. The other kind of meaning of the term *norms,* which may lead to quite different interpretations of the same performance, is the *statistical* meaning and is the one in terms of which educational and psychological measurements are most often interpreted. Thus a test performance is said to be high or low nearly always in relation to a defined group of other individuals and only rarely in terms of a previously set standard. The fact that the two kinds of "normative" interpretations can be quite different may be illustrated by noting that the same Mr. Jones who may be clinically overweight by 15 pounds may be 10 pounds underweight when compared with other men of the same age, height, and morphological structure. Clearly, then, the comparison group is also clinically overweight, even more so than Mr. Jones.

In the context of educational and psychological measurement, the term norms typically refers to the *statistical information* which describes the distribution of scores of a well-defined population (or representative sample) of examinees on a particular test, and hence, provides evaluative information about an examinee's level of performance (represented by his test score), vis-à-vis the norm population, on that test.

The *statistical information* referred to in this definition may be presented in a variety of forms, including (a) summary statistics like means and standard deviations, (b) conversion or norms tables which show the association in the norm population between each possible raw score value and the corresponding values on one or more derived scales (e.g., T, stanine), and (c) profile charts which show at a glance the performances of the norm group on a number of dimensions simultaneously. The relative utility of these and other approaches to recording normative data for future use depends, of course, on the way in which the test in question will ultimately be used. For example, the classroom teacher who "grades on a curve" will probably be most interested in the percentile rank scale because that is all he needs in order to implement that type of grade assignment policy in his class. On the other hand, most publishers of standardized tests tend to present normative data in several forms (e.g., percentile rank, T, and stanine) in order to maximize the interpretability and ease of use for a diverse consumer population.

The *population* referred to in the definition depends, of course, on the purpose for which the test is being used. Some examples are

1. The total membership of Mr. Jones' eighth grade geography class (if, for example, Mr. Jones uses a "grading on a curve" grade assignment policy).
2. The total membership of the eighth grade class at P.S. 193 (if, for example, the P.S. 193 administration espouses a tracking or homogeneous-grouping philosophy).

3. The total membership of all eighth grade classes in the United States (if, for example, comparisons with the national norms are of interest).
4. The total male membership of all eighth grade classes in the United States (if, for example, one wishes to make the same type of comparisons as described in *3* above, but where the measure of concern has an appreciable correlation with sex of examinee).

The term *examinee* included in the definition may refer to any type of well-defined sampling unit such as an individual, a classroom, a school, a school district, a geographic region, etc. The question, "Are the eighth grade students currently living in the state of Delaware reading above the national norm?" requires the comparison of some summary measure of the Delaware eighth grade student performance (e.g., the median) with the distribution of similarly defined summary measures of eighth grade reading scores in the various states comprising the norm population. Here, each state is regarded as an examinee and the average score of a state is taken as the measure of examinee performance. Regardless of the type of sampling unit involved, one fact which should be obvious is that a particular score has as many normative interpretations as there are norm groups with which to compare it. Thus, the selection of an appropriate norm group is necessary for a valid interpretation of any norm-referenced test score. Even if the reliability and validity credentials of a test are impeccable, referencing a test score to an inappropriate norm population will result in an invalid interpretation of that score.[2]

CONSIDERATIONS IN EVALUATING NORMS

In evaluating normative data, consideration must be given to (a) the definition and relevance of the norm population, (b) the procedure used to construct the norm sample, and (c) the usability of the norms.

First of all, the norm population must be well-defined, i.e., it must be possible to tell who does and does not belong to the norm population. Unless this is the case, there exists no adequate basis for determining the appropriateness of the norms for any given measurement application.

Second, because of time, expense and other factors, it is frequently impractical or impossible to administer a test to every member of a norm population. When this is the case, normative data must be obtained from a *representative* sample of the norm population. By representative, we mean that the sample resembles the population from which it was drawn in all relevant and

---

2. A common problem associated with norm-referenced classroom achievement testing is that individual student test scores are interpreted relative to the distribution of scores generated by the class in which they hold membership. As a result, an average student may be evaluated (and, hence, graded) as either "below average," "average," or "above average" depending solely on the caliber of his classmates. (This is one of the compelling reasons for seriously considering a criterion-referenced approach to the measurement of achievement in the classroom.)

important respects. Since various textbooks provide detailed directions for constructing representative samples (see, for example, Stuart, 1962), those technical details are not discussed here. However, several relevant observations are in order before leaving this topic.

Many people erroneously believe that the size of the norm sample is the most important consideration in its evaluation. While certain minimal sample size requirements must be met in constructing a norm sample, the primary consideration in evaluating its quality is *representativeness.* Consequently, a national norm sample must be based on an adequate description of the national population, i.e., U.S. census data. Please note that since (a) such data are collected only at ten year intervals, and (b) the population of the United States is a transient and rapidly changing one, even the most recent census data may be inadequate several years after compilation. At a minimum, population changes would seem to dictate the renorming of tests every five to ten years, or sooner wherever feasible.

Also, publishers of standardized tests sometimes publish norms based on arbitrarily defined samples. In using that kind of normative data for test score interpretation, the test user should realize that the population represented by such a sample is strictly a hypothetical one and may not be appropriate to the test user's goals.

Finally, one must consider the usability of the norms. Some types of test score interpretation require conversion tables while other types require individual difference score norms (as, for example, in studies of student growth or change) or individual profile data. The level of sophistication of the potential user of normative data as well as the manner in which the test scores are to be interpreted bear directly on the usability issue.

In evaluating any norm-referenced test, the definition and relevance of the norm population, the representativeness of the norm sample, and the usability of the normative data are all important considerations. Since any one test may be used for many purposes (e.g., assigning students to classes within a school, selecting applicants for admission to graduate school, diagnosing aptitude or achievement deficits), the norm population appropriate for one purpose may be totally unsuitable for another. In some cases, national norms are required; in other cases, regional, local or user-defined norms are most suitable. Further consideration of selected types of norms is the focus of the next section.

SELECTED TYPES OF NORMS

In this section, we briefly examine several types of norms.[3] For convenience, this is done in the context of achievement testing.

National Norms

Perhaps the most frequently encountered and most frequently used are national norms, i.e., norms based on the test performances of a well-defined national sample

---

3. See Angoff (1971) for a detailed discussion of the various types of norms.

of examinees. If such a norm sample were available for a particular standardized measure of reading achievement, it would consist of data reflecting not only a national cross section of individuals at a given age or grade level, but a national cross section of reading programs as well. Therefore, the use of the national norms in an achievement testing context implies that one is chiefly interested in determining how pupils in program X fare on this test when compared to pupils exposed to a wide variety of programs. While national norms are usually appropriate and meaningful in interpreting intelligence and special aptitude test scores, they are frequently inappropriate in an achievement context unless the important question concerns cross-program comparisons.

Local Norms

Frequently, local school personnel (e.g., teachers, counselors, administrators) are interested in how pupils in their school or district, all of whom receive essentially the same educational treatment (i.e., they are in the same educational program, attending the same school or university, or residing in the same school or political district) compare with each other. In such a case, locally developed, user-defined norms are relevant; national norms are not. Since such norms are quite useful for grouping students by ability or achievement level, identifying exceptionally "slow" and "fast" learners, etc., the development of such norms frequently justifies their cost.

Classroom Norms

One type of local norm which deserves special attention is the classroom variety. Because of philosophical or practical reasons, norm-referenced classroom achievement testing may be appropriate. In many physical education activities, competition is an integral part of achievement; hence, norm-referenced measurement techniques in such a setting are philosophically justifiable. Also, there are many subject matter areas where the specification of masterable objectives is difficult, or perhaps impossible, given the present state of the art, e.g., courses in poetry, painting, and other fine arts. In such cases, norm-referenced measurement techniques are defensible on practical grounds. In any event, the student's class (with him included) serves as the norm group against which his performance is compared. Because of the dependency of an individual's assessment on the rather fortuitous composition of the class to which he belongs, this procedure is not recommended except where justifications of the type noted above exist.

Conclusion and Final Comments

It seems appropriate to conclude this section with the following remarks:

1. Assuming the availability of a test having acceptable reliability and validity for measuring the characteristic of interest, and further assuming one is interested in interpreting individual scores, the choice of norms is largely dictated by the type of decision one is going to make using the test information. Several types of

decisions and their implications for norm selection were discussed in the previous several paragraphs. Using norms just because they are available is very poor measurement practice.

2. If the raw measurements (scores) correlate appreciably with age, sex, geographic region, etc., the norm population (be it national or local) should be stratified on such variables and separate norms compiled for each distinct subpopulation. In this way, one is able to compare the examinee's score with the most appropriately defined norm population to which he belongs. An added advantage to such a procedure is that it provides information about examinee performance independent of the variables used for stratification purposes.

3. There are times when one is interested in comparing a single student's performances in several academic areas, e.g., science vs. mathematics. To do this properly requires difference score norms, i.e., norms developed by (a) transforming raw scores to Z scores for each test separately, (b) calculating the difference score for each individual, and (c) transforming the results to a suitable scale. These types of norms are not usually available, and hence, profile comparisons like this are difficult to make. A very common practice is to interpret the difference between the available scores using the normative data which are available. This must be done cautiously because the opportunity for misinterpretation is appreciable. If such a technique is used, comparing interval estimates of two scores rather than point estimates tends to minimize the probability of gross misinterpretations. Additional material on the interpretation of profiles is contained in Gardner's article "Interpreting Achievement Profiles — Uses and Warnings" reprinted as Chapter 18 in this text.

4. Finally, the term *norm* is frequently encountered in statements like "School district X is below the national norm in reading." Statements like this one tend to be interpreted to mean that school district X is deficient in some important respect(s), e.g., reading program quality. There is no justification for this kind of interpretation unless it can be corroborated with other independent assessments of program quality. By definition, the term *norm* refers to the arithmetic mean (or the median) of the norm population distribution and, hence, approximately one-half of the examinees in the norm population must be below the norm. It is patently absurd to conclude that being below the norm necessarily implies an important deficit.

We conclude this chapter by examining two examples of norms tables from a standardized test manual.

EXAMPLES OF NORMS TABLES FROM A STANDARDIZED TEST MANUAL

In this section, we present selected information from one standardized test manual to illustrate some of the forms commonly used to present normative data. Tables 11-1 and 11-2 show the percentile rank and stanine conversion tables appearing in the technical manual for forms A and B of the Metropolitan Readiness Tests, a test designed "... to measure the extent to which school beginners have developed in the several skills and abilities that contribute to readiness for first-grade

TABLE 11-1. *Percentile Ranks Corresponding* to Beginning-First-Grade Total Scores on Form A or Form B.*

Total Score	Percentile Rank	Total Score	Percentile Rank
Above 88	99+		
86–88	99	49	38
84–85	98	48	36
82–83	97	47	35
81	96	46	33
80	95	45	31
79	94	44	29
78	93	43	27
77	92	42	26
76	91	41	25
75	89	40	23
74	88	39	22
73	86	38	20
72	84	37	19
71	83	36	17
70	81	35	16
69	79	34	15
68	77	33	14
67	75	32	13
66	73	31	12
65	71	29–30	11
64	69	28	10
63	67	27	9
62	65	26	8
61	63	24–25	7
60	61	23	6
59	59	21–22	5
58	57	19–20	4
57	55	17–18	3
56	53	14–16	2
55	51	9–13	1
54	48	Below 9	1–
53	46		
52	44		
51	42		
50	40		

* Reproduced from the *Metropolitan Reading Tests* copyright © 1965 by Harcourt, Brace, and Jovanovich, Inc. Reproduced by special permission.

TABLE 11-2. *Stanine Level Corresponding to Total Score on Form A or Form B.* *

Total Score	Stanine
81–102	9
76– 80	8
69– 75	7
61– 68	6
51– 60	5
41– 50	4
30– 40	3
21– 29	2
Below 21	1

* Reproduced from *Metropolitan Reading Tests*, copyright © 1965 by Harcourt, Brace, and Jovanovich, Inc. Reproduced by special permission.

instruction" (Hildreth *et al.*, 1969, p. 2). According to these tables, a raw score of 70 is equivalent to a percentile rank of 81 and a stanine score of 7. This indicates that a child obtaining a score of 70 has performed as well as or better than 81% of the children *in the norm sample.* Whether this information is meaningful or not depends upon the particular application.

SUMMARY

In this chapter, we defined the term *norms* as it is used in an educational measurement context, examined a number of factors which must be considered in evaluating or constructing norms, differentiated among several useful classes of norms, and briefly examined two examples of norms tables taken from a standardized test technical manual. Additional information concerning the use and misuse of norms can be found in the articles by Gardner and Deutsch *et al.* reprinted as Chapter 18 in this text.

SELF-EVALUATION

1. In educational measurement, the term *norms* usually refers to
   a. An absolute standard against which a score is compared for interpretive purposes.
   b. A record of a population of scores against which an individual score is compared for interpretive purposes.

2. In constructing a norm sample, one's goal should be _____ .
   a. obtaining as large a sample as possible
   b. constructing as representative a sample as possible
   c. the use of a random sampling procedure
   d. either a, b, or c because they are equivalent

3. If one is interested in comparing the achievement of public school students in District X with students in a cross section of schools having different organizational structures, philosophies, and/or curricula, _____ norms are most appropriate.
   a. national   b. local   c. classroom

4. Norm-referenced assessment of pupil achievement leading to a report card grade is typically based on _____ norms.
   a. national   b. local   c. classroom

5. _____ norms are most appropriate for evaluating a candidate's application to XYZ University.
   a. national   b. local   c. classroom

6. According to Table 11-1, an individual obtaining a total raw score of 75 on the Metropolitan Readiness Test has done as well as or better than _____% of the norm group. The stanine equivalent of this is _____ .

ANSWER KEY

1. b	4. c
2. b	5. b
3. a	6. 89; 9

REFERENCES

Angoff, W. H. (1971). Scales, Norms, and Equivalent Scores, in *Educational Measurement* (R. L. Thorndike, ed.), 2nd ed., Washington, D.C.: American Council on Education.

Hildreth, G. H., N. L. Griffiths, and M. E. McGauvran (1969). *Manual of Directions for Metropolitan Readiness Tests (Forms A and B)*. New York: Harcourt, Brace, and World.

Stuart, A. (1962). *Basic Ideas of Scientific Sampling*. New York: Hafner.

12

Norm-Referenced Item Analysis

Item analysis is a systematic examination of the responses of a group of examinees to the items in a test. The purposes of item analysis are twofold: (a) to assess the quality of test items and (b) to detect the existence of student content deficiencies or misunderstandings. In the discussion which follows, we describe and illustrate a procedure for extracting information from examinee performance on a norm-referenced test item and indicate how such information is used to accomplish the two purposes stated above. Although this procedure is appropriately used with all norm-referenced tests, it is examined within the multiple-choice achievement test context primarily because (a) a great deal of information regarding item quality and/or instructional (or learning) problems is accessible when this procedure and multiple-choice items are used in concert, and (b) this approach gives us the opportunity to examine some of the problems encountered when the procedure is used to assess the adequacy of criterion-referenced test items. In the following discussion, we define and illustrate two important concepts (*p*-level and discrimination power) and a useful item performance summary device (the item response chart). We then simulate the analysis of two hypothetical items using a procedure based on these components. We begin with a discussion of the item *p*-level.

THE ITEM *p*-LEVEL

The *p-level* (frequently called the *difficulty level*) of an item for a particular examinee group is the proportion of correct responses made to that item by the members of that group. To calculate the *p*-level (or difficulty level) for any item, divide the number of examinees selecting the keyed correct response by the total number of examinees in the group.

For example, suppose 25 students responded to a particular multiple-choice item with the following result: 20 students chose the correct alternative, 3 students chose incorrect alternatives, and 2 students failed to respond. The p-level for this item *in this examinee group* is 20/25, or 0.80. Since the p-level is a proportion, p values are always contained in the interval 0.00 to 1.00, inclusive. The closer the value of p is to 1.00, the easier the item; the closer p is to 0.00, the more difficult the item. Therefore, one must conclude that this item is relatively easy for this group of examinees. (It is worth emphasizing at this point that the p-level, like all other norm-referenced measurement statistics, is group specific. The p-level for a particular test item may differ considerably across examinee groups. For example, suppose a problem in adding fractions having unlike denominators was given to two groups of students differing in past mathematical achievement, say an accelerated seventh grade class and a "slow" seventh grade class in the same school. Would you expect the p-level for that item to be the same for each group? Of course not! Therefore, the interpretation of an item p-level must take into account the characteristics of the group to which the item was administered).

In a norm-referenced framework, the test constructor tries to write items with p-levels near 0.50. The reason is that an item's ability to discriminate between the more and less knowledgeable students depends on variability. Recall from the discussion of KR20 (see Chapter 9) that the variance of an item distribution (where the response to an item is scored 1 if it is correct and 0 otherwise) is the product of p and $1 - p$. If $p = 0.50$, then $p(1 - p) = 0.5\,(0.5) = 0.25$. As the value of p approaches 0 or 1, the value of $p(1 - p)$ approaches 0. Thus, the closer an item p-level is to 0.50, the greater the variance in the distribution of scores on that item. While the maximization of item variability does not guarantee that it will discriminate among examinees as desired, it is clear that items displaying little or no variation in examinee performance cannot perform the discrimination function so necessary in norm-referenced measurement. From a classical, norm-referenced measurement viewpoint, items having p-levels close to 0 or 1 are deadwood. Such items are ordinarily not included in norm-referenced tests unless there are other compelling reasons to do so, as in cases where (a) an item measures the acquisition of an important fact, concept, etc., (b) the test is designed to measure examinee performance in a skill or knowledge hierarchy, or (c) the test is to be used to describe student achievement in a particular content domain. Since it is impossible to write items having the "ideal" p-level, the prevailing practice in norm-referenced test construction is to attempt to generate items which will have p-levels in the 0.30–0.70 range.

In concluding this discussion of the item p-level, it is interesting to contrast the implications of various values of p within the norm-referenced and criterion-referenced frameworks. If an item has a p-level greater than 0.70 (or less than 0.30), the norm-referenced examiner typically asks "Why is that item so easy (or difficult)?" and begins to study the item to find the answer. In a criterion-referenced framework, the test constructor tries to write items which measure examinee status in a well-defined content domain or achievement of the stated instructional objectives. On a test following instruction relevant to the content domain (or instructional objectives), he expects the item p-levels to be high. After all, if the content is masterable (or the objectives are attainable) and the instructor was high quality, it is quite reasonable to expect most students to pass most of the items. In this context, the test constructor is most disturbed when the item p-levels are not close to 1.00. In other words, a p-level of 0.50 would cause him to ask "Why did so many students miss this item?"

ITEM DISCRIMINATION POWER

Item discrimination power refers to an item's ability to differentiate (or discriminate) between the examinees performing well on the test as a whole and the examinees performing poorly on the test as a whole. In other words, an item is a good discriminator if performance on the item is positively correlated with performance on the entire test. This is the single most important characteristic of a norm-referenced test item. Norm-referenced test items which do not discriminate or which correlate negatively with total test performance reduce the amount of variability in the total test score distribution and, hence, adversely affect test reliability and validity. Therefore, it is good test construction practice to revise or replace such items if the test is to be reused at a later time.

Two commonly used discrimination indexes are the item-test point biserial correlation coefficient (see Chapter 6) and a statistic called D. The first of these is just the Pearson correlation coefficient used to measure the degree of correlation between student performance on an item and student performance on the total test. It is somewhat laborious to compute without the aid of a calculator; therefore, simpler indexes like D have been devised for use by the classroom teacher. In this unit, we limit our attention to D as the measure of an item's discrimination power.

The procedure for calculating D for a particular test item is as follows:

1. Rank-order all test papers from the highest total test score to the lowest total test score. Separate the papers into three groups containing the highest 27%, middle 46%, and lowest 27% of the scores, respectively.
2. Find the proportion of persons in the top 27% group who answered the item correctly. Call this value p_U. Notice that this is simply the item p-level for the upper group.
3. Find the proportion of persons in the lower 27% of the total test distribution who answered the item correctly. Call this value p_L.
4. $D = p_U - p_L$

Where relatively small examinee groups are the rule, as in the typical classroom situation, use 50% instead of 27%. That is, after ordering the papers according to the total test score, divide it into just two stacks, each containing one half of the papers. Then follow steps 2 through 4 outlined above with the value 50% replacing the value 27% in each case.

Like its point biserial correlation counterpart, the limits of D are -1.00 and $+1.00$. A positive D value indicates the item is discriminating, more or less, like the whole test. A negative D value indicates just the opposite, i.e., people having low scores on the total test tend to get the item correct, while those scoring high on the total test tend to select incorrect responses for the item. Often, this is the mark of a defective item, i.e., one that either is misinterpreted by the more knowledgeable student or provides a clue to the less knowledgeable (and, therefore, clue-seeking) examinee. A near zero value indicates the item lacks discrimination power. In norm-referenced testing, D values greater than 0.20 are usually desirable.

As defined here, D is a very useful index in norm-referenced situations. Because of its dependence on variability in examinee performance, however, it is not very useful and may be misleading if used in analyzing performance on criterion-referenced test items. Finally, as in the case of the item p-level, the value for D in a given examinee group is specific to that group.

THE ITEM RESPONSE CHART

An item response chart is a table showing the number of examinees in the upper 27%, middle 46%, and lower 27% (or upper 50% and lower 50%) of the total test score distribution selecting each option to a particular multiple-choice test item. An example based on the responses of 200 examinees to one 3-option multiple-choice item is given in Table 12-1. Notice, the bottom row of that table indicates that 150 examinees selected the keyed corrected alternative a, 10 examinees selected alternative b, 35 examinees selected c, and 5 examinees did not respond to this item. At a glance, the item appears to be relatively easy

TABLE 12-1. *Example of an Item Response Chart for a 3-Option, Multiple-Choice Item.***

Position in Test Score Distribution	Option			No Response	Total
	a*	*b*	*c*		
Upper 27%	40	4	8	2	54
Middle 46%	80	2	7	3	92
Lower 27%	30	4	20	0	54
Total	150	10	35	5	200

* *a* is the keyed correct response.
** *Item.* Suppose test score distribution A has a mean equal to 50 and a variance equal to 100 while test score distribution B has a mean equal to 75 and a standard deviation of 20. One must then conclude that distribution A is _____ distribution B.
  (a) less variable than
  (b) more variable than
  (c) as variable as

$(p = 150/200 = 0.75)$ and a positive, but somewhat weak, discriminator $(D = p_U - p_L = 40/54 - 30/54 = 10/54 = +0.19)$. In addition, distracter c appears to be doing its job while b is not. Based on this information, a reasonable course of action would be to first examine the item to see if these results are due to some item flaw or defect (e.g., perhaps option b is grammatically inconsistent with the stem, or option a contains a clue which is used by many of the poor achievers). If one or more defects were found, the appropriate action would be to revise the item. If the item appeared to be sound, the appropriate action would be to seek an explanation in the content and instructional procedures to which this item is related. Once this is done, a decision regarding the future use of this item in its present form can be made. Please note that this type of chart would not be very useful in a criterion-referenced situation because of its dependence on variability in the total test score distribution. A modified version of this chart based on a division of the examinees into mastery and nonmastery groups would possibly be more informative.

Let us conclude this discussion with the analysis of a multiple-choice item in the area of educational measurement. Suppose the item was administered as part of a larger test to 100 students and the data shown in Table 12-2 were obtained.

The p-level for this item is $28/100 = 0.28$; the value of D is $15/27 - 2/27 = 13/27 = +0.50$, approximately. These two indicators tell us that the item is performing acceptably. However, the relatively low p-level and the distribution of responses to the item shown in this chart suggest the existence in our examinee group of two possible misconceptions about the effect of group homogeneity on the magnitude of a correlation coefficient. This is very useful information to a classroom teacher because it suggests that a reexamination of the instruction related to this concept is in order. Notice, however, using norm-referenced test

TABLE 12-2. *Item Response Chart for a Hypothetical Multiple-Choice Test Item in Educational Measurement.***

Position in Test Score Distribution	Option			No Response	Total
	a	b	$c*$		
Upper 27%	6	5	15	1	27
Middle 46%	15	20	11	0	46
Lower 27%	12	11	2	2	27
Total	33	36	28	3	100

* c is the keyed correct response.
** *Item.* Suppose the value of $r(IQ, SES) = +0.30$ for the 20-year-old students at Foggy Bottom University. The value of $r(IQ, SES)$ among the entire population of 20-year-olds would most likely be _____ +0.30.
    (a) less than
    (b) about equal to
    (c) greater than

information this way leads one into a dilemma. Improving performance on the item (through improved instruction) will ultimately result in a high p-level and near zero D value, thus, converting the item into psychometric deadwood. If one is wed to the norm-referenced approach, this item would then have to be replaced or revised and the entire cycle would begin again. The criterion-referenced achievement examiner does not have to contend with this problem.

SUMMARY AND FINAL COMMENTS

In this chapter we defined item analysis, described its utility, and presented a procedure for analyzing norm-referenced test items. Several final comments concerning norm-referenced item analysis seem in order.

1. p-levels and D values should not be used mechanically in selecting or evaluating the worth of test items. Remember, there are perfectly legitimate reasons for including some items in a norm-referenced test which are weak discriminators.
2. The p-level, D, and the item response chart are just one facet of item analysis. A complete analysis requires the evaluation of information provided by these three summary devices vis-à-vis the nature of the examinee group, and the test items and instructional activities related to these indexes.
3. The stability of p and D for a particular item depends upon the size and composition of the groups to which the item is administered. Ideally, item analysis should be carried out using a large sample (several hundred examinees) which is very heterogeneous with respect to the characteristic (i.e., ability, knowledge, etc.) the item is designed to measure. Since this is not possible in most classroom situations, an appropriate measure of caution and common sense should be employed when doing an item analysis.

EXERCISE SET 12-1

Items 1–3 are based on the following response chart for one multiple-choice item (option c is correct).

	Options			
	a	b	c	d
Upper Group	10	1	30	9
Lower Group	5	15	20	10

1. The p-level for this item is _____ .
2. The D value for this item is _____ .
3. What does the pattern of responses tell you about the quality of this test item?

4. The table below shows the response charts for three multiple-choice items. The distributions are shown for the top and bottom half of a class.

Item	Group	A	B	C	D	No Response
#1	High	40*	3	0	7	0
	Low	37*	5	6	0	2
#2	High	22	0	20*	7	1
	Low	9	0	30*	9	2
#3	High	0	40*	0	8	2
	Low	0	25*	0	20	5

* Keyed correct response.

a. Calculate the difficulty index for each item.
b. Calculate the discrimination index for each item.
c. What item revisions are suggested by analysis of these patterns, assuming a norm-referenced framework?

SELF-EVALUATION

1. The p-level of a dichotomously scored test item (e.g., an item scored 1 for a correct response and 0 otherwise) is the proportion of examinees who
   a. answered the item correctly.
   b. answered the item incorrectly.
   c. answered the item correctly and passed the test.
   d. answered the item incorrectly and passed the test.

2. If 40 students are given an achievement test and $p = 0.30$ for item number seven in that test, we must conclude that _____ students answered item seven correctly.
   a. 40   b. 30   c. 12

3. An item p-level of 0.90 means the item is _____ .
   a. very difficult
   b. moderately difficult
   c. very easy

4. The point biserial correlation and D are both appropriate measures of _____ in a norm-referenced context.
   a. item difficulty
   b. item discrimination power

5. In a norm-referenced test, extremely easy and extremely difficult items tend to be _____ discriminators.
   a. good   b. fair   c. poor

6. Items which do not discriminate between "good" and "poor" students _____ variability and, hence, _____ test reliability
   a. reduce, reduce
   b. reduce, increase
   c. increase, reduce
   d. increase, increase

Base the answers to items 7 and 8 on the following table.

Position in Test Score Distribution	Option				
	a	b	c*	d	Total
Upper 27%	7	3	40	4	54
Middle 46%	9	12	80	11	112
Lower 27%	20	5	10	19	54

* Keyed correct response.

7. The p-level and D index for this item are _____ and _____, respectively.
8. This response chart indicates that the item on which it is based is _____ .

   a. too difficult for the examinees represented in this table
   b. not discriminating adequately and, hence, must be revised
   c. functioning properly and does not appear to require revision

9. *True or False.* The response pattern in the table shown below suggests that option c may be the correct response and the item has been miskeyed.

Position in Test Score Distribution	Option					
	a*	b	c	d	e	Total
Upper 50%	0	5	15	0	0	20
Lower 50%	1	2	10	4	3	20

* Keyed correct response.

10. *True or False.* An item having a p-level of either 0.00 or 1.00 must have a D index equal to 0.00.

ANSWER KEY

1. a	7. 0.59, 0.56
2. c	8. c
3. c	9. True (The popularity of
4. b	option c suggests that it may
5. c	be the correct response.)
6. a	10. True

EXERCISE SET 12-1: ANSWERS

1. 0.50
2. +0.20
3. The p-level and D values are acceptable, but the response chart shows that option a attracted more upper than lower group examinees. Therefore, option a should be examined to see if the reason for this can be determined.
4. a. 0.77; 0.50; 0.65
   b. +0.06; −0.20; +0.30
   c. Item 1 does not discriminate between upper and lower groups; therefore, it provides no useful information about examinees. It should be examined.

   Item 2 discriminates negatively. It probably needs to be revised. Option b is useless because it attracts no one. Option a attracts too many examinees in the high group and, therefore, ought to be checked.

   Item 3 is a good discriminator and ought to be retained. However, options a and c are not very appealing and probably ought to be replaced or deleted.

13

A Taxonomy of Cognitive Instructional Objectives and Test Items

In preparing a test construction plan (or a plan for instruction), a useful first step is to develop a set of objectives which can then be used as a guide for test construction and/or lesson planning. In an instructional context, such objectives are frequently translated into questions which may then be used by the teacher to stimulate classroom discussion or to obtain a rough assessment of student status at different stages of a lesson. In a test construction situation, the objectives are usually used as a basis for generating test questions which are then used to measure student achievement of those objectives. Among the factors to be considered in formulating a set of objectives are (a) the subject matter (i.e., information) to which the objectives (or questions) relate and (b) the mental operations the examinee (or student) must use in order to achieve the objectives (or answer the questions).

The subject matter to be acquired can be broken down into definitions, facts, principles, generalizations, etc. As conceptualized by Benjamin Bloom (1956) and his colleagues, the mental operations can be grouped into a small number of simple-to-complex, hierarchically-ordered categories: knowledge, comprehension, application, analysis, synthesis, and evaluation. (Hierarchical order means that a given level of mental activity, e.g., application, involves all of the lower level activities also, e.g., knowledge and comprehension.)

In this chapter a highly simplified version of *Bloom's Taxonomy* is presented.[1] Each category is defined and examples of correctly classified

---

1. The organization and format of this chapter are patterned after those employed in a mimeo handout entitled "Synopsis of Taxonomy of Questions," which I came across several years ago. Unfortunately, that document did not bear the author's name and, hence, I am unable to give proper credit at this time.

elementary school questions are provided. Careful examination of the definitions and examples should help the student see the hierarchical relationship *presumed* to exist among the levels of this taxonomy.[2]

KNOWLEDGE

A *knowledge* level (or *memory* level) item measures the student's ability to recall or recognize information (e.g., terminology, facts, principles, problem-solving strategies) in essentially the same form as it was presented to him. The essential student behavior elicited by questions at this level is remembering. At all higher levels of the taxonomy, remembering is only one of several behaviors required to successfully answer the items presented to the student. Consider the following examples:

1. PRIOR LEARNING CONDITIONS: The students have been told that George Washington was the first president of the United States.

   QUESTION: Who was the first president of the United States?

2. PRIOR LEARNING CONDITIONS: The students have been given the definitions of "solid," "liquid," and "gas," and shown several examples of each.

   QUESTION: The teacher holds up one of the objects used as an example of a solid and asks, "Is this a solid, liquid, or gas?"
   (*Note:* If the teacher held up a solid object not used previously as an example of a solid and asked the same question, the taxonomic level of the question would be higher.)

3. PRIOR LEARNING CONDITIONS: The teacher has outlined the procedure for constructing an isosceles triangle.

   QUESTION: List the steps necessary for constructing an isosceles triangle.

COMPREHENSION

Comprehension level items measure understanding at the most rudimentary level. Items at this level measure the student's ability to use previously acquired information to solve a novel problem. A key feature of measurement at this level

---

2. Bloom and his colleagues point out that the taxonomy under consideration appears to be a hierarchy, but before it may be regarded as such, empirical evidence is required. While it is possible to use the taxonomy to produce hierarchical sets of items [see, for example, R. B. Smith, A Discussion of an Attempt at Constructing Reproducible Item Sets, *Journal of Educational Measurement*, 1968, 5(1), pp. 55–60], research evidence currently available falls considerably short of verifying the existence of a strict hierarchical relationship among the levels of this taxonomy.

is that *the item or the context in which it is asked is structured in such a way that the student is made aware of the information required to solve the problem.* In other words, items at this level are designed to find out whether the student can solve a novel problem if some clue is given about the information to be used.

Examples of questions which exactly fit this general comprehension definition are given later in the section which deals with application items. At this point examples are provided for two subclasses of the comprehension level which are sufficiently different from the general definition that special treatment of them seems required. These two subclasses are *translation and interpretation.* In the complete version of the taxonomy, there is a third subclass called extrapolation which is not included in the following presentation. The reader is referred to Bloom (1956) for information concerning extrapolation-type items.

Translation

A *translation* item measures the student's ability to paraphrase a communication or present it in a different symbolic form (i.e., a foreign language, mathematical notation, etc.), or to recognize paraphrases or symbolic form changes. Consider the following examples:

1. PRIOR LEARNING CONDITIONS: The student has read a paragraph in the textbook.

   QUESTION: Now tell me in your own words what you read.

2. PRIOR LEARNING CONDITIONS: The students have just viewed a film showing a volcanic eruption.

   QUESTION: Write a short story describing the volcanic eruption shown in the film you just saw.

3. PRIOR LEARNING CONDITIONS: The students have been shown (by example) that the area of a rectangle is obtained by multiplying the length of the figure by its width.

   QUESTION: Using the letters x for area, y for length, and z for width, write the formula for calculating the area of a rectangle.

Interpretation

Interpretation level items usually measure the student's ability to make an inference based on the information in a communication, to explain what is meant by the communication, or to summarize the information in the communication. Interpretation level items differ from translation level items in that they require more than just a part-for-part transformation of the communication. Consider the following examples:

1. PRIOR LEARNING CONDITIONS: The math teacher has taught his students how to read simple line graphs. He presents them with the following material:

Miss Barker decided to find out if John could memorize the names of the 50 states better than Mary. To do this, she used the following procedure:

One day she tested John and Mary to find out how many names of states they could remember. (This test is called a *pretest*.) Then, John and Mary practiced the whole list three times. Each practice period was ten minutes long. At the end of each practice period, both students were tested to see how many names they could remember. (A test which follows a practice period is called a *posttest*.) John's and Mary's scores on each test were the number of state names each remembered. Miss Barker used these scores to make the graph shown below.

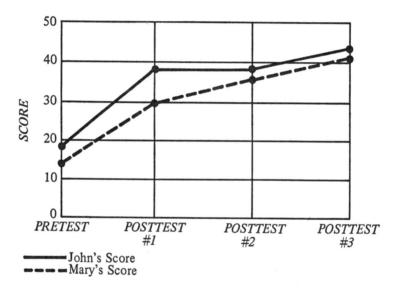

FIGURE 13-1. *John's and Mary's Scores on four tests.*

QUESTION: (*True or False*) After the first five minutes of practice, Mary probably knew more than 30 state names.

QUESTION: (*True or False*) Learning the names of states seems to improve with practice.

2. PRIOR LEARNING CONDITIONS: The sixth grade class has just completed reading and discussing a number of newspaper and magazine articles on the state of the national economy.

QUESTION: Write a short paper summarizing our discussions of the national economy.

APPLICATION

An *application* item, like the comprehension item, requires the student to use previously acquired information in solving a novel problem. *Unlike the comprehension item, however, neither the question nor the context in which it is asked helps the student decide what previously acquired information must be used to solve the problem.* Questions at this level are aimed at determining whether the student is able to select the appropriate knowledge as well as use it correctly in solving the novel problem. Consider the following examples:

1. PRIOR LEARNING CONDITIONS: In language arts class, the students have just learned how to use a dictionary.

   QUESTION: (in history class) What does the following statement mean, "James Buchanan approached his presidential duties in a perfunctory manner"?

2. PRIOR LEARNING CONDITIONS: Early in an advanced eighth grade math class, the students are taught how to solve simple systems of linear equations.

   QUESTION: (on the final exam) John can mow one acre of lawn in six hours, and Sam can mow half an acre in four hours. How long would it take John and Sam to mow one-quarter of an acre working together? (*Note:* The question would have measured comprehension if asked when problems of this type were being studied or if prefaced with the statement, "Use one of the methods you learned for solving systems of linear equations to find the answer to the following problem.")

3. PRIOR LEARNING CONDITIONS: In language arts class, the students have just learned how to use the school library card catalog.

   QUESTION: (by the history teacher) Find a book written by Cotton Mather in the school library. (*Note:* This would have been a comprehension level question if prefaced by "Using the library card catalog" or if it were asked by the language arts teacher during or soon after instruction in using the card catalog.)

ANALYSIS

An *analysis* level item may require the student to (a) identify a logical error in a communication (e.g., a contradiction, an error in deduction, an erroneous causal inference) or (b) identify, classify, and/or recognize the relationships among the elements (i.e., facts, assumptions, hypotheses, conclusions, ideas, etc.) in a communication. Items at this level usually assume specific training in the logical process to be used. Consider the following examples:

1. PRIOR LEARNING CONDITIONS: A primary school teacher explained to her class that some ideas do not go together (contradiction). For example, it is silly to believe a man is both tall and short.

QUESTION: What is silly or funny about this story?

Johnny had one dime. He went to the grocery store and spent the dime to buy candy. Next he went to the drug store and spent the dime for a comic book. After this he was tired so he went home and put the dime in his piggy bank.

2. PRIOR LEARNING CONDITIONS: The teacher has explained the logic of deductive arguments.

QUESTION: What is wrong with this argument? All men are mortal. JoJo is mortal.   Therefore, JoJo must be a man.

3. PRIOR LEARNING CONDITIONS: The students are instructed to watch a 15-minute film on the effects of pollution on our environment.

QUESTION: List all of the statements made by people in the film about the effects of pollution on the environment.   Underline each statement which is based on fact. Do not mark the statements which are opinions.

SYNTHESIS

A *synthesis* level item requires the student to create (a) a unique verbal or nonverbal communication (e.g., a story about a personal experience, an extemporaneous speech, a poster showing the evils of drug abuse), or (b) a plan or procedure for accomplishing a particular task (e.g., designing a simple experiment to test an interesting hypothesis, formulating a plan for erecting a tent).   Consider the following examples:

1. PRIOR LEARNING CONDITIONS: The fourth grade class has just returned from a field trip to a dairy farm.

QUESTION: Pretend you live on a farm like the one you just visited, and write a story about what you would do on days off from school.

2. PRIOR LEARNING CONDITIONS: The students have been shown Modigliani's painting, "Gypsy Woman with Baby."

QUESTION: Write a short story telling about the place where the woman and baby shown in this picture live.

3 PRIOR LEARNING CONDITIONS: The students have read in their science text that every action produces an equal and opposite reaction.

QUESTION: How can we experimentally demonstrate the principle that "Every action has an equal and opposite reaction?"

An *evaluation* level item requires the student to judge the value of ideas, people, products, methods, etc. for a specific purpose and state *valid* reasons for his judgment. Consider the following examples:

1. PRIOR LEARNING CONDITIONS: The students have just read the story of "Jack and the Beanstalk."

    QUESTION: Do you think Jack did the right thing when he took the gold, the harp, and the chicken from the giant? Why?

2. PRIOR LEARNING CONDITIONS: The students are shown two films, one about the need for additional oil production and one about the harmful ecological effects of oil spills.

    QUESTION: Do you think we ought to have more or less offshore oil exploration? Why?

3. PRIOR LEARNING CONDITIONS: The students have been considering the various alternatives proposed thus far for eliminating *de facto* school segregation.

    QUESTION: Do you think busing to achieve racial desegregation in our schools is a reasonable procedure? Why?

SUMMARY

In this chapter, we have examined a simplified version of *Bloom's Taxonomy*. Rather than classifying objectives, we concentrated on the classification of test questions given information about the student's level of knowledge or prior experience in the relevant content area(s). The reasons for this approach were (a) the nature of the hierarchy (especially at the lower levels) seemed easy to illustrate this way, (b) it stresses the need to consider the examinee's prior knowledge or experience in attempting to classify a question, and (c) skill in classifying questions should transfer rather directly to the task of classifying objectives.

In closing, it must be realized that this version of *Bloom's Taxonomy* is a substantial simplification of the original work, the reading of which would be quite profitable to the average teacher.

Check you comprehension of the material in this chapter using the self-evaluations provided for this purpose.

SELF-EVALUATION

Form A
Directions: This exercise consists of ten test items and a description of the prior learning conditions for each item. Identify the taxonomic level of each question.

1. PRIOR LEARNING CONDITIONS: The history class has been reading about the life and times of Benjamin Franklin.

   QUESTION: Franklin once said, "There was never a good war or a bad peace." Do you agree with this statement? Give reasons for your answer.

2. PRIOR LEARNING CONDITIONS: The sixth grade science class has just finished an experiment to determine whether adding fertilizer to the soil has any effect on plant growth. It was found that fertilized plants were larger and healthier than unfertilized plants. The teacher then asks the following question:

   QUESTION: Plan an experiment which would allow us to find out whether the proper use of toothpaste X results in 50% fewer cavities?

3. PRIOR LEARNING CONDITIONS: The science teacher has just demonstrated that the addition of salt to ice causes the ice to melt.

   QUESTION: Why does one put rock salt on the sidewalk on a winter morning as a safety measure?

4. PRIOR LEARNING CONDITIONS: The teacher shows the class a picture of two men loading hay onto a truck.

   QUESTION: What are the men in this picture doing?

5. PRIOR LEARNING CONDITIONS: A science class has been studying the process of inference.

   QUESTION: Both parts of the following statements are true. In each case tell whether the *second* part explains why the *first* part is true.
   a. Cows are mammals *because* they give milk.
   b. Trees are members of the plant kingdom *because* they are living things.

6. PRIOR LEARNING CONDITIONS: The teacher has told the class that an acid solution will turn blue litmus paper red, but will have no effect on red litmus paper.

   QUESTION: (*True or False*) An acid solution turns red litmus paper blue.

7. PRIOR LEARNING CONDITIONS: The fifth grade science class has finished a unit on ecology.

   QUESTION: Suppose you are the teacher. Make up a list of ten questions about water and air pollution.

8. PRIOR LEARNING CONDITIONS: The class has read that the steamboat was invented by Robert Fulton.

   QUESTION: Who invented the steamboat?

9. PRIOR LEARNING CONDITIONS: The sixth grade arithmetic class has just finished studying the associative law for addition.

   QUESTION: Express the following equality in words:

   $$(3 + 5) + 4 = 3 + (5 + 4)$$

10 PRIOR LEARNING CONDITIONS: The sixth grade social studies teacher has taught the students how to use an encyclopedia.

   QUESTION: (in geography class) Locate a topographical map of Oregon.

Form B

Directions: This exercise consists of ten test items and a description of the prior learning conditions for each item. Identify the taxonomic level of each question.

1. PRIOR LEARNING CONDITIONS: Ann is studying music composition in school.

   QUESTION: Write the words and music for a song celebrating the first day of spring.

2. PRIOR LEARNING CONDITIONS: The class has learned that addition of salt to water lowers the freezing point of water.

   QUESTION: Why does ocean water not freeze as quickly as drinking water in the winter?

3. PRIOR LEARNING CONDITIONS: The students know how to read line graphs. The science teacher displays the following graph to the class.

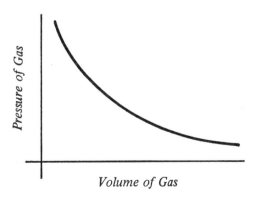

Volume of Gas

FIGURE 13-2. *The relationship of gas pressure to gas volume.*

QUESTION: When the pressure on a gas at constant temperature is increased, the volume of the gas _____.
a. increases
b. decreases
c. remains the same

4. PRIOR LEARNING CONDITIONS: The science class has been studying velocity and acceleration. The following table was constructed by the class after rolling a ball down an incline

Time (seconds)	0	1	2	3	4	5	6
Distance (feet)	0	1	4	9	16	25	36

QUESTION: Write a formula expressing the relationship between D and T.

5. PRIOR LEARNING CONDITIONS: The teacher has presented examples of "compounds" and "mixtures" during science class and has given definitions of these terms.

QUESTION: What is the definition of compound? of mixture?

6. PRIOR LEARNING CONDITIONS: The teacher in music class plays two recordings: one by the Boston Symphony, the other by the Beatles.

QUESTION: Which recording is the better one? Why?

7. PRIOR LEARNING CONDITIONS: The fourth grade has been working on a unit on map-reading and the teacher has just shown them how to use the "scale of miles."

QUESTION: How many miles is it from Boston to Philadelphia?

8. PRIOR LEARNING CONDITIONS: The class has been learning about analogies.

QUESTION: What is wrong with this analogy?

Dog : puppy :: horse : lamb

9. PRIOR LEARNING CONDITIONS: The science class has just completed a unit on "foods and health."

QUESTION: Make a poster illustrating the importance of a balanced diet to good health.

10. PRIOR LEARNING CONDITIONS: The sixth grade has been studying modern communication media. As part of its assignment, it was required to watch "Lassie" on a certain evening.

QUESTION: Imagine that you are the TV critic for the Evening Journal. Write a short critical review of the most recent episode of "Lassie." Give reasons for your favorable and unfavorable comments.

Form A

1. Evaluation
2. Synthesis
3. Comprehension (This item measures ability to use previously acquired information to solve a novel problem; the *context* is structured so that the student knows what information is required.)
4. Comprehension (The student is asked to present in verbal form a communication given pictorially.)
5. Analysis (The student is asked to identify an error in deduction.)
6. Knowledge
7. Synthesis
8. Knowledge
9. Comprehension (The student is asked to translate a communication from *one* symbolic form, *mathematical*, to another form, *verbal*.)
10. Application (Previously acquired information — how to use an encyclopedia — must be used to solve a novel problem. However, *neither* the question *nor* the context in which it is asked helps the student decide *what* information is to be used.)

Form B

1. Synthesis
2. Application (Previously acquired information — the fact that a solute, salt, lowers the freezing point of the solvent, water, must be used to solve a novel problem. However, the context in which the problem is posed is different; thus, the student must *select* the appropriate knowledge before using it to solve the problem.)
3. Comprehension (Translation from the *graphic* to the *verbal* mode of communication is called for.)
4. Analysis (The student is asked to recognize the relationship between time and distance.
5. Knowledge
6. Evaluation
7. Comprehension (The student is asked to infer the distance from Boston to Philadelphia based on the information on the map.)
8. Analysis (The student must identify a logical error in the analogy.)
9. Synthesis
10. Evaluation

REFERENCE

Bloom, B. S. (ed.) (1956). *Taxonomy of Educational Objectives: The Classification of Educational Goals, Handbook I: Cognitive Domain.* New York: David McKay.

14

The Traditional Approach
to Test Construction

The purpose of this chapter is to examine the traditional approach to test construction as it has evolved within the norm-referenced testing framework. Although this approach is quite general and has been used extensively in developing all types of tests, it is presented here within an achievement testing context. In this way, the present discussion not only supplies basic information concerning the traditional approach to test construction, but also provides a useful backdrop for the material in the next several chapters dealing with some recent approaches to test construction which have been developed almost exclusively within a criterion-referenced achievement testing context.

In subsequent sections of the present chapter, we examine topics related to (a) planning the test, (b) item writing, and (c) scoring. The essay and multiple-choice item formats are singled out for special attention in the item-writing portion of the discussion.

PLANNING THE ACHIEVEMENT TEST

Prior to the beginning of the criterion-referenced measurement movement, the recommended procedure for constructing an achievement test consisted of the following steps:

1. Making a content outline based on a thorough analysis of the content to be tested.

2. Making an objectives outline reflecting the goals the examinees were expected to achieve or a behavior outline reflecting the different ways in which the examinees were expected to process, manipulate or act on the content.
3. With the results of steps 1 and 2, constructing a content-*by*-objectives (or, alternatively, a content-*by*-process) matrix in which each intersection or cell represents a particular content-objective (or content-process) pairing.
4. Entering a numeral in each cell of the matrix to indicate the number (or percentage) of each type of item to be included in the test.

Two examples of the application of this technique are illustrated in Tables 14-1 and 14-2. In Table 14-1, the content dimension is defined in terms of 12 historical topics; the objectives dimension, in terms of eight objectives. The result is an eight-row *by* 12-column matrix containing 96 cells which presumably describe the universe or population of test items in which the examiner is interested. The numerals in the cells reflect either the assumed relative frequency of each item type in the hypothetical item population represented by this grid or the relative importance of each of the content-behavior (or content-objective) pairings.

Given the matrix shown in Table 14-1, the test constructor would proceed to write the number of items prescribed in each cell, e.g., two items which measure the examinee's "knowledge and understanding of historical terms related to Hellenic civilization," six items which measure the examinee's "ability to use 18th century historical maps," etc. This would continue until 300 "good" items, distributed as shown by the matrix, had been produced.

Similarly, Table 14-2 is the "blueprint" for a 100-item final examination in natural science. In this matrix, 10 content categories are paired with each of four objectives (or behavior) categories, where the latter represent the lowest four levels of Bloom's *Taxonomy*. As before, the numerals in the cells indicate the number of each item type to be produced by the test constructor.

Following construction of the test, content validity would be assessed by having content specialists judge (a) the adequacy of the matrix itself and (b) the "goodness-of-fit" of the test to the matrix on which it is based. Further checks on item quality and test adequacy might then be carried out with the aid of norm-referenced item analysis and test reliability statistics following a pilot administration of the test. In some cases, the pilot-testing statistical-analysis item revision procedure might be repeated several times before the test is declared to be in final form. Let us now take a closer look at some of the important considerations in item writing and test scoring.

EXERCISE SET 14-1

1. Table 14-1 calls for the production of _____ item(s) to measure examinee ability to recognize chronological relationships during the Renaissance.
2. Table 14-2 calls for the production of _____ items in all, _____ of which measure comprehension of cellular reproduction and mitosis.

TABLE 14-1.   A Two-Way Outline for an Examination in History of Civilization.

CONTENT / OBJECTIVES	I Nature of Civili-zation	II Hellenic Civili-zation	III Hellen-istic Civili-zation	IV Roman Civili-zation	V Medi-eval Civili-zation, the Church	VI Medi-eval Civili-zation, Feudal-ism	VII The Medi-eval Mind	VIII The Renais-sance	IX The Refor-mation	X The 18th Century	XI The French Revolu-tion	XII The Last Century	TOTAL
Knowledge and Understanding of													
1. Historical Terms	–	2	1	1	3	–	1	2	1	5	5	4	25
2. Cause-Effect Relationships	1	1	–	3	2	3	4	1	6	3	3	3	30
3. Motivating Ideals	–	1	–	1	6	5	6	1	10	3	1	7	41
4. Miscellaneous	9	11	4	6	4	6	12	9	5	8	11	13	98
Ability to													
5. Recognize Chronological Relationships	–	5	1	3	5	–	3	1	1	1	2	3	25
6. Use Historical Maps	–	–	2	1	2	1	–	2	1	6	3	5	23
7. Evaluate Differences in Civilizations	1	4	1	1	1	1	6	–	–	5	6	6	32
8. Read Historical Materials	–	–	–	5	–	6	–	5	–	–	–	10	26
TOTAL	11	24	9	21	23	22	32	21	24	31	31	51	300

NOTE: Reprinted by permission from Paul L. Dressel et al, *Comprehensive Examinations in a Program of General Education*.   East Lansing: Michigan State University Press, 1949, p. 91.

TABLE 14-2. *Two-Axis Chart of Specifications for a Final Examination in Natural Science — Term 1.*

Objectives[a] \ Course Content	Knowl-edge	Comprehension (Translation, Interpretation, Extrapolation)	Application	Analysis	Total
I. Perception, symboliza-tion, and the methods of science	5	5			10
II. The cell — structure and function; cell principle; spontaneous generation and biogenesis	5			5	10
III. sexual repro-duction in animals and plants; hu-man repro-duction and sex hormones	4	6			10
IV. Cellular re-production; mitosis	4	6			10
V. Meiosis; chro-mosomes and genes	3	3	4		10
VI. Monohybrid cross		4	6		10
VII. Dihybrid cross		3	3	4	10
VIII. Blood group inheritance; heredity in man		4	6		10
IX. linkage and crossing-over	3	3	4		10
X. Sex determi-nation and sex linkage	1	1	2	6	10
Total	25	35	25	15	100

a Based on *Taxonomy of Educational Objectives.* New York: Longmans, Green and Company, 1954.

NOTE: Reprinted by permission from Paul L. Dressel, Evaluation in Higher Education. Boston: Houghton Mifflin Company, 1961, p. 117.

Once the matrix or "blueprint" has been constructed, test items must be written. A question which arises immediately is whether one ought to use a constructed response-type item (i.e., one which literally requires the examinee to construct or generate a response, e.g., completion, essay) or a response selection-type item (i.e., one which requires the examinee to choose a subset of a larger set of possible correct or "best" responses, e.g., true-false or multiple choice). Although there are many types of constructed response and response selection item formats, we will restrict our attention to the most versatile and most popular in each class, i.e., essay and multiple choice. Regardless of the choice of item format, the following remark by Wesman (1971, p. 81) describes the essential nature of item writing as viewed from the traditional perspective.

> Item writing is essentially creative — it is an art. Just as there can be no set of formulas for producing a good story or a good painting, so there can be no set of rules that guarantees the production of good test items. Principles can be established and suggestions offered, but it is the item writer's judgment in the application — and occasional disregard — of these principles and suggestions that determines whether good items or mediocre ones are produced. Each item, as it is being written, presents new problems and new opportunities.

In the next two sections of this chapter, the focus is on the essay and multiple-choice item formats. In the first section, a fairly comprehensive treatment of the essay format is provided by Coffman's article in which some of the supporting arguments for the use of the essay format, the various sources of scoring unreliability associated with this mode of testing, and some specific recommendations for improving the reliability of essay ratings are examined. In the next section, some of the supporting arguments for the use of the multiple-choice format are presented, followed by (a) examples of several varieties of the multiple-choice format, (b) a set of guidelines for writing and/or editing multiple-choice items, (c) some procedures for generating distracters, and (d) some alternative scoring procedures.

> ## On The Reliability of Ratings of Essay Examinations[1]
>
> For more than half a century, critics have been calling attention to the deficiencies of essay examinations, yet teachers continue to use them. To some extent, the persistence of the essay examination may be only a reflection of the typical tendency of any large enterprise with a long tradition to resist change. On the other hand, the very vigor of essay testing in the face of strong criticism suggests that there may be strong arguments in its favor.

1. This section is a slightly revised version of William E. Coffman's "On the Reliability of Ratings of Essay Examinations in English," originally printed in *Research in the Teaching of English*, Vol. 5, No. 1, Spring 1971. Copyright © 1971 by the National Council of Teachers of English. Reprinted by permission of the publisher and the author. Some of this material first appeared in the author's chapter in *Educational Measurement*, American Council on Education, 1971.

ARGUMENTS FOR ESSAYS

In the first place, a case can be made for the essay examination as a special type of performance test. A major purpose of education is to prepare individuals to interact effectively with other individuals in the realm of ideas. The basic tool of interaction is language, and the educated man is the one who can react appropriately to questions or problems in his field of competence. The scholar performs by speaking and writing. The essay examination constitutes a sample of scholarly performance; hence, it provides a direct measure of educational achievement.

In the second place, the persistence of essay examinations appears to reflect the judgment of teachers that no effective alternatives are available. The typical teacher has grown up with essay examinations; he has encountered a wide variety of them in his own experience as a student, and so far as he can tell, the essay examinations he has prepared seem to have done a satisfactory job. In contrast, when the teacher has tried to prepare objective tests, he has encountered frustration. After a few attempts at building objective tests to measure complex skills and understandings, the typical teacher is likely to return to the familiar essay examination whenever he wishes to do more than measure the student's knowledge of facts.

In the third place, there has been deep concern about the effects of the typical teacher-made objective test on students' study habits. Such concern is not without foundation. In many cases, the student obtains his ideas about the things he is expected to learn from the kinds of questions he encounters on examinations; so he governs his study procedures accordingly. Many years ago, Meyer (1934, 1935) reported that the form of the examination expected by students determined the way they went about preparing for the examination. Furthermore, he found that greater achievement on any type of examination followed study in anticipation of an essay examination.

Now there are counter-arguments to each of these. The typical essay examination, with its strict time limits and emotional tensions, is a far cry from the typical setting in which scholarly work proceeds; teachers can, with practice under guidance, learn to prepare good objective tests of important educational objectives; and well-constructed objective tests can provide sound guides to teaching and learning. On the other hand, essay examinations are likely to remain a significant force for a long time to come, particularly in the classroom setting. It therefore seems appropriate to consider ways of minimizing deficiencies in the essay examination when it is used by the individual teacher in measuring outcomes of instruction.

SOURCES OF ERROR

There is extensive evidence that it is difficult to achieve consistency in grading essay examinations. The problem is complex, and appropriate procedures for analyzing it are difficult to design. The accumulated evidence leads, however, to three inescapable conclusions: (1) Different raters tend to assign different grades to the same paper. (2) A single rater tends to assign different grades to the same paper on different occasions. (3) The differences tend to increase as the essay question permits greater freedom of response (Hartog and Rhodes, 1936; Vernon and Millican, 1954; Findlayson, 1951; Pearson, 1955; and Noyes, 1963).

INTERRATER VARIABILITY

Each of these conclusions is more complex than the simple statement indicates. For example, the grades assigned by different raters may differ as a result of various influences. First, raters may differ in their severity. One may tend to assign relatively high grades while another may tend to assign generally low grades. If some papers are rated by one rater and other papers are rated by another rater, then the level of the mark an examinee receives will depend on which rater happens to rate his paper. Second, raters may differ in the extent to which they distribute grades throughout the score scale. Some tend to distribute scores closely around their average; others will spread scores much more widely. The good student hopes that his paper will be read by the rater who distributes scores widely; the poor student hopes that his paper will be read by the rater who gives few low (or high) scores. Finally, raters differ in the relative values they assign to different papers. A paper judged high by one rater may be judged low by another.

It has sometimes been argued that while the demonstrated differences in ratings assigned by different raters may be relevant to the grading of large-scale essay examinations, they are irrelevant to the grading of classroom tests. Such tests are designed to measure a particular teacher's goals of instruction. The fact that other teachers in other settings might assign different scores to a paper is of no concern. The important point is that the classroom teacher has made his judgment, based on his own goals of instruction and on his own value system.

There is something to be said for this position. The essay examination in the classroom setting is fundamentally different from the essay examination as part of a national testing program. The classroom teacher has direct knowledge of what has been taught and can select questions that require students to apply their knowledge to problems not already dealt with in class. Furthermore, he can instruct the students in how they should deal with questions of particular types. The external examiner, on the other hand, cannot possibly know the details of instruction of the students and has no way of insuring that a question will present the same problem to all examinees. Some of the factors that contribute to error in national testing are not present in classroom testing.

On the other hand, one should not ignore the fact that there remains a problem of scoring reliability. One would hardly defend the right of the teacher to impose an idiosyncratic value system. Ratings that differ too greatly from those of other teachers in the same school will be considered unreliable. Furthermore, ratings will vary from time to time. Whenever a teacher has graded a set of papers, put the papers aside for a period of time, and then graded them a second time, the agreement between the two sets of grades has been less than perfect. The extent to which the ratings will vary from time to time will depend on the individual teacher, the kinds of questions to be graded, and the particular procedure followed in making the ratings. The professional teacher will take steps to find out just how much his own ratings may be expected to vary from time to time.

INTRARATER VARIABILITY

This intrarater variability, like the interrater variability discussed above, consists of three components, one related to the relative standard for different papers, one to the general grading standard, and the third to the variability of the ratings. In other words, if a teacher rates a set of papers twice, without setting up objective controls of some sort, the relative standing of some pupils will shift. In addition, the average rating will be higher one time than the other, and there will be differences in the extent to which the scores are spread out over the range of the ratings.

The extent to which each of these sources of error will be of concern will depend on how the ratings are to be used. If ratings are used only to determine the rank order of pupils, only the first source of error is of concern. If, however, the ratings are treated as direct measures of quality, then all three sources of error become critical. Suppose, for example, that the ratings are made on a percentage basis and that an evaluative scale has been established in advance. Such a situation might be one where the passing grade had been set at 65% and the honor grade at 90%. In such a case, all students would hope that this time the teacher would give generally high rather than low grades. In addition, the poor students would hope that the variability of the scores would be small, that is, that there would be few low (and high) scores; and the good student would wish that the variability would be large, that is, that there would be many high (and low) scores.

The traditional manner of reporting reliability – as a product-moment coefficient of correlation between two sets of ratings – does not adequately assess all of these sources of error in ratings. It takes into account only the fluctuations in relative standing. The formula for computing the coefficient makes an adjustment for any differences in the grading standard or variability between the two sets of ratings. There is, however, a mathematical approach through the analysis-of-variance that provides a way of assessing all three sources of error and of computing different reliability coefficients depending on the way in which the ratings are to be used (Guilford, 1954; Stanley, 1962). It is unlikely, however, that many classroom teachers will have either the technical background to understand this procedure or the computational facility to use it if they did. There is, however, a feasible and meaningful procedure the classroom teacher can use to evaluate his own skill in rating essay examinations.

A RATING EXPERIMENT

The first step in the procedure is to have the pupils identify themselves by number only, so that the ratings won't be influenced improperly by knowledge of which pupil wrote which paper. Next, rate the papers by whatever procedure has been used in the past, but do not record the ratings on the papers. Record them on a separate grading sheet along with the corresponding identification numbers, and then put the papers away in a safe place until there has been time to forget the details of the rating. Use the ratings to make whatever decisions are to be made, that is, determine who made high grades, who made low grades, who failed, or whatever evaluation is usually made, and make a record of these decisions. Several weeks later, repeat the procedure, again assigning ratings and applying the same decision rules. Then count the number of pupils who are placed in a different decision class by the two procedures. What part of the class would be placed in a different group the second time? If the part is small, the reliability is high; if the part is large, the reliability is low.

A good way to summarize such an experiment is illustrated in Table 14-3. The data are hypothetical, but they are not inconsistent with what is known about variability in ratings from one time to another. The product-moment correlation between the two sets of ratings is 0.871. Findlayson (1951) reports coefficients ranging from 0.636 to 0.957 for four raters who re-read two sets of essays. Actually, the reliability for the data in Table 14-3 based on the analysis-of-variance is 0.848, somewhat lower than 0.871 because the second set of scores has a lower average than the first and a greater spread around the average, characteristics that are not reflected in the product-moment correlation.

The full effect of this difference in reliability depends, however, on how the ratings are to be used. If grades had been assigned on the first set of scores as indicated in the final column of the table, and if grades were then assigned on the basis of the same cutting points for the second set of scores, the table summarizing the two sets of grades would look like Table 14-4. Twelve of the 25 students would be in different grade categories on the two sets. Eight would have received lower grades and four would have received higher grades, reflecting the fact that the second set of ratings is lower on the average. Notice, however, that only one would have received grades that differed by more than one category (the one that received a C on the first rating and an A on the second). The product-moment correlation of these two sets of grades is 0.767, a figure considerably lower than the 0.848 obtained with the 15-point scale.

The consistency of the two sets of grades would be increased if one were to use different cutting scores for the second set of ratings. If, for example, the cutting scores between A and B were changed from 11–12 to 12–13, that between B and C from 9–10 to 8–9, and that between C and D from 6–7 to 5–6, the summary table would look like Table 14-5. Here three students would receive lower grades on the second rating and five would receive higher grades. Furthermore, no student's grades on the two sets of ratings would differ by more than one grade category. In other words, by making an adjustment for differences in the averages and in the spread of scores on the two ratings, the percentage of students receiving different ratings would be reduced from 48% (12 out of 25) to 32% (8 out of 25). The product-moment correlation in this case is 0.869, approximately, the same as that of the original ratings.

This kind of adjustment, however, is after the fact, and takes advantage of any chance factors in the situation. A more systematic way of increasing

TABLE 14-3. *Bivariate Frequency Distribution of Hypothetical First and Second Ratings of 25 Papers.*

Score First Rating	Score—Second rating															Freq.	Grade
	1	2	3	4	5	6	7	8	9	10	11	12	13	14	15		
15																	
14																	
13														1		1	A
12													1		1	2	A
11											1					1	B
10									2		1					3	B
9							1	2		1		1				5	C
8							3	1	1							5	C
7						1	1									2	D
6					1	1										2	D
5						1										1	F
4			1		1											2	F
3				1												1	F
2																	F
1																	F
Frequency			1	1	2	3	5	3	3	1	2	1	1	1	1	25	

TABLE 14-4. *Bivariate Frequency Distribution of Grades Based on Ratings of Table 14-3, Assuming No Adjustment in Cutting Scores.*

First Rating	Second Rating				
	F	D	C	B	A
A				1	2
B			3	1	
C		3	7	1	1
D	1	1	1		
F	2	1			

$r_{12} = .767$

TABLE 14-5. *Bivariate Frequency Distribution of Grades Based on Ratings of Table 14-3, After Adjusting Cutting Scores.*

First Rating	Second Rating				
	F	D	C	B	A
A				1	2
B				4	
C		1	9	2	
D	1		2		
F	2	1			

$r_{12} = .869$

the reliability of the rating would be to always rate a set of papers twice and add the two sets of ratings together before distributing the grades. Such a procedure, however, would require postponing the reporting of ratings until the second rating could be made. It would scarcely be worth the effort, because there is a much more significant source of error in essay examinations than the error of intraindividual rating variability. That is the error attributable to the sampling of questions.

SAMPLING ERROR

Basic to the concept of sampling reliability is the notion that each sampling unit should be independent and equally likely to be chosen in the sample. In this sense, the basic sampling unit for an essay examination is the question; the size of the sample is determined by the number of different questions in the examination. If the examinee is asked to deal with a number of different aspects of a single topic, the different aspects cannot be considered strictly independent; rather, it is likely that the ability to deal with one aspect of a question is more closely related to the ability to deal with another aspect of the same question than it is with the ability to deal with an aspect of a different question.

There is some evidence that there is an increment in reliability per question if questions are "longer" rather than "shorter" but the increment is not proportional to the time required for longer answers. For example, Godshalk, Swineford, and Coffman (1966) report data indicating that the reliability of a score based on five independent ratings of a twenty-minute essay would be 0.485 and that a score based on the sum of two such essays would be 0.655. In contrast, the reliability of a score based on a single forty-minute essay requiring the same amount of testing time as the two twenty-minute essays was only 0.592 (Godshalk, Swineford, and Coffman, 1966). In general, the greater the number of different questions included in the examination, the higher the reliability of the scores, assuming the same amount of testing time. A major problem facing the teacher who is preparing an essay examination is to effect a satisfactory compromise between the desire to increase the adequacy of the sample by asking many different questions and the desire to ask questions that probe deeply the understanding the student has developed.

It should be recognized that the problem of how large a sample of questions to include is more critical in some situations than in others. If, for example, the test is only one in a series of classroom tests administered as a basis for making tentative decisions about progress to date and next steps to be taken in instruction, then relatively low reliability can be tolerated. Misclassifications at this stage can be corrected on the basis of other tests in the sequence. If, however, the examination is to carry a heavy weight in determining the student's status, as is often the case with a final examination in a course, then it is very important that a sufficiently representative sample of questions be included in the test. Some idea of the relative importance of rating variability and question variability in contributing to the misclassification of students can be developed by preparing two tests considered to be equivalent and then making two ratings of each, say Forms I and II and ratings A and B. Then make four bivariate frequency distributions like the one in Table 14-3. The distribution for IA and IB and the distribution for IIA and IIB will estimate rating variability. The distributions for IA and IIB and for IIA and IB will estimate score reliability. There will surely be a greater number of discrepancies for the latter two than for the former two.

REDUCING RATING ERROR

Assuming that the problem of sampling questions has been solved, what can the busy teacher do to reduce the error attributable to rating? Four steps seem worthy of consideration: First, use a sufficiently fine scale for recording the ratings. Second, develop clear reference points to anchor the scale. Third, distribute the error randomly rather than systematically. Finally, include multiple rating where feasible. Each of these will be discussed briefly.

1. *Use a Sufficiently Fine Scale.* A comparison of Table 14-3 and Table 14-4 illustrates the importance of a sufficiently fine scale. The reliability of the fifteen-point ratings of Table 14-3 is 0.848; that of the five-point grade scale is 0.767. It would be a mistake to combine grades on a number of tests using only a five-point grade scale if the original ratings had been made on a finer scale. On the other hand, too fine a scale may be introducing the appearance of reliability without really achieving any reliable differentiation among the students. Generally, the evidence seems to be that a scale having from seven to fifteen units provides useful information.

2. *Develop Clear Reference Points.* The greater the number of different points on the scale, the more important it is to have clear notions about the characteristics of answers falling at each point. If the examination is concerned with knowledge, one can often define points on the scale by listing the things one would count as evidence. For example, for a question in literature, one might list nine things that could be included in a satisfactory answer and then define the points on a five-point scale in the following manner:

5. Discusses at least four points, describes each accurately, and gives acceptable reasons for each being important; or lists at least seven points.
4. Discusses three points, describes each accurately, and gives acceptable reasons for each being important; or lists at least five.
3. Discusses two points, describes each accurately, and gives acceptable reasons for each being important; or lists at least four.
2. Discusses one point, describes it accurately, and gives an acceptable reason for it being important; or lists at least three.
1. Lists at least two points.

The more clearly the different points on the scale can be defined, the more reliable the rating is likely to be.

If the examination is concerned with the ability to develop a synthesis of several ideas or with other characteristics that are difficult to count, one may anchor the scale by developing model answers. One way of doing this is to write out a top quality answer at the time the examination is prepared and then look through the papers written by the students for a "middle-level" paper, and perhaps for papers illustrating other points on the scale, before beginning the actual rating. Another way of developing an anchor is to let the papers themselves determine the anchor by sorting the papers according to a predetermined distribution that is to be used for every examination for the same class. For example, with a class of twenty-five pupils and a nine-point scale, one might assign the worst paper a one and the best a nine and so on according to the following scheme:

Scale	1	2	3	4	5	6	7	8	9
Number of Papers	1	2	3	4	5	4	3	2	1

Such a system has the advantage that it insures that there will be no shift in either the average score or in the spread of scores regardless of when the papers are rated. It has the disadvantage that one is often forced to assign different ratings to papers that one cannot honestly differentiate. It seems unjust to force the papers into a predetermined distribution, perhaps by flipping a coin. One may consider, however, that the alternative is often to run the risk of creating a greater injustice by the way rating standards may shift from time to time.

3. *Distribute Error Randomly.* One can reduce the probability that errors will be distributed in a biased manner by rating question by question rather than student by student and by giving a number of different tests through the term. Each time a question is to be rated the papers should be arranged in a different order. If such a procedure is adopted it is likely that a student whose essay was rated too high one time will probably have his paper rated somewhat too low another time so that the sum of his scores over a number of questions (or examinations) will more nearly reflect his actual ability. On the other hand, if all questions on a paper are rated before moving to the next paper, there is the likelihood that whatever errors are being made at the time will be reflected in all of the ratings for a single student. Furthermore, it is likely that systematic error will be introduced in the sense that the impression made by an answer to one question will influence the rating of answers to succeeding questions.

4. *Include Multiple Ratings.* A teacher can never completely escape the systematic error reflecting his own special biases; he can, however, reduce the effect of variations in his standards from time to time by adopting the procedures outlined above. In addition, he can reduce the effects of personal bias by working cooperatively with other teachers in the rating of essay examinations. One way that this might be accomplished is described by Diederich and Link (1967). In essence, the procedure calls for the development of common examinations to be used throughout a school, each examination to be rated by more than one teacher. In general, two ratings, even if they are made rapidly in order to permit time for a greater number of ratings to be made, will be preferable to a single rating. The sum of the two ratings will be more reliable than a single rating. There is an additional advantage to cooperative grading projects. By making bivariate frequency distributions of the type described in Table 14-3 using ratings from pairs of teachers, a staff can become aware of the extent to which individuals differ in the three sources of rating error; that is, differences in standards, differences in the tendency to spread scores around the average, and differences in the relative value assigned to different papers. In general, when made aware of discrepancies, teachers tend to move their own ratings in the direction of the average ratings of the group. Over a period of time, the ratings of the staff as a group tend to become more reliable.

SUMMARY

The sources of error in essay examinations are complex. Some error arises because the questions in an examination are only a sample of all the possible questions that might be asked. Some error is the result of differences between raters. Some is due to variability in the judgments of a rater from one time to another. Both interindividual and intraindividual variability can be further broken down into at least three components. The extent to which any of these various sources of error are present depends on how the essay questions are prepared, on how the responses are rated, and on how the scores are used. Awareness on the part of the teacher of the factors contributing to unreliability — an awareness that can be increased by simple experiments — is a first step in improving the reliability of the teacher's essay examinations.

EXERCISE SET 14-2

1. a. In Table 14-3, how many papers received a rating of 9 on the first occasion? Of these, how many also received a rating of 9 on the second occasion?
   b. How many papers received exactly the same rating on both occasions?
2. a. In Table 14-4, how many papers received a grade of C based on the first rating? Of these, how many also received a grade of C based on the second rating?
   b. How many papers received the same grade on both occasions?
3. Based on the results of items 1 and 2, does the Pearson r seem to be useful as a measure of agreement between two sets of ratings? (By agreement, we mean the "sameness of the ratings" on different occasions or by separate judges.)

The Multiple-Choice Format

Contrary to popular belief, the existing item-writing literature suggests that multiple-choice items can be constructed to measure many complex cognitive tasks. In addition, multiple-choice tests tend to be more objective (i.e., exhibit less interrater and intrarater variability), more efficient (i.e., require less examinee and scorer time per unit of information obtained), and less subject to item sampling errors (i.e., for a fixed amount of test time, they permit the construction of a more representative sample of the item population of interest). Thus, in the opinion of many test specialists, the multiple-choice format is the preferred item format unless there are compelling reasons for using the essay approach.

Some Variations on the Multiple-Choice Format. An item presented in the multiple-choice format consists of a *stem* (typically a leading question or incomplete statement) and a set of response *alternatives* or *options*. The correct response alternative or set of alternatives is called the *answer* and the remaining alternatives are called *distracters, misleads,* or *foils.* Some of the more common multiple-choice item variants are illustrated in the following excerpt from Wesman (1971, pp. 94–98):[2]

---

2. Reprinted from A. G. Wesman's "Writing the Test Item," in *Educational Measurement*, 2nd ed. (R. L. Thorndike, ed.), 1971, by permission of The American Council on Education.

1. THE CORRECT-ANSWER VARIETY

This variety of the multiple-choice form consists of an item stem followed by several responses, one of which is absolutely correct while the others are incorrect.

1. Who invented the sewing machine?
   a. Singer
   b. Howe
   c. Whitney
   d. White
   e. Fulton   _____b_____

2. THE BEST-ANSWER VARIETY

This variety consists of a stem followed by two or more suggested responses that are correct, appropriate in varying degrees, or downright wrong. The examinee is directed to select the best (most nearly correct) response.

1. What was the basic purpose of the Marshall Plan?
   a. Military defense of Western Europe
   b. Reestablishment of business and industry in Western Europe
   c. Settlement of differences with Russia
   d. Direct help to the hungry and homeless in Europe   _____b_____

The difference between the best-answer and the correct-answer variety is more one of topic than of form. The name of the inventor of the sewing machine is recorded in history beyond question or doubt. The purpose of the Marshall Plan cannot be stated with any such precision. In using the best-answer variety, it is sometimes necessary, in fairness to the examinee, to include in the item stem the specification of the authority or other source that defines "best" in the context of the item. Thus, if the examinee is expected to respond with the opinion of the author of a textbook (and other authorities may differ as to what the "basic cause" or "most influential factor" is), the examinee should be informed of the desired frame of reference. Failure so to specify may penalize the student who has read more extensively on the topic. If, on the other hand, the intent of an item is to assess whether or not the student has thought issues through and reached the conclusion that the examiner considers "best" or "most important," no such qualification of the stem need be made. In that case, of course, the test maker has the responsibility of determining that all competent experts would agree as to what is the *best* answer.

3. THE MULTIPLE-RESPONSE VARIETY

When the item writer is dealing with questions to which a number of clearly correct answers exist, it is sometimes desirable to include two or more correct answers in the choices offered. When this is done, and the examinee is instructed to mark all correct responses, the item variety is designated as the multiple-response form.

1. What factor or factors are principally responsible for the clotting of the blood?
   a. Oxidation of hemoglobin
   b. Contact of blood with injured tissue
   c. Presence of unchanged prothrombin
   d. Contact of blood with a foreign surface   <u>b, c</u>

A multiple-response item is most often a correct-answer item. It may, in some settings, serve for best-answer purposes. Thus, the examinee may be instructed to choose from a list of contributing causes to a social event those that were basic, most influential, or the like. The number of choices to be so identified should ordinarily be specified; if left to the judgment of the examinee, he may be faced with the additional task of judging the threshold of acceptability.

4. THE INCOMPLETE-STATEMENT VARIETY

Quite frequently the introductory portion of a multiple-choice item (the item stem) consists of a portion of a statement rather than a direct question.

1. Millions of dollars worth of corn, oats, wheat, and rye are destroyed annually in the United States by
   a. rust
   b. mildews
   c. smuts
   d. molds   <u>c</u>

5. THE NEGATIVE VARIETY

To handle questions that would normally have several equally good answers, item writers sometimes use a negative approach. The responses include several correct answers together with one that is not correct or that is definitely weaker than the others. The examinee is then instructed to mark the response that does *not* correctly answer the question or that provides the least satisfactory answer.

1. Which of these is *not* true of a virus?
   a. It can live only in plant and animal cells.
   b. It can reproduce itself.
   c. It is composed of very large living cells.
   d. It can cause disease.   <u>c</u>

Special care is required in the preparation of items of the negative variety. The stem should be worded with the greatest possible clarity to avoid reading confusion on the part of the examinee. One occasionally finds a stem (or one or more options) phrased in a negative context with instructions to the student to identify the option for which the stem statement is not correct. This may lead students to respond with the wrong answer because they have been tripped up by tricky or careless item writing[3] rather than through lack of knowledge. It is also highly desirable to call the examinee's attention to the fact that an item is of the negative variety by italicising or underlining the negative word (usually "not").

6. THE SUBSTITUTION VARIETY

The multiple-choice form has been utilized by item writers in testing a student's ability to express himself correctly and effectively. Samples of originally well written prose or poetry are systematically altered to include errors in punctuation, spelling, word usage, and similar conventions. Selected words or phrases in these rewritten passages are underlined and identified by number. Several possible substitutions for each critical phrase are provided. The examinee is directed to select the phrase (original or alternative) that provides the best expression.

Selection

Surely the forces of education should be fully utilized to acquaint youth

with the real nature of the dangers to democracy, <u>for</u> no other place offers
1

<u>as good or better opportunities than</u> the school for a <u>rational</u> consideration
2   3

of the problems involved.

Item

1. a. , for
   b. . For
   c. −for
   d. no punctuation   *a*

2. a. As good or better opportunities than
   b. as good opportunities or better than
   c. as good opportunities as or better than
   d. better opportunities than   *d*

3. a. rational
   b. radical
   c. reasonable
   d. realistic   *a*

---

3. Which of the following was *not* true of George Washington?
a. He was not born in 1708.
b. He did not accept a third term as president.
c. He was never a British subject.
d. He was an experienced military officer before the Revolutionary War.

7. THE INCOMPLETE-ALTERNATIVES VARIETY

In some cases, an item writer may feel that the suggestion of a correct response would make the answer so obvious that the item would function poorly or not at all. He then may resort to incomplete or coded alternatives; for example, the examinee may be asked to think of a one-word response and to indicate that response on the basis of its first letter:

1. The name of Socrates' most famous disciple began with the letter
   1. A to E
   2. F to J
   3. K to O
   4. P to T
   5. U to Z   <u>   4   </u>

The correct answer is Plato, so response 4 is marked.

The use of incomplete responses makes possible the objective measurement of such traits as active vocabulary. In tests for this purpose it is essential to force the examinee to think of the appropriate response himself. The following item illustrates this application.

2. An apple that has a sharp, pungent, but not disagreeably sour or bitter, taste is said to be 4^a
   1. p
   2. q
   3. t
   4. v
   5. w   <u>   3   </u>

[a]The figure indicates the number of letters in the word (in this case "tart"). This restriction serves to rule out many borderline correct responses.

Incomplete responses also may be used in arithmetical problems. The student may be directed to mark a choice on the basis of a certain digit in his answer, such as the third digit from the left. Thus:

3. When one computes the square root of 18, what number should appear in the second decimal place?
   A. 3
   B. 4
   C. 5
   D. 6
   E. 7   <u>   B   </u>

The use of incomplete responses for arithmetic problems prevents a student from using proffered responses as starting points for reverse, short-cut solutions of the problems. (If sophisticated scoring equipment is employed, the student may be instructed to code his answer completely on an appropriate answer sheet. Modern scanners can readily process answers marked in this manner.)

The incomplete-response variety represents a hybrid between the short-answer and multiple-choice form. It has the advantage of perfectly objective scoring. However, like the short-answer form, it is limited to questions for which unique simple correct answers exist. Furthermore, unless the response categories are delimited sharply, credit may be given for wrong answers that happen to fall in the correct response category.

8. THE COMBINED-RESPONSE VARIETY

This variety consists of an item stem followed by several responses, one or more of which may be correct. A second set of code letters indicates various possible combinations of correct responses. The examinee is directed to choose the set of code letters which designates the correct responses and to mark his answer accordingly. The following is an example of the combined-response variety. It embodies a weakness that frequently characterizes this variety of item, in that the stem does not really formulate a problem — it merely acts as a base on which to mount the statements that follow. It may also be noted that this item form is much the same as the multiple-response variety described on pp. 213–214.

1. Our present constitution
   a. was the outgrowth of a previous failure.
   b. was drafted in Philadelphia during the summer (May to September) of 1787.
   c. was submitted by the Congress to the states for adoption.
   d. was adopted by the required number of states and put into effect in 1789.

   1. a.
   2. a, b
   3. a, b, c
   4. b, c, d
   5. a, b, c, d   <u>5</u>

Another version of the combined-response variety (sometimes referred to as the rearrangement or sequence form) requires that the student rearrange material according to some specified principle. The stem for such an item might read: "Arrange the following historical events in correct chronological order, marking the earliest 1, the next 2, etc.," or "Rank the following chemical elements in order of their atomic weights, marking the heaviest a, the next b, etc."

Still another version of the combined-response variety is represented by the item in which the examinee is required to organize fragments into a desirable whole. An illustration of this version may set the student the task of reassembling a set of scrambled sentences to show the correct order which would constitute a coherent paragraph.

2. A. A sharp distinction must be drawn between table manners and sporting manners.
   B. This kind of handling of a spoon at the table, however, is likely to produce nothing more than an angry protest against squirting grapefruit juice about.
   C. Thus, for example, a fly ball caught by an outfielder in baseball or a completed pass in football is a subject for applause.
   D. Similarly, the dexterous handling of a spoon in golf to release a ball from a sand trap may win a championship match.
   E. But a biscuit or a muffin tossed and caught at the table produces scorn and reproach.

The student is required to indicate the proper position of each sentence. The correct order in this case is *A, C, E, D, B*.

It will be obvious that the combined-response variety is one of the more complex forms of multiple-choice items. It is also one of the more difficult to write well and, sometimes, to score. It permits ready appraisal of mastery of sets of facts or of complex abilities such as organization and comparative evaluation of facts or concepts. Since items of this type are essentially combinations of several true-false items, a single score point for the combination response may obscure as much information as it reveals. The student who answers correctly receives a point of score; the student who is right on all but one of the inherent true-false questions gets no more credit than the student who is wrong on all parts. Whether the advantages of the combined-response item in a particular instance of test construction outweigh the disadvantages is a matter for individual decision; educational philosophy is likely to play a more important role in that decision than do purely psychometric principles.

The multiple-choice form is widely applicable. An idea presented in short-answer, true-false, or matching item form can always be converted into one or more multiple-choice items. Frequently this conversion improves the effectiveness of the item. Since there is only one correct choice that an examinee can make to a well-constructed multiple-choice item in its standard form, the difficulty and subjectivity of scoring which plague most short-answer items readily can be avoided. Since the multiple-choice form is adapted to the best-answer approach, it avoids the ambiguity associated with the application of a standard of absolute truth, which constitutes the chief weakness of the true-false form. Since each multiple-choice item may be independent, the problem of finding a number of parallel relationships, which frequently causes difficulty in the matching form, may be avoided.

How Many Alternatives. Once a particular variation on the multiple-choice format has been selected for use, a decision must be made concerning the number of alternatives (or options) which ought to be employed. The important factors entering into this decision are discussed in the following excerpt from Wesman (1971, pp. 99–102)[4]:

---

4. See footnote 2.

What is the optimum number of distracters to use when devising a multiple-choice — or matching — item? Are two distracters better than three? Is a five-option multiple-choice item better than a four-option? There is no clear definitive answer to these questions, but there are considerations involved that are worthy of attention.

Theoretically, the larger the number of distracters, the more reliable is the item. Psychometricians are well agreed on this point of theory. It is analogous to the readily demonstrated fact that a longer test is more reliable than a shorter one if the two tests are composed of equally good items. In theory, the analogy is sound; in practice, however, the theory is not often supported.

When a test is being put together, the universe of relevant, meaningful items is ordinarily broad enough to permit tryout of large quantities of potentially effective items and to select from among them the desired number to make up a test of predetermined length. When an individual item is being written, the number of potentially meaningful, relevant distracters is far more limited; the law of diminishing returns very quickly takes over, even for a highly imaginative item writer. This is not to say that one cannot find additional distracters; more often than not statements can be found to stretch an item to four, five, six, or more distracters. The question is whether the stretching process genuinely contributes to the effective measurement capabilities of the item or whether the additional distracters merely act as filler. Too often the latter is the case. In the usual multiple-choice situation, the item writer who can incorporate two or three really effective distracters may well feel pleased. Items for which as many as four distracters operate effectively are relatively infrequent; the search for additional distracters *after* three or four good ones have already been found is likely to be frustrating and fruitless.

One argument for more options on the original item preparation for tryout is that one does not really know which options will work. If one tries the item out with five or more options, one can drop the distracters that prove to be mere filler (or occasionally a distracter chosen by a larger proportion of able students than of less able) before preparing the final test form. However, when more options are tried than are to be included in the final form, another preliminary item tryout is desirable to ascertain the difficulty and discrimination power of the item in its revised version. Eliminating options changes the task set before the examinee.

To return to the earlier analogy, then, the parallelism may be clarified. A lengthened test is more reliable than the shorter one only if the additional items are of good quality; adding items that are ridiculously difficult, extremely easy, or otherwise nondiscriminating can add little to the value of the original test. So it is with item writing — adding distracters that fail to distract cannot improve the utility of the item.

Examples of the futility of attempting to include large numbers of distracters are not difficult to come by. The reader who wishes to demonstrate the phenomenon to himself needs only to give a set of arithmetic items in short-answer form to an appropriate sample of examinees. He will find that, among the incorrect responses, two or three or perhaps four responses appear with sufficient frequency to indicate their possible utility as distracters for converting the item to multiple-choice form. The remaining incorrect responses will be scattered, with too few examinees agreeing on any further erroneous response to make its employment as an additional distracter worthwhile.

An interesting demonstration from the verbal-information area of measurement was found with the items in the Verbal Reasoning portion of the *Differential Aptitude Tests*. In the original published forms of the test (A and B), each item offered the student 16 choices from which to select a response. The item stem consisted of an analogy from which the first and fourth terms were omitted. An example item was:

X. _____ is to water as eat is to _____

1. continue	A. drive
2. drink	B. enemy
3. foot	C. Food
4. girl	D. industry

2C

The student's task was to select one of the four numbered choices to fill in the blank at the beginning of the stem and one of the four lettered choices to fill in the blank at the end of the stem. The 16 combinations thus available, it was hoped, would make for particularly reliable items, since the likelihood that the correct combination would be chosen by chance was so small. That the total group of 50 items in each form comprised a satisfactorily reliable test was demonstrated by average single-grade single-sex reliability coefficients of approximately 0.90.

When revised forms (L and M) of the test were undertaken, the authors decided to study the effectiveness of offering all 16 choices per item. A large and representative sample of answer sheets was analyzed with respect to the combinations of incorrect responses which students actually selected. The analysis revealed that for almost every item more than 95 percent of the incorrect responses were encompassed by the four or five most popular pairs of words; the remaining combinations were just filler. In the revised forms, therefore, the student was offered only four distracter word pairs in addition to the correct response. That test reliability suffered not at all from the smaller number of options was shown by the reliability coefficients, similarly computed, for the revised forms: again the average coefficient was about 0.90. Thus, it is as one might expect − it is not the number of choices but their effectiveness that determines the contribution of the item. Distracters that are not chosen by examinees contribute nothing to an item, except in rare instances: in some items a distracter may be included to enhance the effectiveness of other distracters or to make the set of distracters logically complete. Or "none of the above" may be included in some items in which it is rarely chosen, to make that response more attractive in other items.

A consideration in decisions as to how many distracters to use is that of economy with respect to time. Since most tests are administered with predetermined time limits, the amount of reading matter presented to the student necessarily influences the number of items to which he can respond. Extra distracters mean extra reading time per item; thus fewer items may appropriately be included as the number of distracters per item is increased. Unless the additional distracters appreciably enhance the quality of the item, they are merely depriving the test constructor of the opportunity to include more good items. For reasons such as this, professional test writers ordinarily are asked to write four- or five-choice items.

There are situations in which the nature of the item largely determines how many options are used. More than one or two good distracters are rarely to be found for a recognition test in spelling. Similarly, the *Bennett Mechanical Comprehension Test*, which shows gears, pulleys and the like and appraises understanding of the effects of simple physical forces, is composed entirely of three-choice problems. For most of the items, as they were constructed, a fourth choice would be meaningless.

The age of the intended examinees may influence the optimal number of options especially if the choices involve appreciable amounts of reading or retention. It appears reasonable that six- and seven-year-old children should not be expected to consider as many response possibilities at a time as may be presented to older children. Two- and three-choice items are probably more appropriate for the younger children than are five-choice items.

A practice that has grown up in the test development field, and which probably deserves more consideration than it has generally received, is that of mixing, in a single test or part, items with differing numbers of distracters. The prevalence of tests in which number of options is uniform throughout the test may be largely attributed to two factors: (a) the relative inflexibility of early scoring machines often made the scoring of items with differing numbers of options a nuisance, and (b) the application of scoring formulas appropriate to items with different numbers of options made hand scoring onerous. A further, but less influential, argument favoring uniformity of number of options was that it made easier the student's task of finding the correct spot on his answer sheet in which to register his response.

That these factors need be granted the importance today which they had in the past is doubtful. Devotion to scoring formulas is less widespread than it was a decade or two ago, and the technology of scoring machines has sped forward so rapidly that slavish adherence to uniform response options is no longer justifiable on this basis alone — certainly not for extensive programs in which test scoring is accomplished by computers.

Thus, the teacher item writer as well as the professional may well consider gaining the flexibility resulting from mixing items with differing numbers of options. As suggested above, the *effectiveness* of distracters is more important to item quality than is the *number* of distracters. Ineffective distracters merely take up reading time that might be more fruitfully employed. The search for additional distracters whose sole function is to complete a predetermined number of options is a waste of time and creative energy for the item writer, who might also be more gainfully occupied. The student might better be reading additional items; the item writer might better be preparing those additional items.

At least some portion of the blame for ineffective and inefficient teacher-made tests may be ascribed to strained attempts to provide additional distracters for purposes of uniformity. In fact, there have been numerous instances in which an otherwise acceptable item has been made defective by inclusion of a distracter that was devised only to give the item the same number of options as other items had. For verification, the reader may inspect the items at the ends of chapters of many textbooks — or go over tests that his fellow teachers have prepared. He should then be convinced that it is better to stop writing distracters when he has run out of good ones than to waste his time and that of his students. (This should not be an excuse for laziness, however.) Item writers should try conscientiously to produce three or four distracters for multiple-choice items. Sometimes good distracters come only after hard searching. Good distracters make good items; some of the best distracters are thought up only after diligent effort.

After making certain simplifying assumptions about the mean and variance of a test score distribution, Ebel (1969) derived a formula from KR21 which allows one to calculate the expected KR21 reliability for a test having k items and a alternatives per item. His computations show two things: (a) the expected value of KR21 increases with increases in k and/or a, and (b) if the total number of alternatives is held constant, a tradeoff which may affect test reliability exists between the number of items and the number of alternatives per item. For example, a 6-item test ($k = 6$) with four alternatives per item ($a = 4$), an 8-item test ($k = 8$) with three alternatives per item ($a = 3$), and a 12-item test ($k = 12$) with two alternatives per item ($a = 2$) all have a total of 24 alternatives. One might ask which of these cases results in the maximum expected value of KR21.

Recently, Grier (1975) addressed this question and found that for fairly long tests in which Ebel's assumptions are reasonable, the maximum expected value of KR21 for a test containing a fixed number of response alternatives is obtained when each item contains three alternatives. Grier is careful to note, however, that the applicability of this result to the short test and to other types of test reliability (e.g., test—retest, parallel form) has not yet been studied. It should also be noted that this theoretical result has not yet been subjected to empirical test. However, when one faces such a tradeoff, the combination of Grier's result, difficulties in distracter generation, and the item sampling problem jointly suggest, for example, that using 80 three-option items rather than 60 four-option items may be a very reasonable decision, assuming of course, that 80 good three-option items can be written.

Some Guidelines for Writing and/or Editing Items. Although there is very little *hard* empirical evidence which shows what happens when one or more of the following guidelines is violated in multiple-choice test construction, they seem to make sense and their use is strongly encouraged by test construction specialists. Again, we turn to Wesman (1971, pp. 113–119)[5]:

> 1. *Use either a direct question or an incomplete statement as the item stem.* There are some item ideas that can be expressed more simply and clearly in the form of incomplete statements than in the form of direct questions.
>
> 1. The present Russian government is a
>   a. democracy.
>   b. constitutional monarchy.
>   c. Communist dictatorship.
>   d. Fascist dictatorship. _____c_____

5. See footnote 2.

If this item were written with a direct question as the stem it would require more words and read less smoothly.

2. The present Russian government is of which of the following types?
    a. A democracy
    b. A constitutional monarchy
    c. A Communist dictatorship
    d. A Fascist dictatorship   _____c_____

On the other hand, some items require direct question stems for most effective expression.

At present there is no adequate experimental evidence on the relative efficiency of the two types of stem. Some experienced item writers exhibit a strong preference for the direct question. Others prefer the incomplete statement. Probably the effect of stem type upon the quality of an item is not large. *There are, however, indications that beginners tend to produce fewer technically weak items when they try to use direct questions than when they use the incomplete statement approach.* Several reasons for this tendency may be suggested:

First, because of its specificity the direct question induces the item writer to produce more specific and homogeneous responses. When an incomplete statement is used as the item stem, the writer's point of view may shift as he writes successive responses. This is evidenced in the frequent tendency on the part of inexperienced item writers to construct incomplete statement items as essentially a series of true-false items with no truly central idea. This tends to confuse the examinee concerning the real point of the item.

Second, it is usually easier for the item writer to express complex ideas (those requiring qualifying statements) in complete question form. The necessity of having the completion come at the end of an incomplete statement restricts the item writer. He is not free to arrange phrases or words to produce the clearest possible statement.

Third and most important of all, the writer of a direct question usually states more explicitly the basis on which the correct response is to be chosen. Contrast these two item stems:

3. In comparing the exports and imports of the United States, we
    find that: _____?_____

4. In the United States, how does the value of exports compare
    with that of imports?   *Exports greater*

Item 4 obviously sets up a much more definite basis for choosing a correct response. The difference here is not inherent in the form, since item 3 could be improved without changing it to a direct question. However, there is a greater tendency for item writers to be vague when using incomplete statements than when using direct questions. A reason for the relative absence of vagueness in the direct question form may be that the form itself requires that the complete problem be stated. It has been suggested that whether an incomplete statement is adequately specific might well be checked by attempting to convert the incomplete statement to a direct question; if new material is required for the conversion, the incomplete statement should be reviewed and modified by adding the material necessary to make it equivalent to the question. Some incomplete item stems are altogether too incomplete, as in

5. Merchants and middlemen
   a. Make their living off producers and consumers, and are, therefore, nonproducers.
   b. Are regulators and determiners of price and, therefore, are producers.
   c. Are producers in that they aid in the distribution of goods and bring the producer and the consumer together.
   d. Are producers in that they assist in the circulation of money. <u>   *a*   </u>

Restatement of this item using a direct question increases the number of words but makes it much easier to understand.

6. Should merchants and middlemen be classified as producers or nonproducers? Why?
   a. As nonproducers, because they make their living off producers and consumers.
   b. As producers, because they are regulators and determiners of price.
   c. As producers, because they aid in the distribution of goods and bring producer and consumer together.
   d. As producers, because they assist in the circulation of money. <u>   *a*   </u>

2. In general, include in the stem any words that otherwise must be repeated in each response. These two forms of a test item illustrate this point:

1. The members of the board of directors of a corporation are usually chosen by which of these?
   a. The bondholders of the corporation
   b. The stockholders of the corporation
   c. The president of the corporation
   d. The employees of the corporation <u>   *b*   </u>

2. Which persons associated with a corporation usually choose its directors?
   a. Bondholders
   b. Stockholders
   c. Officials
   d. Employees <u>   *b*   </u>

It is not always possible, or desirable, however, to eliminate all words common to the responses. In a preceding example (1.6 above), dealing with the activities of merchants and middlemen, it was necessary to introduce each response with the word *as* to make grammatical sense. If the retention of common words in all of the responses makes the item easier to understand, they should by retained. In most cases, however, it will be found that the common words can be transferred to the stem without loss of clarity.

3. *Avoid a negatively stated item stem if possible.* Experience indicates that this approach is likely to confuse the examinee. He is accustomed to selecting a *correct* response and finds it difficult to remember, in a particular isolated instance, to choose an *incorrect* response. The negative approach and the difficulty it frequently causes may be apparent in these sample items:

1. Which of these is *not* one of the purposes of Russia in consolidating the Communist party organization throughout Eastern Europe?
   a. To balance the influence of the Western democracies
   b. To bolster her economic position
   c. To improve Russian-American relations
   d. To improve her political bargaining position   *c*

2. Which of these is *not* true of a virus?
   a. It is composed of very large living cells.
   b. It can reproduce itself.
   c. It can live only in plants and animal cells.
   d. It can cause disease.   *a*

The use of a negative approach can sometimes be avoided by rewording the item, by reducing the number of responses, or both. Where use of negatively stated items appears to constitute the only satisfactory approach, underlining, italicizing, or otherwise emphasizing the "not" is essential.

4. *Provide a response that competent critics can agree on as the best.* The correct response to a multiple-choice item must be determinate. While this requirement is obvious, it is not always easy to fulfill. Sometimes through lack of information but more often through failure to consider all circumstances, writers produce items that confuse and divide even competent authorities. For example, experts disagreed sharply over the best response to each of these questions:

1. What is the chief difference in research work between colleges and industrial firms?
   a. Colleges do much research, industrial firms little.
   b. Colleges are more concerned with basic research, industrial firms with applications.
   c. Colleges lack the well-equipped laboratories that industrial firms maintain.
   d. Colleges publish results, while industrial firms keep their findings secret.   *?*

2. What is the chief obstacle to free exchange of scientific information between scientists in different countries?
   a. The information is printed in different languages.
   b. The scientists wish to keep the information secret for their own use.
   c. Scientists do not wish to use second-hand information from other countries.
   d. Countries wish to keep some of the information secret for use in time of war.   _____?_____

The most obvious remedy for this type of weakness is to have the items carefully reviewed by competent authorities. Items on which the experts cannot agree in selecting a best response should be revised or discarded.

Expert reviewers may frequently suggest desirable improvements in the wording of the item, but the item writer should not feel bound to accept these suggestions if they do not affect choice of the answer. Some suggested changes may actually weaken the item. Expert reviewers have a tendency to "split hairs at the Ph.D. level" and to prefer the technical jargon and stereotypes with which they are most familiar. The changes in wording they suggest sometimes may make the item more verbose and confusing to the examinees for whom it is intended or may destroy its ability to discriminate those who understand from those who simply possess verbal facility.

5. *Make all the responses appropriate to the item stem.* Writers sometimes produce items in which no one of the responses is reasonably correct.

1. In which of the following cases is loss due to hail greatest?
   a. To livestock
   b. To skylights
   c. To growing crops   _____?_____

2. Why do living organisms need oxygen?
   a. Purification of the blood
   b. Oxidation of wastes
   c. Release of energy
   d. Assimilation of foods   _____?_____

3. What process is exactly the opposite of photosynthesis?
   a. Digestion
   b. Respiration
   c. Assimilation
   d. Catabolism   _____?_____

The responses to item 1 are not "cases." The responses to item 2 are not stated as reasons, as required by the stem. Item 3 illustrates a different type of difficulty. It asks a question that has no possible correct answer, since no process is *exactly* the opposite to photosynthesis. In all three, the items can be improved by rewording.

4. The greatest economic loss in hailstorms for the country as a whole results from damage to
   a. livestock.
   b. skylights.
   c. growing crops.   _____c_____

5. Why do living organisms need oxygen?
   a. To purify the blood
   b. To oxidize wastes
   c. To release energy
   d. To assimilate food   _____c_____

6. What process is most nearly the opposite of photosynthesis chemically?
   a. Digestion
   b. Respiration
   c. Assimilation
   d. Catabolism   _____d_____

One fairly obvious indication of inappropriate or carelessly written responses is lack of parallelism in grammatical structure. This is illustrated by:

7. Which would do most to advance the application of atomic discoveries to medicine?
   a. Standardized techniques for treatment of patients
   b. Train the average doctor to apply radioactive treatment
   c. Reducing radioactive therapy to a routine procedure
   d. Establish hospitals staffed by highly trained radioactive-therapy specialists   _____d_____

The responses to a multiple-choice item should always be expressed in parallel form. Sometimes this can be achieved by a simple change in wording. In other cases, it requires substitution of a more appropriate response. The revised and improved item is given:

8. Which would do most to advance the application of atomic discoveries to medicine?
   a. Development of standardized techniques for treatment of patients
   b. Training of the average doctor in application of radioactive treatments
   c. Removal of restriction on the use of radioactive substances
   d. Addition of trained radioactive-therapy specialists to hospital staffs   _____d_____

6. *Make all distracters plausible and attractive to examinees who lack the information or ability tested by the item.* In addition to inappropriate

distracters resulting from careless writing, there are others resulting from failure to consider plausibility. Consider:

1. Which element has been most influential in recent textile technology?
   a. Scientific research
   b. Psychological change
   c. Convention attendance
   d. Advertising promotion   _____a_____

Only the first response is plausible as an answer to question 1. Another example is provided by item 2.

2. Why is physical education a vital part of general education?
   a. It guarantees good health.
   b. It provides good disciplinary training.
   c. It balances mental, social, and physical activities.
   d. It provides needed strenuous physical exercise.   _____c_____

The alert examinee would reason that nothing can *guarantee* good health, that *disciplinary training* is now in low repute educationally, and that *strenuous* physical exercise is seldom recommended. Such an item might function well as a test of understanding of verbal meaning, but it would not discriminate between those who do and those who do not understand the place of physical education in general education.

Each distracter should be designed specifically to attract those examinees who have certain common misconceptions or who tend to make certain common errors. This mathematics test item illustrates the point:

3. The ratio of 25 cents to 5 dollars is
   a. 1/20
   b. 1/5
   c. 5/1
   d. 20/1
   e. none of these   _____a_____

The examinee who carelessly overlooks the distinction between cents and dollars, or inverts the ratio, will arrive at one of the distracters rather than at the answer. For some purposes, a very productive procedure for obtaining effective distracters for multiple-choice purposes is to administer the item first in completion form. If the sample of examinees used in this preliminary tryout is representative of the examinees for whom the test is eventually intended, a study of the incorrect responses should reveal the most common errors made and hence the most useful distracters. The item writer who depends solely on his own imagination and experience to guess what mistakes examinees are likely to make rarely will find as good distracters as the examinees' actual errors can provide. The method is especially applicable when factual information is being tested and a single word or number represents the correct response. Solution of arithmetic problems, identification of correctly and incorrectly spelled words, and selection of foreign language vocabulary synonyms are examples of testing situations that lend themselves readily to this method.

Occasionally, one is fortunate enough to find ready-made distracters available through others' researches. In the construction of the *Differential Aptitude Tests*, the selection of potentially effective incorrectly spelled words was considerably facilitated by the availability of Gates' *A List of Spelling Difficulties in 3,876 Words* (1937). The test author who is knowledgeable in a subject-matter field (or seeks the counsel of those who are) will now and again find, in published studies or unpublished dissertations, similarly helpful materials. More often, it will be necessary to do one's own experimenting by giving items in completion format to appropriate samples of examinees.

7. *Avoid highly technical distracters.* Item writers, needing additional distracters, sometimes are tempted to insert a response of which the meaning or applicability is completely beyond the ability of the examinee to understand.

1. Electric shock is most commonly administered in the treatment of
   a. rheumatism.
   b. paralysis.
   c. insanity.
   d. erythema.   _____c_____

The first three suggested responses are fairly common terms. The fourth is almost never encountered. It is definitely a "space filler" in this item, but it presents a frustrating problem to the examinee since he is forced to choose a best answer without knowing the meaning of one of the answers. *The level of information or ability required to reject a wrong response should be no higher than the level of ability required to select a correct response.* When this is true, an examinee may sometimes arrive at his choice by successively eliminating incorrect answers. Response by elimination has been criticized, but it has one possible advantage over response by direct selection. The examinee may need more pertinent information to eliminate three plausible distracters than he would need to select one correct verbal stereotype.

8. *Avoid responses that overlap or include each other.* An example of this defect is provided by:

1. The average height of adult U.S. males is
   a. less than 5 feet 3 inches.
   b. less than 5 feet 5 inches.
   c. more than 5 feet 7 inches.
   d. more than 5 feet 9 inches.   _____c_____

This item is, in effect, a two-response item. The choice lies between *b* and *c*. For if *a* is correct then *b* is also correct, and if *d* is correct then *c* is also correct. More subtle examples of this defect are occasionally encountered in item writing.

9. *Use "none of these" as a response only in items to which an absolutely correct answer can be given. Use it as an obvious answer several times early in*

the test but use it sparingly thereafter. Avoid using it as the answer to items in which it may cover a large proportion of incorrect responses. "None of these" is quite appropriate as a response to the correct-answer variety of multiple-choice item. It is inappropriate in best-answer items. An examinee may properly reject all suggested responses if he is working under instructions to choose only completely correct answers. He cannot reasonably be asked to mark "none of these" when his general instruction is to pick the *best* of several admittedly imperfect responses.

"None of these" is a useful response for items in arithmetic, spelling, punctuation, and similar fields where conventions of correctness can be applied rigorously. It provides an easy-to-write fourth or fifth response when one is needed and may be more plausible than any other that can be found. It sometimes enables the item writer to avoid stating an answer that is too obviously correct.

Two dangers are connected with the use of "none of these." The first is that it may not be seriously considered as a possible answer. The second is that the examinee who chooses "none of these" as the correct response may be given credit when he has really arrived at a wrong answer. To avoid the first danger, the examinee must be convinced at the beginning of the test that "none of these" is likely to be the answer to some items. This can be achieved by using it as the correct response to several easy items early in the test.

The second danger can be avoided by sparing use of "none of these" *as the correct answer* after the beginning of the test and by limiting its use as the answer to items in which the distracters encompass most of the probable incorrect responses. "None of these" would be an appropriate answer to:

1. What is the area of a right triangle whose sides adjacent to the right angle are 3 inches and 4 inches long respectively?
   a. 7
   b. 12
   c. None of these

   <u>   c   </u>

Some examinees may miss this item by simply adding 3 and 4. Others might multiply 3 by 4 and forget division by 2. Still others might add 3, 4, and 5. Since the number of possible incorrect responses to this item is limited, they may all be included as distracters, so that only examinees who solve the problem correctly will be likely to choose "none of these."

This situation does not prevail in item 2.

2. What is the sum of

37,859	a. 176,216
46,212	b. 183,127
39,843	c. 186,226
62,312	d. None
?	of these <u> c </u>

It is obviously impossible to anticipate all of the possible errors students might make in responding to this item. Hence, with no further information, it would be undesirable to use "none of these" as the answer with only a few of the possible incorrect responses listed as distracters. It is more appropriate to use it as a distracter. As mentioned earlier, however, it is sometimes possible to anticipate a very large proportion of the incorrect responses for an item if it has previously been administered in completion form. Such items might well be favored for use with "none of these" as the correct response in later portions of the test.

10. *Arrange the responses in logical order, if one exists, but avoid consistent preference for any particular response position.* When the responses consist of numbers, they should ordinarily be put in ascending or descending order. If the responses are small numbers such as 1, 2, 3, 4, or 5, the 1 should occur in the first position, 2 in the second position, and so on. If this is not done, there will be a strong tendency for the examinees to confuse the absolute value of the answer with the response position used to indicate it.

If an item contains one or more pairs of responses dealing with the same concept, these should usually be placed together. In the following item, it is preferable to arrange the responses as shown rather than to distribute them at random among the choice positions.

1. Which of these would you expect to be anti-inflationary in the United States?
   a. Increased consumption of goods.
   b. Increased exports to Europe.
   c. Limitation of credit to consumers.
   d. Limitation of the size of savings accounts. _____c_____

In many items, however, there is no objection to assigning the responses at random to the response positions. This gives the item writer an opportunity to balance roughly the number of answers occurring in each position.

Some writers have advocated that obvious answers should be placed last so that the examinee will be forced to read and consider the distracters before seeing the correct response. There is no evidence concerning the effectiveness of this procedure, and it appears to be of doubtful value. If the answer is so obvious that the examinee will choose it the moment he sees it, placing it last is not likely to help the item much.

11. *If the item deals with the definition of a term, it is usually preferable to include the term to be defined in the stem and present alternative definitions in the responses.* The reason for this suggestion is that it usually provides more opportunities for attractive distracters and tends to reduce the opportunity for correct response by verbal association. Consider these illustrations:

1. What name is given to the group of complex organic compounds that occur in small quantities in natural foods and are essential to normal nutrition?
   a. Nutrients
   b. Calories
   c. Vitamins
   d. Minerals _____c_____

2. What is a vitamin?
   a. A complex substance necessary for normal animal develop-
      ment, which is found in small quantities in certain foods
   b. A complex substance prepared in biological laboratories to
      improve the nutrient qualities of ordinary foods
   c. A substance extracted from ordinary foods, which is useful
      in destroying disease germs in the body
   d. A highly concentrated form of food energy, which should
      be used only on a doctor's prescription _____*a*_____

In the second item, more of the common misconceptions about the meaning of the term *vitamin* can be suggested and made attractive to the superficial learner.

12. *Do not present a collection of true-false statements as a multiple-choice item.* Such items usually reveal the item writer's failure to identify or specify a single problem. In some cases, the true-false statements are grouped about a single problem and could be easily reworded to make that problem specific. In other cases, the statements are so loosely related that they hardly constitute a single problem at all. This situation is illustrated by

1. What does physiology teach?
   a. The development of a vital organ is dependent upon
      muscular activity.
   b. Strength is independent of muscle size.
   c. The mind and body are not influenced by each other.
   d. Work is not exercise. _____*a*_____

Here two of the responses show some similarity. The other two are quite diverse. Grouping all in a single item leads the examinee to look for a common principle. It is difficult for him to arrive at any rational basis for selecting a best response. One beneficial change would be to replace *c* and *d* by others dealing with muscles or muscle activity and to reword the stem to point toward this problem.

A Note on Distracter Generation.   In an earlier section, Wesman pointed out the fact that distracters are an important part of the multiple-choice item. In fact, it seems obvious that the quality of a multiple-choice item depends quite heavily on the quality of its distracters. Additionally, systematic distracter construction procedures, coupled with the item analysis techniques discussed in Chapters 12 and 17, constitute a fairly powerful diagnostic tool. Let us briefly review some fairly common strategies for distracter construction. These are

1. The use of incorrect paraphrases of the correct response option.
2. The use of substantive words contained in the stem. This seems especially
   useful in foreign language competency exams and content areas having a
   distinctive technical vocabulary.
3. The administration of the stem using the well-known completion format. The
   most frequently occurring and/or logically appealing wrong responses supplied
   by the examinees can, with judicious editing, be used as distracters in
   subsequent administrations of the item.

4. A logical analysis of the task posed to the examinee by the item. Incorrect, but frequently used, examinee reasoning patterns identified in this way provide distracter generation mechanisms. This technique works especially well in mathematics where, for example, the item "3 + 2 = ?" might be accompanied by the correct response and distracters based on incorrect operations like subtraction, multiplication, and division.

Of these four strategies, the last provides the best example of what one should be aiming for in distracter generation because it produces distracters which differ from the answer in a systematic and easily described way. As a result, the distracters provide useful diagnostic information. In the arithmetic illustration, for example, examinees who respond in a more or less random fashion and those who systematically misinterpret the meaning of the + symbol would be easy to identify. With the latter type of error, useful remedial information would be available. More is said on this topic in Chapter 16.

Item Order and Placement of the Correct Answer. Assuming that we have written the required number of multiple-choice items for a particular test, the next tasks are (a) ordering the items and (b) choosing the location of the answer for each item.

If the items vary in difficulty, a reasonable approach to the first task would be to arrange the items according to their anticipated p-levels (difficulty levels) with the easiest items appearing first and the most difficult, last. Since most examinees seem to respond to test items in order, this approach allows the examinees to ease into the test and helps minimize the anxiety and frustration which tend to accompany an encounter with difficult items at the beginning of a test. If the items are of approximately the same level of difficulty, then any ordering will do.

Once the order has been established, a conscious effort must be made to vary the position of the correct answer in order to prevent the occurrence of a systematic answer pattern. For example, in a 40-item, 4-option multiple-choice test one might accomplish this by using each answer position a, b, c, and d approximately ten times with the items to be associated with each of these answer positions being determined using a random procedure.[6] As Wesman indicated (see previous section), an exception to this would be the item in which a particular ordering makes the examinee's task easier. For example, in items having numerical response alternatives, the alternatives should be arranged in ascending or descending numerical order.

Some Scoring Considerations. In most situations, multiple-choice items are scored 1 if correct and 0 otherwise, the total score for an examinee simply being

---

6. In this example, once the items are arranged in sequence the following procedure might be used to locate the answers for the first four items:
a. Roll a die. If side 1 through 4 occurs, place the answer for that item in position a. If sides 5 or 6 occur, ignore them and roll again.
b. Assume the first roll turned out to be 3. Roll again until a 1, 2, or 4 turns up. Locate the answer to that item in position b.
c. Assume a 1 turned up. Roll again until a 2 or 4 occurs. Locate the answer to that item in position c. The answer for the remaining item is automatically assigned to position d.
Repeat this procedure for each subsequent set of 4 items.

the number of items answered correctly. Other scoring procedures have been proposed over the years to suppress guessing behavior and/or to provide a mechanism for giving additional credit for partial information. A brief review and an assessment of the value of these procedures seems appropriate at this time. We begin with an excerpt from a note by R. L. Thorndike (1971, pp. 59–61)[7] which presents a cogent discussion of the issues related to the problem of guessing on tests.

> "Guessing" is a loose, general term for an array of behaviors that occur when an examinee responds to an alternate choice question to which he does not "know" the answer. The behaviors that may, and probably do, occur are many and varied. They include, among others:
>
> 1. Eliminating one or more answer choices judged to be definitely wrong.
> 2. Making use of unintended semantic or syntactic cues available from the wording of the question or the response options.
> 3. Falling into traps set by the ingenious item writer, e.g., cliché-like choices that sound plausible but are wrong.
> 4. Responding on the basis of some element in one of the response choices that attracts him, but at a relatively low level of confidence.
> 5. Using some essentially random fashion of responding – in the extreme, flipping a coin or marking some specific response position or pattern of positions.
>
> Of course, examinees may also omit items on which they do not feel sure of the correct response, and differences appear for different individuals, different schools, and different national cultures in tendency to omit the item when one is not sure of the answer.
>
> SCORING FORMULAS
>
> Obviously, if individuals respond purely at random, as by rolling a die or using a table of random numbers, they will get some items right. On the average the number right will be k/n, where k is the number on which they guessed, and n is the number of choices per item. The number of items on which random guessing occurred that will be gotten wrong will average $k - k/n$ or
>
> $$\frac{k(n-1)}{n} \quad \text{or} \quad (n-1)\frac{k}{n}.$$
>
> Since one can never know directly how many were gotten right by guessing, the number is inferred from the number wrong as being $W/(n-1)$, where W is the number wrong. Given this estimate of the number gotten right by guessing, it is possible to "correct" or adjust for this effect, using the formula
>
> $$R - \frac{W}{n-1}$$

---

7. Reprinted by permission of The American Council on Education.

to provide an estimate of the number of items to which the person "really knew" the answer. Similarly, it is possible to correct statistics on single test items using an expression such as

$$P_c = \frac{R - \dfrac{W}{n-1}}{R + W + O}$$

Where P_c = corrected percent of right answers,
             R = number getting item right,
             W = number getting item wrong,
             O = number omitting item,
             n = number of answer choices in an item,

to get an estimate of the percent of examinees who "really knew" the answer to the item.

      This logic, however, applies only when the behavior of the examinee is as described in behavior 5 above; that is, he responded as if he were using a table of random numbers. Even then it is applicable only as the *expected average number* of right responses, and values for a single examinee or a single item will show a fairly wide dispersion around the value to be expected on the average. So the adjustment as applied to the score for a specific person or to the proportion succeeding on a specific item is at best a crude and approximate adjustment — because of chance variations in a statistic based on a small sample of data, on the one hand, and because the basic assumption of random choice is rarely met, on the other.

      It should be noted that if every examinee answers every item, there will be a simple linear relationship between a score that is simply the number of right answers and one that is calculated by subtracting from the rights a fraction of the wrongs. Since, in this case, $R + W = N$, where N is the number of items, the corrected score becomes

$$\frac{nR - N}{n-1}$$

and depends only upon R, since the other factors are constant over all examinees. Thus, correction for guessing has a significant influence on individual differences in score only when items are omitted and when the number omitted varies appreciably from one examinee to another or from one item to another.

INSTRUCTION TO EXAMINEES

One can attack the problem of guessing at two points, through adjustments in scoring procedure after the individual has responded on the one hand and through instructions that attempt to control his response before he has responded on the other. Thus, a second aspect of the problem concerns the instructions that should be provided to the examinee. Should he be firmly instructed to answer every item, even if he has no idea which is the correct answer? Should he be instructed to answer only if he is "sure" of the right answer? Should he be given some intermediate instruction, inviting him to respond if he has some idea of what the correct answer is (or some assurance that one or more choices is wrong)?

To instruct the examinee to respond only if he is "sure" of the right answer has received little support among test-makers, though one suspects that this instruction is more prevalent among classroom teachers. On the one hand, there will certainly be individual differences in standards of certainty, so that the instruction will be interpreted differently by different examinees. At the same time, the instruction would seem generally to prevent examinees from displaying knowledge that they actually possess. The timid and insecure would seem to be most severely penalized by such an instruction.

More common has been an intermediate instruction worded somewhat as follows: "You may respond even if you are not sure of the right answer, but do not guess blindly." There is often some such additional instruction as: "A penalty of a fraction of a point will be assessed for wrong answers." This type of instruction is appropriately used only when a penalty *is* in fact assessed for wrong answers, and in that case a wording similar to the one given should presumably be provided. This instruction will not, and does not really try to establish for all examinees a uniform standard of confidence, at which point they will elect to mark an answer. To establish such uniformity is probably impossible, and one criticism of *any* approach that leaves to the examinee the decision of whether he has enough knowledge about a question to hazard a choice is that individuals may deviate by varying degrees from an optimum strategy. (In general, the deviation seems likely to be in the direction of being too conservative, unless the test-maker is very skilled at making seductive wrong options. In many test items there are cues that permit a person with only limited knowledge to exclude one or more options so that the odds in his favor are improved.) Basically, one has no real alternative to using some such instruction if the correction formula is to be used. The presumption is that when this type of instruction is combined with use of the correction formula, differing individual thresholds of willingness to respond will be of relatively little importance, because the correction formula will compensate for them.

The argument in favor of instructing examinees to answer every item is that if the instruction is followed (and if time is available for all to complete the test), correction of scores for guessing ceases to be of any importance. As was indicated above, corrected and uncorrected scores arrange people in identically the same order and correlate perfectly with one another. Two further arguments are that standards for responding are more uniform for all examinees, and that the scoring of tests is simpler and less subject to clerical error.

Arguments against instructing examinees to answer every question are of three types, which might be designated psychometric, pragmatic and "moral." From the psychometric point of view, it is argued that guessing, to the extent that it approaches random response, introduces variance that is pure error into the final score, and that this variance may be expected to lower the reliability of the score. To the extent that guessing *is* truly random, this argument is unimpeachable. However, when the individual responds with one of the other modes of response listed earlier, it is hard to say just what is the nature of the variance that is introduced. Systematic elimination of options and random selection from among the remainder imply partial knowledge, and such behavior may generate valid variance between individuals. Susceptibility to seductive wrong options certainly does not represent random behavior, but how it relates to the ability that the test is measuring is hard to say. Choices made at a low level of confidence probably represent a mixture of subthreshold knowledge and irrelevant past experience. So it is hard to state with assurance just what mixture of variance is generated by the instruction to answer every item, though there is good reason to be concerned that enough of it may approach random error so that the reliability of the resulting score will be reduced.

The pragmatic argument is that even though urged to do so, some examinees will fail to answer every item. They may fail to do so because of lack of time; they may fail to do so because they are temperamentally incapable of committing themselves to a choice on a question to which they do not know the answer. Liberal time limits reduce the first problem, and a warning that only two or three minutes remain and that one should quickly mark any unmarked items could eliminate the residue of that problem. However, such marking would clearly generate the type of random error variance referred to in the previous paragraph.

Overcoming the extreme reluctance to guess that seems to characterize some examinees is a more difficult problem. It is especially acute when pupils have been reinforced, as they are in some school systems, for being cautious and not committing themselves until they are sure. One suspects that if a culture were consistent in rewarding the examinee for answering all items, few would fail to respond in that way, but so long as practice remains divided one is likely to encounter some examinees who will resist the instruction to respond to all items.

The argument labeled "moral" would affirm that it is somehow "wrong" to guess at random. One argument offered in support of this wrongness is that in marking a wrong response one is "practicing error" and strengthening the tendency to give this response in the future. Connectionist learning theory of 40 years ago could be interpreted as asserting that occurrence of a connection strengthens that connection, even if no reward or reinforcement is provided. The issue here is what the connection is that is strengthened. If the examinee's mental process is "I think A is the answer, so I will choose it," the connection between the question and answer A appears to be explicit and its strengthening to have some probability. However, this is not random guessing; this is responding in terms of misinformation. When the mental process is "I haven't the foggiest idea what the answer is, so I might as well mark A," there seems to be little connection between the substance of the question and that of answer choice A. So where guessing is most random, the likelihood of any deleterious educational influence seems least.

CURRENT PRACTICE

Practice in United States testing organizations and among test publishers with respect to using the correction formula remains divided. The College

Entrance Examination Board continues to use such a correction on their Scholastic Aptitude Test, college admissions achievement tests and Advanced Placement Tests. However, the American College Testing Program uses for its tests a score that is simply the number right. Almost without exception, test publishers distributing tests for use by local school systems use a simple "rights" score on their tests.

The fact that among test publishers, as distinct from organizations administering large-scale testing programs, use of simply the number of correct answers as the score is almost universal may be attributable as much to practical convenience as to psychometric conviction. The publishers are selling their tests to many local users, who may do their scoring locally either by hand or by using any of a variety of types of scoring equipment. The requirement to apply a correction formula represents one additional complication and one additional possible source of clerical error. It has probably been as much to simplify the scoring procedure as for any more profound theoretical reason that the simple "rights" score has been adopted by these groups.

With a complex of educational, psychometric and practical issues involved, it is perhaps not surprising that test-makers have failed to reach a consensus on the correction-for-guessing problem. The issues have been recognized and debated throughout the short history of objective testing, but agreement does not seem an immediate prospect. One point on which there does seem to be agreement is that the instructions given the examinee should be consistent with the scoring procedure that is actually used, so that the examinee may have a clear picture of how his errors will be treated.

EXERCISE SET 14-3

1. a. If the formula $R - [W/(n-1)]$ is used to correct a test score for random guessing, what is the corrected raw score for an examinee who responds to 75 items correctly and 15 items incorrectly, and omits the remaining 10 on a 100-item, four-option, multiple-choice test?
   b. What is the corrected percentage score?

2. a. Suppose the same formula were used to correct for guessing in a situation where an examinee responds to 20 items correctly and 6 items incorrectly, and omits the remaining items on a 40-item true-false test. What is his corrected raw score?
   b. What is his corrected percentage score?

Confidence Weighting[8]. Any scoring procedure which requires the examinee to choose an answer and indicate in some prescribed manner (e.g., using a 10-point scale) the level of confidence he has in the correctness of his choice is called a *confidence weighting* procedure. The examinee's score in such cases is a function of the correctness of his responses and the measure of confidence (called a

---

8. A comprehensive review and assessment of the research in this area may be found in G. J. Echternacht, "The Use of Confidence Testing in Objective Tests," *Review of Educational Research*, 1972, 42(2), 217–236.

confidence weight) he attaches to his responses. Typically, the sum of the weights attached to incorrect responses is subtracted from the sum of the weights attached to correct responses to produce a total raw score. Although procedures of this type seem to have a sound conceptual base, there is some evidence that the scores which result using such procedures are contaminated by a personality factor which is uncorrelated with the examinee's status in the content area being tested (see, for example, Ebel, 1965). As a result, although these procedures tend to increase score variability and, in some cases, test reliability, validity may decrease due to the introduction of systematic, but irrelevant, "confidence" variance.

Identifying a Set of Possibly Correct Responses.   A somewhat different technique aimed more directly at the assessment of partial information involves either selecting as many of the alternatives to a multiple-choice item as seem plausible or eliminating (or striking out) as many of the alternatives as seem implausible. In either case, the scoring procedure typically awards the largest amount of credit to an examinee when his item response contains only the answer for the item. If his response contains more than one alternative or fails to contain the answer, his item score is reduced appropriately. Although examinees tend to view such procedures favorably, the personality variance which results may reduce validity and hence offset any beneficial gains in reliability which might be realized.

Probabilistic Approaches.   A third approach is based on the concept of personal probability. One implementation of such a procedure requires the examinee to "place a bet" on each response alternative. For example, he may be given 10 points to bet on each item which he can distribute in any fashion across the various alternatives. If he is absolutely certain that alternative a is the correct response, he would most likely bet all 10 points on alternative a and zero points on each of the remaining alternatives. If he thought a was the most plausible alternative, c somewhat less plausible, and b totally implausible in a 3-option item, he might choose to bet 7 points on a, 3 points on c, and 0 points on b.

The advantage of this approach over the confidence weighting notion discussed earlier is that, with certain assumptions about examinee behavior and the axioms of probability theory, one can devise very elegant and rational scoring rules. However, considerable research is required before the true value of this and the previous approaches can be assessed.

SUMMARY

In most research studies done in this area, test reliability has been the primary criterion for assessing the usefulness of these alternative multiple-choice test scoring procedures. The questions of validity and testing efficiency have not been adequately addressed. In most achievement testing applications, it may be the case that lengthening the test will more easily accomplish the purposes for which these procedures have been developed. Experimenting with them in a classroom testing situation does, however, introduce some measure of novelty into the testing situation and may serve as a useful motivational device. In such cases, limited use of these techniques may be justifiable.

Essay and Multiple-Choice Formats Compared[9]

In deciding whether to use the essay or multiple-choice formats, the following factors should be considered:

1. The essay format is especially well-suited for testing an examinee's ability to communicate within the context of a particular content area. To the extent that this is viewed as an important objective of instruction, the essay format ought to be employed.
2. Where the choice between the essay and multiple-choice formats is essentially a "toss-up," factors like reliability, item sampling errors, and efficiency (from both the examinee and test scorer point-of-view) tend to tip the balance in favor of the multiple-choice format.
3. Both item formats are legitimate. Rather than rigidly adhering to one or the other as the standard mode of testing, a great deal of flexibility can be gained by evaluating each format relative to the objective on which achievement is being measured, the nature of the examinee group, and various other practical factors.

FINAL COMMENTS

A great deal can be said about the layout of a test and its administration, much of which lies in the domain of common sense. Since a thorough review of these aspects of test construction is available in a variety of standard sources [e.g., *Educational Measurement* (second edition) edited by R. L. Thorndike], they are not dealt with in this text.

SUMMARY AND A LOOK AHEAD

In this chapter, we have examined the traditional approach to achievement test construction including planning, item-writing, and test-scoring considerations. Particular attention was paid to the essay and multiple-choice item formats. Armed with this technology, reasonably good tests can be constructed. In Chapter 6, we begin to examine several new approaches to test planning and item writing which attempt to make the test construction process more objective and reproducible, and to generate test items having a demonstrable, logical link to a

---

9. Specific guidelines for preparing items using other formats (e.g., true-false, completion, matching), as well as an assessment of the strengths and weaknesses of the formats are discussed by Wesman (1971).

well-defined content domain. Before proceeding to that chapter, test your comprehension of the material in the present chapter using the self-evaluation form provided for this purpose.

SELF-EVALUATION

1. Which of the following specific factors must be considered by the item writer when he is deciding on the number of options to be used for each item included in a multiple-choice test?
   a. His ability to produce high quality options
   b. The number of items in the test
   c. The age of the examinees
   d. All of the above

2. Application of the formula $R - [W/(n - 1)]$ to a set of test scores assumes that:
   a. all items in the test have the same number of alternatives.
   b. all examinees responded to every item.
   c. all responses are based on relevant knowledge or a systematic response strategy.

3. Suppose a particular examinee responds to just 24 items on a 30-item, 5-option, multiple-choice test. Twenty of his responses are correct. Using the formula $R - [W/(n - 1)]$, his adjusted score is _____ .
   a. 16   b. 17   c. 19   d. 21

4. The extent to which the formula $R - [W/(n - 1)]$ alters the relative standings within a group of examinees is directly related to _____ .
   a. the variability in the number of items omitted by the examinees
   b. the number of items included in the test
   c. both a and b
   d. neither a nor b

5. Which of the following practices is (are) generally recommended when essay items are used in testing?
   a. Allow the examinee as much latitude as possible in constructing responses.
   b. Ask only one or two questions and require an "in-depth" response to each.
   c. Provide a large number of questions and instruct each examinee to answer the subset about which he knows most.
   d. None of the above.

6. Research on the reliability of essay response rating procedures indicates:
   a. equally competent raters, working independently, usually rank order the responses to an essay item in the same way.
   b. a single competent rater tends to assign different scores to the same essay item response on different scoring occasions.
   c. both a and b are true.

7. In rating the responses of 30 examinees to five essay items, the teacher makes five separate passes through the stack of test papers. On each pass, he rates the responses of all examinees to a particular item. According to Coffman, this is a _____ practice.
   a. good   b. questionable   c. poor

8. In grading student responses to an essay item, teacher **X**:
   i. uses a 10-point rating scale.
   ii. prepares model answers worth one, five and ten points.
   iii. reads each response twice (at different times) and assigns the average score in each case.
   Teacher X's approach to essay response scoring is _____.
   a. good   b. of questionable value   c. poor

9. Multiple-choice test reliability is affected by the number of _____.
   a. items in the test   b. alternatives per item
   c. a and b

10. Among the following item types, the most satisfactory level of reliability tends to be achieved with the _____ item.
    a. essay   b. true-false   c. 3-option, multiple-choice

11. The muliple-choice item format most appropriate for a geography item which asks the students for the location of Mt. McKinley is the _____ variety.
    a. correct-answer   b. best-answer   c. multiple-answers

12. The multiple-choice item format which is especially suitable for assessing an examinee's skill at editing a prose passage is the _____ variety.
    a. negative   b. substitution   c. incomplete-statement

13. Item 9 above is an example of the _____ variety multiple-choice format.
    a. correct-answer   b. multiple-response   c. a and b

14. In writing multiple-choice test items, Wesman recommends that the item writer _____ .
    a. use a negatively stated stem wherever possible
    b. reserve use of the alternative "none of the above" for items presented in the best-answer format
    c. make all alternatives grammatically compatible with the stem.
    d. a, b, and c

15. *True or False.* Confidence weighting procedures capitalize on the examinee's knowledge of what he knows and, hence, usually increase the reliability and validity of the testing process.

ANSWER KEY

1. d	6. b	11. a
2. a	7. a	12. b
3. c	8. a	13. c
4. a	9. c	14. c
5. d	10. c	15. False

EXERCISE SET 14-1: ANSWERS

1. one
2. 100, 6

EXERCISE SET 14-2: ANSWERS

1. a. 5; none   b. 2
2. a. 12; 7   b. 13
3. No. In Table 14-3, the correlation is 0.871 despite the fact that only 2 out of 25 ratings were the same on both occasions. This should emphasize the fact that r is primarily a function of rank order consistency. A measure of agreement, the kappa statistic, is discussed in Chapter 17.

EXERCISE SET 14-3: ANSWERS

1. a. Here, $R = 75$, $W = 15$, and $n = 4$. Therefore, the corrected score is $75 - (15/3)$, or 70.
   b. The formula for the corrected percentage score simply tells you to divide the corrected raw score by the total number of items in the test. Therefore, the corrected value for this problem is 70/100, or 70%.
2. a. $20 - [6/(2 - 1)] = 20 - 6 = 14$ b. $14/40 = 0.35$, or 35%

REFERENCES

Coffman, W. E. (1971). On the Reliability of Ratings of Essay Examinations in English. *Research in the Teaching of English*, 5(1), 24–36.

Diederich, P. B. and F. R. Link (1967). Cooperative Evaluation in English. *Evaluation as Feedback and Guide*, Edited by Fred T. Wilhelms. Washington, D.C.: Association for Supervision and Curriculum Development, NEA.

Ebel, R. L. (1965). Confidence Weighting and Test Reliability. *Journal of Educational Measurement*, 2, 49–57.

Ebel, R. L. (1969). Expected Reliability as a Function of Choices per Item. *Educational and Psychological Measurement*, 29, 565–570.

Findlayson, D. S. (1951). The Reliability of the Marking of Essays. *British Journal of Educational Psychology*, 21, 126–134.

Godshalk, F. I., F. Swineford, and W. E. Coffman (1966). *The Measurement of Writing Ability*. New York: College Entrance Examination Board.

Grier, J. B. (1975). The Number of Alternatives for Optimum Test Reliability. *Journal of Educational Measurement*, 12(2), 109–112.

Guilford, J. P. (1954). *Psychometric Methods*, 2nd ed. New York: McGraw-Hill.

Hartog, P. and E. C. Rhodes (1936). *The Marks of Examiners*. New York: MacMillan.

Meyer, G. (1935). An Experimental Study of the Old and New Types of Examination: II. Methods of Study. *Journal of Educational Psychology*, 26, 30–40.

Meyer, G. (1934). An Experimental Study of the Old and New Types of Examination: I. The Effect of the Examination Set on Memory. *Journal of Educational Psychology*, 25, 641–661.

Noyes, E. S. (1963). Essay and Objective Tests in English. *College Board Review*, 49, 7–10.

Pearson, R. (1955). The Test Fails as an Entrance Examination. *College Board Review*, 25, 2–9.

Stanley, J. C. (1962). Analysis-of-Variance Principles Applied to the Grading of Essay Tests. *Journal of Experimental Education*, 30, 279–283.

Thorndike, R. L. (1971). Editors Note: The Problem of Guessing, in *Educational Measurement*, 2nd ed. (R. L. Thorndike, ed.). Washington, D.C.: America Council on Education.

Vernon, P. E. and G. D. Millican (1954). A Further Study of the Reliability of English Essays. *British Journal of Statistical Psychology*, 7, 65–74.

Wesman, A. G. (1971). Writing the Test Item, in *Educational Measurement*, 2nd ed. (R. L. Thorndike, ed.). Washington, D.C.: American Council on Education.

15

Instructional Objectives

In their article, *Criterion-Referenced Testing in the Classroom* (reprinted in Chapter 18 of this text), Airasian and Madaus document a number of reasons for the emergence of *objectives-based* instruction and measurement in American education, cite the advantages of a criterion-referenced (rather than a norm-referenced) approach to test score interpretation within an objectives-based context, and suggest how one might implement such an approach in classroom instruction. The present chapter, which would profitably be studied in conjunction with the Airasian and Madaus article, focuses on the form and substance of *objectives statements* which can provide a basis for the type of system they describe.

Traditionally, statements of objectives have been formulated in ways which do not provide very explicit guidance either for lesson planning or test construction. As Tyler (1949) has noted:[1]

> Objectives are sometimes stated as things which the instructor is to do; as for example, to present the theory of evolution [or] to demonstrate the nature of inductive proof.... The real purpose of education is not to have the instructor perform certain activities but to bring about significant changes in the students' patterns of behavior.... The difficulty of an objective stated in the form of activities to be carried on by the teacher lies in the fact that there is no way of judging whether these activities should really be carried on. They are not the ultimate purposes of the educational program and are not, therefore, really the objectives....
>
> A second form in which objectives are often stated is in listing topics, concepts, generalizations, or other elements of content that are to be dealt with in the course.... Objectives stated ... [in this form] do indicate the

---

1. Reprinted by permission of University of Chicago Press.

areas of content to be dealt with by the students but they are not satisfactory objectives since they do not specify what the students are expected to do with these elements. In the case of generalizations, for example, is it expected that the student is to memorize [them] . . . , or to be able to apply them to concrete illustrations in his daily life . . . , or is there some other kind of use to which the student is expected to put these generalizations? In the case of a list of topics the desired changes in students are still more uncertain. . . .

A third way in which objectives are sometimes stated is in the form of generalized patterns of behavior which fail to indicate more specifically the area of life or the content to which the behavior applies. For example, one may find objectives stated as "To Develop Critical Thinking." . . . Objectives stated in this form do indicate that education is expected to bring about some changes in the students and they also indicate in general the kinds of changes with which the educational program is expected to deal. However, from what we know about transfer of training it is very unlikely that efforts to aim at objectives so highly generalized as this will be fruitful. . . .

The purpose of the present discussion is to describe and illustrate one procedure for generating new statements or refining inadequate, existing statements of instructional objectives. The statements formulated in this way turn out to be quite useful as guides for curriculum development, classroom instruction, and the construction of achievement tests. The recipe presented in this chapter is patterned after and represents a refinement of the earlier work of Mager (1962) in this area. Let us now turn our attention to the characteristics of well-formed instructional objectives, several illustrative examples, and a few comments concerning the value of this approach.

THREE CHARACTERISTICS OF WELL-FORMED STATEMENTS OF INSTRUCTIONAL OBJECTIVES

A *well-formed* instructional objective must provide (a) a clear specification of the target behavior (Mager's terminal performance), (b) a clear specification of the performance standard (or criterion of acceptable performance), and (c) a description of the conditions (or constraints) which will prevail at the time student achievement of the objective is to be assessed. Let us first consider each of these characteristics in turn and then examine several examples which show the type of objective that results when this recipe is sensibly applied.

The Target Behavior

The most important element of an instructional objective is a clear specification of the target behavior. In classroom situations, a target behavior is an observable action presumed to be an important consequence of instruction. It is something that can be seen, and hence, it is measurable. Action verb phrases, such as *ties his shoelaces, reads aloud, writes original stories,* are examples of target behaviors. They are observable, and hence, provide important instructional and measurement implications. Each clearly tells the instructor what overt act is to be introduced into the student's behavior repertoire or modified as a result of instruction; each also tells the test constructor what his test procedure is to measure. By way of contrast, consider several passive verb phrases like *appreciates music, understands the principles of reinforcement,* and *likes to read* which do not describe overt acts, are not observable, and hence, are not directly measurable. They offer little guidance in instructional and measurement matters.

One of the principal tasks of the curriculum developer, classroom teacher, commercial test constructor, and others is to deduce from national, state, and local educational objectives that are typically stated in passive terms, the well-formed objectives specifying the observable, measurable acts implied by the more general objectives. For example, consider the following general objective: "The student likes to read." While most people would agree that this is an important objective, it is an inadequate guide for instruction and test construction as it stands because it does not specify a target behavior. One way of achieving a remedy for this problem is to ask the question, "If the student likes to read, then what kinds of overt acts is he likely to demonstrate as a result of this?" In the case of an average third grade student, the following deductions might be made: (a) given the opportunity in reading class, he volunteers to read excerpts from his textbook aloud, (b) given ample opportunity to visit the school library, he frequently checks out library books, and (c) given a choice between reading and a number of other school related activities, he consistently expresses a preference for the reading activity.

Approaching the problem in this way, one can take a general objective stated in nonperformance terms and translate it into a number of specific objectives, each pinpointing a particular target behavior believed to be an indicator of the general characteristic of interest. In this example, *voluntarily reading aloud, checking out books,* and *selecting the reading activity* in a free choice situation are all indicators of the student's "liking to read."

The Performance Standard

Once a target behavior has been identified, the next question to be answered concerns the quality of the performance which must be exhibited before it will be concluded that the objective has been achieved. This characteristic of an instructional objective is referred to by Mager and others as the standard or criterion of acceptable performance. Consider, for example, the following objective: "The student voluntarily reads at least 5,000 words of textual material per week." Here, the target behavior *reads . . . textual material* and the performance standard (or criterion of acceptable performance) *at least 5,000 words . . . per week* are both specified. The former identifies the act; the latter describes the quality of the act which must be exhibited before one is willing to conclude that the objective has been achieved.

An important problem, unresolved at this time, concerns the formulation of rational procedures for establishing performance standards. In most situations, the teacher involved in preparing the instructional objective or the test constructor engaged in clarifying an objective uses his knowledge of the students and subject matter involved in attempting to set reasonable standards. If one were dealing with the mastery of arithmetic skills, the performance standard might be specified in terms of a particular percentage score on an examination covering those skills. On the other hand, if one were concerned with a single task rather than a multiple-item test, the performance standard might very well deal with the quality of performance with respect to that task. For example, one objective for a preschool class might be "The student ties his shoelaces so the knot or bow remains intact during at least five minutes of playground activity." In this case, the performance standard describes the quality of performance which must be exhibited on a single task rather than as a percentage of successes on a series of tasks. In each case, however, specification of the performance standard or the minimum acceptable quality of performance which must be exhibited is left to the judgment of the writer of the objective.

Test Conditions: The Conditions Under Which the Target Behavior Must Be Exhibited

In addition to specifying the target behavior and providing an unambiguous specification of the performance standard, a well-formed instructional objective should also describe the relevant aspects of the situation under which the target behavior is to be exhibited by the examinee or student. These include relevant information about (a) the form of the test, (b) test time limit, and (c) the "givens" and restrictions.

The form of the test can have a significant effect on examinee performance in many situations. Some students consistently perform better on multiple-choice items than on essay or completion items; some socioeconomic groups consistently perform better on the nonverbal rather than the verbal measures of specific aptitudes. Whenever a dependency is known or expected to exist between test form and examinee performance, the relevant features of the form of the test to be used should be clearly specified in the statement of the objective.

If the task or test must be completed within a specific time period, such information is relevant and should be included in the statement of the objective. Sometimes, time specifications are considered to be performance standards (i.e., whenever time is an important indicator of performance quality); other times, they are regarded as test constraints or conditions. For example, the time specification in the objective "The student runs the quarter mile in less than two minutes" is strongly related to the quality of the performance and, hence, is most appropriately regarded as a performance standard. In running, swimming, shorthand, etc., time is an important indicator of performance quality and, hence, must be given full consideration in the decision regarding the establishment of performance standards. Similarly, the time specification in the more consumer oriented objective

"The appliance will operate properly without service for a minimum of one year" is a performance standard. In all other situations, the time specification is most appropriately regarded as a condition or a constraint. Perhaps the best example of this is the typical time limit placed on most classroom and standardized achievement examinations. Time in such situations is not usually regarded as important indicator of performance quality. However, it is a relevant constraint which should be noted in the objective since the duration of the test period is important to both the test constructor and the examinee. The important point here is, regardless of whether the time specification is regarded as a performance standard or as a test constraint, it should appear in the statement of the objective when relevant.

The term *givens* refers to a variety of resources the examinee may use at the time his achievement of the objective is being assessed; the term *restrictions* refers to the resources he is prohibited from using at that time. Of course, the types of resources which are relevant depend on the situation and the nature of the task. For example, information about whether students are allowed to use or prohibited from using their texts, notes, pocket calculators, etc., would be relevant in a mathematics achievement situation; information about the use of a dictionary, thesaurus, encyclopedia, etc., may be most relevant in a social studies setting; and information about clothing may be most relevant in the performance of a particular physical education task. The individual writing the objective should determine the relevant resources and classify each into the *given* or *restriction* category. Only then is it likely that such information will be considered when structuring instructional activities and constructing measures of achievement related to those activities.

SOME EXAMPLES OF WELL-FORMED INSTRUCTIONAL OBJECTIVES

In writing objectives using this recipe, a good deal of common sense must be applied. Objectives which are too vague offer little guidance to the instructor/test constructor. On the other hand, the prospect of spelling out everything in detail may "turn off" the prospective producer/user of instructional objectives. With practice, a satisfactory middle ground will be found and the resulting objective statements will provide the information necessary for sound instruction and measurement. Consider the following:

1. *A ninth grade physical education example.* Dressed in a standard gym outfit, the student will do at least 20 push-ups in three minutes or less. During this exercise, his body must remain rigid and, aside from his toes and palms, only his nose is allowed to touch the floor.
   Target Behavior: Do push-ups.
   Performance Standard: At least 20; 3 minutes or less; body must remain rigid; only toes, nose and palms allowed to touch the floor.
   Test Conditions: Outfitted in a standard gym suit.

2. *A sixth grade arithmetic example.* Using the text conversion table, the student transforms American weight measures into their metric counterparts. Ninety-five percent or more correct responses indicate mastery.

Target Behavior: Transforms American weight measures to their metric counterparts.

Performance Standard: Ninety-five percent accuracy.

Test Conditions: Using the text conversion table.

3. *A third grade reading example.* Given the opportunity, the student will volunteer to read excerpts from his reading text on at least three different occasions each week for one month.

Target Behavior: Volunteers to read excerpts.

Performance Standard: On at least three different occasions each week for one month.

Test Conditions: Given his reading text and the opportunity to volunteer.

SUMMARY AND FINAL COMMENTS

In this chapter, we examined Tyler's criticisms of several "older" approaches to writing objectives and then shifted our attention to a procedure for writing well-formed instructional objectives in terms of target behaviors, performance standards, and test conditions.

It is important to keep in mind that the production of well-formed instructional objectives is not an end in itself, but rather an attempt to make the goals of instruction explicit so that adequate measures of the achievement of these goals can be realized. Unfortunately, lesson planning and test construction are frequently carried out in a very haphazard way. Although there are times when this is unavoidable, the conscientious professional teacher/test constructor constantly works at clarifying the relevant goals and constructing measures of those goals which exhibit satisfactory levels of validity and reliability. The well-formed objectives approach described in this section provides a reasonable methodology for accomplishing that end. While the sensible use of this methodology does not guarantee success as a teacher or as a test constructor, it provides a very useful tool for lesson planning and test construction.

In a subsequent chapter, we will deal with procedures for transforming these objectives into test items. You should now conclude your activity in this chapter by assessing your comprehension of and skills in using this methodology. The self-evaluation form which follows is included for this purpose.

SELF-EVALUATION

1. Which of the following objectives is (are) stated in performance terms?
   a. The student knows how to plan a test.
   b. The student really understands the necessity for closely adhering to the rules of thumb for item writing.

c. The student defines the technical measurement terms appearing in Chapter 1 of this textbook.

d. The student sees the importance of measurement in curriculum evaluation.

2. For each of the following objectives indicate whether the *target behavior*, *performance standard*, *both*, or *neither*, are specified.

a. The student must know the correct form of an instructional objective.

b. The student points out or identifies instructional objectives stated in nonperformance terms.

c. Without the aid of textbook or notes, the student solves at least 90% of the following kinds of problems:

$$3x = 14$$

d. The student correctly answers 25 out of 30 five-option, multiple-choice items on the procedure for constructing classroom achievement tests.

3. Consider the following objective:

The student understands the concept "average." Which of the following statements specify student performances which are relevant to deciding whether the student has attained the general objective stated above.

a. The student correctly answers 8 out of 10 multiple-choice questions about the arithmetic mean, median, and mode.

b. The student defines the term "average."

c. The student outlines the procedure for calculating an arithmetic mean.

d. The student spells the word "average" correctly.

4. Consider the following general objective:

The student knows the meaning of the numeral "5." What specific performances on the part of the student would help the teacher decide whether he (the student) has achieved the objective as stated.

5. Rewrite the following objective using the three criteria for well-formed instructional objectives:

The student knows how to estimate the square root of a number.

ANSWER KEY

1. c
2. a. neither
   b. target behavior
   c. both
   d. both
3. There is no correct answer for this item. If you ask a number of people to answer this item, their responses will vary considerably. Some will choose a only; others will choose a and c; etc. The purpose of the item is to demonstrate the fact that the word "understands" is subject to many interpretations.

4. You can probably think of many ways of finding out whether a student knows the meaning of "5." One example is giving him a set of more than 5 objects and asking him to pick up the number of objects indicated by the numeral "5."

5. The target behavior is given. Many students mistakenly change *estimate* to *calculate* in the belief that the latter is less ambiguous than the former. *Estimate* has a very definite meaning and is not synonymous with the word *calculate*.

Special instructions or conditions which might be included in the objective pertain to (a) the use of aids, (b) the type of number, e.g., whole numbers, fractions, and/or (c) the time restrictions.

A performance standard for each item (e.g., each item must be correct to the nearest whole number) and for the test as a whole (e.g., at least 80% of the problems must be correct for a passing grade) should be added.

EXAMPLE

Within five minutes, the student must estimate the square root of 10 different counting numbers falling in the interval from 0 to 100, inclusive. Each estimate must be correct to the nearest whole number and at least eight answers must be correct for unit credit to be awarded. The use of scratch paper is not permitted.

REFERENCES

Mager, R. F. (1962). *Preparing Instructional Objectives.* Belmont, California: Fearon.

Tyler, R. W. (1949). *Basic Principles of Curriculum and Instruction.* Chicago: University of Chicago Press.

16

Some New Approaches
to Achievement Test
Construction

In Chapter 14, we examined the traditional approach to achievement test construction which involves (a) the formulation of a content-*by*-objectives (or content-*by*-behavior) matrix (see, for example, Tables 14-1 and 14-2), (b) the numerical weighting of each matrix cell to indicate the frequency or importance of the content-objective (or content-behavior) pairing it represents in the population of items (or tasks) deemed relevant for the test, (c) the production of test items, and (d) content validation of both the test and the matrix on which it is based via the judgment of content specialists.

Bormuth (1970) and others (e.g., Anderson, 1972) have cogently pointed out the limitations of the traditional test construction paradigm. These include

1. The content categories appearing as matrix headings are quite arbitrary and tend to reflect the individual test constructor's idiosyncratic conceptualization of the content area. As a result, two equally competent content experts may very well categorize the content differently and, hence, construct different test "blueprints" for the same body of content.
2. The behavior dimension typically contains terms like "knows" and "understands" or construct labels like "knowledge," "application," and "synthesis" which are subject to many interpretations. This factor, along with the one discussed above, tends to result in ambiguous domain definitions. One consequence of this is that two equally competent test constructors may interpret the same content-*by*-behavior matrix quite differently and, as a result, produce tests which are nonequivalent, i.e., tests having different means and standard deviations, and even a low to moderate correlation.

3. Even if the "blueprint" were interpreted in the same way by different test constructors, the process of translating it into a set of test items is heavily dependent on the individual item writer's technical skill, ingenuity, vocabulary, and a host of other factors. Hence, for most content areas there is no way one can unequivocally show the existence of a logical connection between an item and the content (or instruction) on which it is presumably based. The best one can do is have content experts judge the appropriateness of an item for a particular test "blueprint."[1]

Several of these criticisms have also been leveled at *objectives-based* tests, i.e., tests in which the blueprint consists of a list of objectives of the type discussed in Chapter 15. As a result, a number of "newer" approaches to domain definition/item generation have been proposed which attempt to further reduce domain ambiguity and provide item-generation mechanisms (rules) that allow the construction of tests which are content valid in a logical as well as a judgmental sense. This is especially important in criterion-referenced testing situations because test score interpretations in this context are difficult when these standards are not met. In a subsequent section, we examine several of these new strategies and attempt to assess their strengths and limitations. We then consider additional questions relating to test length, item selection, and the establishment of a cut score (if a criterion-referenced interpretation is intended). But first, a word about the concept of *domain-referenced testing*.

DOMAIN-REFERENCED TESTING

Generally, the term *domain-referenced test* refers to a test consisting of a representative sample of tasks (or items) from a well-defined population of tasks (or items). The ambiguities inherent in the traditional domain-definition approach using the content-*by*-behavior matrix have been noted and, hence, a test generated using the traditional approach would not be domain-referenced by the present definition. This statement will become more evident as, in the next several sections, we examine some strategies for generating domain-referenced tests.

A second important point concerns the distinction between the terms *criterion-referenced* and *domain-referenced*. Strictly speaking, the term *criterion-referenced* refers to the manner in which the examinee's test score is interpreted (e.g., pass/fail is defined in terms of some preset performance standard or cut score); the term *domain-referenced* refers to the logical relationship which exists between a set of items in a test and a well-defined domain represented by those items. Thus, domain-referenced tests can be used in either norm-referenced or criterion-referenced situations although, as Millman (1974) points out, the optimization of a test for one type of interpretation will tend to diminish its

---

1. Obviously, there are some content domains for which this criticism does not hold (e.g., the addition of two whole numbers taken from the set $\{0, 1, 2, \ldots, 9\}$), but these are relatively few in number.

usefulness for the other type. For example, to maximize a test's discrimination power for norm-referenced applications one would be forced to eliminate the easy and difficult items. This would not only reduce its utility for criterion-referenced applications, but it would also destroy its domain-referenced character, i.e., the test would no longer be a representative subset of the population or domain of items it was originally intended to represent. Of course, one can always redefine the domain in terms of the modified test, but whether such a course is desirable depends upon the goal of the test constructor.

The third point to be emphasized is that domain-referenced tests can be used to (a) estimate an individual's domain status, i.e., the proportion (or percentage) of items (or tasks) in the domain to which he is capable of correctly responding, or (b) to make criterion-referenced mastery decisions. The term *criterion-referenced test* seems an appropriate descriptive label for a domain-referenced test used in the latter sense.

Finally, it must be understood that the domain definition problem has not been completely solved. The approaches to be considered in this chapter do not singly or in combination provide all of the answers to the problems of criterion-referenced measurement. Each approach has serious limitations; however, these strategies represent an important step in the right direction and merit serious study.

SELECTED APPROACHES TO DOMAIN DEFINITION/ITEM WRITING

In this section we examine several approaches to the construction of domain-referenced tests. These include (a) the linguistic transformation approach, (b) the item form/item frame approach, (c) the amplified objectives approach, and (d) the facet design approach.

The Linguistic Transformation Approach

Bormuth (1970) first proposed an approach to item generation which involves the formulation of rules which, when applied directly to a segment of text or other written instructional material, transform the content of that segment directly into one or more test items. An attractive feature of this approach is that given a common text segment and a particular transformational rule, different item writers working independently will produce the same item(s). Thus, the text segment and the transformational rule provide an unambiguous definition of the relevant item domain.

Consider the following example of a very simple linguistic transformation, i.e., the *echo* transformation. An *echo* item is generated by replacing the period at the end of the original or base sentence with a question mark.

Base Sentence: Jane picked up the ball.

Item: Jane picked up the ball?

Next, examine the effects of several other types of transformations on the same base sentence:

Transformation Name	Item
1. Tag	Jane picked up the ball, didn't she?
2. Yes/No	Did Jane pick up the ball?
3. Noun deletion	Who picked up the ball?

The actual steps of the transformations illustrated here are not presented in this discussion, but careful examination of the base sentence and each item should allow one to intuit the approximate nature of each. The interested reader is referred to Bormuth (1970) for explicit representations of these and numerous other more complex transformational rules.

Subsequently, Anderson (1972) proposed examples of procedures for generating items to measure comprehension, as opposed to recall. He defines a verbatim question as one in which "a statement is taken in literal word-by-word form from the text or transcript of the instruction" (Anderson, 1972, p. 149), and then is either treated as a true-false item or transformed using procedures like those illustrated above. He offers the following illustration of the fact that verbatim items do not measure comprehension.

> Suppose the nonsense sentence, *The sleg juped the horm*, were presented. A person competent in the language could answer [the question], *Who juped the horm?* . . ., but he wouldn't comprehend the message. (Anderson, 1972, p. 150).

One procedure he recommends for measuring comprehension involves the use of paraphrase. In Anderson's (1972, p. 150) words,

> Two statements are defined as paraphrases of one another if (1) they have no substantive words (nouns, verbs, modifiers) in common and (2) they are equivalent in meaning. The first condition can be tested mechanically. As for whether two statements are equivalent in meaning, we can rely on the intuitive, unformalized knowledge possessed by any mature user of the language . . .; in order to answer a question based on a paraphrase, a person has to have comprehended the original sentence, since a paraphrase is related to the original sentence with respect to meaning but unrelated with respect to the shape or the sound of the words.

Consider the following simple examples of this technique:

1. *Base Sentence*: Jane picked up the ball.
   Noun Deletion Item: Who picked up the ball?
   Paraphrased Item: Who lifted the spherical object?
2. *Base Sentence*: Jane picked up the ball.
   Yes/No Item: Did Jane pick up the ball?
   Paraphrased Item: Did a girl lift the spherical object?

To test for comprehension of concepts, Anderson suggests that items generated using the paraphrase technique and items which require the examinee to identify or create new examples of the concept are appropriate. Consider the following examples:

1. *Definition*: A right triangle is a three-sided closed figure having only one 90° angle.
   Question:
   a. Draw a picture of a right triangle.
   b. Which of the following figures is an example of a right triangle (followed by a list of figures, only one of which is a correct response to the question)?
2. *Definition*: To incarcerate is to imprison or to confine.
   Question: Which of the following situations is the best example of incarceration?
   a. The boy threw a rock at the animal.
   b. The naughty child was sent to his room.
   c. The rags in the closet burst into flame.

Additional suggestions for item generation are provided by Bormuth (1970) and Anderson(1972). As you can see, this general approach, which involves transforming a segment of text or instruction using a rule, makes both the nature of the domain and the item-domain relationship quite explicit. It must be realized, however, that unambiguous transformational rules (of the type discussed by Bormuth) have been worked out for a relatively small class of item types. Additionally, attempts to produce rules for generating items to measure comprehension tend to be a bit more subjective in nature and their utility tends to be restricted somewhat by the vocabularies of the test constructor and the examinee population, as well as by the nature of the content. For example, many technical and scientific terms have very precise meanings, and hence, have no synonyms. As a result, assessing knowledge of them may be impossible to accomplish using the paraphrase technique.

The Item Form/Item Frame Approach

Unadorned instructional objectives, even when well-formed, tend to leave a number of questions unanswered. For example, consider the following objective: "The student will compare the weights of two objects using an equal-arm balance and choose the appropriate symbol to complete a statement which describes their weight relationship." The objective says nothing about the sizes, shapes, or weights of the objects to be used, the manner in which they are to be presented to the examinees, etc. One procedure for ameliorating this problem proposed by Osburn (1968) and Hively *et al.* (1973) involves the use of item forms. According to Osburn (1968, p. 98), "An item form has the following characteristics: (1) it generates items with a fixed syntactical structure; (2) it contains one or more variable elements; and (3) it defines a class of item sentences by specifying the replacement sets for the variable elements."

To begin, consider the following very simple example appropriate for use in an elementary history unit dealing with significant American inventors.

Item Form Shell: _____(a)_____ invented the _____(b)_____ .

Replacement Sets:

(a)	(b)
Marconi	radio
Whitney	cotton gin
Fulton	steam engine

Using this information, one could randomly select one element from replacement set (a) and one from replacement set (b), place two selected elements in the item form shell shown above, and use the resulting statement as a true-false item. Notice, this procedure is capable of generating nine items having exactly the same grammatical structure. This set of nine items would constitute a content domain.

A much more detailed and sophisticated item form, related to the equal-arm balance objective stated above, is shown in Figure 16-1 (From Hively *et al.*, 1973). Notice, this item form contains all of the elements necessary to generate the entire domain of items.

To begin our examination of Figure 16-1, first read the statement of the objective and General Description appearing in the upper left corner. This provides an overview of the item form and its intent. Next, notice the locations of the sections Item Form Shell, Cell Matrix, Replacement Scheme, and Replacement Sets.

The *Item Form Shell* describes the common (unchanging) elements of all items in the domain. Here, the materials, the directions to the examiner, and the script (what the examiner says to the examinee in presenting an item) are provided.

Next, consider the Cell Matrix, Replacement Scheme, and Replacement Sets. To generate an item for cell (1) in the *Cell Matrix*, the *Replacement Scheme* tells us to use objects o and a from the table contained in the *Description of Materials* section. Since a represents a small, 23-gm object and o, a large, 25-gm object, the resulting item requires the examinee to compare these two objects which differ in both size and weight. In accordance with the specification of cell (1) in the *Cell Matrix* (which says $S_1 > S_r$ and $W_1 > W_r$), the weight presented on the examinee's left side will be the larger of the two ($S_1 > S_r$) and the heavier of the two ($W_1 > W_r$).

As a second example, if cell (6) of the *Cell Matrix* were used, the row heading ($S_1 = S_r$) says the objects must be equal in size while the column heading ($W_1 < W_r$) indicates the left object must be lighter than the right one. The *Replacement Scheme* tells us to use *Replacement Set* 16.14 which in turn specifies the object pairs a and m or b and o as shown in the *Description of Materials* section. Consulting the table there, we see that a and m represent small 23- and 25-gm objects, respectively, and b and o represent large 23- and 25-gm objects, respectively. Once the test has been generated, the *Item Form Shell* sections provide test administration and scoring directions.

Using a modification of this approach, Price *et al.* (1974), generated several domain-referenced tests for measuring the acquisition of specific kinds of

ITEM FORM 16.14*

Comparing two objects on equal-arm balance and choosing a symbol to complete a statement of the weight relation.

GENERAL DESCRIPTION

The child is asked to compare the weights of the two objects that may be (1) indistinguishable by hefting but easily distinguished on the balance, (2) indistinguishable even on the balance. In each of these situations, size varies as an irrelevant dimension. An equal-arm balance is available but instructions for its use are non-directive. The child is asked to select one of the three symbols (>, <, and =) and place it in the blank space provided between the two weight symbols.

STIMULUS AND RESPONSE CHARACTERISTICS

Constant for All Cells

The equal-arm balance is of similar construction to that used in MINNEMAST Unit 16, made of Tinkertoys, cardboard, string, a metal weight, and a foot ruler.

The objects are opaque, cylindrical bottles, identical except for weight (either 23 gm. or 25 gm.) and size (either 2" × 5/8" or 2½" × 1¾"). Each is identified by a lowercase letter assigned at random.

The child is asked to complete a symbolic statement, corresponding to the weight relation, by choosing the correct relation symbol.

Distinguishing among Cells

Three weight relations (detectable by balance only, not by hefting or "feel") defined in terms of the location of the objects when placed in front of the child:

left > right; left < right; left = right.

Three size relations:

left > right; left < right; left = right.

CELL MATRIX

| | Weight Relations (Detectable by Balance Only) | | |
Size Relations	$W_1 > W_r$	$W_1 < W_r$	$W_1 = W_r$
$S_1 > S_r$	(1)	(4)	(7)
$S_1 < S_r$	(2)	(5)	(8)
$S_1 = S_r$	(3)	(6)	(9)

*Originally developed by Wells Hively.

ITEM FORM SHELL

MATERIALS

Beam Balance
Objects l and r
from T.O. 16.14.0
Stimulus-Response sheet (attached)
Pencil

DIRECTIONS TO E

Place materials in front of child. (Keep order of objects given above.)

- Balance
- Objects
- S-R Sheet
- Subject

SCRIPT

Here are two objects. They have symbols attached to them. Compare them by weight and write one of these three signs (point) in the blank (point) to form the comparison sentence.

You may use this balance if you need to.

RECORDING

Attach Stimulus-Response sheet to this page. Describe what child did.

If balance was used, insert object symbols in schematic drawing of the balance given below, and mark the position of the plumb-line at the time of child's judgement.

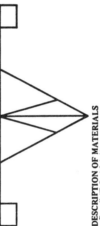

DESCRIPTION OF MATERIALS

Pencil (T.O. 16.1.1)

Beam balance (T.O. 16.13.1): Equal-arm beam balance made from Tinkertoy materials as described in MINNEMAST Unit 16.

Set of Weight Comparison Objects (T.O. 16.14.0); Set of opaque plastic cylindrical bottles with firmly fitting lids. Two sizes of bottles have been chosen. The small bottle has a length of 2" and a diameter of 5/8". The large bottle has a length of 2½" and a diameter of 1¾". Two weight values have been chosen so that the objects cannot typically be distinguished by hefting but can be distinguished on the balance. Each object is designated by a randomly chosen lowercase letter.

| Size | Weight | |
	23 gm	25 gm
small	a	m, k
large	b	n, o

Stimulus-Response sheet (attached to item) (T.O. 16.14.1); a sheet of paper approximately 6" × 4" with the following display:

Write >, <, or = in the blank

$$W_1 \; \underline{\quad} \; W_r$$

where l and r are the appropriate subscripts (from Replacement Scheme).

REPLACEMENT SCHEME

(l, r) Objects

- Cell 1: (o, a)
- Cell 2: (m, b)
- Cell 3: Choose from R.S. 16.13
- Cell 4: (b, m)
- Cell 5: (a, o)
- Cell 6: Choose from R.S. 16.14
- Cell 7: Choose from R.S. 16.15
- Cell 8: Choose from R.S. 16.16
- Cell 9: Choose from R.S. 16.17

REPLACEMENT SETS

R.S. 16.13	Ordered pairs	(m, a); (o, b)
R.S. 16.14	Ordered pairs	(a, m); (b, o)
R.S. 16.15	Ordered pairs	(b, a); (o, m)
R.S. 16.16	Ordered pairs	(a, b); (m, o)
R.S. 16.17	Ordered pairs	(m, k); (o, n)

SCORING SPECIFICATIONS

A correct response is made by writing the correct symbol (>, <, or =) in the blank space to complete the comparison sentence. This should be > in Cells 1, 2, and 3; < in Cells 4, 5, and 6; = in Cells 7, 8, and 9.

FIGURE 16-1. *Example of an item form (from Hively et al., 1973; reproduced with permission of the Center for the Study of Evaluation, University of California, Los Angeles).*

information from a line graph display. Each test was produced using an item frame and a set of rules. Figure 16-2 shows the complete recipe for generating one eight-item true-false test. Some specific examples of items are

1. The average value per share of Circle Electronics stock was greater than five dollars during the year 1966.
2. The average value per share of Cross Appliances stock was less than five dollars during the year 1968.

Using this approach, one could generate a number of randomly parallel eight-item tests (i.e., tests consisting of a random samples of items from the domain of interest), each measuring the examinee's ability to verify or recall a specific kind of information contained in the line graph.

Unquestionably, item forms and item frames are considerably less ambiguous than an unadorned objective with respect to both domain definition and item generation. However, it is quite apparent that this approach works best for highly structured types of content and may be completely unfeasible in many important situations. Even where this approach is useful, the development of an item form may be quite time consuming and, as a result, may seem totally impractical for the development of classroom tests. However, it is within the realm of possibility that item form/item frame banks may be assembled in specific content areas over the next several years in much the same manner that banks of instructional objectives have been formed (e.g., those compiled by the Instructional Objectives Exchange or by Westinghouse Learning Press). These could then be used by classroom teachers and professional test developers alike to construct tests for various purposes.

The Amplified Objectives Approach

Perhaps the most popular and widely used of the newer techniques for the construction of criterion-referenced/domain-referenced achievement tests at this time is the amplified objectives approach advocated by James Popham. Like the item form, this approach begins with an instructional objective. Additional information is then added to reduce as much as possible the ambiguities typically associated with the testing situation, response alternatives, and criterion of correctness. An example is provided in Figure 16-3. This figure merits careful examination because it shows a number of ways in which the objective on which it is based can be "amplified" to further clarify it. A slightly more structured approach, one more in keeping with the spirit of Hively's item form technique, is described by Popham and Baker (1973) and is illustrated in Figure 16-4. Notice, the amplified objective in this approach consists of (a) a response description (which is rather directly related to the instructional objective of interest), (b) content limits (essentially a rule for determining or identifying the content relevant to the achievement of the objective), (c) an item format specification (a detailed description of the characteristics of the item and the appropriate means of responding to it), (d) scoring criteria (the standards which must be met for the item

a. Graphical Display

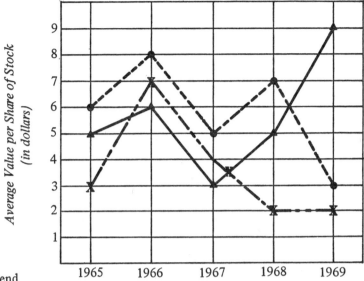

Legend
- ● Circle Electronics
- ▲ Pyramid Industries
- X Cross Appliances

Five Successive Years

b. Item Frame: The average value per share of (*name*) stock was (± *comparative*) than (*value*) during the year (*year*).

c. Generation Rules:

1. Company names for the eight items were selected randomly with the restriction that each company name was used at least twice and no more than three times.
2. The year values for the eight items were chosen randomly with the restriction that each year value was used at least once and no more than twice.
3. The comparative (greater than-less than) was assigned randomly to the items so that each appeared in four items of the subtest.
4. Within the four items containing the "greater than" comparative, the truth value was randomly assigned such that two propositions would be true and two would be false. The same procedure was used for the four "less than" comparative items.
5. For each item, the set of stock values that would satisfy the truth value for that item was determined, and one element of the set was randomly selected for inclusion in the item.

FIGURE 16-2. *Example of the item frame approach (Price, Martuza, and Crouse, 1974). Elements b and c are direct quotations from the published report. Element a (the figure) did not appear in the report but was obtained from the authors.*

Objective: Given a sentence with a noun or verb omitted, the student will select from two alternatives the word which most specifically or concretely completes the sentence.

Sample Item

Directions: Mark an "X" through one of the words in parentheses which makes the sentence describe a clearer picture.

Example: The racer (~~tumbled~~, went) down the hill.

Amplified Objective

Testing Situation

1. The student will be given simple sentences with the noun or verb omitted and will be asked to mark an "X" through the one word of a given pair of alternative words which more specifically or concretely completes the sentence.

2. Each test will omit nouns and verbs in approximately equal numbers.

3. Vocabulary will be familiar to a third- or fouth-grade pupil.

Response Alternatives

1. The student will be given pairs of nouns or pairs of verbs with distinctly varied degrees of descriptive power.

2. In pairs of verbs, one verb will either be a linking verb or an action verb descriptive of general action (e.g., is, goes), and one verb will be an an action verb descriptive of the manner of movement involved (e.g., scrambled, skipped).

3. In pairs of nouns, one noun will be abstract or vague (e.g., man, thing), and one noun will be concrete or specific (e.g., carpenter, computer).

Criterion of Correctness

The correct answer will be an "X" marked through the more concrete, specific noun or through the more descriptive action verb in each given pair.

FIGURE 16-3. *Amplified objective. (Reproduced with permission of the Instructional Objectives Exchange, Los Angeles, CA 90024.)*

to be judged correct or to be awarded a specific point value), (e) item directions (instructions telling the examinee how to respond to the item), and (f) a sample item (in Figure 16-4, the sample item consists of the item directions and the map of a continent).

The primary shortcoming of the amplified objectives approach is that it does not result in an item-writing recipe which can then be used to mechanically generate content valid test items. Hence, this approach may not lead to as explicit

Response Description: To be able to identify physical features on a map.

Content Limits: Maps will not include political features; elevation, vegetation, and waterways will be included with a range in their height, density, and length, respectively.

Item Format: Presented with a map of a country, to identify the point of greatest elevation, the longest waterway, the most dense vegetation by drawing a line to the appropriate features.

Criteria: Only the single correct answer for each feature should be indicated.

Item Directions: Draw a line which indicates the highest point on the map; draw a dotted line to the longest waterway; draw a broken line to the area of densest vegetation.

FIGURE 16-4. *Example of an amplified objective. (Reproduced with the permission of Prentice-Hall, Inc.)*

a domain definition as the linguistic and item forms approaches discussed previously. However, because this approach is widely applicable (e.g., it does not require as structured a content as the item forms approach) and because it is a natural extension of the well-formed objectives approach discussed earlier, it appears to be the most practical and perhaps most appealing approach to domain definition in a wide variety of instructional and measurement contexts.

The Facet Design Approach

Facet design, invented by Guttman (1969) for the purpose of mapping out a research domain, has a great deal of potential for the development of domain-referenced tests. If one can conceive of a population of items having both fixed and variable components, the facet approach provides a good conceptual framework for domain definition and item production.

In this approach, the test constructor begins by doing a conceptual analysis of the content to be tested. His goal is to identify a set of related facets (i.e., dimensions along which the items in the potential item population differ) which are then linked by what is called a *mapping sentence*. The Price *et al.* item frame example provided earlier (see Figure 16-2) may be regarded as a particular case of a facet-designed item. In that example, the item frame is the mapping sentence and the variable components represent the facets of the domain. Items can be generated rather mechanically by changing the elements in one or more facets. In most applications, however, the content is not as highly structured; hence, the mapping sentences tend to be considerably more vague than in the Price *et al.* example. Consider the illustration in Figure 16-5 which shows a more typical example. The "lettered" portions of the mapping sentence represent the facets.

	A. Referent		B. Referent's Commitment
The subject attributes to the	1. self 2. music educators 3. general public 4. students	the	1. belief 2. feeling

	C. Level		D. Actor's (i.e., music curriculum's) Behavior	
that the	1. elementary 2. secondary	school music curriculum	1. should be 2. is	taught by

E. Teacher		F. General Student Needs
1. classroom 2. specialist	for the purpose of fulfilling	1. relaxation 2. means of expression 3. break from academics 4. emotional stimulation 5. self-dicipline 6. fun time 7. contact with a human 8. group activity 9. uncover unknown talents 10. public performance 11. creative outlet 12. success 13. bring out shy students

FIGURE 16-5. *Example of a mapping sentence.* [*Millman, Jason, Criterion-Referenced Measurement. In* Evaluation in Education, Current Application *(W. J. Popham, ed), 1973, p. 333. Copyright 1974, American Educational Research Association, Washington, D. C. Reproduced by permission.*]

If the first element of each facet were chosen in this case (i.e., A-1 self, B-1 belief, etc.), the following item could be produced: "Do you believe that the elementary school music curriculum should be taught by a classroom teacher for the purpose of relaxing the students?" Similarly, the last element from each facet can be used to produce the following statement to which the respondent would answer *agree* or *disagree*: "Students feel that the secondary school music curriculum is taught by a specialist for the purpose of bringing out shy students." As you can see, the mapping sentence permits the generation of a large number of items which differ from each other in an easily described manner. One particularly attractive feature of this approach is it can be used to generate multiple-choice items in which the distracters differ systematically from the answer. For example, consider the mapping sentence shown in Figure 16-6 which was used by Engel (1975, p. 65) to generate the following multiple-choice item:

The following table lists scores on an attitude pretest and posttest for 3 students [in a course designated] BU307. Select the Pearson *r* for this set of data.

Attitude Questionnaire	
Pretest	Posttest
1	6
1	3
4	3

*a. −0.50
 b. 0.67
 c. 0.50
 d. −0.17

According to Engel,

If a student were to consistently select distractor type "c," then the content and facet structure of the distractor type could be related to that of the correct answer as follows:

*a. F1, G1, H1, I1, J1
 c. F1, G2, H1, I1, J1

Notice that compared to the correct answer, the distractor type varies in the G-facet. This facet element (G2) indicates that this incorrect answer was generated by an incorrect multiplication of signed numbers. Consistent selection of this distractor type would lead to a specific strategy for remediation.

Further refinement of Engel's approach (which uses the amplified objectives methodology to generate the mapping sentence, and the mapping sentence and linguistic notions to produce the items) may result in a useful approach for the construction of diagnostic tests in a variety of content areas.

	A. Presentation Form			B. Content Form
Given a	1. table		in	1. verbatim
	2. prose passage			2. concept

C. A Set of Ordered Pairs of Values on Variables

with   1. 3 pairs   "X"

              2. 4 pairs

              3. 5 pairs

D. Variable X		E. Variable Y
1. one digit		1. one digit
2. two digits	and "Y"	2. two digits
3. three digits		3. three digits

the student will select the correct value of $r(X, Y)$ from
a set of alternatives that vary with respect to

F. **Type of Score**
     1. deviation
     2. raw

G. **Multiplication of Signed Numbers**
     1. correct
     2. incorrect:
         $-x + = +$
         $+x - = +$
         $-x - = -$

H. **Division of SP(X, Y)**
     1. no
     2. yes, i.e., SP(X, Y)/N

I. **Square Root of SS(X) · SS(Y)**
     1. yes
     2. no

J. **Type of Unit**
     1. no unit
     2. linear unit
     3. square unit

FIGURE 16-6.   *Example of a mapping sentence (Engel, 1975).*

SOME REMARKS

In reviewing the newer approaches to test construction, one becomes aware of a trade-off which appears to exist between the precision with which a domain can be defined and the applicability of the approach to the broad range of achievement tasks which our society values. At one end of the continuum we have the ultimate in domain clarity and item reproducibility represented by Bormuth's transformational rules; at the other end, the broader range of applicability enjoyed by the amplified objectives technique. The remaining "new" procedures seem to lie between these points.[2] None of these approaches are as refined, well-articulated, and broadly applicable as we would like them to be and are certainly not capable of completely supplanting the traditional method in all its aspects. A sensible approach to classroom test construction would be to consider the applicability and practicality of each strategy to a given situation and to make use of the best each has to offer. Keep in mind that the greater the degree of clarity and reproducibility attainable, (a) the easier the item validity issue is to deal with, (b) the easier it is to generate parallel measures of a given objective, and (c) the more meaningful the individual test score is. The latter factor is especially critical in a criterion-referenced measurement context.

WHAT NEXT?

After the domain definition and item production strategies have been decided upon, the steps remaining in the construction of a domain-referenced/criterion-referenced test are

1. *Constructing a content valid test.* Recall, the two principal concerns here are (1) domain definition and (2) the production of a test consisting of a representative sample of items from the domain of interest.

    If, for example, the single item form shown in Figure 16-1 is used, the first of these criteria is automatically satisfied. The second can then easily be met by selecting a simple or stratified random sample of the replacement scheme/replacement set entries provided in the item form. The items generated using the results of this selection process will then constitute a representative sample (within the limits of sampling variability) of the target domain. The payoff is, of course, the assurance one has that an individual's score on the test is a content valid estimate of his competence in the entire domain. Of course, the precision of the estimate depends upon the number of items included in the test.

    On the other hand, if the amplified objectives approach is used, content specialists can be used to judge the goodness of the match between an objective and the items written to measure its achievement. The logical link between item and domain is somewhat tenuous because "hard and fast" logic is not provided for deriving an item from an objective. This is not a flaw in the approach. After all, this technique was proposed specifically to deal with situations not amenable to the more rigorous approaches. The main point here is that judgmental and/or experimental methods must be used to obtain validity data. (Some potentially useful methods for doing this are outlined in Chapter 17.)

---

2. A more technical and comprehensive comparison of the item form, linguistic transformation (or operational) and facet approaches, as well as a description of Scandura's algorithmic approach to domain definition/item generation is given by T. Hsu, Approaches to the Construction of Achievement Test Items. *The Researcher*, 1975, 14(1), 31–50.

Following the establishment of a large pool of content valid items, a one- or two-stage simple or stratified random sampling procedure may be used in item selection. Consider the following possibilities:

a. If a test is being constructed to measure achievement of a single objective and a fairly large number of items have been generated, a simple random sample of a predetermined size can be used.

b. If one is interested in measuring achievement of a small set of unrelated objectives and a fairly large number of items per objective have been generated, a simple random item sample of predetermined size should be taken for each objective. (*Note*: It is not necessary that each sample contain the same number of items. Keep in mind, however, that the precision with which an observed score estimates a person's true score is directly related to test length.)

c. If the measurement of student achievement of a large set of objectives is desirable, but because of practical constraints (e.g., test time available) is not feasible, one may first select a random sample of objectives to be tested and then select a random item sample for each of those objectives. Examinee performance on each item sample provides an estimate of achievement with respect to one objective and examinee performance across item samples provides an estimate of the percentage of the total set of objectives achieved by the examinee. For example, if an examinee meets this criterion on 8 out of 10 objectives sampled for testing and these 10 objectives are a random sample of some larger set, say 30 objectives, then 8/10, or 80%, is a reasonable estimate of the number of objectives he has achieved in the total set.

Obviously, this list is not exhaustive; other schemes can be used for item selection. In some situations a more systematic approach may be quite acceptable. For example, in constructing a test to measure achievement in the domain of arithmetic problems involving the addition of two single-digit numbers, one might deliberately write a set of items which insures that each digit is included in the test and that all of the digits were used approximately the same number of times. Remember, the goal is to construct a test which is representative of the content domain, and whatever procedure accomplishes that goal is acceptable. The most appropriate scheme for any given situation will depend on a number of factors including the number of items per objective, the level of precision required for estimating examinee domain status, the amount of time available for testing, and so on.

2. *Pilot testing the items.* The first time an item or test is used must be considered a tryout or pilot test exercise. This is true whether the item is constructed by a professional item writer for use in a standardized test or by a classroom teacher for use in a classroom achievement test. Even if an item is derived using a Bormuth-type transformation and reviewed by a competent content specialist, there simply is no way one can be sure that the item is completely free of flaws and is unambiguous to the knowledgeable examinee without an empirical tryout. Many problems can be avoided if guidelines like those provided by Wesman (see Chapter 14) are used to edit the items before use. However, items which appear to be near perfect sometimes fail the empirical test, and hence, data obtained from the initial administration of an item should be used cautiously in making decisions about an examinee. A sound strategy would be to use the item analysis techniques outlined in Chapters 12 and 17, as appropriate, to see whether an item functions as intended.

More often than not, achievement tests are administered for the purpose of estimating examinee achievement in a particular content domain or collection of content domains. When this is the case, item statistics (i.e., difficulty or discrimination indexes) should not be used as the sole basis for assessing item quality. This is most apt to happen in a norm-referenced situation because norm-referenced test reliability is directly related to item difficulty. Since the exclusion of very easy and/or very difficult items tends to optimize test discrimination power and, hence, test reliability, the temptation is strong to do so. In the process, items which measure the achievement of "easy-to-achieve" or "difficult-to-achieve" objectives are eliminated, thus jeopardizing the test's content validity. The decision to eliminate an item should always involve other considerations like the intended use of the test scores and the probable effect of such an action on content validity and domain definition.

3. *Estimating examinee domain status.* In Chapter 8, we discussed the use of the observed raw score (X) as an estimate of an individual's true score (T) in the context of classical measurement theory. While the raw score can be used in criterion-referenced testing, there are some advantages to using the proportion (or percentage) of correct responses instead, e.g., the proportion correct is interpretable even if test length is unknown, while the raw score is not.

Two noteworthy approaches to the estimation of domain status are (a) using the proportion (or percentage) correct on the test as the estimate of domain status[3] and (b) using collateral information such as the examinee's past achievement and the performance of his peers on the same or parallel tests to produce a refined estimate of domain status. Taking the first approach, Millman (1972) compiled a set of tables based on the *binomial probability model* which can be used to (a) determine the precision of the "test proportion correct" as an estimate of the "domain proportion correct" and (b) determine the number of items which ought to be included in a particular test for specified cut score values. Using the second approach, Novick and Lewis (1974) have shown that collateral information, such as the examinee's past academic performance and the performance of his peers on the same or parallel test(s), can be used to increase the precision with which one can estimate domain performance. For additional technical details regarding these approaches, the reader is referred to the articles cited above, or to Millman (1974) and Hambleton *et al.* (1975). (The latter two sources would probably be more readable to the novice in this area.)

4. *Establishment of a performance standard or cut score.*[4] A performance

---

3. Millman (1974) suggests that a correction for guessing be applied before converting the raw score to a proportion or percentage whenever the type of item used is one which allows examinees to increment their scores by guessing as, for example, when true-false or multiple-choice type items are used. While the application of such a correction in the norm-referenced case usually has little or no effect on examinee rank order in an achievement testing context, it would materially alter estimates of domain status and, in the criterion-referenced case, possibly change the examinee's location relative to the cut score.

4. Millman (1974) points out that in cases where one is interested only in estimating examinee status in a particular domain and is not concerned with grade assignment or making a pass/fail decision, there is no need to establish a cut score. He indicates that this would be true if, for example, one wanted to compare the status of different students at the same time or the status of the same student at different times with respect to a particular content domain. In the present discussion, we are assuming that test results are being used for decision-making purposes and, hence, the establishment of a cut score is necessary.

standard or cut score (i.e., the domain score which must be surpassed by the examinee if he is to be credited with achieving the stated objective (or mastering the content in a particular domain) must be established if the test results are to be subjected to a criterion-referenced interpretation.

One rational procedure for carrying out this task involves (a) examining each item in the test carefully and rating its importance on a 10-point scale ranging from "of little importance" to "extremely important" (with help from other content experts, if possible), (b) averaging these ratings across all items in the test, and (c) converting the result to a proportion. The proportion could then be used as the cut score for the test. For example, suppose a domain-referenced pencil-and-paper driver's license exam contained items related to (a) the meaning of a speed limit sign, (b) the meaning of a solid center line separating lanes on a two-lane highway, (c) knowledge of the exact stopping distance at 50 mph on a dry road, and (d) knowledge of the automobile license expiration date. Items in the first two categories are very important and probably would be rated at (or near) 10 on a 10-point scale, while items in the latter two categories are of lesser importance and might be rated at 8 and 7, respectively. The results could then quite easily be converted into a cut score using the method described. Note, this score may be adjusted upward or downward depending on a number of factors like (a) the possible effects of guessing on the test score [e.g., if multiple-choice or true-false items are used, Millman (1973) recommends either (1) correcting the observed scores to remove the constant positive bias due to guessing or (2) raising the cut score to compensate for the presence of the bias], (b) the possible effects of a sampling error, i.e., the possible selection of a set of test items which are unrepresentative of the domain making the test either too easy (in which case the cut score should be raised) or too difficult (in which case the cut score should be lowered), and (c) the relative cost (in terms of money, instructional and learning efficiency, and psychological effects on the learner and instructor) of erroneous master/nonmaster (or pass/fail) decisions. If the overall cost of erroneously passing nonmasters (called *false-positive* decisions) is greater than the overall cost of retaining (or failing) masters (called *false-negative* decisions), then raising the cut score will tend to minimize losses. If *false negatives* are more costly than *false positives*, then lowering the cut score will tend to minimize losses. So, if the relative costs can be assessed, such information can be used to choose a cut score that will minimize costs due to decision errors. In most classroom applications, the assumption of equal costs is probably a necessity given the current state of the art in this area. Hopefully, this will change shortly.

Additional discussions concerning these and other factors relevant to setting cut scores may be found in Millman (1973, 1974), Hambleton, *et al.* (1975), and Novick and Lewis (1974). The latter reference provides explicit suggestions regarding the appropriate value of the cut score for varying test lengths and false-positive/false-negative cost ratios. A tabular summary of some of these results is given by Millman (1974).

After considering a number of reasons why tests constructed using traditional procedures tend to be unsatisfactory for estimating examinee domain status and for making criterion-referenced mastery decisions, we formally introduced the concept of domain-referenced testing and used this concept to make more explicit the definition of a criterion-referenced test. We then examined a number of new approaches to the domain-definition/item-writing problem which, where applicable, enjoy a number of advantages over the traditional approach discussed in Chapter 14. Additionally, we considered a number of other factors which must be attended to in the test construction process where the estimation of examinee domain status and/or the making of a criterion-referenced mastery decisions are intended. These included item sampling, item tryout, estimation of examinee domain status, and establishment of a cut score.

Looking back over the discussions in Chapters 14 to 16, one can see that there are a variety of approaches to domain definition and item writing, the most critical distinguishing feature among them being the degree of explicitness achieved by these approaches. At one extreme, we have the traditional approach (with its test "blueprint" and "artistic approach" to item writing); at the other, the linguistic transformation approach of Bormuth (in which a linguistic transformation rule along with the specified transcript serves both as a domain definition and an item-generation rule). The remaining approaches seem to fall somewhere in between these two.

It must be realized that not one of these approaches is "best" or "worst" for all testing applications. Each has strong points as well as limitations. The choice of approach in a particular test construction situation should be determined by the intended use of the test and the utility of each approach relative to that usage. For example, the traditional approach may be judged quite adequate for a variety of situations (e.g., constructing tests to measure specific personality traits or to develop predictors for selected criterion variables), while one or a combination of newer approaches may be most suitable for other applications (e.g., making criterion-referenced mastery decisions in a self-paced, modularized achievement context).

In the typical classroom setting, there is an emphasis on achievement in some describable subject matter or skill area. Within such a context, there tends to be a concern with estimating examinee level of knowledge (i.e., domain status) and/or making decisions based on such information regarding the next most logical instructional step for a particular student or group of students. Here, domain-referenced test construction procedures seem to be most appropriate. Using the well-formed objectives approach of Chapter 15 and/or the techniques of the current chapter to (a) describe the domain(s) as explicitly as possible and (b) produce items whose logical relation to the domain(s) can be established enables one to construct tests which yield scores with clear meanings, making them especially well-suited for criterion-referenced interpretations.

In the next chapter, we round out the discussion of domain-referenced test construction and evaluation methodology by considering selected approaches to the assessment of reliability and validity of such tests. Before moving on, check your comprehension of the material in this chapter using the self-evaluation form provided for this purpose.

SELF-EVALUATION

1. Critics of traditional test construction methodology strongly suggest that _____ is(are) required in constructing tests to measure individual levels of knowledge.
   a. more explicit definitions of the content
   b. more "objective" procedures for producing test items
   c. both a and b
   d. neither a nor b

2. The term *domain-referenced* pertains to _____; the term *criterion-referenced* pertains to _____ .
   a. test construction . . . test score interpretation
   b. test score interpretation . . . test construction

3. Suppose a 10-item test is generated by the following procedure: Starting with the item frame $a \times b = c$,
   i Randomly select a, b, or c and insert in its place the letter N.
   ii Fill in each of the remaining two blanks by randomly selecting a counting number from 0 to 30, inclusive.
   iii Repeat this process ten times.
   This resulting test would most appropriately be called a _____ test.
   a. norm-referenced
   b. domain-referenced
   c. criterion-referenced

4. If a raw score of 8 or more were required to pass a test of the type described in item 3, the type of test score interpretation being made is appropriately labeled _____ .
   a. norm-referenced
   b. domain-referenced
   c. criterion-referenced

5. The test construction procedure described in item 3 is an example of the _____ approach.
   a. traditional
   b. well-formed objectives
   c. amplified objectives
   d. item form/item frame

6. The establishment of a cut score is necessary only when _____ test score interpretations are desired.
   a. norm-referenced
   b. domain-referenced
   c. criterion-referenced

7. Suppose an examinee's test score reflects an overestimate of his ability to correctly respond to the items (or tasks) in some well-defined population and,

as a result, he is erroneously declared a master with respect to that population. This is an example of a _____ error.
a. false-positive
b. false-negative

8. Suppose the cut score for a criterion-referenced testing application is set at 0.80 on the assumption that the cost of a false-positive error equals the cost of a false-negative error. The value of the cut score would most likely be decreased if it were subsequently determined that the cost of a _____ error is substantially greater than the cost of a _____ error.
a. false-positive . . . false-negative
b. false-negative . . . false-positive

9. Of the following approaches to domain definition/item writing, the one which seems viable in the greatest number of distinctly different subject matter areas is the _____ approach.
a. facet analysis
b. item frame
c. amplified objectives

10. The linguistic transformation approach to domain definition/item writing seems quite appropriate if one wishes to assess an examinee's
a. comprehension of a concept like "orange."
b. ability to discriminate between correct and incorrect applications of a particular grammatical rule.
c. recall of an important geographical fact.
d. a, b, and c.

ANSWER KEY

1. c	2. a	3. b
4. c	5. d	6. c
7. a	8. b	9. c
10. d		

REFERENCES

Anderson, R. C. (1972). How to Construct Achievement Tests to Assess Comprehension, *Review of Educational Research*, 42, 145–170.

Block, J. H. (1972). Student learning and the setting of mastery performance standards. *Educational Horizons*, 50, 183–190.

Bormuth, J. R. (1970). *On the Theory of Achievement Test Items*. Chicago: University of Chicago Press.

Engel, J. D. (1975). The Development and Investigation of a Methodology to Systematically Construct Multiple-Choice Achievement Test Items. Unpublished dissertation.

Guttman, L. (1969). Integration of Test Design and Analysis. *Proceedings of the 1969 Invitational Conference on Testing Problems.* Princeton: Educational Testing Service.

Hambleton, R. K. and M. R. Novick (1973). Toward an Integration of Theory and Method for Criterion-Referenced Tests. *Journal of Educational Measurement,* 10, 159–170.

Hambleton, R. K., H. Swaminathan, J. Algina, and D. Coulson (1975). Criterion-Referenced Testing and Measurement: Review of Technical Issues and Developments. An invited symposium presented at the annual meeting of the American Educational Research Association. Washington, D.C.

Hively, W., G. Maxwell, G. Rabehl, D. Sension, and S. Lundin (1973). *Domain-Referenced Curriculum Evaluation: A Technical Handbook and a Case Study from the Minnemast Project.* CSE Monograph Series in Evaluation, No. 1. Los Angeles: Center for the Study of Evaluation, University of California.

Millman, J. (1972). *Determining Test Length: Passing Scores and Test Lengths for Objectives-Based Tests.* Los Angeles: Instructional Objectives Exchange.

Millman, J. (1972). *Tables Needed for Determining Number of Items Needed on Domain-Referenced Tests and Number of Students to be Tested.* Los Angeles: Instructional Objectives Exchange.

Millman, J. (1973). Passing Scores and Test Lengths for Domain-Referenced Measures. *Review of Educational Research,* 43(2), 205–216.

Millman, J. (1974). Criterion-Referenced Measurement, in *Evaluation in Education, Current Applications* (W. J. Popham, ed.). Berkeley: McCutchan.

Novick, M. R., and C. Lewis (1974). Prescribing Test Length for Criterion-Referenced Measurements, in *Problems in Criterion-Referenced Measurement* (C. W. Harris, M. C. Alkin, and W. J. Popham, eds.), Monograph Series in Evaluation, No. 3. Los Angeles: Center for the Study of Evaluation, University of California.

Osburn, H. G. (1968). Item Sampling for Achievement Testing. *Educational and Psychological Measurement,* 28, 95–104.

Popham, W. J., and E. L. Baker (1973). Writing Tests Which Measure Objectives, *The Prentice-Hall Teacher Competency System.* Englewood Cliffs: Prentice-Hall.

Price, J. R., V. R. Martuza, and J. H. Crouse (1974). Construct Validity of Test Items Measuring Acquisition of Information from Line Graphs. *Journal of Educational Psychology,* 66(1), 152–156.

17

Reliability and Validity of Domain-Referenced Tests

As mentioned previously, a *domain-referenced* test is a representative sample of items (or tasks) from a well-defined population of items (or tasks). The population definition can be made sufficiently explicit in a number of ways, for example, (a) by listing or enumerating all of the items (or tasks) which comprise the domain or (b) by devising procedures or rules capable of generating all of the items in the domain. Examples of the latter approach were provided in Chapter 16. The major asset of a domain-referenced test is the special relation it has to the explicitly defined domain from which it was derived. The payoff is a test score which can be used in (a) estimating examinee status in the domain and/or (b) making meaningful criterion-referenced test score interpretations.

Please note that it is possible to attempt criterion-referenced interpretations using any test, however it is constructed; but unless the test is of the domain-referenced variety, such interpretations will not usually be satisfactory. For example, the most widely used standardized achievement tests, though well-planned and constructed, are not well-suited to criterion-referenced interpretations because (a) the domain definitions used in constructing such tests are not sufficiently explicit and (b) the item-writing and item-selection procedures typically used tend to place a premium on item discrimination power. Hence, the domain(s) represented by the entire set (or selected subsets) of items in a particular test of this type is(are) difficult to describe with any degree of precision. Furthermore, even if subsets of items within a standardized achievement test do appear to provide measures of achievement in describable domains, these subsets typically contain too few items to allow one to estimate domain status with an acceptable level of precision. As a result, attempts to estimate domain status or make criterion-referenced interpretations using all or portions of a test designed for norm-referenced interpretations tend not to be very fruitful. This does not mean that such tests are without value. Remember, they are specifically designed to produce test scores most suitable for norm-referenced interpretation and usually perform that function satisfactorily. The point is that a special type of test (i.e., a domain-referenced test) is most suitable if the scores are to be used to estimate domain status or to make criterion-referenced mastery decisions.

The purpose of the present chapter is to examine selected approaches to examining the quality of the items and tests designed for use in estimating domain status and/or making criterion-referenced mastery decisions. For the sake of brevity, the first of these usages, i.e., the estimation of domain status, will occasionally be referred to as a *domain-status* interpretation; the latter, as a *criterion-referenced* interpretation. Before proceeding to the heart of this presentation, let us first be certain of having the correct perspective regarding this presentation.

Whenever test scores are given either a domain-status or criterion-referenced interpretation, the *concepts* of reliability and validity are as important as in the norm-referenced case; however, the methodologies appropriate for assessing reliability and validity differ from those typically used in the norm-referenced case. For example, the correlational procedures which enjoy extensive use in the assessment of norm-referenced reliability and validity are not well-suited to the assessment of reliability and validity of tests intended to yield domain status or criterion-referenced interpretations. What is needed here are techniques which yield meaningful, interpretable results *regardless of the amount of variability present* in the test score distribution. In the remainder of this chapter, we look at a selected set of these procedures in some detail. Be aware of the fact that they do not represent all of the conceptualizations of domain-referenced reliability and validity discussed in the measurement literature to date, nor do they reflect the existence of a well-established, universally accepted set of domain-referenced or criterion-referenced measurement principles. However, the general approaches to assessing validity and reliability of domain-referenced tests (as well as the specific techniques) described herein appear, at present, to be among the most promising of those currently available. As will be noted, some of the techniques have important limitations; nevertheless, when used in combination and with a modicum of common sense, they provide the domain-referenced test constructor with a systematic methodology for assessing the quality of his tests and the validity of his test score interpretations. Let us begin by considering selected approaches to reliability estimation.

RELIABILITY

As in the norm-referenced case, the term *reliability* refers to the absence of measurement error or, equivalently, the quality of the observed scores assigned by the test as estimates of examinee true scores. However, as suggested previously, the statistical procedures used for estimating reliability of norm-referenced tests are not well-suited for use with tests intended to provide domain-status or criterion-referenced interpretations. Let us begin with the case involving estimation of domain status.

Estimating Domain Status

In situations where the emphasis is on the estimation of domain status, rather than on making a criterion-referenced decision, the ability of a domain-referenced test to estimate individual domain scores, i.e., percentage scores which would be obtained if the entire domain of items were presented to the examinees, is of paramount importance. To examine a test's reliability in such a situation, Millman (1974) proposes the following procedure: (a) generate two tests of equivalent length from the same domain, (e.g., select two random samples of items from the same domain), (b) intermingle the two sets of items in one form, (c) administer this form to the examinee population of interest (or a large representative sample thereof), (d) compute the absolute difference between percentage scores on the two tests for each examinee, and (e) construct a table or graph of the results to facilitate interpretation. An alternative to the last step is to compute the mean of the absolute differences. The closer this mean absolute difference is to zero, the better examinee observed percentage scores estimate their true percentage scores in this domain, and hence, the more reliable the test is in this examinee population. Millman warns us that the value obtained with this type of index is affected by the difficulty levels of the two tests; hence, information about test difficulty must be considered in interpretation.

Notice that there is a striking similarity between this procedure and both the split-half and parallel form procedures discussed earlier within a norm-referenced context. The principal difference is in how the test scores are used to provide the reliability estimate. In the norm-referenced case, the correlation coefficient was the statistic used (along with the Spearman-Brown formula in the split-half case). In the present case, a statistic which seems more meaningful is the mean absolute difference in percentages on the two tests. To illustrate the rationale for this, consider the following hypothetical example: Two 10-item tests are administered to three students using the procedure just described. On test I, their raw scores are 8, 7, and 6, respectively; on test II, their raw scores are 5, 4, and 3, respectively. For these data, the Pearson r value equals 1.00 which indicates that both tests assign the same *relative* scores to the examinees in question; however inspection of the scores and the mean absolute difference in percentages, $(|80\% - 50\%| + |70\% - 40\%| + |60\% - 30\%|)/3$, or 30%, clearly indicate the test's unsuitability for estimation of domain status.

Notice that this index will have a value of 0% when the scores are completely reproducible (i.e., the percentage score on one test is exactly the same as the percentage score on the other for each examinee) and under highly unusual circumstances may attain a maximum value of 100% (an extreme value like this occurring only in the unlikely case that each examinee scores 0% or 100% on one form and receives the opposite score on the other). Since experience with this index is somewhat limited, a general set of guidelines for its interpretation is not presently available. In general, however, the closer to zero, the better.

In a typical criterion-referenced achievement situation, a student strives to achieve a series of objectives. On each objective (or collection of related objectives), his achievement must be assessed and a decision made regarding one of two possible actions to be taken: (1) declare that the student has achieved (mastered) the objective(s) and allow him to move on, or (2) declare that he has not achieved (not mastered) the objective(s) and prescribe some remedial work.[2] Since such a decision has important consequences for the examinee, evidence of decision-making reliability or consistency is desirable. Retaining an individual who has achieved the objective (a false-negative decision) will unnecessarily retard his progress and may produce a variety of unwanted side effects like boredom, disenchantment with the content and/or structure of the curriculum, or a profound distrust of the evaluation procedures being used. On the other hand, passing a student on before a satisfactory level of achievement has been reached (a false-positive decision) may result in considerable frustration for the student, especially where success on subsequent objectives depends on prior achievement of the objective(s) in question. In the paragraphs which follow, we examine some criterion-referenced analogues to the norm-referenced procedures for assessing test reliability and rater consistency. We begin with a rather detailed exposition within the test-retest framework and subsequently discuss modifications required by the parallel form procedure. Then we examine the modifications necessary for assessing interrater and intrarater agreement.[3]

The Test-Retest Procedure. As in the norm-referenced case, the test-retest procedure may be used to assess the stability of a decision-making process. Unlike the norm-referenced case, where the primary concern is the ability of the test to assign the same relative scores in a single group of examinees on two separate occasions, the locus of attention in the criterion-referenced case is the ability of the decision process (which in many cases consists of a single criterion-referenced test) to classify students consistently as achievers (masters) or nonachievers (nonmasters) on two separate measurement occasions. The extent to which a test or decision-making process displays this type of consistency is an indication of its freedom from random measurement errors.

------

1. The material in this section follows the approach proposed by Hambleton and Novick (1973) using the statistical methods suggested by H. Swaminathan, R. K. Hambleton, and J. Algina (1974).
2. For an extension of this approach to the "more than two" category case involving examinee classification into categories like "master," "partial master," and "nonmaster," see Hambleton *et al.* (1975).
3. Whenever a decision-theoretic approach is used, the decisions made on the basis of all available information (including the probabilities and relative costs of false-positive and false-negative errors) are the proper focal point of reliability estimation. Whenever the decision is made solely on the basis of test performance or a subjective rating procedure and the costs of the two types of decision errors are either assumed equal or ignored, the reliability of the decision process is the reliability of the test or the rating process used. To avoid unnecessary complications and because the reliability of the test or rating process used is always important in its own right, the examples in this chapter are developed within the latter context.

Two statistics which may be used to quantify decision-making consistency are (1) P_o, defined as the proportion of examinees classified in the same category on both occasions, and (2) kappa (K), defined as P_o corrected for chance agreements. Let us examine the applications of each of these statistics in a hypothetical situation.

Suppose a particular criterion-referenced test was administered to 50 students on two separate occasions and the decisions shown in Table 17-1 resulted. For convenience, we first convert all of the tabled values to proportions by dividing through by the total number of decisions, 50 in this case. The results are shown in Table 17-2. To determine the value of P_o, compute the sum of the values in cells a and d of Table 17-2. In this example, 0.80 (or 80%) of the decisions made on the two occasions were in agreement. However, this value really represents an overestimate of the stability of this test (or decision-making process) for the simple reason that some fraction of these decisions can be attributed to chance. In general, the proportion of chance agreements in a table like this one is computed using the recipe $(a + b)(a + c) + (c + d)(b + d)$. In this example, the proportion of chance agreements (P_c) is $0.74(0.66) + 0.26(0.34)$, or 0.58. So, although P_o has

TABLE 17-1. *Example of a Decision Matrix for 50 Hypothetical Examinees.*

		Administration 1		
		Master	Nonmaster	Totals
	Master	(a) 30	(b) 7	(a + b) 37
Administration 2	Non-Master	(c) 3	(d) 10	(c + d) 13
	Totals	(a + c) 33	(b + d) 17	(a + b + c + d) 50

TABLE 17-2. *Data of Table 17-1 Expressed as Proportions.*

		Administration 1		
		Master	Nonmaster	Totals
	Master	(a) 0.60	(b) 0.14	(a + b) 0.74
Administration 2	Non-Master	(c) 0.06	(d) 0.20	(c + d) 0.26
	Totals	(a + c) 0.66	(b + d) 0.34	(a + b + c + d) 1.00

the desirable property of always being in the interval 0.00 (reflecting total disagreement) to 1.00 (reflecting total agreement), its tendency to overestimate the number of systematic or nonchance agreements tends to reduce its utility.

Cohen's (1960) kappa statistic (K), which measures the degree of agreement uncontaminated by chance, is defined as follows:

$$K = \frac{P_o - P_c}{1 - P_c}$$

where P_o and P_c are the proportions of observed and chance agreements, respectively, as computed above. In the present example,

$$K = \frac{0.80 - 0.58}{1 - 0.58} = \frac{0.22}{0.42} = 0.52$$

which reflects 52% agreement over and above that attributable to chance. In order to properly use and interpret K, the following factors must be kept in mind:

1. The value of K is always in the interval from 1.00 (reflecting total consistency) to some value near −1.00 (reflecting total inconsistency). The theoretical upper-bound value of 1.00 is fixed; the theoretical lower-bound value may fluctuate from situation to situation depending on a number of factors. However, since values of K less than 0.00 reflect decision making inconsistency, the lack of a fixed lower bound is unimportant in practical applications. Unlike P_o, K represents only the proportion of systematic or nonchance agreements. An examination of the formula for K shows that its value is always less than or equal to the value of P_o; the size of this difference being a function of the susceptibility of the decision process to chance influences.

2. A K value of 1.00 can be realized only when the marginal distributions for the two administrations have the same shape, i.e., when the proportion of "masters" in the right margin of the table equals the proportion of "masters" in the bottom margin of the table. The maximum value of K for the present case is determined by (a) adjusting the cell values in Table 17-2 to reflect the maximum possible number of agreements consistent with the observed marginal proportions and (b) calculating K using these adjusted values. For the present example, Table 17-3 reflects the appropriate adjustments. Here,

$$K_{max} = \frac{0.92 - 0.58}{1 - 0.58} = \frac{0.34}{0.42} = 0.81$$

This shows that the theoretical upper limit of 1.00 for K cannot be realized when the marginal proportions are as shown in Table 17-2. Though the procedure becomes a bit more cumbersome when K_{max} is routinely computed along with K, this extra step is probably a good one because it provides additional information for interpreting a specific K value. In particular, the ratio K/K_{max} provides a mechanism for interpreting K on a "standard scale" which has some advantages, e.g., the upper limit of this ratio is 1.00 regardless of the marginal distributions obtained in a particular application.

3. P_o and K are dependent on a number of factors associated with the decision process, e.g., the value of the cut score (i.e., the score used to classify examinees

TABLE 17-3. *Illustration of Tabular Adjustments Required in Table 17-2 for Calculation of* K_{max}.

		Administration 1		
		Master	Nonmaster	Totals
Administration 2	Master	(a) 0.66	(b) 0.08	(a + b) 0.74
	Non-Master	(c) 0.00	(d) 0.26	(c + d) 0.26
	Totals	(a + c) 0.66	(b + d) 0.34	(a + b + c + d) 1.00

as masters or nonmasters), test length (i.e., the number of items included in the test), the number of alternatives per item if multiple choice items are used, and the homogeneity of the examinee group in which the decisions concerning mastery and nonmastery are being made. As a result, the values K and P_o are interpretable only when information concerning these factors is available. The necessary research has not been carried out to date which would enable the formulation of guidelines for interpreting the values of P_o and K across a variety of situations differing with respect to these factors. As a result, whenever criterion-referenced test reliability is described using either P_o or K, explicit information regarding these factors should also be provided.

In the next several subsections we consider the criterion-referenced analogues to the norm-referenced parallel form reliability, interrater agreement, and intrarater agreement.

The Parallel Form Procedure. In most achievement testing situations, the utility of the test-retest procedure is questionable regardless of the measurement framework adopted. The reason is that new learning, forgetting, etc., tend to occur differentially across examinees from the first to the second measurement occasion and, hence, to differentially affect examinee true scores. Therefore, a more appropriate procedure involves the administration of parallel forms of a test to a single group of examinees on either one or two separate, closely spaced occasions. A question of interest then is whether the two forms show a substantial degree of agreement in classifying the members of the examinee group as masters and nonmasters. The data from administration of the two forms can be used to classify the subjects in a matrix like that shown in Table 17-1 with the following label changes: (a) *Administration 1* to *Form 1* and (b) *Administration 2* to *Form 2*. P_o and K would then be calculated in exactly the same way as they were in the test-retest case. If both forms agreed perfectly, all individuals would be classified in cell *a* and/or cell *d*. If both forms disagreed completely, all examinees would be classified in cell *b* and/or cell *c*. If one were to use *randomly parallel forms* (i.e., forms consisting of items randomly selected from the same domain), the expected distribution of classifications would be characterized by a heavy concentration of classifications in cells *a* and *d* and relatively light concentrations in cells *b* and *c*. This would result in values of P_O and K considerably greater than 0.00. In the parallel form case, P_O and K provide information concerning the relative invariance of the decision process across different item samples from the same domain.

Intrarater and Interrater Agreement. If mastery of an objective (or set of related objectives) is assessed for a group of examinees by one rater on two different occasions or by several raters on the same (or different) occasion(s), both P_O and K can be used to obtain measures of rater consistency.

In the intrarater (within rater) case, the single rater classifies all examinees as either masters or nonmasters on each occasion after taking appropriate steps to minimize the effects of the first rating on the second (for example, by shuffling the pages, obscuring examinee names and initial grade assignments). The resulting data are again arrayed as shown in Table 17-1 with minor labeling changes, i.e., changing *Administration 1* to *First Rating* and *Administration 2* to *Second Rating*. Either P_O or K may then be used as the index of *intrarater* agreement.

In the interrater (between rater) case, two (or more) raters independently classify all examinees as either masters or nonmasters one time. Again, the resulting data can be arrayed as shown in Table 17-1 with minor labeling changes, specifically, *Administration 1* changes to *Rater 1* and *Administration 2* changes to *Rater 2*. In this instance, P_O and K provide measures of interrater agreement. Note that P_O and K can be calculated in instances where more than two raters are involved. Such applications are described in a number of sources (see, for example, Light, 1973).

EXERCISE SET 17-1

Using the following data set, calculate
a. P_O b. K   c. K_{max}

		Rater 1		
		Master	Nonmaster	Totals
Rater 2	Master	20	10	30
	Nonmaster	10	20	30
	Totals	30	30	60

VALIDITY

As mentioned previously, a test (or test item) is *valid* to the extent that the scores it assigns to examinees are free of constant (or systematic) errors and, hence, the inferences based on those scores are justified. If the inference concerns examinee status in a well-defined domain, content validity is of concern; if the inference concerns examinee location on some hypothetical trait or construct continuum, construct validity is of concern; and, if the inference concerns examinee performance on a different test or task, criterion-related validity is of concern. When, as is usually the case, domain-referenced test scores are subjected to domain-status or criterion-referenced interpretations, content validity is especially important.[4]

Various approaches to assessing or demonstrating content validity have been proposed (see, for example, Rovinelli and Hambleton, 1973; Millman, 1974; and Hambleton *et al.*, 1975) including (a) the formulation of item generation rules which lead directly to the construction or derivation of content valid items, (b) the assessment of item and/or test validity using judgmental data obtained from content specialists, and (c) the assessment of item and/or test validity based on examinee responses to tests under different "experimental" conditions. Any systematic, thorough approach to domain-referenced test construction and/or revision, as well as the critical evaluation of existing tests, will probably require a combination of these approaches. Let us now consider each in turn.

Item Generation Rules

This approach to item validity involves the formulation of explicit rules which can be used to produce items in a rather mechanical fashion. One example of this technique is Bormuth's approach (see Chapter 16) in which rules enable one to systematically and objectively transform a segment of text or a portion of an instructional transcript into a test item. Other examples include Hively's item form and the Price *et al.* item frame approaches to domain definitions and item generation. When item-generation rules of this type can be formulated and used, a logical connection between the items and the content on which they are based can be demonstrated. However, the application of these techniques in a routine fashion to the many and varied content areas valued by our society is not always possible. Even where these techniques are applicable, it is doubtful that any content domain can be defined with absolute precision. Therefore, empirical validity assessment techniques, such as those discussed in the following two sections, should also be utilized by domain-referenced test constructors and test users.

Judgment by Content Specialists

One approach to the empirical validation of domain-referenced test items which have been written to measure the achievement of an instructional objective involves (a) having two or more content specialists judge the relevance of each item to the objective it is intended to measure and (b) using some index of interjudge agreement as the measure of item content validity.

---

4. If construct inferences are intended, i.e., if one intends to explain observable test performance in terms of one or more hypothetical constructs, evidence of construct validity is crucial. Some measurement specialists have been critical of domain-referenced testing. For example, Messick argues for the development of construct-referenced, rather than domain-referenced, tests in which case the focus would most properly be on construct validity. For his statement on this issue, see S. Messick, The Standard Problem: Meaning and Values in Measurement and Evaluation. *American Psychologist*, 1975, 30(10), 955–966.

One technique, developed by Hemphill and Westie (1950) and first applied to criterion-referenced item validity assessment by Rovinelli and Hambleton (1973), requires a group of content specialists to judge whether or not each item in a test measures each of the instructional objectives represented in the test. A value of +1 is assigned whenever an item is judged to be a measure of the objective; a value of −1, whenever the item is judged as definitely not a measure of the objective; and a value of zero, otherwise. The resulting data then are used to compute an *index of homogeneity of placement*. According to Rovinelli and Hambleton (1976), the Hemphill-Westie index has two important limitations; namely, it ranges in value between −0.40 and +0.67, and, more importantly, it is affected by the number of objectives and the number of content specialists involved in the particular application. To ameliorate these problems, Rovinelli and Hambleton (1976) derived a version of the Hemphill-Westie index that they call the *Index of Item-Objective Congruence*. Their formula may be stated as follows:

$$I_{io} = \frac{(M-1)S_o - S_o'}{2N(M-1)}$$

where I_{io} = the index of congruence for item i and objective o.

J = the number of objectives.

N = the number of content specialists.

S_o = the sum of the ratings assigned to objective o.

S_o' = the sum of the ratings assigned to all objectives *except* objective o.

An illustration of the computations involved in using this formula appears in Table 17-4.

TABLE 17-4. *Illustration of the Index of Item-Objective Congruence for Hypothetical Item #1.*

Judge	Objective 1	Objective 2	Objective 3	Objective 4	
A	+1	−1	−1	−1	
B	+1	−1	−1	−1	
C	0	0	−1	−1	
D	+1	−1	−1	−1	
E	0	0	0	0	
S_o	+3	−3	−4	−4	$S_1 = +3$ $S_1' = -11$

1. In the notation of equation (17-1), $I_{io} = I_{11}$, $M = 4$, $N = 5$, $S_1 = +3$, and $S_1' = -11$.

2. Therefore, the index of congruence for item *1* and objective *1* is:

$$I_{11} = \frac{(4-1)(+3) - (-11)}{2(5)(4-1)} = \frac{9+11}{30} = \frac{20}{30} = 0.67$$

According to Rovinelli and Hambleton, the limits of this index are -1.00 to $+1.00$ (the latter occurring only when there is unanimous agreement among content specialists that item i definitely measures objective o and no other objective). More importantly, this index yields the same result regardless of the number of content specialists and/or objectives involved in the application.

By computing the Index of Item-Objective Congruence for each item-objective combination, one would gain useful information concerning whether each item measures achievement of: (a) only its intended objective, (b) several objectives, or (c) none of the objectives. In test development, this kind of information would be useful in identifying items and/or objectives that may need revision, and in revealing heretofore unknown relationships among the objectives represented in the test.

A second approach, related to a technique described by Hambleton et al. (1975), involves supplying the domain definition and test items to two content specialists and having them independently rate the relevance of each item to the domain as defined. If a four-point rating scale (e.g., 1 = not relevant, 2 = somewhat relevant, 3 = quite relevant, and 4 = very relevant) is used, the joint ratings of the items involved can be displayed as shown in Table 17-5. One can then compute a measure of interrater agreement and an index of content validity. For example, suppose the relevance of each of 20 items in a test to a particular domain is independently rated by two content specialists using the four-point scale

TABLE 17-5. *Joint Ratings of the Relevance of 20 Test Items to a Particular Domain.*

		Rater 1		
		1 or 2	3 or 4	Totals
Rater 2	1 or 2	2	3	5
	3 or 4	1	14	15
	Totals	3	17	20

(a) *Interrater Agreement*

(1) $P_o = \dfrac{2 + 14}{20} = 0.800$

(2) $P_c = \left(\dfrac{5}{20}\right)\left(\dfrac{3}{20}\right) + \left(\dfrac{15}{20}\right)\left(\dfrac{17}{20}\right)$

$\qquad = 0.038 + 0.638$

$\qquad = 0.676$

(3) $K = \dfrac{P_o - P_c}{1 - P_c} = \dfrac{0.800 - 0.676}{1 - 0.676} = 0.38$

described above. Furthermore, suppose the joint ratings obtained are as shown in Table 17-5. Using P_o or K we can first assess interrater reliability.[5] If either or both of these values are too low, this may be a sign that the domain definition is somewhat ambiguous and/or the raters misunderstand what they are being asked to do, interpret the rating scale labels differently, or use the rating scales in a different fashion (e.g., one rater uses the full scale range, while the other tends to use the lower categories more often than the higher ones). If the root of the problem is domain-definition ambiguity, then refinement of the definition is in order. If the problem is a result of rater misperceptions of the task or differential use of the scale involved, steps should be taken to increase interrater reliability to an acceptable level. Once an acceptable level of interrater reliability has been achieved, a measure of content validity can be computed. Assuming that $P_o = 0.80$ indicates an acceptable level of interrater agreement in the present example, the index of content validity (CVI) can be taken as the proportion of items given a rating of 3 or 4 by both of the raters involved, here, $14/20 = 0.70$.

Notice, if all items are given ratings of 3 or 4 by both raters interrater agreement would be perfect (e.g., $P_o = 1.00$), and the value of the content validity index (CVI) would be 1.00. On the other hand, if one-half of the items are jointly classified as 1 or 2 while the others are jointly classified as 3 or 4, the value of P_o would be 1.00 (indicating perfect interrater agreement), but the value of CVI would be only 0.50 (indicating an unacceptable level of content validity).

Several comments concerning the use of this type of procedure are worth noting. First, what one considers to be an acceptable level of interrater agreement may vary from one situation to another. Some experience with these indices is necessary before one is able to assess the appropriate level for his/her particular situation. Until that experience has been gained, P_o greater than or equal to 0.80 or K greater than or equal to 0.25 should be useful guides.

Second, the content validity index used here suffers from the same *chance* inflation as P_o. An index of content validity which does not include chance classifications can be derived but this one seems quite suitable for most practical applications.

Third, the values of P_o, K, and CVI in a given situation depend on the number of rating categories used and the manner in which rating categories are combined. For example, if a 10-point scale had been used or if the present scale ratings were not dichotomized, the values of these indexes would probably be different, the exact nature of the difference being unknown.

Despite these apparent limitations, this general approach to quantifying content validity appears to be useful.

---

5. The properties of K are a bit more difficult to fully appreciate than those of P_o. As pointed out in this chapter, the maximum (and minimum) possible values of K are not constant from one application to the next and this tends to make interpretation somewhat difficult at times. One possible solution, as indicated previously, is to form the ratio K/K_{max} and use that index instead of K. Another is to use P_o augmented by visual inspection of the table on which it is based. Selecting a suitably stringent minimum value of P_o for use as a minimum acceptable level of agreement, e.g., 0.80, would be appropriate and in keeping with the motivation underlying the use of K.

1. What would be the index of item-objective congruence if Table 17-1 showed +1 for all judges on objective 1 and values of −1 everywhere else?
2. Suppose the rating procedure illustrated in Table 17-5 were used and the following data obtained. Calculate P_o and CVI and interpret their meaning.

Rater 1

		1 or 2	3 or 4	Totals
	1 or 2	20	0	20
Rater 2	3 or 4	2	3	5
	Totals	22	3	25

Objective Methods

Whether the scores from a domain-referenced test are given a domain status or a criterion-referenced interpretation, useful information can be gained through inspection of examinee performance on the individual items as well as the test as a whole. Let us first focus on procedures appropriate at the item level:

One general approach involves a comparison of the *expected* and *observed* p-levels for each item. This technique requires a rational estimate of each item p-level prior to looking at the test data. To illustrate, suppose careful consideration of a particular item and the examinee group to be tested resulted an expected p-level of 0.40 for that item.[6] If the actual p-level turned out to be near 0.40, no further check would be necessary. If, however, the discrepancy between the expected and observed p-levels turned out to be substantial,[7] further

---

6. Research indicates that teachers tend to judge items as being easier than they actually are for their students; a factor which should be kept in mind when using this technique. An investigation of one's own bias in this regard should prove to be an interesting and profitable exercise for most teachers.

7. With large samples of examinees, an "eyeball" comparison of the observed and expected p-levels is usually sufficient. With relatively small samples, statistical criteria for deciding whether the discrepancy is substantial can be established. For example, if N (the number of examinees) is, say, 30 or more and NP_e and $N(1 - P_e)$ are both greater than 5, a "substantial" discrepancy might be said to exist if

$$\frac{P_o - P_e}{\sqrt{P_e(1 - P_e)/N}}$$

is greater than 2.00 or less than −2.00. Here, P_o represents the observed item p-level, P_e represents the expected or predicted item p-level, and N is the number of examinees in the group.
If, in the present example, $P_e = 0.60$ and $N = 50$, then

$$\frac{0.40 - 0.60}{\sqrt{0.60(0.40)/50}} = \frac{-0.20}{\sqrt{0.0048}} = -2.89$$

The discrepancy in p-level would be considered substantial enough to warrant further examination of the item.

examination of the item would be in order. If the item had the familiar multiple-choice format, an examination of the item with special attention to the proportion of examinees selecting each distractor might provide clues to possible item flaws.

As a second illustration of this general approach, consider the situation in which the test under consideration is to be used for making criterion-referenced mastery decisions and all of the items in the domain (and, hence, in the test) are expected to have approximately the same p-level. This would occur when the items were naturally homogeneous in difficulty level (e.g., addition of pairs of digits where each is in the set zero to five, inclusive) or when an instructional treatment designed to produce a very high level of mastery in the domain preceded the test. In the latter case, observation of an item p-level substantially less than the test cut-score (expressed as a proportion) would indicate that a more penetrating analysis of that item is warranted. A useful adjunct technique in this case involves the use of P_O or K to measure the extent to which any test item agrees with the total test in classifying the examinees with respect to mastery level. For example, suppose the data (expressed as proportions) in Table 17-6 reflect the joint classifications of 100 examinees by a particular criterion-referenced test and item 1 in that test. In this case we find 23% agreement between item 1 and the total test above and beyond that expected on strictly a chance basis.

As before, we can calculate the value of K_{max} to see what the maximum possible agreement is if the marginal proportions of Table 17-6 are preserved (see Table 17-7). In this example, the value of K suggests that the item is functioning in a manner consistent with the total test.

Finally, suppose a particular set of items is designed to measure the achievement of knowledge or skills related in a hierarchical fashion. In such a circumstance, it would be reasonable to expect examinees correctly responding to items "high up" in the hierarchy to also respond correctly to the related lower-level items in the same hierarchy. For example, examinees correctly answering a high

TABLE 17-6. *The Joint Classifications of 100 Examinees by One Item and the Total Test Score.*

Test Decision

		Master	Nonmaster	Totals
Item Decision	Master	0.75	0.05	0.80
	Nonmaster	0.15	0.05	0.20
	Total	0.90	0.10	1.00

$$K = \frac{P_o - P_c}{1 - P_c} = \frac{[0.75 + 0.05] - [(0.80)(0.90) + (0.20)(0.10)]}{1 - [(0.80)(0.90) + (0.20)(0.10)]}$$
$$= \frac{0.80 - 0.74}{1 - 0.74} = \frac{0.06}{0.26} = 0.23$$

TABLE 17-7. *Illustration of Tabular Adjustments Required in Table 17-5 for Computation of* K_{max}.

Test Decision

		Master	Nonmaster	Total
Item Decision	Master	0.80	0.00	0.80
	Nonmaster	0.10	0.10	0.20
	Total	0.90	0.10	1.00

$$K_{max} = \frac{[0.80 + 0.10] - [(0.80)(0.90) + (0.20)(0.10)]}{1 - [(0.80)(0.90) + (0.20)(0.10)]} = \frac{0.90 - 0.74}{1 - 0.74} = 0.62$$

percentage of application-level items (in the Bloom-*Taxonomy* sense) on a particular topic would also be expected to correctly answer a relatively high percentage of comprehension and knowledge level items on the same topic as compared to examinees performing poorly on the application items. Similarly, elementary school students who correctly compute the answers to problems like $\sqrt{2753}$ would be expected to respond correctly to addition, subtraction, and multiplication problems which test the component skills in the higher-level square-root problem.

Notice that each of these techniques involves making a prediction about the item *p*-level and then checking that prediction against examinee performance. If the prediction for an item is supported, further examination of that item is unnecessary; if the prediction is not supported, closer examination of the item and/or the basis for the prediction would be in order.

Earlier we said that test score variance was not a prerequisite to reliability and validity of domain-referenced tests. However, one can conceive of situations in which selected groups of examinees would be expected to exhibit different levels of performance on either a particular item or on an entire domain-referenced test. We now consider three related approaches of this type which, as you will see, bear a strong resemblance to the experimental and contrasted groups validity strategies discussed in Chapter 10.

If two groups of examinees known to differ with respect to mastery in a particular domain can be identified or created, relevant data on item validity can be obtained. For example, beginning with a group of examinees who know relatively little with respect to the content domain, one can administer the domain-referenced test to them before and after a relevant instructional treatment. Assuming the instruction is effective, a significant increase in the proportion of correct responses on items related to the instructional treatment would be expected. For example, suppose a group of 100 examinees respond to a particular item on both a pretest (i.e., a test administered before exposure to an instructional treatment) and a posttest (i.e., the same test administered after exposure to the instructional treatment). Suppose their responses are as shown in Table 17-8. Notice, cell *a* in

TABLE 17-8. *Data for Illustrative Example.*

		Posttest		Total
		Correct	Incorrect	
Pretest	Incorrect	(a) 70	(b) 10	(a + b) 80
	Correct	(c) 15	(d) 5	(c + d) 20
	Total	(a + c) 85	(b + d) 15	(a + b + c + d) 100

this table indicates the number of examinees who responded to the item incorrectly on the pretest and correctly on the posttest, cell b indicates the number of examinees responding incorrectly on both occasions, and so on. In Table 17-9, these values are expressed in proportions. If the instructional treatment relevant to the objective this item is intended to measure is known to be reasonably effective, then a substantial increase in the item p-level from pretest to posttest would be positive evidence of item validity. In the absence of such a finding, an examination of the item would be in order. The difference between the posttest and the pretest p-levels, sometimes referred to as the pretest/posttest difference index (PPDI), can be obtained as the difference between the values in cells $a + c$ and $c + d$ or between the values in cells a and c. In the present example, the value of PPDI = 0.65.

Equivalently, randomly dividing a group of naive examinees into two groups, applying the instructional treatment to just one of these groups, and then testing both groups produces data permitting the same type of comparison. Again, assuming the instructional treatment is effective, a greater proportion of correct responses on items directly related to the instructional treatment should be observed in the instructed group.

While both of these techniques are useful, they are not without limitations. For example, in the first procedure, exposure to the pretest may influence posttest

TABLE 17-9. *Data of Table 17-8 Expressed as Proportions.*

		Posttest		Total
		Correct	Incorrect	
Pretest	Incorrect	(a) 0.70	(b) 0.10	(a + b) 0.80
	Correct	(c) 0.15	(d) 0.05	(c + d) 0.20
	Total	(a + c) 0.85	(b + d) 0.15	(a + b + c + d) 1.00

performance by sensitizing the examinees (i.e., making them more receptive) to the instructional treatment. Additionally, valid items based on difficult content or hard-to-master skills may not show up well simply because the instructional treatment was inadequate in some respect. Problems like these should not be taken to mean that the techniques under consideration are without value; rather, they indicate that a reasonable amount of caution is necessary in their application.

Finally, contrasted groups can sometimes be created "after the fact" in a criterion-referenced application by classifying examinees as masters and nonmasters based on their total test scores.[8] Evidence that an item discriminates between masters and nonmasters in such a situation is a positive indication of item validity. Please note, however, that failure of an item to discriminate does not necessarily indicate lack of validity; but an item which discriminates in a negative fashion would certainly merit closer examination.

In all of the procedures discussed thus far in this chapter, two basic strategies were used: (1) make a prediction about item p-level and check this against the data, and (2) identify or create groups of examinees expected to perform differently on a particular item and compare this expectation with their actual performance. If item generation procedures of the type described earlier are used to produce the test, statistical techniques like these provide a useful methodology for detecting subtle as well as gross types of item flaws so they can be remedied. While item analysis techniques like these are most valuable when constructing a test, the routine examination of the item p-level and item response chart (see Chapter 12) with previously validated items may provide useful insights regarding possible omissions or ambiguities in an instructional treatment, especially when multiple-choice items are used.

In concluding this section on validity, some attention to the assessment of validity at the test level, rather than the item level, seems appropriate. Just as predictions about p-levels of items provide a basis for assessing item validity, predictions can be made and empirically checked for the entire test. For example, on a test designed to measure student ability to add fractions having different denominators, one would expect a group of examinees instructed on this arithmetic procedure to outperform a comparable group *not* receiving such instruction. Hence, an experiment set up to test such a prediction would provide relevant validity evidence.

Finally, a procedure more akin to the correlational approach to criterion-related validity (see Chapter 10 for a refresher, if necessary) might also be used to check the validity of the inferences made using a domain-referenced test. For example, it may be reasonable to expect a moderate correlation to exist in the examinee population between performance on a particular domain-referenced test and performance on some other kind of task, or to expect significant differences in performance among masters and nonmasters in a domain of related, but different, tasks. In such cases, either the Pearson correlation coefficient, P_o, or K might

---

8. The existence of a group of nonmasters may mean that these students are unable or lack the motivation to achieve mastery of the domain in question, in which case reexamination of the objective(s) and instructional treatment would seem to be in order.

provide an appropriate index of validity depending, of course, on the particular form of the expectation. For the first type described above, r would be appropriate; for the second, either P_o or K.

In concluding this section, it is appropriate to emphasize once again the fact that the process of validation is a complex one. Not all approaches apply in any particular testing application. In mapping any validation strategy, the techniques must be chosen which produce the kinds of evidence required to determine the quality of the intended test score interpretation and concurrently point out defective items so they can be remedied before they are reused. Usually a combination of methods like those discussed in this section is required.

SUMMARY AND FINAL COMMENTS

In this chapter, we examined selected approaches to assessing reliability and validity of domain-referenced tests used for (a) estimating domain status (domain-status interpretations) and (b) making criterion-referenced mastery decisions. It was pointed out that when test scores are subjected to a domain-status interpretation, estimation of the examinee's actual domain percentage score is important; when they are subjected to a criterion-referenced interpretation, estimation of the correct domain classification (i.e., master vs nonmaster) of each examinee is of concern. Hence, the reliability estimation strategies for the two cases are somewhat different.

It was also pointed out that the type of inferences made using domain-referenced test scores in either of the above ways requires evidence of content validity. Three general approaches to this problem were described in some detail. Any serious test construction project or test validity study would most likely involve consideration of all three of these approaches to the content validity problem.

The methods described in this and the preceding chapter provide the domain-referenced test constructor with a useful test-construction/test-evaluation methodology. However, to take full advantage of it, one must be quite familiar with both the strengths and limitations of the component parts of this methodology. Despite the relative recency of interest in this type of testing, a great deal of progress has been made. Nevertheless, there is considerable room for refinement and the development of new and better approaches, particularly in the area of domain definition/item writing where new theoretical advances would be most welcome.

SELF-EVALUATION

1. The type of validity of primary concern in criterion-referenced measurement is _____ validity.
   a. content   b. construct   c. criterion-related

2. While item validity is always important, it is of special concern in _____ measurement.
   a. norm-referenced   b. criterion-referenced

3. Which one of the following statistics is most suitable for measuring the extent to which two judges independently classify a group of students with respect to a specific criterion or cut score?
   a. The index of item-objective congruence
   b. The Pearson correlation coefficient
   c. P_O

4. Of the statistics listed below, which one can be used to obtain a measure of agreement between separate classifications of the same examinee group above and beyond that expected on the basis of chance alone?
   a. P_O b. K   c. r

5. The value of P_O will usually be _____ the value of K.
   a. greater than
   b. approximately equal to
   c. less than

6. When we say that a criterion-referenced test is very reliable, we mean it is capable of reproducing examinee _____ with a high degree of accuracy.
   a. rank order
   b. raw scores
   c. mastery classifications

7. Suppose an English teacher reads a set of essays written by his class and on this basis assigns each student to one of two categories: pass or fail. Two weeks later, the same teacher reorders the essays and, after rereading each, again classifies each student into either the pass or fail category. Which of the following indexes is (are) most suitable for measuring the teacher's consistency in classifying his students?
   a. The index of item-objective congruence
   b. The Pearson r
   c. P_O
   d. K

8. Suppose 200 examinees are given alternate forms of a 10-item criterion-referenced test on the same day and the following decisions result:

		Form A		
		Master	Nonmaster	Total
Form B	Master	90	20	110
	Nonmaster	40	50	90
	Total	130	70	200

   a. What is the value of P_O?
   b. What is the value of K?
   c. What is the value of K_{max}?
   d. What can you say about the equivalence of these two forms?

9. Suppose 100 students responded to a particular criterion-referenced test item included in both a pretest and posttest, and the following data were obtained.

		Posttest		
		Correct	Incorrect	Total
Pretest	Incorrect	20	40	60
	Correct	30	10	40
	Total	50	50	100

a. Calculate the posttest p-level.
b. Calculate PPDI.
c. What hypotheses can you make about the test item, content, or instructional procedures which provided the basis for these data.

10. Suppose 150 students are randomly divided into *instruction* and *noninstruction* groups. The students in the *instruction* group are given instruction relevant to a particular objective, while those in the *noninstruction* group are given some irrelevant activity to perform for about the same amount of time. Both groups are tested for achievement of the objective in question and the following data are obtained.

	Group		
	Instruction	Non-Instruction	Total
Correct	50	15	65
Incorrect	25	60	85
Total	75	75	150

a. What is the p-level for each group?
b. What conclusions can you draw about the item's ability to discriminate between those who achieved the objective and those who did not?

1. a   2. b   3. c
4. b   5. a   6. c
7. c, d
8. a. $(90 + 50)/200 = 0.70$

b. $P_c = \dfrac{110}{(200)}\dfrac{130}{(200)} + \dfrac{90}{(200)}\dfrac{70}{(200)} = 0.52$

$K = \dfrac{0.70 - 0.52}{1.00 - 0.52} = \dfrac{0.18}{0.48} = 0.38$

c. The tabled values for K_{max} are

110	0	110
20	70	90
130	70	200

$P_o = \dfrac{110 + 70}{200} = \dfrac{180}{200} = 0.90$

$P_c = 0.52$ (as above)

$K_{max} = \dfrac{0.90 - 0.52}{1 - 0.52} = \dfrac{0.38}{0.48} = 0.79$

d. Both P_o and P_c indicate a moderate amount of agreement between the two forms. Whether the forms would be judged equivalent in this case is debatable. Instances like this point up the need for additional study of K and other agreement statistics for use in criterion-referenced measurement so reasonable guidelines for interpretation can be formulated.

9. a. Posttest p-level = 0.50 (not very good for a criterion-referenced test).
   b. PPDI = $20/100 - 10/100 = 0.10$ (positive, but not very high).
   c. Forty percent of the examinees apparently did not benefit from instruction; 30% (or a slightly smaller number if you adjust this figure for guessing) apparently achieved the objective prior to instruction (maybe it was covered on Sesame Street); even though the PPDI is positive, only 30% of the examinees' performances changed from pretest to posttest. This suggests that either the instruction was ineffective or the item is insensitive to achievement of this objective. All factors considered, examination of the test item and the instructional approach are in order.

10. a. Instruction p-level = $50/75 = 0.67$; noninstruction p-level = $15/75 = 0.20$.
    b. The difference in p-levels ($0.67 - 0.20 = 0.47$) suggests that this item discriminates between those who achieved the objective and those who did not. Of course, we are assuming that more students in the instructional treatment have achieved the objective than in the other group. However, the relatively low instruction-group p-level ($p = 0.67$) suggests that item and/or instructional quality might still be improved.

In fraction form, the table values become

		Rater 1		
		Master	Nonmaster	Totals
Rater 2	Master	1/3	1/6	1/2
	Nonmaster	1/6	1/3	1/2
	Totals	1/2	1/2	1.00

a. $P_O = 1/3 + 1/3 = 2/3$, or 0.67

b. $P_c = (1/2)(1/2) + (1/2)(1/2) = 2/4 = 1/2 = 0.50$

$$K = \frac{(P_O - P_c)}{(1 - P_c)} = \frac{(0.67 - 0.50)}{(1.00 - 0.50)} = \frac{0.17}{0.50} = 0.34$$

c. To find K_{max}, (i) change the smallest off-diagonal entry in the original table to 0, (ii) keep the marginal totals as they are, and (iii) fill in the remaining cells by subtraction. The resulting table values are

		Rater 1		
		Master	Nonmaster	Totals
Rater 2	Master	30	0	30
	Nonmaster	0	30	30
	Totals	30	30	60

Here,

$$P_O = \frac{30}{60} + \frac{30}{60} = 1.00$$

$$P_c = \frac{30}{(60)} \frac{30}{(60)} + \frac{30}{(60)} \frac{30}{(60)} = 0.50$$

$$K_{max} = \frac{P_O - P_c}{1 - P_c} = \frac{1.00 - 0.50}{1.00 - 0.50} = 1.00$$

This example illustrates the fact that when the marginal distributions are rectangular or flat, $K_{max} = 1.00$.

REFERENCES

Cohen, J. (1960). A Coefficient for Agreement of Nominal Scales, *Educational and Psychological Measurement*, **20**, 37–46.

Hambleton, R. K. and M. R. Novick (1973). Toward an Integration of Theory and Method for Criterion-Referenced Tests, *Journal of Educational Measurement*, **10**(3), 159–170.

Hambleton, R. K., H. Swaminathan, J. Algina, and D. Coulson (1975). Criterion-Referenced Testing and Measurement: Review of Technical Issues and Developments. An invited symposium presented at the annual meeting of the American Educational Research Association, Washington, D.C.

Hemphill, J. and C. M. Westie (1950). The Measurement of Group Dimensions, *Journal of Psychology*, **29**, 325–342.

Light, R. J. (1973). Issues in the Analysis of Qualitative Data, in *Second Handbook of Research on Teaching* (R. Traver, ed.). Chicago: Rand McNally, pp. 318–381.

Millman, J. (1974). Criterion-referenced Measurement. In W. J. Popham (ed.) *Evaluation in Education, Current Applications*. Berkeley, Calif.: McCutchen.

Rovinelli, R. and R. K. Hambleton (1973). Some Procedures for the Validation of Criterion-Referenced Test Items. Final Report. Albany: Bureau of School and Cultural Research, New York State Education Department.

——————. (1976) On the Use of Content Specialists in the Assessment of Criterion-Referenced Test Item Validity. *Laboratory of Psychometrics and Evaluative Research Report No. 24*. Amherst, Mass.: The University of Massachusetts.

Swaminathan, H., R. K. Hambleton, and J. Algina (1974). Reliability of Criterion-Referenced Tests: A Decision Theoretic Formulation, *Journal of Educational Measurement*, **2**(4), 263–267.

18

Selected Readings

This chapter consists of reprints of three articles that not only amplify and extend important concepts discussed in Chapters 1 through 17 but also provide a refined perspective and some practical considerations related to the use of standardized and teacher-made tests in an educational context.

In *Guidelines for Testing Minority Group Children*, Deutsch *et al.* identify and discuss the special problems which arise when standardized tests currently on the market are used to measure the "potential" or performance of minority group children. Problems of reliability and validity, particularly as they affect test score interpretation, are examined rather closely. Although the discussion is aimed rather directly at the user of standardized tests, the problems discussed are quite general and should be of considerable interest to the classroom teacher.

In *Interpreting Achievement Profiles — Uses and Warnings*, Gardner examines both the advantages and potential problems associated with the use of profiles to visually convey examinee performance in a number of different areas simultaneously. This article is an excellent supplement to Chapter 11 "Interpretation of Norm-Referenced Measurements."

In *Criterion-Referenced Testing in the Classroom*, Airasian and Madaus sketch the background, identify the trends leading to the current popularity in criterion-referenced measurement, and discuss the implementation of the criterion-referenced approach in the classroom. This article should be of interest to teachers contemplating the adoption of a criterion-referenced approach to instruction and measurement.

Guidelines for Testing Minority Group Children*

Martin Deutsch
Joshua A. Fishman
Leonard Kogan
Robert North
Martin Whiteman

INTRODUCTION

American educators have long recognized that they can best guide the development of intellect and character of the children in their charge if they take the time to understand these children thoroughly and sympathetically. This is particularly true with respect to the socially and culturally disadvantaged child.

Educators must realize that they hold positions of considerable responsibility and power. If they apply their services and skills wisely they can help minority group children to overcome their early disadvantages, to live more constructively, and to contribute more fully to American society.

Educational and psychological tests may help in the attainment of these goals if they are used carefully and intelligently. Persons who have a genuine commitment to democratic processes and who have a deep respect for the individal, will certainly seek to use educational and psychological tests with minority group children in ways that will enable these children to attain the full promise that America holds out to all its children.

Educational and psychological tests are among the most widely used and most useful tools of teachers, educational supervisors, school administrators, guidance workers, and counselors. As is the case with many professional tools, however, special training and diagnostic sensitivity are required for the intelligent and responsible use of these instruments. That is why most colleges and universities offer courses in educational and psychological testing. It is also the reason for the growing number of books and brochures designed to acquaint educators and their associates with the principles and procedures of proper test selection, use, and interpretation.[1]

Responsible educational authorities recognize that it is as unwise to put tests in the hands of untrained and unskilled personnel as it is to permit the automobile or any highly technical and powerful tool to be handled by individuals who are untrained in its use and unaware of the damage that it can cause if improperly used.

---

* Prepared by a Work Group of the Society for the Psychological Study of Social Issues (Division 9 of the American Psychological Association). Reprint of Deutsch, J. A. Fishman, L. Kogan, R. North, and M. Whitemen. "Guidelines for Testing Minority Group Children," *Journal of Social Issues*, Vol. 20, No. 2, Supplement, pp. 129–145. Reprinted with permission of the publisher.

1. See, for example, Katz (1958), Froelich and Hoyt (1959), Cronbach (1960), Anastasi (1961), Thorndike and Hagen (1961).

The necessity for caution is doubly merited when educational and psychological tests are administered to members of minority groups. Unfortunately, there is no single and readily available reference source to which test users can turn in order to become more fully acquainted with the requirements and cautions to be observed in such cases. The purpose of this committee's effort is to provide an introduction to the many considerations germane to selection, use and interpretation of educational and psychological tests with minority group children, as well as to refer educators and their associates to other more technical discussions of various aspects of the same topic.

The term "minority group" as we are using it here is not primarily a quantitative designation. Rather it is a status designation referring to cultural or social disadvantage. Since many negro, Indian, lower-class white, and immigrant children have not had most of the usual middle-class opportunities to grow up in home, neighborhood, and school environments that might enable them to utilize their ability and personality potentials fully, they are at a disadvantage in school, and in after-school and out-of-school situations as well. It is because of these disadvantages, reflecting environmental deprivations and experiential atypicalities, that certain children may be referred to as minority group children.

The following discussion is based in part on some of the technical recommendations developed for various kinds of tests by committees of the American Psychological Association, the American Educational Research Association, and the National Council on Measurement in Education (1954, 1955). Our contribution is directed toward specifying the particular considerations that must be kept in mind when professional educators and those who work with them use educational and psychological tests with minority group children.

Critical Issues in Testing Minority Groups

Standardized tests currently in use present three principal difficulties when they are used with disadvantaged minority groups: (1) they may not provide reliable differentiation in the range of the minority group's scores, (2) their predictive validity for minority groups may be quite different from that for the standardization and validation groups, and (3) the validity of their interpretation is strongly dependent upon an adequate understanding of the social and cultural background of the group in question.

I. RELIABILITY OF DIFFERENTIATION

In the literature of educational and psychological testing, relatively little attention has been given to the possible dependence of test reliability upon subcultural differences. It is considered essential for a test publisher to describe the reliability sample (the reference group upon which reliability statements are based) in terms of factors such as age, sex, and grade level composition, and there is a growing tendency on the part of test publishers to report subgroup reliabilities. But to the best of our knowledge, none of the test manuals for the widely used tests give separate reliability data for specific minority groups. Institutions that use tests regularly and routinely for particular minority groups would do well to make their own reliability studies in order to determine whether the tests are reliable enough when used with these groups.

Reliability Affected by Spread of Scores. In addition to being dependent on test length and the specific procedure used for estimating reliability (e.g., split-half or retest), the reliability coefficient for a particular test is strongly affected by the spread of test scores in the group for which the reliability is established. In general, the greater the spread of scores in the reliability sample, the higher the reliability coefficient. Consequently, if the tester attempts to make differentiations within a group which is more homogeneous than the reference or norm group for which reliability is reported, the actual effectiveness of the test will find to be lower than the reported reliability coefficient appears to promise. For many tests, there is abundant evidence that children from the lower socioeconomic levels commonly associated with minority group status tend to have a smaller spread of scores than do children from middle-income families, and such restriction in the distribution of scores tends to lower reliability so far as differentiation of measurement with such groups is concerned.[2]

Characteristics of Minority Group Children that Affect Test Performance. Most of the evidence relating to the contention that the majority of educational and psychological tests tend to be more unreliable, i.e., more characterized by what is technically called "error variance," for minority group children, is indirect, being based on studies of social class and socioeconomic differences rather than on minority group performance *per se.* Nevertheless, the particular kinds of minority groups that we have in mind are closely associated with the lower levels of socioeconomic status. The results of studies by Warner, Davis, Deutsch, Deutsch and Brown, Havighurst, Hollingshead, Sears, Maccoby, and many others are cases in point. Many of these studies are discussed by Anastasi (1958), Tyler (1956), and Deutsch (1960).

For children who come from lower socioeconomic levels, what characteristics may be expected to affect test performance in general, and the accuracy or precision of test results in particular? The list of reported characteristics is long, and it is not always consistent from one investigation to another. But, at least, it may be hypothesized that in contrast to the middle-class child the lower-class child will tend to be less verbal, more fearful of strangers, less self-confident, less motivated toward scholastic and academic achievement, less competitive in the intellectual realm, more "irritable," less conforming to middle-class norms of behavior and conduct, more apt to be bilingual, less exposed to intellectually stimulating materials in the home, less varied in recreational outlets, less knowledgeable about the world outside his immediate neighborhood, and more likely to attend inferior schools.

Some Examples. Can it be doubted that such characteristics — even if only some of them apply to each "deprived" minority group — will indeed be reflected in

---

2. See Anastasi (1958) and Tyler (1956).

test-taking and test performance? Obviously, the primary effect will be shown in terms of test validity for such children. In many cases, however, the lowering of test validity may be indirectly a result of lowered test reliability. This would be particularly true if such characteristics interfere with the consistency of performance from test to retest for a single examiner, or for different examiners. Consider the following examples and probable results:

EXAMPLE

A Negro child has had little contact with white adults other than as distant and punitive authority figures. *Probable Result:* Such a child might have difficulty in gaining rapport with a white examiner or reacting without emotional upset to his close presence. Even in an individual testing situation, he might not respond other than with monosyllables, failing to give adequate answers even when he knows them. The examiner, reacting in terms of his own stereotypes, might also lower the reliability and validity of the test results by assuming that the child's performance will naturally be inferior, and by revealing this attitude to the child.

EXAMPLE

Children from a particular minority group are given little reason to believe that doing well in the school situation will affect their chance for attaining better jobs and higher income later in life. *Probable Result:* Such children will see little purpose in schooling, dislike school, and will reject anything associated with school. In taking tests, their primary objective is to get through as rapidly as possible and escape from what for them might be an uncomfortable situation. Their test performance might, therefore, be characterized by a much greater amount of guessing, skipping, and random responses than is shown by the middle-class child who never doubts the importance of the test, wants to please his teacher and parents, and tries his best.

Special Norms Often Needed. When the national norms do not provide adequate differentiation at the lower end of the aptitude or ability scale, special norms, established locally, are often useful. For instance, if a substantial number of underprivileged or foreign-background pupils in a school or school district rank in the lowest five per cent on the national norms, local norms might serve to provide a special scale within this range. If the score distribution with the first few percentiles of the national norms is mainly a function of chance factors, however, a lower level of the test or an easier type of test is needed for accurate measurement of the low-scoring children.

Responsibilities of Test Users. The sensitive test user should be alert to reliability considerations in regard to the particular group involved and the intended use of the tests. In assessing reports on test reliability provided by test manuals and other sources, he will not be satisfied with high reliability coefficients alone. He will consider not only the size of the reliability samples, but also the nature and composition of the samples and the procedures used to estimate reliability. He will try to determine whether the standard error of measurement varies with score levels, and whether his testing conditions are similar to those of the reliability samples. He will ask whether the evidence on reliability is relevant to the persons and purposes with which he is concerned. He will know that high reliability does not guarantee validity of the measures for the purpose in hand, but he will realize that low reliability may destroy validity.

The examiner should be well aware that test results are characteristically influenced by cultural and subcultural differentials and that the performance of under-privileged minority group children is often handicapped by what should be test-extraneous preconditions and response patterns. He should not necessarily assume that the child from a minority group family will be as test-sophisticated and motivated to do his best as are the majority of environment-rich middle-class children.

If the examiner finds — and this will be typical — that the reliability sample does not provide him with information about the reliability of the test for the kind of children he is testing, he should urge that the test results not be taken at face value in connection with critical decisions concerning the children. Very often, careful examination of responses to individual test items will indicate to him that the apparent performance of the child is not adequately reflecting the child's actual competence or personality because of certain subcultural group factors.

II. PREDICTIVE VALIDITY

Of course, if an individual's test scores were to be used only to describe his relative standing with respect to a specified norm group, the fact that the individual had a minority-group background would not be important. It is when an explanation of his standing is attempted, or when long-range predictions enter the picture (as they usually do), that background factors become important.

For example, no inequity is necessarily involved if a culturally disadvantaged child is simply reported to have an IQ of 84 and a percentile rank of 16 on the national norms for a certain intelligence test. However, if this is interpreted as meaning that the child ranks or will rank no higher in learning ability than does a middle-class, native born American child of the same IQ, the interpretation might well be erroneous.

Factors Impairing Test Validity. Three kinds of factors may impair a test's predictive validity. First, there are test-related factors — factors or conditions that affect the test scores but which may have relatively little relation to the criterion. Such factors may include test-taking skills, anxiety, motivation, speed, understanding of test instructions, degree of item or format novelty, examiner-examinee rapport, and other general or specific abilities that underlie test performance but which are irrelevant to the criterion. Examples of the operation of such factors are found in the literature describing the problems of white examiners testing Negro children (Dreger and Miller, 1960), of American Indian children taking unfamiliar, timed tests (Klineberg, 1935), and of children of certain disadvantaged groups being exposed for the first time to test-taking procedures (Haggard, 1954).

It should be noted that some test-related factors may not be prejudicial to disadvantaged groups. For example, test-taking anxiety of a disruptive nature (Sarason *et al.*, 1960) may be more prevalent in some middle-class groups than in lower-class groups. In general, however, the bias attributable to test-related factors accrues to the detriment of the culturally disadvantaged groups.

The problem of making valid predictions for minority group children is faced by the Boys' Club of New York in its Educational Program,[3] which is designed to give promising boys from tenement districts opportunities to overcome their environmental handicaps through scholarships to outstanding schools and colleges. Although the majority of the boys currently enrolled in this program had mediocre aptitude and achievement test scores up to the time they were given scholarships, practically all of the boys have achieved creditable academic success at challenging secondary boarding schools and colleges. In this program, normative scores on the Otis Quick-Scoring Mental Ability Test and the Stanford Achievement Test are used for screening purposes, but they are regarded as minimal estimates of the boys' abilities. The Wechsler Intelligence Scale for Children (WISC) is frequently used in this program to supplement the group tests. The boys typically score 5 to 10 points higher on the WISC than on the Otis, probably because the WISC gives less weight to educational and language factors.

Interest and Personality Inventory Scores. When standardized interest inventories are used, special caution should be observed in making normative interpretations of the scores of culturally disadvantaged individuals. When a child has not had opportunities to gain satisfaction or rewards from certain pursuits, he is not likely to show interest in these areas. For example, adolescent children in a particular slum neighborhood might rank consistently low in scientific, literary, musical, and artistic interests on the Kuder Preference Record if their home and school environments fail to stimulate them in these areas. With improved cultural opportunities, these children might rapidly develop interests in vocations or avocations related to these areas.

Scores on personality inventories may also have very different significance for minority group members than for the population in general (Auld, 1952). Whenever the inventory items tap areas such as home or social adjustment, motivation, religious beliefs, or social customs, the appropriateness of the national norms for minority groups should be questioned. Local norms for the various minority groups involved might again be very much in order here.

Predicting Complex Criteria. A second class of factors contributing to low predictive validity is associated with the complexity of criteria. Criteria generally represent "real life" indices of adjustment or achievement and therefore they

---

3. Information about this program is obtainable from The Boys Club of New York, 287 East 10th Street, New York, N.Y.

commonly sample more complex and more variegated behaviors than do the tests. An obvious example is the criterion of school grades. Grades are likely to reflect motivation, classroom behavior, personal appearance, and study habits, as well as intelligence and achievement. Even if a test measured scholastic aptitude sensitively and accurately, its validity for predicting school marks would be attenuated because of the contribution of many other factors to the criterion. It is important, therefore, to recognize the influence of other factors, not measured by the tests, which may contribute to criterion success. Since disadvantaged groups tend to fare poorly on ability and achievement tests (Anastasi, 1958; Tyler, 1956; Masland, Sarason, and Gladwin, 1958; Eels et al., 1951; Haggard, 1954), there is particular merit in exploring the background, personality, and motivation of members of such groups for compensatory factors, untapped by the tests, which may be related to criterion performance.

In some instances, such as in making scholarship awards on a statewide or national basis, test scores are used rigidly for screening or cut-off purposes to satisfy demands for objectivity and "impartiality." The culturally disadvantaged child (quite possibly a "diamond in the rough") is often the victim of this automatic and autocratic system. Recourse lies in providing opportunities where the hurdles are less standardized and where a more individualized evaluation of his qualifications for meeting the criterion may prove to be fairer for him.

For example, the following characteristics that may be typical of minority group children who have above-average ability or talent are among those cited by DeHaan and Kough (1956), who have been working with the North Central Association Project on Guidance and Motivation of Superior and Talented Secondary School Students:

They learn rapidly, but not necessarily those lessons assigned in school.
They reason soundly, think clearly, recognize relationships, comprehend meanings, and may or may not come to conclusions expected by the teacher.
They are able to influence others to work toward desirable or undesirable goals.

Effects of Intervening Events on Predictions. A third set of contributors to low criterion validity is related to the nature of intervening events and contingencies. This class of conditions is particularly important when the criterion measure is obtained considerably later than the testing — when predictive rather than concurrent validity is at stake. If the time interval between the test administration and the criterial assessment is lengthy, a host of situational, motivational, and maturational changes may occur in the interim. An illness, an inspiring teacher, a shift in aspiration level or in direction of interest, remedial training, an economic misfortune, an emotional crisis, a growth spurt or retrogression in the abilities sampled by the test — any of these changes intervening between the testing and the point or points of criterion assessment may decrease the predictive power of the test.

One of the more consistent findings in research with disadvantaged children is the decline in academic aptitude and achievement test scores of such children with time (Masland, Sarason, and Gladwin, 1958). The decline is, of course, in relation to the performance of advantaged groups or of the general population. It is plausible to assume that this decline represents the cumulative effects of the diminished opportunities and decreasing motivation for acquiring academic knowledge and skills. When such cumulative effects are not taken into consideration, the predictive power of academic aptitude and achievement tests is impaired. If it were known in advance that certain individuals or groups would be exposed to deleterious environmental conditions, and if allowances could be made for such contingencies in connection with predictions, the test's criterion validity could be improved.

Looking in another direction, the normative interpretation of the test results cannot reveal how much the status of underprivileged individuals might be changed if their environmental opportunities and incentives for learning and acquiring skills were to be improved significantly. In the case of the Boy's Club boys mentioned above, estimates of academic growth potential are made on the basis of knowledge of the educational and cultural limitations of the boys' home and neighborhood environment, observational appraisals of the boys' behavior in club activities, and knowledge of the enhanced educational and motivational opportunities that can be offered to the boys in selected college preparatory schools. With this information available, the normative interpretation of the boys' scores on standardized tests can be tempered with experienced judgment, and better estimates of the boys' academic potential can thus be made.

In situations where minority group members are likely to have to continue competing with others under much the same cultural handicaps that they have faced in the past, normative interpretation of their aptitude and achievement test scores will probably yield a fairly dependable basis for short-term predictive purposes. When special guidance or training is offered to help such individuals overcome their handicaps, however, achievement beyond the normative expectancies may well be obtained, and predictions should be based on expectancies derived specifically from the local situation. In this connection, it should be recognized that attempts to appraise human "potential" without defining the milieu in which it will be given an opportunity to materialize are as futile as attempts to specify the horsepower of an engine without knowing how it will be energized.

"Culture Fair" and "Unfair" – in the Test and in Society. The fact that a test differentiates between culturally disadvantaged and advantaged groups does not necessarily mean that the test is invalid. "Culturally unfair" tests may be valid predictors of culturally unfair but nevertheless highly important criteria. Educational attainment, to the degree that it reflects social inequities rather than intrinsic merit, might be considered culturally unfair. However, a test must share this bias to qualify as a valid predictor. Making a test culture-fair may decrease its bias, but may also eliminate its criterion validity. The remedy may lie in the elimination of unequal learning opportunities, which may remove the bias in the criterion as well as in the test. This becomes more a matter of social policy and amelioration rather than a psychometric problem, however.

The situation is quite different for a test that differentiates between disadvantaged and advantaged groups even *more* sharply than does the criterion. The extreme case would be a test that discriminated between disadvantaged and advantaged groups but did not have any validity for the desired criterion. An example of this would be an academic aptitude test that called for the identification of objects, where this task would be particularly difficult for disadvantaged children but would not be a valid predictor of academic achievement. Here, one could justifiably speak of a true "test bias." The test would be spuriously responsive to factors associated with cultural disadvantage but unrelated to the criterion. Such a test would not only be useless for predicting academic achievement, but would be stigmatizing as well.

While certain aptitude and ability tests may have excellent criterion validity for some purposes, even the best of them are unlikely to reflect the true *capacity for development* of underprivileged children. For, to the extent that these tests measure factors that are related to academic success, they must tap abilities that have been molded by the cultural setting. Furthermore, the test content, the mode of communication involved in responding to test items, and the motivation needed for making the responses are intrinsically dependent upon the cultural context.

Elixir of "Culture-Fair" Tests. The elixir of the "culture-fair" or "culture-free" test has been pursued through attempts to minimize the educational loading of test content and to reduce the premium on speed of response. However, these efforts have usually resulted in tests that have low validities for academic prediction purposes and little power to uncover hidden potentialities of children who do poorly on the common run of academic aptitude and achievement tests.

In spite of their typical cultural bias, standardized tests should not be sold short as a means for making objective assessments of the traits of minority-group children. Many bright, nonconforming pupils, with backgrounds different from those of their teachers, make favorable showings on achievement tests, in contrast to their low classroom marks. These are very often children whose cultural handicaps are most evident in their overt social and interpersonal behavior. Without the intervention of standardized tests, many such children would be stigmatized by the adverse subjective ratings of teachers who tend to reward conformist behavior of middle-class character.

III. THE VALIDITY OF TEST INTERPRETATION

The most important consideration of all is one that applies to the use of tests in general, namely, that test results should be interpreted by competently trained and knowledgeable persons wherever important issues or decisions are at stake. Here, an analogy may be drawn from medical case history information that is entered on a child's record. Certain features of this record, such as the contagious-disease history, constitute factual data that are easily understood by school staff members who have not had medical training. But other aspects of the medical record, as well as the constellation of factors that contribute to the child's general state of health, are not readily interpretable by persons outside the medical profession.

Consequently, the judgment of a doctor is customarily sought when an overall evaluation of the child's physical condition is needed for important diagnostic or predictive purposes. So, too, the psychological and educational test records of children should be interpreted by competently trained professional personnel when the test results are to be used as a basis for decisions that are likely to have a major influence on the child's future.

There are several sources of error in test interpretation stemming from a lack of recognition of the special features of culturally disadvantaged groups. One of these may be called the "deviation error." By this is meant the tendency to infer maladjustment or personality difficulty from responses which are deviant from the viewpoint of a majority culture, but which may be typical of a minority group. The results of a test might accurately reflect a child's performance or quality of ideation, but still the results should be interpreted in the light of the child's particular circumstance in life and the range of his experiences. For example, a minister's son whose test responses indicate that he sees all women as prostitutes and a prostitute's son whose test responses give the same indication may both be accurately characterized in one sense by the test. The two boys may or may not be equally disturbed, however. Clinically, a safer inference might be that the minister's son is the one who is more likely to be seriously disturbed by fantasies involving sex and women.

There is evidence to indicate that members of a tribe that has experienced periodic famines would be likely to give an inordinate number of food responses on the Rorschach. So too might dieting Palm Beach matrons, but their underlying anxiety patterns would be quite different than those of the tribesmen. Or, to take still another example, the verbalized self-concept of the son of an unemployed immigrant might have to be interpreted very differently from that of a similar verbalization of a boy from a comfortable, middle-class, native-American home.

A performance IQ that is high in relation to the individual's verbal IQ on the Wechsler scales *may* signify psychopathic tendencies but it also may signify a poverty of educational experience. Perceiving drunken males beating up women on the Thematic Apperception Test may imply a projection of idiosyncratic fantasy or wish, but it may also imply a background of rather realistic observation and experience common to some minority group children.

For children in certain situations, test responses indicating a low degree of motivation or an oversubmissive self-image are realistic reflections of their life conditions. If these children were to give responses more typical of the general population, they might well be regarded as subgroup deviants. In short, whether test responses reflect secondary defenses against anxiety or are the direct result of a socialization process has profound diagnostic import so that knowledge of the social and cultural background of the individual becomes quite significant.

What Does the Test Really Measure. A second type of error, from the viewpoint of construct and content validity,[4] might be called the "simple determinant

---

4. For a discussion of various types of test validity, see Anastasi (1961), Cronbach (1960), Guilford (1954), Thorndike and Hagen (1961), Lindquist (1950).

error." The error consists in thinking of the test content as reflecting some absolute or pure trait, process, factor, or construct, irrespective of the conditions of measurement or of the population being studied. Thus, a fifth-grade achievement test may measure arithmetical knowledge in a middle-class neighborhood where most children are reading up to grade level, but the same test, with the same content, may be strongly affected by a reading comprehension factor in a lower-class school and therefore may be measuring something quite different than what appears to be indicated by the test scores.

Generally, the test-taking motivation present in a middle-class group allows the responses to test content to reflect the differences in intelligence, achievement, or whatever the test is designed to measure. On the other hand in a population where test success has much less reward-value and where degree of test-taking effort is much more variable from individual to individual, the test content may tap motivation as well as the trait purportedly being measured.

Caution and knowledge are necessary for understanding and taking into account testing conditions and test-taking behavior when test results are being interpreted for children from varying backgrounds. A child coming from a particular cultural subgroup might have very little motivation to do well in most test situations, but under certain conditions or with special kinds of materials he might have a relatively high level of motivation. As a result, considerable variability might be evident in his test scores from one situation to another, and his scores might be difficult to reconcile and interpret.

How a question is asked is undoubtedly another important factor to consider in interpreting test results. A child might be able to recognize an object, but not be able to name it. Or, he might be able to identify a geometric figure, but not be able to reproduce it. Thus, different results might be obtained in a test depending upon whether the child is asked to point to the triangle in a set of geometric figures or whether he is required to draw a triangle.

Response Sets May Affect Test Results. In attitude or personality questionnaires, response sets[5] such as the tendency to agree indiscriminately with items, or to give socially desirable responses, may contribute error variance from the viewpoint of the content or behavior it is desired to sample. To the extent that such sets discriminate between socially advantaged and disadvantaged groups, the target content area may be confounded by specific test format. Thus, a scale of authoritarianism may be found to differentiate among social classes, but if the scale is so keyed that a high score on authoritarianism is obtained from agreement with items, the social class differences may be more reflective of an agreement set rather than an authoritarian tendency. If authoritarian content is logically distinct from agreement content, these two sources of test variance should be kept distinct either through statistical control, by a change in the item format, or by having more than one approach to measurement of the trait in question.

From the standpoint of content validity, there is a third type of error. This may be termed the "incompleteness of content-coverage" error. This refers to a

---

5. For a discussion of this and related concepts, see Anastasi (1961), Cronbach (1960).

circumscribed sampling of the content areas in a particular domain. In the area of intelligence, for instance, Guilford (1954) has identified many factors besides the "primary mental abilities" of Thurstone and certainly more than is implied in the unitary concept of intelligence reflected by a single IQ score. As Dreger and Miller (1960) point out, differences in intellectual functioning among various groups cannot be clearly defined or understood until all components of a particular content area have been systematically measured.

Familiarity with the cultural and social background of minority-group children not only helps to avoid under-evaluating the test performance of some children, but also helps to prevent over-evaluating the performance of others. For example, children who have been trained in certain religious observances involving particular vocabularies and objects, or those who have been encouraged to develop particular skills because of their cultural orientations, might conceivably score "spuriously" high on some tests or on particular items. In other words, any special overlap between the subgroup value-system of the child and the performances tapped by the test is likely to be an important determinant of the outcome of the test.

Failure Barriers May Be Encountered. Failure inducing barriers are often set up for the minority-group child in a testing situation by requiring him to solve problems with unfamiliar tools, or by asking him to use tools in a manner that is too advanced for him. To draw an analogy, if a medical student were handed a scalpel to lance a wound, and if the student were to do the lancing properly but were to fail to sterilize the instrument first, how should he be scored for his accomplishment? If he had never heard of sterilization, should his skillful performance with the instrument nevertheless be given a "zero" score? Similarly, if a child from a disadvantaged social group shows a considerable degree of verbal facility in oral communication with his peers but does very poorly on tests that stress academic vocabulary, can he justifiably be ranked low in verbal aptitude?

In a broad sense, most intelligence test items tap abilities involving language and symbol systems, although opportunities for developing these abilities vary considerably from one social group to another. One might reasonably expect that a child living in a community that minimizes language skills – or, as depicted by Bernstein (1960), a community that uses a language form that is highly concrete – will earn a score that has a meaning very different from that of the score of a child in a community where language skills are highly developed and replete with abstract symbolism. It is important, therefore, to interpret test results in relation to the range of situations and behaviors found in the environments of specific minority groups.

Some Suggested Remedies. While this analysis of the problems involved in the use and interpretation of tests for minority group children may lead to considerable uneasiness and skepticism about the value of the results for such children, it also points up potential ways of improving the situation. For example, one of these ways might consist of measuring separate skills first, gradually building up to more and more complex items and tests which require the exercise of more than one basic skill at a time. With enough effort and ingenuity, a sizable universe of items might be developed by this procedure. Special attention should also be given to the selection or development of items and tests that maximize criterial differentiations and minimize irrelevant discriminations. If a test is likely to be biased against certain types of minority groups, or if its validity for minority groups has not been ascertained, a distinct *caveat* to that effect should appear in the manual for the test.

Furthermore, we should depart from too narrow a conception of the purpose and function of testing. We should reemphasize the concept of the test as an integral component of teaching and training whereby a floor of communication and understanding is established and *learning* capabilities are measured in repeated and cyclical fashion.

Finally, we should think in terms of making more use of everyday behavior as evidence of the coping abilities and competence of children who do not come from the cultural mainstream. Conventional tests may be fair predictors of academic success in a narrow sense, but when children are being selected for special aid programs or when academic prediction is not the primary concern, other kinds of behavioral evidence are commonly needed to modulate the results and implications of standardized tests.

CONCLUSION

Tests are among the most important evaluative and prognostic tools that educators have at their disposal. How unfortunate, then, that these tools are often used so routinely and mechanically that some educators have stopped *thinking* about their limitations and their benefits. Since the minority group child is so often handicapped in many ways his test scores may have meanings different from those of non-minority children, even when they are numerically the same. The task of the conscientious educator is to ponder what lies behind the test scores. Rather than accepting test scores as indicating fixed levels of either performance or potential, educators should plan remedial activities which will free the child from as many of his handicaps as possible. Good schools will employ well qualified persons to use good tests as one means of accomplishing this task.

In testing the minority group child it is sometimes appropriate to compare his performance with that of advantaged children to determine the magnitude of the deprivation to be overcome. At other times it is appropriate to compare his test performance with that of other disadvantaged children — to determine his relative deprivation in comparison with others who have also been denied good homes, good neighborhoods, good diets, good schools and good teachers. In most instances it is especially appropriate to compare the child's test performance with his previous test performance. Utilizing the individual child as his own control and using the test norms principally as "bench marks," we are best able to gauge the success of our efforts to move the minority group child forward on the long, hard road of overcoming the deficiencies which have been forced upon him. Many comparisons depend upon tests, but they also depend upon *our* intelligence, our good will, and our sense of responsibility to make the proper comparison at the proper time and to undertake proper remedial and compensatory action as a result. The misuse of tests with minority group children, or in any situation, is a serious breach of professional ethics. Their proper use is a sign of professional and personal maturity.

REFERENCES

American Educational Research Association and National Committee on Measurements Used in Education. (1955). *Technical Recommendations for Achievement Tests.* .Washington, D.C.: National Educational Association.

American Psychological Association. (1954). Technical Recommendations for Psychological Tests and Diagnostic Techniques, *Psychol. Bull.*, **51**, No. 2.

Anastasi, A. (1961). *Psychological testing*, 2nd ed. New York: Macmillan.

Anastasi, A. (1958). *Differential psychology*, 3rd ed. New York: Macmillan.

Auld, F., Jr. (1952). Influence of Social Class on Personality Test Responses, *Psychol. Bull.*, **49**, 318–332.

Bernstein, B. (1961). Aspects of Language and Learning in the Genesis of the Social Process, *J. Child Psychol. Psychiat.*, **1**, 313–324.

Bernstein, B. (1960). Language and Social Class. *Brit. J. Sociol.*, **11**, 271–276.

Chronbach, L. (1960). *Essentials of psychological testing*, 2nd ed. New York: Harper.

DeHaan, R., and J. Kough (1956). *Teacher's Guidance Handbook: Identifying Students with Special Needs*, (Vol. I Secondary School Edition). Chicago: Science Research Associates.

Deutsch, M. (1960). *Minority Group and Class Status as Related to Social and Personality Factors in Scholastic Achievement* (Monograph No. 2). Ithaca, New York: The Society for Applied Anthropology.

Deutsch, M. (1963). The Disadvantaged Child and the Learning Process: Some Social, Psychological, and Developmental Considerations, in *Education in Depressed Areas* (H. Passow, ed.). New York: Teachers College Press.

Deutsch, M., and B. Brown. Some Data on Social Influences in Negro-White Intelligence Differences, *J. Social Issues*, **XX**, No. 2, 24–35.

Dreger, R., and K. Miller (1960). Comparative Psychological Studies of Negroes and Whites in the United States, *Psychol. Bull.*, **57**, 361–402.

Eells, K., et al. (1951). *Intelligence and Cultural Differences.* Chicago: University of Chicago Press.

Fishman, J. A., and P. I. Clifford (1964). What Can Mass Testing Programes Do for and to the Pursuit of Excellence in American Education? *Harvard Educ. Rev.*, **34**, 63–79.

Froehlich, C., and K. Hoyt (1959). *Guidance testing*, 3rd ed. Chicago: Science Research Associates.

Guilford, J. (1954). *Psychometric methods*, 2nd ed. New York: McGraw-Hill.

Haggard, E. (1954). Social Status and Intelligence: an Experimental Study of Certain Cultural Determinants of Measured Intelligence. *Genet. Psychol. Monogr.*, 49, 141–186.

Klineberg, O. (1935). *Race differences.* New York: Harper.

Katz, M. (1958). *Selecting an Achievement Test: Principles and Procedures.* Princeton: Educational Testing Service.

Lindquist, E. (ed.) (1950). *Educational Measurement.* Washington: American Council of Education.

Masland, R., S. Sarason, and T. Gladwin (1958). *Mental Subnormality.* New York: Basic Books.

Sarason, S. et al. (1960). *Anxiety in Elementary School Children.* New York: Wiley.

Thorndike, R., and E. Hagen (1961). *Measurement and Evaluation in Psychology and Education*, 2nd ed. New York: Wiley.

Tyler, L. (1956). *The Psychology of Individual Differences*, 2nd ed. New York: Appleton-Century-Crofts.

GLOSSARY OF TERMS AS USED IN THE TEXT

Criterion. A standard that provides a basis for evaluating the validity of a test.

Cultural bias. Propensity of a test to reflect favorable or unfavorable effects of certain types of cultural backgrounds.

Culture-fair test. A test yielding results that are not culturally biased.

Culture-free test. A test yielding results that are not influenced in any way by cultural background factors.

Error variance. The portion of the variance of test scores that is related to the unreliability of the test.

Educational loading. Weighing of a test's content with factors specifically related to formal education.

Norms. Statistics that depict the test performance of specific groups. Grade, age, and percentile are the most common type of norms.

Normative scores. Scores derived from the test's norms.

Reliability. The degree of consistency, stability, or dependability of measurement afforded by a test.

Reliability coefficient. A correlation statistic reflecting a test's consistency or stability of measurement.

Standard deviation. A statistic used to depict the dispersion of a group of scores.

Standard error of measurement. An estimate of the standard deviation of a person's scores that would result from repeated testing with the same or a similar test, ruling out the effects of practice, learning, or fatigue.

Validity. The extent to which a test measures the trait for which it is designed, or for which it is being used, rather than some other trait.

Interpreting Achievement Profiles—
Uses and Warnings*

Eric F. Gardner

The old Chinese saying that a picture is worth one thousand words is especially applicable to test profiles. Profiles are convenient ways of showing test scores; they are graphic devices enabling us to see the over-all performance of an individual or group of individuals at a glance. They provide an excellent means for gaining a comprehensive picture of a person's or class' strengths and weaknesses. Profiles can be very helpful provided we use suitable caution in their interpretation. In one sense, a profile is like a good map which reflects features existing in reality, however, the appearance of such features on the profile does not *guarantee* their reality. An important point to remember is that although many of us find it surprisingly easy to believe that a score must be accurate if we have seen it on a test profile, its appearance on the profile does not make the score any more or less accurate or valid.

In general, profiles are used when we wish to show two or more scores for the same person or two or more scores for groups of people. We may be interested in sets of scores obtained at the same time or sets of scores obtained at fixed intervals such as those of a student on a group of tests taken in successive grades.

Profiles show the tests along one axis of the graph and the score values along the other axis. Profile forms may show score values along the vertical axis or along the horizontal; there is no particular reason for preferring the one over the other so far as ease of reading is concerned. If, for example, we wish to prepare a profile sheet for our own class we would probably want to list our test variables down the left hand side of the sheet and to plot our scores along the horizontal axis of the profile. We would do this because it is easier to write the complete test identification along a line than to write it along the narrow confines of a column.

Since raw (or obtained scores) test scores may vary considerably in meaning, it is obvious that raw scores cannot be used in plotting a profile. Before a profile can be plotted, then, it is clearly necessary to transform the scores to sets of comparable values. There are two ways of doing this. One is to scale the raw scores on the profile itself so that each scale has an equivalent mean and equivalent units of measurement. The other is to convert the raw scores into some type of derived scores before plotting them. The most common method is to use either

---

* Reprint of E. F. Gardner, "Interpreting Achievement Profiles – Uses and Warnings." *NCME*, 1(2), 1970. Reprinted by permission of the National Council on Measurement in Education, Inc., East Lansing, Michigan.

standard scores, percentile ranks scaled to proportional standard score distances, or stanines. Note that when this procedure has been followed, the standard scores, stanines, or percentile ranks must be based on the same or strictly comparable populations all of whom have been tested at the same time. A discussion of comparability and other warnings about the construction of profiles and their interpretation will be presented later on in this paper. Let us now consider and illustrate several different kinds of useful profiles.

SOME USES OF PROFILES

1. To Obtain a Picture of the Relative Performance of a Pupil in Several Different Subjects or Areas. What should you look for in a profile? Is there a systematic way that you can analyze test results? The following three steps of analysis represent a good approach to the interpretation of test results: diagnose, evaluate, plan. The analysis of the test profile in Figure 18-1 illustrates how these steps can be applied.[1]

Stanford Achievement Test
Intermediate Complete Battery

Name	Date of Testing	Grade Placement	Age
K., Susan B.	2-26	4.6	9 yr. 6 mo.

Otis Quick-Scoring Mental Ability Test IQ 124, Stanine 8

	GRADE SCORE	%-ILE RANK	STANINE
Word Meaning	70	94	1 2 3 4 5 6 7 ⑧ 9
Paragraph Meaning	82	98	1 2 3 4 5 6 7 8 ⑨
Spelling	76	96	1 2 3 4 5 6 7 8 ⑨
Word Study Skills	71	90	1 2 3 4 5 6 7 ⑧ 9
Language	72	90	1 2 3 4 5 6 7 ⑧ 9
Arithmetic Computation	54	80	1 2 3 4 5 6 ⑦ 8 9
Arithmetic Concepts	40	34	1 2 3 ④ 5 6 7 8 9
Arithmetic Applications	49	62	1 2 3 4 5 ⑥ 7 8 9
Social Studies	77	98	1 2 3 4 5 6 7 8 ⑨
Science	45	46	1 2 3 4 ⑤ 6 7 8 9

FIGURE 18-1. *Stanine profile for Susan K.*

---

1. The following illustration has been taken from *Stanford Achievement Test, Teachers' Guide for Interpretation and Use of Test Results,* Harcourt, Brace and World, Inc., 1965.

Analysis of Susan K.'s Profile

Figure 18-1 is a sample copy of the Pupil Stanine Profile. The three steps of analysis are applied to this profile as an illustration of how test scores of a pupil can be meaningfully interpreted. At this point I would like to call attention to the statement in the Stanford Achievement Manual which says, "When comparing two subtest stanines for an individual pupil, only differences of two or more stanine levels should be considered significant by the teacher."

Diagnose – Examine the profile for the most obvious subject strengths and weaknesses shown by the pupil's performance on this test battery.

Susan, with plotted stanines of either 8 or 9, is achieving best in the areas of word meaning, paragraph meaning, spelling, word study skills, language, and the social studies. When compared with other girls and boys of her grade level, Susan shows average achievement in arithmetic concepts and in science, where she has stanines of either 4, 5, or 6. She shows evidence of understanding the application of arithmetic with a stanine of 6 and shows considerable competence in arithmetic computation with a stanine of 7. With an IQ of 124 and a corresponding stanine of 8, Susan would normally be expected to achieve stanines of 7 or above in the various subjects.

Evaluate – Relate the pupil's scores on the achievement test to such variables as your estimate of the pupil, his grades, his performance on a test of mental ability, and the like.

Susan's test results indicate that she is a superior student in the language arts and in social studies. Her school marks and judgments of previous teachers should reflect this superiority. If the test was taken in the spring, have school marks through the school year reflected this superiority? If not, why not? What are Susan's personal attitudes? Is she a non-conformist? Does she excel in aspects of a subject not measured by the tests? Is Susan a highly verbal memorizer? Is she a poor reasoner in mathematics and science? What are her interests? Doesn't Susan need special encouragement and help in mathematics and science? These and other questions arise when test scores and other evaluations do not correspond.

Plan – Plan a program of classroom activities that will remedy some of the obvious shortcomings and will build upon the greater strengths of each pupil.

Diversity of interest in subject areas and of levels of achievement in them is inevitable and even desirable among pupils and within each individual pupil. But no pupil in the elementary grades, especially one of Susan's general level of ability, should fail to learn the fundamental subjects such as arithmetic.

Because of Susan's outstanding work in the language arts, her teacher can be reasonably assured that her inability to score much above average in the area of science or in arithmetic concepts does not stem from any reading difficulty. This then leaves the teacher at least two factors to consider: (1) lack of interest and (2) lack of fundamental knowledge about the underlying concepts in science and in arithmetic. These possible deficiencies could have resulted from inadequate experience with these subjects, inadequate interest evidenced in the home in these content areas, lack of a stimulating teacher of these subjects, and the like.

The instructional problem here is a relatively simple one. A careful, thorough discussion with Susan should elicit from her the level of interest in these areas and also some reasons for a lack of understanding in the basic concepts. Her shortages in knowledge of mathematics concepts need to be diagnosed. As a result of such understanding, Susan's teacher will be able to build an instructional program that will improve Susan's performance in these areas.

2. To Compare the Performance of a Single Grade on Several Subjects and with the National Norm. One common use of achievement test batteries is in connection with some phase of administration or supervision. The supervisor is interested in knowing strengths and weaknesses in specific subjects so that they can be given greater attention. Frequently the national performance is accepted as a standard. Although national norms are useful as one frame of reference, it is important to recognize that achievement at the national average may well be an unreasonable goal for a particular school, class, or system. Norms are not designed to be standards nor should they be so designated unless a consideration of all relevant variables indicates they represent an appropriate level of average achievement for a particular group of students. Even then, by the very definition of a norm, it is expected that half the pupils will exceed it and half will fall below.

The authors of most achievement test batteries provide several scales for comparing local achievement with national norms. We can usually expect to be furnished with grade equivalents, percentile ranks, standard scores, and stanines. In spite of their deficiencies and decrease in popularity, the grade equivalent is still the most commonly used frame of reference for evaluating local achievement.

In Figure 18-2 a single-grade profile is shown in which the deviations of the local school system medians from the corresponding national normative values are plotted in months of grade equivalent above or below the norm at the time of testing. This profile, which represents the performance of all fourth grade pupils tested the first of November (grade 4.2) from a community of slightly better-than-average socioeconomic level and moderate size, indicates that achievement is above the national norm in all areas.

We have to note, however, that the average IQ of this system was 110 on the *Pintner General Ability Test,* and the average age in this grade was three months younger than the national normative group. Hence, it is pertinent to ask, "Is this group exceeding the national norm as much as would be expected?" Many factors previously mentioned and others to be discussed later are at issue, e.g., (1) comparability of grade equivalent units across subjects, (2) mental tests generally correlate differently with subject-matter achievement tests from area to area, (3) reliability of test scores.

3. School-by-School Comparisons in Terms of Achievement Tests. The superintendent of schools, usually the person who eventually has to approve the purchase of test materials and the allocation of time for testing, is interested in knowing how his schools compare with each other and the national norm. As one

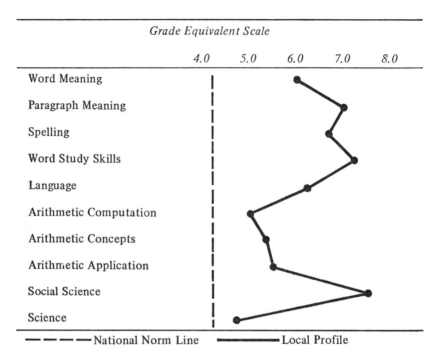

FIGURE 18-2. *Profile of fourth grade students (tested November 1st). Plotted in terms of median standard scores expressed as grade equivalents.*

important datum it is often helpful for him and the supervisor to have a school-by-school comparison based on standardized test results.

Figure 18-3 shows such a distribution of standard scores by school for one subject (Spelling) in a small school system.[2]   Medians have been computed for each school and these median standard scores have been circled and joined in order to make a profile.   Although the standard score scales used here lack some of the deficiencies of grade equivalent scales and although we are dealing with medians rather than individual scores, we still have the typical problems associated with determining how large an observed difference must be to be meaningful.   Some of these differences are so small that they can be considered chance differences. Others are so substantial that they would undoubtedly maintain upon retesting. A similar profile could be made for each class within a specific grade.

It is desirable for a school system to carry out such a testing program for several years using alternate forms of the same batteries.   By relating this kind of achievement test information to other factors such as socioeconomic status, aptitude measures, ethnic composition and differences in the characteristics of the instructional staff, the administration will gain an increasingly dependable idea of

---

2. Adapted from the manual of the *Metropolitan Achievement Test*, Harcourt, Brace and World, 1962.

Standard Score	SCHOOLS					
	A	B	C	D	E	F
80	1		1			1
76		1	3			2
72	1	1			1	1
70		3	8			
69	1	4	1		2	3
68	1	4		1	2	2
66	3	3		1	1	
65	2	3	2		2	
63	3	4		1	2	1
62	3	3	1		1	3
61	3	(5)	4	1	1	4
60	1	1	2		(2)	4
59	3	4	4	1	2	2
58	(1)	2	4	1		
57	1	1	(2)	1	1	(3)
56	2	4	3	(1)	1	3
55	1	2	1			1
54	2	1	2			1
53	3	1	2			1
52		2	2	1	1	1
51	1	1	2		1	
50	1	3	1	3		1
49	2	1	4		2	1
48		2	2			3
47	2	1	1	1	1	2
46	2		1	1	1	
45	2	2				
44						
43			1			2
42	1	2	1			2
41	1		5			1
40					1	
39			1			
38		1	1			
37						
36	1			1		
35						
34			1			
33	1					
32						2
31						
30						
28					1	
N	46	62	63	15	26	47
Median Stan. Sc.	58	61	57	56	60	57
Corres. Gr. Eq.	7.6	8.4	7.3	7.1	8.1	7.3

FIGURE 18-3. *School-by-school comparison of test results for Grade 6.7 in a single community, showing distributions of standard scores for the spelling test in the Metropolitan Intermediate Battery.*

such school by school variations. Some of these differences, which may be rooted in the background of abilities that the children bring to school, require the focusing of special efforts and resources in particular schools to achieve satisfactory remediation.

4. Comparing a Pupil's Performance in Successive Years.   Not only is the profile a useful device for portraying the differential performance of a pupil (class or school) on the subtests of an achievement test battery, it can be used to show profiles of the same pupil for several years.   The Teachers's Manual for the *Iowa Tests of Basic Skills* presents a standard permanent profile chart on which are plotted the test profiles of a pupil for two consecutive years.   The chart utilizes the principle of plotting scores for all tests in the battery along a "standard scale" – in this case, grade equivalents.   This principle is illustrated in Figure 18-4.   The dotted line represents the performance of Frank Smith tested as a fourth grade pupil; the solid line represents his performance when tested at the same time in the fifth grade.[3]

By comparing the dotted and solid lines one may discover what relative progress he has made during the intervening school year in the various areas tested. It appears that Frank's gains on the language tests are larger than the typical gain of 10 points per grade but that they are less on other tests particularly Test W.   The usual questions about the confidence one can place in this observation alone are relevant.   An examination of the fifth-grade profile confirms the impression from

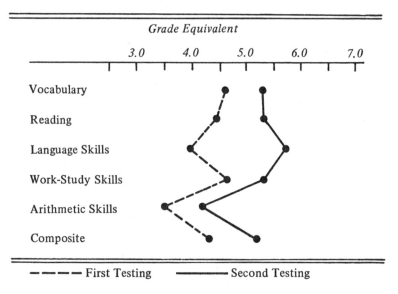

FIGURE 18-4.   *Performance of Frank Smith tested as a fourth and later as a fifth grade student.*

---

3. Adapted from the profile chart shown on p. 18 of the *Teacher's Manual for the Iowa Tests of Basic Skills*, Houghton Mifflin Co., 1956.

the previous profile that Frank is relatively poor in arithmetic skills. The use of such profiles for consecutive years, not only gives a more complete picture of a pupil's performance, but also gives information about consistency of performance.

WARNINGS ON THE USE OF PROFILES

Since profiles are relatively simple to construct and are at least superficially easy to interpret, they constitute one of the most popular methods of summarizing the results of multiple measurement. They have the obvious advantage that the graphic presentation enables one to view the total set of test scores and their possible interpretations at a glance. In the use of profiles, more than any other aspect of test interpretation, we need to beware of seeming simplicity and to understand the numerous pitfalls into which a naive interpretation would lead us.

For example, the failure to question whether or not the plotted scores are based upon common scales, which permit comparisons, may result in a distorted picture which has absolutely no meaning. Furthermore, most of us find it especially easy to interpret *apparent* differences in scores as real differences. By not being sensitive to the effect on our conclusions of the size of the profile scale we may arrive at erroneous decisions merely because our profile occupies a full page rather than a 2" by 3" corner. By failing to question the reliability of differences between scores and by relying solely on observed differences in arriving at conclusions, we ignore the possible unreliability and invalidity of the overall summation which would be instantly revealed if less "simple" methods were used.

These issues along with others must be understood by those who use or make profiles if the conclusions drawn are to be valid. This comment should not lead to the abandonment of the profile, but to an awareness of the precautions which should be followed in its use. The following portion of this paper will comment in some detail on the background and supplemental information one must consider for adequate interpretation of a profile. The material will be presented in the form of a number of warnings for proper construction and use of a profile.

1. Be Sure the Scores Plotted Are in Comparable Units. Since raw test scores may vary considerably in meaning, it is obvious that raw or obtained scores do not possess the kind of comparability needed in plotting profiles. For example, the pupils in one class may have scores which range from 40 to 60 on a vocabulary test and from 5 to 25 on an arithmetic test. Hence, it would be impossible for anyone in the class to appear better in arithmetic than in vocabulary. Before any profile can be plotted which will permit desired comparisons it is clearly necessary to convert the scores to scales having comparable values.

Comparable scores are obtained usually by some scaling procedure so that all scores may be expressed in terms of a common reference point and a common unit of measurement. The authors of most tests fill this need by providing tables for interpreting a raw score in relation to "normal" or typical performance. These tables of "norms" are based on statistical operations on scores of a normative or standardization group. A variety of definitions of comparability have given rise to a number of numerical indices used to express such comparability. Such measures as percentiles, standard scores, stanines, and grade equivalents have been derived to be consistent with specific definitions of comparability, and although different from each other, have proved to be useful in the interpretation of performance on tests. Note that comparisons using profiles must use the same unit across variables, even though it may be possible to present the same profile using several different measurement units. (See Figure 18-5)

2. Be Sure the Score Scales on the Profile Are Based on the Same or Strictly Comparable Populations Which Have Been Tested at the Same Time. The importance of the particular reference population used to determine any such scale cannot be overemphasized. The performance of a student who scores at the 84th percentile or obtains a stanine of 6 in a reading comprehension test where these scores are based on a set of typical 7th grade scores is obviously not the same as the performance of one whose standing at the 84th percentile on the same test is calculated from the distribution of a below-average 7th grade. Likewise, a pupil with a vocabulary grade score of 5.2 obtained for a representative sample of 5th graders in one locality may not be at all comparable to a pupil who makes a score of 5.2 based on a representative national sample.

Note that comparable scores, either standard scores, percentile ranks, or stanines must be based on the same or strictly comparable populations. Also, note that a percentile score of 84 or a stanine of 6 based on a normative population tested in October does not represent as high a level of performance as a percentile score of 84 or a stanine of 6 based on a normative population tested the following April. Figure 18-6 presents data from which no meaningful statements can be made as to the relationships among the scores of John Jones whether we consider raw scores, percentile ranks, or standard score equivalents.

3. Do Not Depend upon Observed Differences Alone. One of the most serious abuses in profile interpretation occurs when teachers, counselors, or school psychologists depend upon *visual scanning only* for their interpretation. Too often, only a quick inspection of the profile is used to determine whether Jim is better in reading than in spelling or arithmetic. Two points that appear to be well separated on the profile are assumed to represent real and significant differences in ability. But such may not be the case. Any difference may be made to appear large by increasing the size of the scale, the way a photographer would make an enlargement of a print. In this way a minute difference may be made to look gigantic.

4. Check on the Reliability and Standard Error of Measurement of Each Test and Each Difference Score. To overcome being unduly influenced by size of scale you should be concerned about the reliability of the measurement and in particular the standard error of measurement of the scores used. Only by considering the size of the errors of measurement associated with the points on the profile can you understand with any certainty the meaning of an observed difference. Suppose

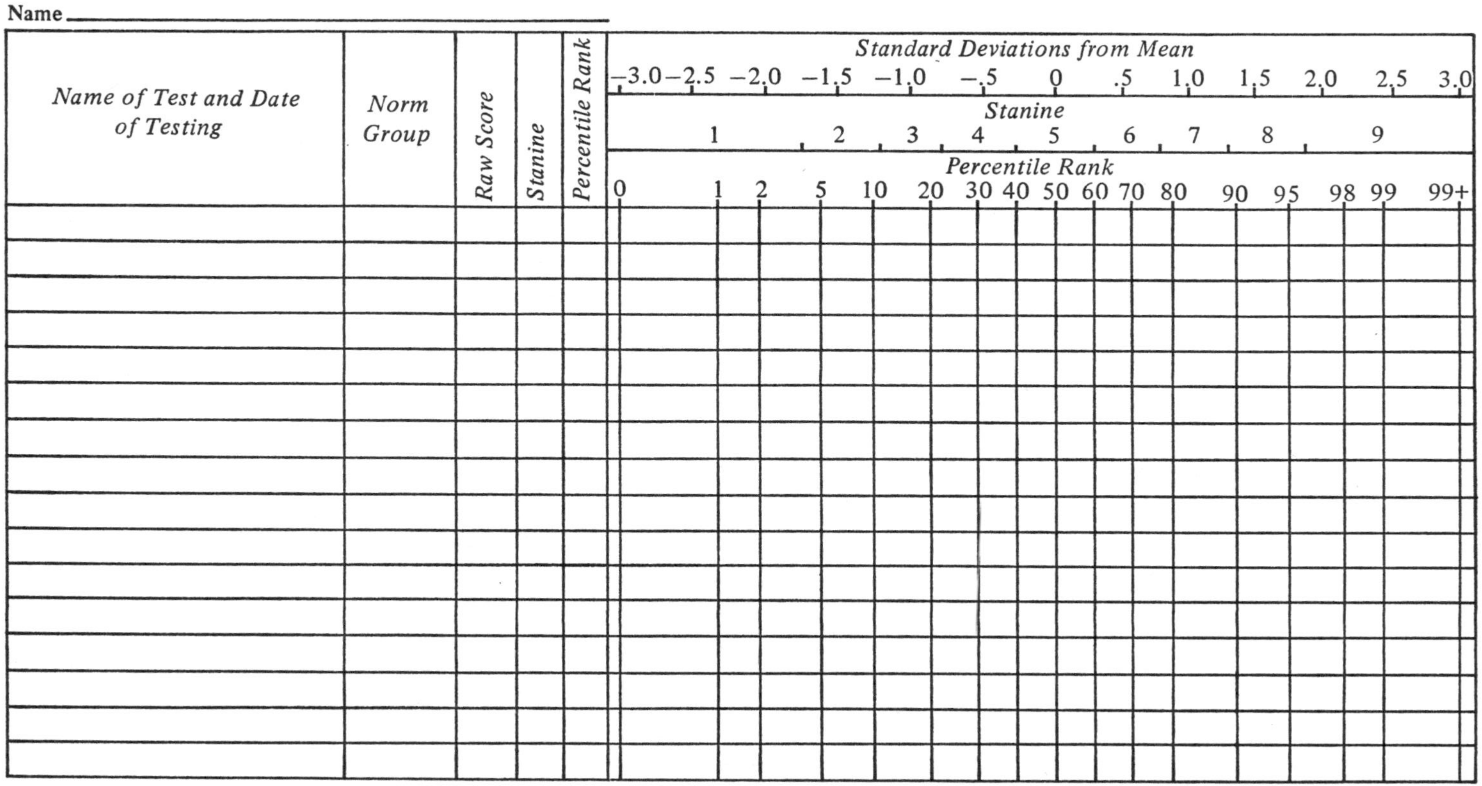

FIGURE 18-5. Test record and profile chart.

Test and Normative Group	Raw Score	Percentile Rank
Learning Aptitude (Freshmen at Ohio St.)	76	45
Reading Comprehension (8th Grade Norms)	42	62
Mathematics (H.S. Algebra Class)	38	40
Mechanical Aptitude (H.S. Shop Class)	53	65
Clerical Aptitude (Employed Clerks)	175	80

FIGURE 18-6.   *Sam Jones: test results in noncomparable form.*

that Johnny had a standard score of 60 in a reading test and a standard score of 55 in an arithmetic test. Suppose further that the reading test had a standard error of 7 and the arithmetic test had a standard error of 8. If you asserted, on the basis of these test scores, that Johnny was better in reading than in arithmetic you would be making a very hazardous statement. The errors of measurement are sufficiently large that on a subsequent retesting the scores could easily be reversed.

Some test publishers have provided a variety of ways to aid the profile user in assessing the reliability of the scores and differences presented on profiles using their particular instrument. For example, the manual for the DAT indicates that the authors and publisher have scaled these tests in such a way that a teacher or counselor can use a ruler to determine reliability of differences on the profile form provided. Plotted points must be separated by a vertical distance of one inch for the difference to be considered significant. The Stanford Achievement Test specifies that in comparing pupil performance a real difference can be assumed only when the two scores compared are more than one stanine apart. The STEP Test sets up a band around each score to indicate the extent of its unreliability.

In each of these instances the authors have computed the standard error of measurement and have incorporated it in their instructions as to how to use the profile for detecting meaningful differences. If such information is not given in the manual then it is necessary for the teacher, counselor, superintendent or other profile user to obtain information about reliability and to personally compute the standard error of measurement for each individual score and the standard error of measurement of differences between rubrics being compared. Otherwise he has no information about how much confidence he can place in his observed differences.

5. Be Concerned about the Independence or Lack of Independence of the Variables Shown on a Profile. When interpreting a profile we are concerned not only with the magnitude of the scores but also with those differences among them which constitute the essence of score pattern. We go beyond the interpretive statement: "Sam is very high in reading comprehension, moderately high in arithmetic computation and only average in science." In addition we often make interpretive statements such as "Sam is higher in paragraph meaning than in arithmetic computation and science; he is higher in arithmetic than in science; and lower in science than either of the others. Therefore, he does not have the score pattern of a person likely to succeed in a field involving arithmetic and science."

Yet even though the individual scores may be reliable for answering certain questions, the unreliability of the differences on which the foregoing interpretation hinges may be such that Sam could actually be equal in all three or higher in paragraph meaning than in arithmetic. Again, the very concreteness of the graphic pattern gives it an appearance of accuracy that is wholly spurious. After all don't we have numerical scores, not only in black and white, but as points on a graph? Can't we rely on the pattern we observe for our interpretation?

Obviously the interpretation of a profile depends not only upon the scores, but upon the interrelationships and differences among them. But the reliability (and the interpretation) of the difference between scores for a single individual on two functions involve not only the reliability of the two tests, but also the correlation between them. The reliability of the difference between two measures which are correlated can easily be shown to be less than the reliability of the difference between the same two measures if they are independent of each other. Hence, when one is dealing with a profile involving a series of measures which are highly correlated, it is even more important to be concerned about the reliability of observed differences than when the measures are relatively independent.

6. Be Sure That All Necessary Supporting Information is Included as Part of the Labeling on a Profile. The greatest advantage of general profile forms is that several different tests may be shown on the same sheet. The great limitation of such forms is the ease with which we may put tests with drastically dissimilar norm groups on the same sheet. Figure 18-5 is an example of a good general profile form for it has percentile, standard score, and stanine scales and calls for: title, normative group, the raw score, two different types of derived scores, and the date of testing. When preparing such a profile we should be careful to give complete information on all tests. What seems self evident at the moment of recording may not be so obvious months later. We need to be especially careful to record a complete designation of the normative group.

7. Remember That Profiles Using Lines Joining Points Are not *Graphs in the Usual Sense.* In its usual form a profile is a graphic representation of a set of test scores for a single individual in which the tests are represented by ordinates spaced along the horizontal base line and the magnitude of each score is represented by plotting the point at the appropriate height on that ordinate. In order to aid the eye in locating the points thus plotted, it is customary to join the points by lines, leading to the more or less "jagged" picture that gives the technique its name. It should be remembered that the line thus drawn is not a graph in the usual sense.

We are accustomed to dealing with graphs of continuous functions even though only a few points may be experimentally determined. In such graphs, the lines have meaning as representing values associated with values intermediate between those plotted. This is not true of ordinary test profiles. What would be the meaning of point "a" in the top profile illustrated in Figure 18-7? Some of these objections may be overcome by plotting profiles without connecting the profile points. Two methods of doing so along with the more common method are illustrated in Figure 18-7.[4] These two profiles avoid the false assumption inherent in the connecting of score points on the tests as well as being less subject to configural misinterpretation.

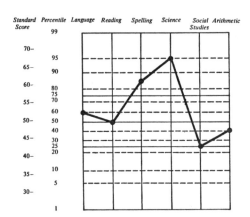
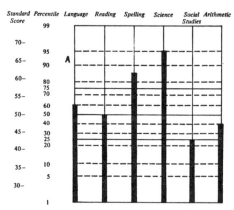
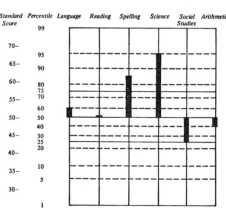

FIGURE 18-7. *Three methods of profiling the same set of scores.*

4. Adapted from the Individual Report Form of the *Differential Aptitude Tests*, The Psychological Corporation, 1947.

8. Base Your Interpretation on Test Scores Aided by the Profile. Since the user of a profile frequently tends to think of a profile as representing a pattern of test results the arrangements of the horizontal ordinates is of importance. In which order should a set of tests be arranged for plotting? Since all of the scores are presented and since the lines between plotted points are meaningless, it may be that order on the base line is wholly immaterial. On the other hand, the interpretation of the "pattern" of the profile is often made as a psychological judgment, based not only on the numerical values of the scores, but on their total perceptual configuration.

To the extent that this latter factor enters, order is important. Consider the impression made by the two profiles shown in Figure 18-8 each based on the same set of test scores. Which is the easier to interpret; which the most open to misinterpretation? To the best of my knowledge no investigation of these problems has been made directly. Without having adequate answers for these questions the practical user of profiles can avoid possible errors by regarding the profile as a method of conveniently presenting the actual test results. Interpretation should be based on test scores aided by the profile, *not on the profile* aided by the scores.

9. Do not Attempt a Simplified Version of Profile Analysis. One of the most extensively researched and complex fields is that of comparing the profile of an individual with the profile of a normative group of individuals having a certain characteristic or who are successful in some particular occupation. On the *Weschler Adult Intelligence Scale* for example, some clinical psychologists have used relationships between scores on certain of the eleven scales as a basis for personality diagnosis. The authors of the California Test Bureau's *Multiple Aptitude Tests* have prepared a number of typical profiles of occupational and other groups, suggesting that important questions can be answered by comparing individual profiles with these examples. In considering the effectiveness of interpretation, many of our questions apply to any normative score, whether on a

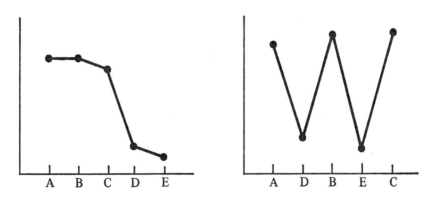

FIGURE 18-8. *Two hypothetical profiles showing different arrangements of the same scores.*

profile or not. It is worth noting, however, that the use of a profile does not solve the questions, and certainly should not lead to ignoring them.

However, assuming adequate reliability certain meaningful statements can be made about the resemblance of an individual's profile to the profiles of specific occupational groups. For example, after administering a battery of tests to Sam, a twelfth grader, we might be able to say that his profile was similar to the profile (pattern of test scores) of the average engineer but was unlike that of the average lawyer. But assuming similarity of profiles, can we say whether he would be successful in either profession? Is the individual engineer more or less successful as his profile lies wholly above or wholly below the average of the group? What shall we say of the individual whose profile, when compared with that for the group in which we are interested, shows several points above the group mean, but one point conspicuously below it? To what extent, then, does superiority in one or more tests compensate for marked deficiency in another?

It is obvious that we are interested in two quite different questions. Question 1 — Do Sam's test scores as profiled permit us to say that he belongs to a particular group, e.g., engineer, when his profile resembles that of the average engineer? Question 2 — If we are able to say that his profile is similar to those of engineers, can we say furthermore that he would be successful as an engineer? To answer these two questions quantitative procedures which are far superior to profile interpretation are available. The first question, namely, group membership, can be answered effectively by the use of the multiple-discriminant function, and the second question — how successful a person is likely to be — can be answered best by multiple regression procedures.

Returning now to the actual situation where we are not able to assume reliability for the profile of either the normative group or that of the individual under consideration, what quantitative answer can we give as to the limits of tolerance within which the individual's profile must agree with the criterion profile with which he is being compared? As yet, no one procedure has been found to be completely satisfactory. However, there has been extensive research in this area and a number of procedures have been proposed. Among the number of techniques proposed for measuring profile similarity are the following:

1. Coefficients of correlation (Burt, 1937)
2. Coefficient of profile similarity (duMas, 1946)
3. Coefficient of intraclass similarity (Webster, 1952)
4. Coefficient of pattern similarity (Cattell, 1949)
5. Distance measure D (Osgood and Suci, 1952)
6. Dissimilarity index D (Cronbach and Gleser, 1953)

The appropriate statistical technique to be used for any particular set of data will depend upon the assumptions underlying the techniques and how well the investigator understands the nature of the scores he is using. No attempt is made in this paper to describe these particular procedures. They are merely presented as preferable alternatives to profiles for interpreting certain types of sets of test scores. Recent papers by Marx (1968), Nunnally (1962), McHugh and Sivanich (1963), and Heermann (1965) have focused on the general problem of profile comparison.

CONCLUSIONS

This paper has attempted to comment on four issues, although equal weight has not been given to each. The main effort has focused on the first two, namely, the use of and pitfalls in interpreting profiles. I have tried to describe and illustrate in some detail the usefulness of profiles as frames of reference for the interpretation of test scores by school personnel; and I have stressed the need to base interpretations on the test scores aided by the profile *not* on the profile configuration aided by the test scores.

Since profiles are relatively simple to construct and appear, at least superficially, easy to interpret, considerable emphasis was placed upon understanding the numerous pitfalls into which a naive interpretation would lead. Comments in the form of nine warnings were presented to assist the school man in using profiles appropriately.

The other two issues were a consideration of the profile configuration itself and a comment on quantitative procedures that for certain purposes are superior to profile analysis. The complexities involved in answering questions by comparing one profile with another or with a vocational normative group were discussed. Even though such comparisons are useful to researchers, I advise the teacher, supervisor, and administrator to avoid simplified versions of profile analysis. Although I have mentioned some of the methods proposed, I have not described them. References have been given which will permit the interested reader to investigate this complex problem for himself.

Finally, only a casual reference was made to two important quantitative procedures — multiple discriminant analysis and multiple regression analysis. These methods are superior to profiles for answering the questions — Which group does a person most resemble? and, How successful is a person likely to be if he is a member of a certain vocational group? Here also references have been given so that an interested reader with a strong statistical background may pursue these problems further.

REFERENCES

Bennett, G. K., H. G. Seashore, and A. G. Wesman (1951). *Counseling from Profiles*. New York: Psychological Corporation.

Burt, C. L. (1937). Correlation Between Persons, *British Journal of Psychology*, 28, 59–96.

Cattell, R. B. (1949). r_p and Other Coefficients of Pattern Similarity, *Psychometrika*, 14, 279–298.

Cronbach, L. and G. Gleser (1953). Assessing Similarity Between Profiles, *Psychological Bulletin*, 50, 456–473.

duMas, F. M. (1949). The Coefficient of Profile Similarity. *Journal of Clinical Psychology*, 5, 123–131.

Heermann, E. F. (1965). Comments on Overall's Multivariate Methods for Profile Analysis, *Psychological Bulletin, 63,* 128.

Marks, E. (1968). Some Profile Methods Useful with Singular Covariance Matrices. *Psychological Bulletin, 70,* 179–184.

McHugh, R. B. and G. Sivanich (1963). Assessing the Temporal Stability of Profile Groups in a Comparative Experiment or Survey, *Psychological Reports, 13,* 145–146.

Nunnally, J. (1962). The Analysis of Profile Data, *Psychological Bulletin, 59,* 311–319.

Osgood, C. E. and G. Suci (1952). A Measure of Relation Determined by Both Mean Difference and Profile Information, *Psychological Bulletin, 49,* 251–262.

Overall, J. E. (1964). Note on Multivariate Methods for Profile Analysis, *Psychological Bulletin, 61,* 195–198.

Tatsuoka, M. M. and D. V. Tiedeman (1954). Discriminant analysis, *Review of Educational Research, 24,* 402–420.

Tiedeman, D. V. (1954). A Model for the Profile Problem, *Proceedings, 1953 Invitational Conference on Testing Problems.* Princeton, N. J.: Educational Testing Service.

Webster, H. (1952). A note on Profile Similarity, *Psychological Bulletin, 49,* 538–539.

Criterion-Referenced Testing in the Classroom*

Peter W. Airasian
George F. Madaus

As education has moved from a luxury to a necessity in American society and as voices for more relevant, less arbitrary stratification systems in education have increased, the problem of grading students has naturally become a focus of attention. For many years student performance has been graded on a norm-referenced, relative, basis. A student's grade is assigned on the basis of how he stands in comparison to his peers, not on the basis of any absolute criterion of what his performance is worth. Within the classroom, such grading practices have had two undesirable effects. First, they have given credence to the notion that for success or achievement to mean anything, there must be a reference group of nonattainers. The rewards system engendered by norm-referenced grading *insures*

---

* Reprint of P. W. Arasian and G. F. Madaus, "Criterion-Referenced Testing in the Classroom." *NCME* 3(4), 1972. Reprinted by permission of the National Council on Measurement in Education, Inc., East Lansing, Mich.

"winners" and "losers" in the achievement race. Second, norm-referenced practices have led to a discrepancy between the rewards system (i.e., grades) and the actual performance of students.

These effects and a series of concomitant trends to be elaborated later, have led to a renewed interest in a concept of criterion-referenced measurement. In this approach emphasis is placed upon the question "What has the student achieved?", rather than upon the question "How much has he achieved?" (Block, 1971a). The interpretation of a student's performance in a criterion-referenced situation is absolute and axiomatic, not dependent upon how other learners perform. Either a student is able to exhibit a particular skill, produce a specific product, or manifest a certain behavior, or he is not. Even in situations where some margin of error is permitted, once this margin has been specified the student's performance can be judged in terms of an "on-off" situation (Popham and Husek, 1971). Both norm- and criterion-referenced systems sort students, but there is an essential difference. In criterion-referenced measurement, interpretation of a student's performance is in no way dependent upon the performance of his classmates. In contrast, the appraisal of norm-referenced performance will differ according to the make-up of the norm group. For example, Mary's scoring higher than 90 percent of a group of academically inferior students on an algebra test will have different implications than her scoring higher than 90 percent in a group of advanced placement students (Bloom, Hastings and Madaus, 1971).

Further, and of equal importance, the criterion-referenced approach focuses attention upon a central aspect of the teaching-learning process, namely, the criterion skills. If the criterion behaviors are important, teachers should be concerned with whether the student has achieved them, not with how much he achieved relative to his peers. The teacher should design his instruction in light of the criterion behaviors and the reward system should reflect this approach.

BACKGROUND

The distinction between norm and criterion-referenced tests is not a new one; few ideas in education are. In 1918, E. L. Thorndike observed that

> There are two somewhat distinct groups of educational measurements: one ... asks primarily how well a pupil performs a certain uniform task; the other ... asks primarily how hard a task a pupil can perform with substantial perfection, or with some other specified degree of success. The former are allied to the so-called method of average error of the psychologists [norm-referenced]; the latter, to what used to be called the method of "right and wrong cases [criterion-referenced]." Each of these groups of methods has its advantages, and each deserves extension and refinement though the latter seems to represent the type which will prevail if education follows the course of development of the physical sciences. (Thorndike, 1918, p. 18.)

Educational measurement, however, did not develop along the lines of the physical sciences, but adopted instead a psychological model based on the concept of individual differences. This psychological lineage, with its emphasis on individual differences, normal distributions, predictions, and the like is a primary reason norm-referenced measurement continues to dominate educational testing to this day.

The work of the Department of Educational Investigation and Measurement of the Boston Public Schools around 1916 offers an excellent example of the course taken by educational measurement in the face of the options Thorndike outlined. Boston teachers were required to draw up a list of words that all students should be able to spell by grade eight. In addition, requirements for English were stated in very precise behavioral terms and all students had to successfully exhibit these behaviors in order to graduate. However, once tests in spelling and English were given to large numbers of students the percentage passing each item or task began to serve as a "standard by which [the teacher] could judge whether her class [was] above or below the *general standard for the city*" (Ballow, 1916, p. 62, italics added). It was only a short step from comparing class performance to comparing individuals' performance to such "general city standards." Thus the emphasis shifted from criterion to norm-referenced evaluation.

The following quote sheds light on some of the reasons underlying such shifts:

> ... Indeed, the measurements which have been made up to this time have more than justified their costs in efforts and money, because they have dispelled forever the idea that schools should produce a uniform product or one that is perfect in its attainment ... With the theoretical ideal of perfection overthrown, there is now an opportunity to set up rational demands. We can venture to tell parents with assurance that their children in the fifth grade are as good as the average if they misspell fifty percent of a certain list of words. We know this just as well as we know that a certain automobile engine cannot draw a ton of weight up a certain hill. No one has a right to make an unscientific demand of the automobile or of the school.
>
> As soon as school officers recognize the fact *that measurements define for them just how much reasonably may be demanded*, they will be unafraid of measurements. (Judd, 1918, pp. 153–154, italics added.)

Clearly the assumption that most students could be brought to a given level of competence in skill subjects such as spelling was rejected. This rejection was due to a belief widely held at that time that *native* limitations in the ability of children — or poor environmental background — precluded such a goal (Judd, 1918). A corollary to this view was that reasonable demands upon student learning should be relative rather than absolute. Standardized test makers began to perfect norm-referenced tests to measure individual differences in achievement. Today, virtually all commercially available standardized tests are norm-referenced instruments.

The last three or four years have witnessed a growing interest in criterion-referenced measures, particularly in the classroom context. The interest is predicated upon a series of trends occurring both inside and outside education.

First there has been a growing criticism of testing, the focus of which has been on standardized tests of achievement and ability (e.g., Hoffman, 1962; Holt,

1968; Illich, 1971; Silberman, 1970). This criticism centers upon questions about the relevancy of tasks tested, what education is really about, and the relevancy of sorting people on any bases. However, even one of testing's most vehement critics, John Holt, admits that in at least two circumstances tests are necessary. There is a need in many occupations to demonstrate the ability to meet standards set by the occupation or profession, e.g., symphony orchestra, surgeon, translator, architect, etc. Further, there is a need for tests that allow people to check their progress toward the attainment of a certain skill or knowledge (Holt, 1968, p. 1). Both of these functions are better served by criterion-referenced than norm-referenced measures.

A second factor, closely related to the first, is the growing controversy surrounding grades. There is a growing distrust of grades *per se* and a reluctance to want to judge others. Critics argue that the fight for good grades engenders a competitive ethic, emphasizing "winning" the good grade race at the expense of the true purpose of education. The argument proceeds that grades become commodities to be bargained in the market place for teacher approval, college admittance, or jobs. The argument concludes, a grade of A or D tells us nothing about what a learner can do, only that he is superior or inferior to some vaguely defined reference group (Farber, 1969; New University Conference, 1972).

A third factor generating interest in criterion-referenced tests has been the growth of the instructional technology movement (Gagne, 1965; Glaser, 1971; Mechner, 1965). Instructional technologists soon realized that norm-referenced tests did not meet their needs in evaluating either individual performance or the efficacy of alternative instructional strategies. A cornerstone in instructional technology is the need for clear statements of instructional objectives. The objectives become a performance standard, for which various instructional strategies are developed. The criterion of success becomes the degree to which the student's performance corresponds to the previously set performance standard.

A fourth factor contributing to the present interest in criterion-referenced measurement is the growing belief on the part of many educators that *all* or *at least most* students can learn, benefit from, or be helped to achieve competency in most subject areas. Educators have argued that the problem of children not learning is not the result of native limitations, but instead a problem of finding better instructional stategies (see, for example, Bloom, 1968; Bruner, 1960; Carroll, 1963; Block, 1971b; Mayo, 1971). The assumption that most children can attain a given performance standard, underlies such approaches to instruction as Individually Prescribed Instruction (Lindvall and Cox, 1970), Performance Contracting (Lessinger, 1970) and Mastery Learning (Block, 1971b). A feature of all such approaches is the use of criterion-referenced measures, both in the formative, ongoing sense, and in the summative, end-of-course sense (Airasian, 1971; Bloom, Hastings and Madaus, 1971). Once one accepts the idea that most students can be helped to criterion performance, the emphasis in testing shifts from comparing individuals on a norm-referenced basis to checking and rewarding student learning in terms of that performance. If all attain the criterion, all should receive A's, passes, etc.

These four trends and their wider implications have nurtured the idea of criterion-referenced measurement. It is within the context of these trends and the value position implied by them that the classroom teacher must view criterion-referenced measurement.

CRITERION-REFERENCED TESTING AND THE CLASSROOM TEACHER

Is criterion-referenced testing a new concept to the teacher? It could be argued that teachers have always employed implicit, but nonetheless criterion-referenced, standards in their evaluations of pupils. For example, there is little doubt that teachers evaluate such student characteristics as cleanliness, dress, speech patterns, conduct, and verbal fluency against an internal model they have developed as a result of their own socialization process. The model serves as a criterion, a standard, against which each individual student is judged. While the standard is internal, and highly individualistic, it nevertheless plays a powerful part in the formation of teacher expectations about a student's worth, potential, and performance (Airasian, Kellaghan, and Madaus, 1971). This type of internal criterion is, of course, different from the common use of the term "criterion-referenced" as found in either the professional literature or in prior sections of this essay. It is not the purpose of this paper to pursue the concept of an internal criterion any further, except to point out that all classrooms are evaluative settings and while criteria may differ from teacher to teacher, and school to school, in the total evaluative context of the classroom judgments based on such internal criteria are undoubtedly pervasive and powerful in terms of their effect on teachers and pupils.

Typically, most teachers grade their classroom tests, either explicitly or implicitly, on a scale of zero to one hundred. Each test item is assigned a point value, with the total number of points generally equalling one hundred. Percentages are then translated into A's, B's, C's, D's, and F's, often with gradations in between, according to widely accepted convention (90−100 = A; 89−80 = B, etc.). In this system an average grade for a marking period is easily determined.

Is the percentage grading approach an example of criterion-referenced measurement? Lynn's score of 85% was, after all, independent of her classmate's performance. She answered 17 of the 20 questions correctly. However, there are several important reasons why this widely accepted marking system does not fit the definition of criterion-referenced measurement described above.

First, the grade or percentage does not describe what Lynn can or cannot do. E. L. Thorndike recognized this problem in 1913 when he observed

> The essential fault of the older schemes for school grades or marks was that the "86" or "B⁻" did not mean any objectively defined amount of knowledge or power or skill − that, for example, John's attainment of 91 in second year German did not inform him (or anyone else) about how difficult a passage he could translate; how many words he knew the English equivalents of and how accurately he could pronounce, or about any other

fact save that he was supposed to be slightly more competent than someone else marked 89 was, or than he would have been if he had been so marked (quoted in Glaser, 1971, pp. 48–49).

Second, very often teacher-made tests are built without the benefit of a prior statement of the behavioral objectives for the instructional unit. Instead, when some body of content is completed, the test items are constructed and become, after the fact, the *de facto* objectives of the teacher. In order to perform a criterion-referenced measurement one must possess a precise definition of objectives prior to instruction.

Third, even when objectives are clearly defined, the use of a single score to represent performance on a number of different objectives can easily mask what a student can actually do. For example, indentical scores of 80% often mask the fact that Sarah did poorly on the 8 items measuring Objective A and well on the 8 items measuring Objective B, while the reverse was true for Eileen.

Fourth, the prior problem is compounded when we recognize that the meaning of identical grades on a test purporting to cover the same content can vary widely across teachers because of such factors as different objectives, item selection and scoring procedures. While it is not necessary — or likely — that every teacher will agree upon the criterion behaviors in English, or math, or reading, it is important that teachers in a department or at a grade level reach some agreement regarding at least minimum skills needed in a subject area. When this task is accomplished, record forms outlining at least the minimal essentials can be developed.

The Mathematics Goal Record Card of the Winnetka, Illinois Public Schools shown in Figure 18-9 is an example of one type of reporting form that is suited to criterion-referenced measurement. A check indicates that a student has mastered the particular skill. Compare the information provided in this approach to the traditional practice of using a single grade or vague verbal description such as:

Distinctly superior work
Above average work
Work of average quality
Meets minimal requirements
Unsatisfactory work

While the goal card could be more specific in terms of defining behaviors (e.g. "understanding") and specifying standards for adequate performance, it does describe what the student can do rather than his rank relative to his peers. The information provided gives a better picture to teachers, students, and parents than vague letter or verbal descriptions. The goal card has a further benefit in that it is more powerful for directing teaching than are the typical norm-referenced categories. Notice also that the goal card can serve to chart student progress and identify individual needs while instruction is in progress. Most of all, however, it serves to focus attention upon the criterion behaviors.

Two additional distinctions between traditional classroom testing practices and criterion-referenced measurement are related to *when* tests are given and *how*

Recognizes number groups up to 5....................................	
Recognizes patterns of objects to 10..............................	
Can count objects to 100..	
Recognizes numbers to 100...	
Can read and write numerals to 50................................	
Recognizes addition and subtraction symbols...............	
Understands meaning of the equality sign.....................	
Understands meaning of the inequality signs................	
Can count objects:	
by 2's to 20...	
by 5's to 100...	
by 10's to 100...	
Recognizes geometric figures:	
triangle...	
circle..	
quadrilateral..	
Recognizes coins (1¢, 5¢, 10¢, 25¢).....................	
Knows addition combinations 10 and under using objects...	
Knows subtraction combinations 10 and under using objects..	
Recognizes addition and subtraction vertically and horizontally.................................	
Shows understanding of numbers and number combinations	
1. Using concrete objects....................................	
2. Beginning to visualize and abstract...............	
3. Makes automatic responses without concrete objects.................................	
Can tell time	
1. Hour..	
2. Half hour...	
3. Quarter hour...	
Addition combinations 10 and under (automatic response).......................................	
Subtraction combinations 10 and under (automatic response).................................	
Can count to 200..	
Can understand zero as a number.....................................	
Can understand place value to tens.............................	
Can read and write numerals to 200..........................	
Can read and write number words to 20.....................	
Use facts in 2-digit column addition (no carrying)...	
Roman numerals to XII..	

FIGURE 18-9. *Portion of the Mathematics Goal Record Card of the Winnetka Public Schools.*

the information derived is used. Teacher-made tests are most often summative measures, in that they are given at the conclusion of a unit of instruction for purposes of grading. Criterion-referenced measurements are ammenable to use before instruction begins to properly place students; while instruction is ongoing for purposes of checking progress so that help can be given if necessary (formative testing); and at the end of the unit to see whether students have achieved the criterion (Airasian and Madaus, 1972). A portrait of group performance on a criterion-referenced test gives information about the efficacy of a particular instructional strategy.

Before describing the steps a teacher or administrator who wishes to employ criterion-based measurement might adopt, a caveat is in order. Criterion-referenced measurement is not a panacea for all the grading or sorting problems in education. The criterion-referenced approach does possess many advantages over norm-referenced approaches within the instructional context. However, criterion-referenced measurement, like all other measurement, is not value free. There is a view of what education is about, what learners are capable of, and the nature of rewards which is implicit in measurement practices based upon absolute rather than normative standards. We have tried to indicate some of these value positions in our discussion of trends which have fostered the criterion-referenced movement. Teachers who opt for criterion-referenced techniques should be aware of the value framework implied. However, advantages of criterion-referenced information in the instructional setting do not rule out the value norm-referenced information can have to administrators, teachers, parents, and students.

IMPLEMENTING CRITERION-REFERENCED TECHNIQUES IN THE CLASSROOM

It should be recognized at the outset that the steps about to be described reflect the present state of the art and that there are a number of conceptual and methodological issues concerning criterion-referenced testing which remain to be solved.

The first step in implementing criterion-referenced measurement is to develop, prior to instruction, a list of objectives which identify the performances, skills, and products which instruction is designed to help students attain. The list becomes the standard for judging learning success. It is the criterion against which each student's performance will be compared to judge learning adequacy. Implicit in the task of specifying criterion behaviors are two questions: *Who* should do the specifying? and *What* features should the criterion performances manifest?

Probably the teacher, taking into account the level and needs of the students, should have the major say in determining what the criterion behaviors will be. However, very often administrators, parents, and students can provide valuable inputs into this decision-making process. In those cases, where a particular course is a prerequisite to another course or where a number of teachers teach the same course, it is advisable that the criterion behaviors be specified by all teachers concerned. Such a recommendation is not advanced to foster total conformity across classrooms, but only to insure cohesion and direction across teachers teaching the same courses or teachers whose courses are sequential in nature.

The criterion performances, or objectives, should be unambiguously stated. A statement of an objective should contain an operational verb, a verb that describes what the student must do to demonstrate he has learned. Often the conditions under which the behavior is expected to occur should be specified as well. For example,

> The student will demonstrate his understanding of the function of the topic sentence in a given paragraph by writing a paragraph about a given subject and underlining the central idea. (Center for the Study of Evaluation, 1970, p. 127).
> When given a newspaper article, the students can distinguish between statements of fact and opinion. When given a situation he has never encountered, the student can explain what is occurring in terms of Boyle's, Charles', or Bernoulli's Law.

Techniques for writing behavioral objectives are described in many books, (Gronlund, 1970; Mager, 1962; Bloom, Hastings and Madaus, 1971), and in film strips developed by Vimcet Associates and by General Program Teaching. While the reader should be aware that there are thoughtful critics of the approach to objectives described in the sources listed above, (i.e., see Eisner, 1969; Doll, 1971; Broudy, 1970), an unambiguous statement of instructional objectives is a necessary first step toward a criterion-based measurement.

The second step in implementing criterion-refenced measurement involves a decision about the standards used to judge whether a student's performance or product indicates mastery of the instructional objectives. Here we need a standard for each objective as well as a standard for the entire set of criterion behaviors. That is, if it is necessary to translate performance on a number of behaviors into pass-fail or yes-no terms, some standard for judging performance across all specific objectives is needed. It is in the area of setting standards, be they for individual objectives or sets of objectives, that criterion-referenced measurement is most in need of research. Thus far, most standards have been arrived at by arbitrary decisions on the part of teachers and researchers. Perfection, that is, perfect mastery, is simply too expensive to obtain. There is evidence (Block, 1972) that standards set in the area of 80 to 90 percent proficiency are most realistic and meaningful. However, the research is somewhat tentative and for the time being teachers will probably have to rely largely upon their own implicit standards for determining levels of adequacy for criterion behaviors.

Given an objective or set of objectives, there usually will be some standard that will define adequate performance. The standard may involve setting a permissible error rate (i.e., answers correctly 80 per cent of the time). Alternatively it may consist of a list of the characteristics associated with an acceptable product or performance. For example, the standard for the previous objective concerning topic sentences and paragraph writing was as follows:

1. The paragraph must be about a single subject.

2. All other sentences in the paragraph must pertain to or support the sentence which the student has underlined.
3. The topic sentence must be underlined.
4. Capitalization and punctuation conventions must be adhered to.

The third step is to devise situations which allow the students a chance to exhibit the desired skill, behavior or product. In many cases this may mean designing paper and pencil instruments. For example, a paper and pencil test is required to assess the following objective: given a set of 10 problems calling for dividing mixed fractions, the student is able to correctly solve the problems with 90% accuracy. In form, the items look identical to items developed for a norm-referenced arithmetic test. Further, the item writing techniques do not differ for norm versus criterion-referenced tests. The reader is referred to Thorndike (1971) for a detailed description of item writing techniques. The essential difference lies in whether the items are used to determine whether a student has mastered division of mixed numbers or where he stands relative to his peers on this skill.

It should be pointed out here that the use of a criterion-referenced approach does not automatically make the testing situation diagnostic, except insofar as it identifies a particular skill a student possesses or fails to possess. In our example of dividing mixed numbers, suppose two students each answered correctly 7 of the 10 items. The conclusion is that the students have not reached the prespecified criterion and therefore have not mastered the arithmetic skill in question. By itself this piece of information is of little diagnostic value. Martha might have missed three items because she incorrectly changed the mixed numbers to fractions while Anthony missed three items because of mistakes in simple multiplication. The point is criterion-referenced information is not intrinsically diagnostic if one stops with an "on-off" statement of results. Popham and Husek (1971) describe the ideal criterion-referenced test as one in which a person's score exactly describes his whole response pattern. No such test is in sight. The point is, then, that generally the more complex the objective, the less prescriptive the test results are likely to be.

There have been efforts in the past few years to specify not only criterion behaviors in school subjects, but also ordering or sequential relationships between behaviors (Airasian, 1971; Gagne, 1965; Resnick, 1967). A body of content or a task is analyzed to determine a sequence in which performances are identified as prerequisites to or necessary products of other performances. Tests based upon such sequences are criterion-referenced, but they also possess a diagnostic value in that they are often able to shed light on the question of why a student failed to demonstrate competence on a given objective, i.e., he failed a prerequisite criterion behavior.

In building a paper and pencil criterion-referenced instrument, all of the items should represent the behavior or behaviors defined in the criterion performances so that accurate inference can be made from test results. Tyler (1967, p. 14), however, points out that there is little theory "to aid in the construction of relatively homogeneous samples of exercises faithfully reflecting an educational objective." Until such techniques are developed, teachers will have to judge the validity of the items or exercises relative to the objective in question. The bases for this judgment can be expert opinion, experience, the face validity of the items, or group consensus. It is precisely on these bases that teachers judge item adequacy at present.

For many objectives, paper and pencil tests will be inappropriate. Actual situations in which the students' performance is observed and rated are required. For example, to determine whether a child has sufficient eye-hand coordination to handle scissors is best measured by giving the child a piece of paper and a pair of scissors. Thus, to assess this capability, Kamii (1971, p. 308) describes the following measurement technique and criteria:

> Give a piece of paper and a pair of scissors to a child and ask him to cut the paper (a) in any way he likes and (b) on a line you have drawn on the paper.
>
> Criteria:
>   Cutting in any way the child likes
>   — Cuts easily without any trouble.
>   — Cuts with some slight difficulty.
>   — Cuts with considerable difficulty.
>   — Simply cannot cut and appears to be "all thumbs."
>   Cutting in a line: (The following criteria refer not to the child's general ability to use scissors but to his specific ability to cut along a given line.)
>   — Cuts easily and accurately on the line.
>   — Cuts easily but with a deviation within ¼ inch from the line.
>   — Cuts with some difficulty with a deviation of more than ¼ inch from the line.

A moment's reflection will reveal that it is possible to convert this measurement, either implicitly or explicitly, into a norm-referenced scale. Even though two students attain criterion performance, it is often difficult to avoid making comparisons between students on the basis of the speed, fluency, smoothness, or adroitness with which they attained the criterion. Dewey (1939) points out that valuing has two aspects, one of prizing, the other appraising. The latter involves comparison and is concerned with the relational property of objects. Whether this relational aspect can be limited to the criterion in question or whether it also inadvertently spills over into comparisons between people is something one must be aware of.

In still other circumstances student products might have to be critically examined in order to infer whether or not the student has in fact attained the required skill or competency. Baldwin (1971) describes such rating scale for a woodworking project in vocational education (Figure 18-10). In terms of rating scales Baldwin points out that the teacher using a rating scale should also demonstrate the objectivity of the instrument for the situation for which it was designed by determining both inter- and intra- rater consistency in light of the criterion performance.

In summary, any classroom approach to criterion-referenced measurement should include the following steps:

1. Evidence of excessive glue under finish/Damage from glue

1	2	3	4	5	6	7
Bubbles of glue under finish		Considerable discoloration		Slight discoloration		No evidence of glue

2. Evidence of clamp damage

1	2	3	4	5	6	7
Splitting		Deep impressions		Marred surface		No evidence of clamps

3. Evidence of inconsistent clamping pressure in assembly (squareness)

1	2	3	4	5	6	7
Parts do not fit		Considerable warp		Some distortion		All parts square

4. Evidence of lamination problems

1	2	3	4	5	6	7
Splitting/ open joint		Buckling/ wide joint		Slight offset		Flat/tight joint

5. Evidence of the improper use of fasteners (screws)

1	2	3	4	5	6	7
Not holding/ head-stripped		Loose/ head damage		Poor seating		Secure/no head damage

6. Evidence of the improper use of fasteners (finish nails)

1	2	3	4	5	6	7
Bent nail/ surface damage		Nail showing		Under or overfilled		Fill blends with surface

FIGURE 18-10. *Evaluation form for a woodworking project.*

1. Competencies to be demonstrated by the student must be stated in explicit terms.
2. Criteria identifying levels or characteristics of successful accomplishment of the competencies must be made explicit.
3. Situations in which the student can demonstrate his competency or lack of competency must be developed.
4. Judgments of any student's learning success must be made in light of the predefined competencies, not in relation to other students' performance.

CONCLUSION

Criterion-referenced testing is not a panacea for all the grading and sorting problems which exist in education. More thoughtful reflection and research is required before all the difficulties associated with criterion-based measurement are resolved. However, the criterion-referenced approach serves two very valuable functions within the instructional context. First, it directs attention to the performances and behaviors which are the main purpose of instruction. Secondly, it rewards students on the basis of their attainment relative to these criterion performances rather than relative to their peers. Under such conditions rewards are distributed on the basis of achievement *vis a vis* the aims of instruction and the frequently meaningless distinctions made between students on the basis of "how much" are replaced by a reward system based upon what has actually been attained.

REFERENCES

Airasian, P. W. (1971). A Study of the Behaviorally Dependent, Classroom-Taught Task Hierarchies, *Educational Technology Research Report Series*, Number 3.

Airasian, P. W. (1971). The Role of Evaluation in Mastery Learning, *Mastery Learning: Theory and Practice* (J. Block, ed.). New York: Holt, Rinehart, and Winston, 81–93.

Airasian, P. W. and G. F. Madaus (1972). Functional Types of Student Evaluation, *Measurement and Evaluation in Guidance*, 221–233.

Airasian, P. W., T. Kellaghan, and G. F. Madaus (1971). *Standardized Test Information, Teacher Expectancies and the Rhetoric of Evaluation.* Working paper for a conference on the design of a societal experiment on the consequences of testing. Dublin, Ireland.

Baldwin, T. S. (1971). Evaluation of learning in industrial education. In Bloom, Hastings, and Madaus. *Handbook on formative and summative evaluation of student learning.* New York: McGraw-Hill, 855–905.

Ballow, F. W. (1916). Work of the Department of Educational Investigation and Measurement, Boston, Massachusetts, in *Standards and tests for the measurement of the efficiency of schools and school systems.* (G. M. Whipple, ed.). Fifteenth Yearbook of the National Society for the Study of Education, Part I. Chicago: University of Chicago Press, 61–68.

Block, J. H. (1971). *Mastery learning: theory and practice.* New York: Holt, Rinehart, and Winston.

Block, J. H. (1971). Criterion-referenced measurement: potential, *School Review*, 79, 289–297.

Ibid. (1972). Student evaluation: towards the setting of mastery performance standards. Paper read at the 1972 Annual Meeting of the American Educational Research Association, Chicago.

Bloom, B. S. (1968). Learning for mastery. UCLA-CSEIP *Evaluation Comment*, 1.

Bloom, B. S., J. T. Hastings, and G. F. Madaus (1971). *Handbook on formative and summative evaluation of student learning.* New York: McGraw-Hill.

Broudy, H. S. (1970). Can research escape the dogma of behavioral objectives? *School Review*, 79, 43–56.

Bruner, J. S. (1960). *The process of education*. Cambridge: Harvard University Press.

Center for the Study of Evaluation (1970). Language Arts, 4–6. *Instructional Objectives Exchange*.

Dewey, J. (1939). *Theory of valuation*. Chicago: University of Chicago Press.

Doll, W. E. (1971). A methodology of experience: an alternative to behavioral objectives. Paper read at the 1971 American Educational Research Association Annual Meeting, New York.

Eisner, E. W. (1969). Instructional and expressive objectives: their formation and use in curriculum. In *Instructional objectives*. American Educational Research Association Monograph on Curriculum Evaluation. Chicago: Rand McNally, 1–31.

Farber, J. (1969). *The student as nigger*. New York: Pocket Books.

Gagne, R. M. (1965). *The conditions of learning*. New York: Holt, Rinehart, and Winston.

Glaser, R. (1971). A criterion-referenced test, in *Criterion-referenced measurement* (J. W. Popham, ed.). Englewood Cliffs Educational Technology Publications, 41–51.

Gronlund, N. E. (1970). *Stating behavioral objectives for classroom instruction*. New York: The Macmillan Co.

Hoffman, B. (1962). *The tyranny of testing*. New York: Collier Books.

Holt, J. W. (1968). *On testing*. Cambridge: Pinck Leodas Assoc.

Illich, I., (1971). *Deschooling society*. New York: Harper and Row.

Judd, C. H. (1918). A look forward, in *The measurement of educational products*. (G. M. Whipple, ed.), Seventeenth Yearbook of the National Society for the Study of Education, Part II. Bloomington, Ill.: Public School Publishing Co., 152–160.

Kamii, C. K. (1971). Evaluation of learning in preschool education in *Handbook on formative and summative evaluation of student learning* (Bloom, Hastings, and Madaus, ed.). New York: McGraw-Hill, 281–344.

Lessinger. L. (1970). *Every kid a winner*. New York: Simon and Schuster.

Lindvall, C. M. and R. Cox (1970). *Evaluation as a tool in curriculum development: the IPI evaluation program*. American Educational Research Association Monograph Series on Curriculum Evaluation. Chicago: Rand McNally.

Mager, R. F. (1962). *Preparing instructional objectives*. Palo Alto, California: Fearon Publishers.

Mayo, S. T. (1970). *Mastery learning and mastery testing*. Measurement in Education, National Council on Measurement in Education, Vol. 1, No. 3.

Mechner, F. (1965). Science education and behavioral technology, in *Teaching machines and programmed learning, II*. (R. Glaser, ed.). Washington, D. C.: National Education Association, 441–507.

New University Conference (1972). *De-grading education*. Jeff Sharlett Chapter of the New University Conference, Bloomington, Ind., January.

Popham, W. J. and T. R. Husek (1971). Implications of criterion-referenced measurement, in *Criterion-referenced measurement*, (W. J. Popham, ed.). Englewood Cliffs: Educational Technology Publishers, 17–37.

Resnick, L. B. (1967). Design of an early learning curriculum. University of Pittsburgh Learning Research and Development Center. Working paper 16.

Silberman, C. E. (1970). *Crisis in the classroom*. New York: Vantage Books.

Thorndike, E. L. (1971). *Educational psychology*, 1913, quoted in R. Glaser, A criterion-referenced test, in *Criterion-referenced measurement*, (J. W. Popham. ed.). Englewood Cliffs: Educational Technology Publications, pp. 48–49.

Thorndike, E. L. (1918). The nature, purposes and general methods of measurements of educational products, in *The measurement of educational products*. (G. M. Whipple, ed.). Seventeenth Yearbook of the National Society for the Study of Education, Part II. Bloomington Public School Publishing Co., 16–24.

Thorndike, R. L. (ed.) (1971). *Educational Measurement*. Washington, D. C.: American Council on Education.

Tyler, R. W. (1967). Changing concepts of educational evaluation, in *Perspectives of curriculum evaluation*. (R. Stake, ed.), American Educational Research Association Monograph Series on Curriculum Evaluation, Chicago: Rand McNally, 13–18.

Index

Normal distribution *(cont.)*
  standard, 43n
  theoretical, 41–42
  unit, 43n
  utility of, 47–48
  Z-score equivalents of percentile
    ranks, 45
Norm–free scales, 169n
Norm population, 171–172
Norms, 169–177
  definition of, 169–171
  evaluating, 171–172
  examples of tables, 174–176
  selected types of, 172–174
    classroom, 173
    local, 173
    national, 172–173

O

Observed scores:
  criterion–referenced, 94–95
  hypothetical distribution of
    potential, 109–110
  partitioning variance, 113–114
Ordered category, 3
Ordinal measurement rules, 3
Otis Quick–Scoring Mental Ability
  Test, 304

P

Parallel forms approach, 125–126, 134
Parallel forms procedure, 281–282
Pearson correlation coefficient, 65,
  72–79
Percentage grade, 7n
Percentage scores, 7n, 31–32
Percentile ranks, 31, 32–33
  calculating, 36–37
  normal distribution converted to, 45
  Z-score equivalents of, 45
Percentiles, 31, 33–34
Percent mastery, 7n
Performance standard, 247–248,
  269–270
Pilot testing, 268–269
Pinter General Ability Test, 317
P-levels:
  expected, 287–288
  item analysis, 178–180
  observed, 287–288
Precision, coefficient of, 124
Predicted criterion–referenced scores,
  94–95

Predictor variables, 85n, 86

Q

Quasi–interval measurement rules, 6

R

Random errors, 8–9, 11
Randomly parallel forms, 281–282
Ratio measurement rules, 4–6
Raw scores, 15–16, 18, 24, 31
  definition of, 15
  distribution of, 16, 18
  linear prediction equation for, 93–94
Reliability of tests *(see* Tests,
    reliability)
Response charts, 181–183
Response sets, 309–310
Restriction category, 249

S

Sampling errors, 208–209
Sampling variability, 123n
Scatterplots, 66–69
Scholastic Aptitude Test (SAT), 4–5
Scores:
  absolute interpretable, 7
  central tendency ("average"), 17–19
    the arithmetic mean, 18–19
    the median, 17–18
    the mode, 17
  criterion–referenced, 7
    observed, 94–95
    predicted, 94–95
  cut, 269–270
  derived, 31, 51–64
    transformations, 52–54, 59–61
  deviation, 19–21, 24–25, 31
  difference, reliability, 139–141
  dispersion of variability, 19–22
    standard deviation, 19, 22
    sum of squares, 19, 21–22
    the variance, 19, 22
  distribution shape, 22–24
    flat, 23–24
    normal, 23–24
    skewed, 23–24
  error component, 108
  interpreting individual, 111–113
  multiple–choice format, 233–238
  observed
    criterion–referenced, 94–95
    hypothetical distribution of